Strategic Leadership in the Public Sector

In good times and bad, in the different situations of renewal, crisis and chronic resource constraints, the strategic leadership of public services is crucial. Good leaders are essential in helping the public sector to adapt and solve 'wicked' problems, and they are also integral to the reform and modernization of public governance.

This new edition of *Strategic Leadership in the Public Sector* continues to provide insights into useful approaches and techniques for strategic leaders, looking at:

- what is expected of leaders
- competency frameworks
- leadership theories
- techniques and processes of strategic leadership
- leading strategic change
- the strategic state
- emerging leadership challenges.

Replete with real-world case studies and examples, and including new material from the USA, Canada, Australia, Europe and India, plus an appendix with practical work-sheets, the book gives students a truly international outlook on the subject and offers a clear understanding of the significance of leadership, strategic management and public services reform.

This textbook represents essential reading for postgraduate students on public management degrees and aspiring or current public managers.

Paul Joyce is Visiting Professor at Leeds Beckett University, UK, an Affiliated Researcher in the Department of Public Management at the Solvay Brussels School of Economics and Management, Belgium, and an Associate at the Institute of Local Government Studies, University of Birmingham, UK.

ROUTLEDGE MASTERS IN PUBLIC MANAGEMENT

Edited by Stephen P. Osborne

Routledge Masters in Public Management series is an integrated set of texts. It is intended to form the backbone for the holistic study of the theory and practice of public management as part of:

- a taught Masters, MBA or MPA course at a university or college;
- a work based, in-service, programme of education and training; or
- a programme of self-guided study.

Each volume stands alone in its treatment of its topic, whether it be strategic management, marketing or procurement, and is co-authored by leading specialists in their field. However, all volumes in the series share both a common pedagogy and a common approach to the structure of the text. Key features of all volumes in the series include:

- a critical approach to combining theory with practice which educates its reader, rather than solely teaching him/her a set of skills;
- clear learning objectives for each chapter;
- the use of figures, tables and boxes to highlight key ideas, concepts and skills;
- an annotated bibliography, guiding students in their further reading; and
- a dedicated case study in the topic of each volume, to serve as a focus for discussion and learning.

Making and Managing Public Policy
Karen Johnston Miller and Duncan McTavish

Ethics and Management in the Public Sector
Alan Lawton, Karin Lasthuizen and Julie Rayner

Managing Local Governments: Designing Management Control Systems that Deliver Value
Emanuele Padovani and David W. Young

Marketing Management and Communications in the Public Sector
Martial Pasquier and Jean-Patrick Villeneuve

Contracting for Public Services
Carsten Greve

Managing Change and Innovation in Public Service Organizations
Stephen P. Osborne and Kerry Brown

Strategic Leadership in the Public Sector, Second Edition
Paul Joyce

Strategic Leadership in the Public Sector

Second edition

Paul Joyce

Routledge
Taylor & Francis Group

LONDON AND NEW YORK

Second edition 2017
by Routledge
2 Park Square, Milton Park, Abingdon, Oxon OX14 4RN

and Routledge
711 Third Avenue, New York, NY 10017

Routledge is an imprint of the Taylor & Francis Group, an informa business

First edition published 2012

British Library Cataloguing in Publication Data
A catalogue record for this book is available from the British Library

Library of Congress Cataloging in Publication Data
Names: Joyce, Paul, 1952-
Title: Strategic leadership in the public sector/Paul Joyce.
Description: Second edition. | London; New York, NY: Routledge, 2017. | Includes bibliographical references and index. | Previous edition title "Strategic leadership in the public services".
Identifiers: LCCN 2016006274 | ISBN 9781138959361 (pbk.) | ISBN 9781315660677 (ebook)
Subjects: LCSH: Leadership. | Strategic planning. | Public administration.
Classification: LCC JF1525.L4 J69 2017 | DDC 352.23/6–dc23
LC record available at http://lccn.loc.gov/2016006274

ISBN: 978-1-138-95935-4 (hbk)
ISBN: 978-1-138-95936-1 (pbk)
ISBN: 978-1-315-66067-7 (ebk)

Typeset in Bembo
by Sunrise Setting Ltd, Brixham, UK

Contents

List of figures, tables and boxes

FIGURES

TABLES

BOXES

Concept Boxes

Research Boxes

Preface

Leadership in the public sector is a big topic. It can also be a very controversial one. I was very aware of this when reading other people's work on 'dark leadership' and 'strong leadership'. But I am finishing this book believing that we do need heroes for the public sector even if we all know that perfect heroes do not exist. We need heroes who keep their promises, are trustworthy and bring about change. We need them to help the public sector solve the 'wicked problems' and the 'critical problems'. We need them to deliver on some of the massive ambitions that have inspired statements of intent to reform public governance, such as the one put out by the Government of India early in 2015. These ambitions require leaders that are able to help the public sector to establish new governance based on anticipating and responding to the needs of people, promoting meaningful participation of citizens, achieving inclusion of all groups in society, and delivering transparency to make the government visible and responsive. (These are some of the intentions of the Government of India.) And we need leaders who are able to provide this help and at the same time enjoy the support of the people and professionals working in the public sector.

In writing this book I did not come across any evidence to back up an elitist model of leadership. Nor did I find any evidence supporting 'distributed leadership' (meaning we are all leaders now). I did find evidence of the need for intelligent, social and ethical leaders. This book, at times, makes the case for seeing leadership as purposeful and conscious. It is sympathetic to the idea that leaders should have an experimental mind-set and should be keen to learn from experience.

Towards the end of the book there is an implication that the developments in public governance over the last 20 years may be creating a new context for public sector leadership, and there is an implicit idea that we may be better off framing public sector leadership by public governance rather than by organization. This reframing brings to the surface the mediating role that public sector leaders have between the people who work in the public sector and the public. There has been, on occasion, so much focus on leaders and followers that the relationship between leaders and the public has been neglected.

Paul Joyce
February 2016

Acknowledgements

I very much value the input to this book by Nahit Bingol, Anne Drumaux and Adrienne Roberts, who provided written contributions. I would like to record additional thanks to Anne Drumaux for the various discussions we have had in recent years about strategy, leadership and the strategic state. My thanks to Pat Kennedy in Dublin for alerting me to the substantial contribution Ken Whitaker made to the change of strategic direction of Ireland in the late 1950s. I would like to give a special thanks to Caitlin Joyce for her very useful advice on issues of followership. Finally, I would like to express my deep appreciation to Theresa Joyce for countless discussions of matters during the writing of this book, and the insights she provided about various aspects of public services.

Part 1

Leading

INTRODUCTION

The first part of this book contains a lot of material on leadership in the public sector. Some of the questions addressed in these early chapters are very basic:

1   What is expected of leaders?
2   How do strategic leaders relate to employees in the public sector?
3   How do leaders operate as strategists?

Some of the complexity of the literature on leadership – either generally or in the public sector specifically – arises because very different motives inspire those who write about leadership. It is by no means all strictly focused on understanding what leaders do and what the consequences of leadership are. Some people write because they are intrigued by the ideas and concepts of leadership. Some are idealists and probably wish there was no need for leaders.

Some of the complexity is simply created by the passage of time and the changes and movements in the aspects of leadership selected for attention (Figure P1.1), the leadership techniques that have come to the fore (Figure P1.2) and the context of leadership (Figure P1.3).

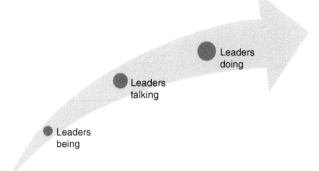

Figure P1.1 *Changing aspects selected for study*

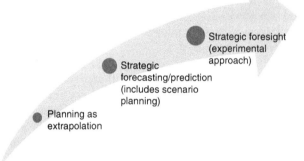

Figure P1.2 *Changing techniques used by leaders*

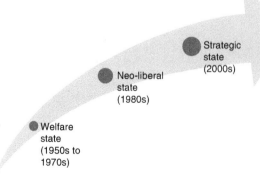

Figure P1.3 *Changing context*

Chapter 1

What is expected of leaders?

LEARNING OBJECTIVES

- To consider some influential ideas of leadership
- To consider what others expect of leaders in the public sector
- To appreciate that strategic leadership is not about infallibility
- To know and understand a working definition of strategic leadership in the public sector

INTRODUCTION

Leadership in the public sector shot to prominence just as the new millennium arrived. It had become a 'hot issue' in the public sector (OECD 2001). The buzz around leadership at this time coincided with a new wave of public sector reform occurring in a number of countries. The 1980s wave had begun shifting the public sector from a culture of 'administrators' and 'policy' to that of 'management' and 'efficiency'. The new 1990s wave of reform seemed spurred by a heightened concern for the effectiveness of the 'state'. It seemed that this was a time for leaders rather than managers (or administrators) because there was a need for change agents who could transform organizations and institutions. Bichard (2000: 44) made the case for leadership rather than management in these terms: 'Yet it is leadership that we need . . . because it is leadership and not good management that transforms organizations'.

The World Bank's advocacy of reform of the state, apparent in the mid 1990s, not only entailed calling for effective leadership but also for farsighted leaders, for leaders who put forward long-term visions, and for leaders who built coalitions and encouraged a wide sense of ownership of reform agendas. The World Bank was talking about politicians as leaders of reform (World Bank 1997: 14):

> Reform-oriented political leaders and elites can speed reform by making decisions that widen people's options, articulate the benefits clearly, and ensure that policies are more inclusive. In recent years farsighted political

3

leaders have transformed the options for their people through decisive reform. They were successful because they made the benefits of change clear to all, and built coalitions that gave greater voice to often-silent beneficiaries. They also succeeded – and this is crucial – because they spelled out a longer-term vision for their society, allowing people to see beyond the immediate pain of adjustment. Effective leaders give their people a sense of owning the reforms – a sense that reform is not something imposed from without.

The 1990s was also a period when thought was given to how leaders could be developed in the civil service. In 1996, a newsletter of the Public Management Service of the OECD, which existed to report and assess new developments in public management, contained a reference to a public sector MBA (PUMA 1996: 5):

> The public and private sectors are coming closer together. We are operating in the same economic and social environment. Future senior civil servants need to understand this environment and its changing pressures in just the same way as future leaders of industry. The mutual exchange of skills and information through initiatives like the Public Sector MBA is a major element in this process. A professionally qualified civil service will be able to continue to meet the changing demands placed upon it.

While a connection between the reforms in the public sector and leadership was clearly and strongly articulated just as the new millennium arrived, it now sometimes seems that our understanding of public sector leadership often takes as its starting point the ideas of American writers and researchers, some of whom were largely thinking about the 1980s and the private business sector of the US. By way of explanation for this US influence we can note two claims made by Bass (1997: 131); first, that the world's language of business is English; and second, that 'much of American management practices and management education have been adopted universally'. The second claim may be an exaggeration, however there is no doubting that US ideas about private sector business leadership have had widespread and persisting influence on the thinking of academics and practitioners in many countries.

SOME INFLUENTIAL AMERICAN IDEAS

Tom Peters wrote about business leadership in a period he saw as defined by fast-pace change and by complex environments. Bernard Bass was the most important writer on transformational leadership. David Osborne and Ted Gaebler used public sector experiences in the US and elsewhere to suggest that public sector leaders should change various things and thereby create entre-preneurial government, which they considered was emerging, and should

4

emerge, from a bureaucratic phase of government. The following sections expand on the ideas of Peters, Bass, and Osborne and Gaebler (Figure 1.1) and are intended to provide a useful background of knowledge and thinking to more recent ideas of leadership in the public sector covered throughout the book.

Tom Peters

Peters, in *Thriving on Chaos* (1987), presents himself as an intellectual revolutionary and claimed that his book would challenge everything people thought they knew about managing. A revolution in management was needed because of the business environment (Peters 1987: 45): 'Today, loving change, tumult, even chaos is a prerequisite for survival, let alone success'. He said predictability was a thing of the past. In fact, at one point he said (Peters 1987: 9), 'Nothing is predictable'. Businesses did not know from day to day what the energy prices would be, what the price of money would be, who their competitors would be, where the competitors would come from, and who would be partnering with whom. Businesses faced uncertainties about technology, about consumers, their tastes and their preferences. The strategies of business organizations were constantly changing (Peters 1987: 8): 'Strategies change daily, and the names of firms, a clear indicator of strategic intent, change with them'.

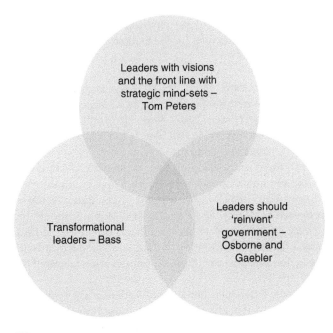

Figure 1.1 *Influential perspectives*

Not surprising in the light of all this, he rejected the possibility of anticipating the future through forecasting (Peters 1987: 11):

> Sum up all these forces and trends, or, more accurately, multiply them, then add in the fact that most are in their infancy, and you end up with a forecaster's nightmare. But the point is much larger, of course, than forecasting. The fact is that no firm can take anything in its market for granted.

Peters said that businesses could be highly successful one year and within just a few years be in difficulties. It might be inferred from this that he was linking change and external volatility to precariousness and threats to the success and survival of businesses.

In the face of all this change and complexity, what should business leaders do? He said they should thrive on this chaos. He wanted businesses to be quick – we might now describe this as 'agile'. Businesses had to react quickly to market opportunities that were short-lived because of all the change occurring. This was to be done through more informality and as a result of front-line managers being at the heart of deciding the future direction of a business. He championed experimentation, with experimentation initiated by the front-line of management, rather than company headquarters (Peters 1987: 390):

> Each day, each manager must practically challenge conventional wisdom . . . Since new truths are not yet clear, the manager must become 'master empiricist', asking each day: What new experiments have been mounted today to test the new principles (in the market, in the accounting department, etc.)?

Business organizations were to experiment, learn, seek change and adapt. 'The organization learns from the best, swipes from the best, adapts, tests, risks, fails, and adjusts – over and over' (Peters 1987: 395). He warned businesses against seeking stability and predictability. He said (Peters 1987: 395), 'Nothing can be "institutionalized"'. Change was constant.

He wanted businesses to focus on developing their skills and capabilities so that they could be flexible and quick in reacting to market opportunities. This concern for skills and capabilities may put us in mind of the resource-based competition model proposed by Hamel and Prahalad (1994), but it should be noted that they took a very different view from Tom Peters on how to address the future. They believed that experimentation should be steered towards an industry foresight – it was not the almost random experimentation favoured by Peters.

Reading between the lines, Peters was not a fan of leaders in the corporate headquarters. Top leaders, as far as Peters was concerned, should concentrate on establishing a framework for front-line management to exercise their initiative. The top managers were to develop visions and values. They were to develop

6

clear visions so that experimentation, testing and risking would be stimulated. He suggested that the experiments and risking might change the vision, so the vision was not to be driven by the top leaders come what may. The visions served the experimentation. It was, he argued, a new type of control, different from the control exercised through a hierarchy of bureaucrats. Leaders would experience corporate life as being far from totally and perfectly controlled by the centre (Peters 1987: 395):

> [Leaders] must preach the vision with verve – over and over. And at the same time, they must insist upon and then revel in the constant tests that re-form (expand, contract, destroy) the very same vision. The ship will seem somewhat out of control by the old standards. That is, the madness of thousands of simultaneous experiments ... is the only plausible path to survival.

Leaders were to campaign to get the support of everybody for the vision. He noted the importance of emotions and of the leader living the vision. He implied that people react emotionally rather than rationally and that they reacted to the 'intensity' of the leader.

His positive views about intensity and emotions can be contrasted with his negative views of the effects of rationality and bureaucracy. He thought bureaucracy and centralized management hierarchy were barriers to organizations becoming quick and experimental at the front line. He was also negative about planners and company headquarters producing formal strategic plans. He was not a great advocate of formal strategic plans or for using them for vertical control of strategic plan implementation. He did not think a strategic plan could be good, but valued a strategic planning process provided that it got everyone involved and forced the asking of new questions. He did not want plans left to the planners or constrained by corporate assumptions. He argued that plans should be modified every year. If they were not modified every year, the strategic plans were in danger of becoming bureaucratic. He saw the only justification of a strategic plan as being to provoke thought. He argued (Peters 1987: 394):

> Strategic planning exercises led by staff are being supplanted by strategic capability building led by the line. The long-range strategic plan, of voluminous length, is less useful than before. But a strategic 'mind-set', which focuses on skill/capability building (e.g., adding value to the work force via training to prepare it to respond more flexibly and be more quality-conscious), is more important than ever.

In summary, Tom Peters considered that fast changing and chaotic environments of the 1980s ruled out the command and control model of leadership, and invalidated the idea of long-term strategic planning carried out in any formal and disciplined way. Quick reactions, front-line leadership and skills and capabilities were his answer. (See Figure 1.2.)

7

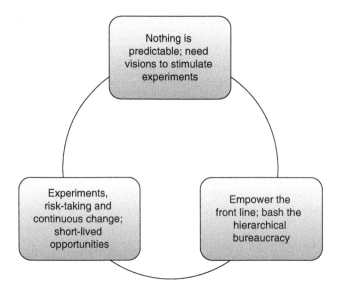

Figure 1.2 *Tom Peters – the madness of thousands of simultaneous experiments*

Bernard Bass

Burns is credited with authorship of the ideas of transformational leadership and transactional leadership (Burns 1978), but Bernard Bass is probably the most significant researcher associated with this theory. Bass worked on the theory of transformational leadership in the 1980s and by the late 1990s he was able to publish meta-reviews of research carried out in a variety of countries and organizations by a number of researchers. The evidence and the analysis he reviewed led him to conclude that the theory had stood up very well for all organizational settings and national cultures.

Bass (1999: 11) defined transformational leadership as follows:

> Transformational leadership refers to the leader moving the follower beyond immediate self-interests through idealized influence (charisma), inspiration, intellectual stimulation, or individualized consideration. It elevates the follower's level of maturity and ideals as well as concerns for achievement, self-actualization, and the well-being of others, the organization, and society.

It might be useful to comment a little more on the meanings of the terms in this definition. Transformational leaders provide idealized influence and inspirational leadership by offering a vision of a desirable future, explaining how it can be realized, acting as a role model, ensuring there are high standards of performance, and displaying determination and confidence. Transformational leaders foster creativity and innovation by means of intellectual stimulation of

8

followers. Finally, transformational leaders are showing individualized consideration for followers when they develop and coach them.

Transactional leadership is said to take more than one form. The most obvious form is where leaders and followers conduct their relationship in such a way as to benefit their self-interests. For example, the leader may offer a contingent reward and explain to the followers what is required from them in order for them to gain the reward. There are three other forms of transactional leadership – active management by exception, passive management by exception and laissez-faire leadership in which leadership action is avoided.

So what are the consequences of individuals acting in line with these prescriptions? What results do transformational leaders achieve? According to Bass (1999) leaders who are more transformational and less transactional are more effective as leaders and their followers find them more satisfying. Bass also notes (1999: 12): 'Transactional leadership can be reasonably satisfying and effective but transformational leadership adds substantially to the impact of transactional leadership'. In fact, the evidence collected on transformational and transactional leaders suggests that the best leaders are both transformational and transactional (Bass 1997).

As noted already, Bass reviewed a number of studies from around the world and concluded that the transformational and transactional model of leadership generally applied in a variety of national cultures and organizations. He checked out, for instance, that the different leadership styles varied in terms of their correlation with effectiveness and that this was consistently true. He was specifically interested in the following pattern: transformational leaders showed the highest correlation with effectiveness; leaders operating using contingent rewards were the next highest in terms of the correlation with effectiveness; then came leaders who used active management by exception; then leaders who used passive management by exception; and finally, showing the lowest correlation with effectiveness, came the laissez-faire leaders. What did the various studies reveal? He reported that the hierarchical pattern appeared consistently (Bass 1997: 134):

> The [pattern], first verified in the United States (Waldman, Bass and Einstein, 1986), is applicable to results from India, Spain, Singapore, Japan, China, Austria and a number of other countries. In Bombay, Dennyson Pereira (1986) found general support for the correlational hierarchy for managers in a large manufacturing organization, as did Roberto Pascual in Bilbao, Spain; Jaime Filella in Barcelona, Spain; Roger Gill in Singapore; Nokko Yokochi in Japan (Yokochi 1989); Steyrer and Mende (1994) in Austria in diverse sectors of business and industrial management; and Davis, Guan, Luo and Maahs (1996) in a Chinese state enterprise.

Elsewhere in the same review he mentions research findings from the army and police, suggesting that the transformational and transactional leadership concepts might be robust even in parts of the public sector where hierarchy and discipline were well developed.

9

As we have seen, Bass believed that in the case of transformational leaders, followers are persuaded to put aside their self-interest (see Figure 1.3). In fact, Bass (1997) also described transformational leaders as socially oriented and suggested that their impact on followers was morally uplifting. Bass's transformational leaders might be seen as able to persuade followers to see things differently, to see things in a new way, to see new possibilities. Bass's point about the suspension of self-interest may be seen as problematic from within a pluralistic frame of reference that regards organizations (and societies) as made up of a coalition of interest groups, and liable to power struggles and negotiations from time to time to adjust those different interests. The leadership model of Bass, in effect, implies that transformational leaders create unitary organizations and dispel pluralism. To describe leaders as socially oriented and having a morally uplifting effect because followers put aside their self-interest might be seen from a pluralistic perspective as a misunderstanding of what was in effect ideological manipulation of followers by leaders.

Osborne and Gaebler

One reading of Osborne and Gaebler's ideas suggests that they had been influenced by the work of Tom Peters just a few years before. For example, they critiqued the existing public sector as being bureaucratic. They supported decentralization. They quoted approvingly the ideas of John Bryson (1988) that it was important to develop a consensus, which they suggested was important in

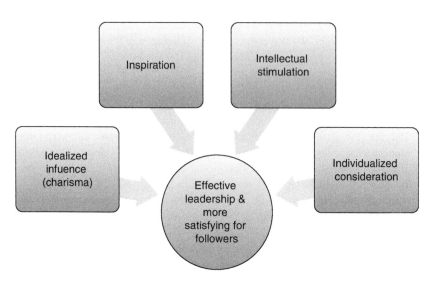

Figure 1.3 Bernard Bass – benefits of transformational leadership

10

connection with strategic planning. Osborne and Gaebler (1992: 234) explain the importance of consensus as follows:

> Strategic planning is not something done once, to develop a plan, but a process that is regularly repeated. The important element is not a plan, but planning. By creating consensus around a vision of the future, an organisation or community builds a sense of where it is going among all its members. This allows everyone – not just leaders – to understand what direction they need to take. It helps them seize unexpected opportunities and deal with unexpected crises, without waiting for word from the top.

This emphasis on a consensus around a vision matches Peters' emphasis on shared vision and shared values. Most importantly, Osborne and Gaebler considered command and control as an outdated approach to leading in the government sector. In place of command and control, they believed that leadership should work by persuasion and incentives.

The Osborne and Gaebler thesis, however, went way beyond a critique of bureaucracy in terms of the internal functioning of the public sector and a critique of command and control leadership. They argued for a fundamental shift from government to governance, which involved the relationship with the public and external stakeholders as well as management relationships inside organizations. They were concerned with reconstructing the relationship between the public sector and the public. Not only did they want to change service relationships to put the public first and get the public sector to treat them as 'customers'; they also wanted to see communities empowered. And they wanted government to evolve its core functions. Governments should do less service delivery (which they labelled as 'rowing') and instead should steer. Governments should commission and pay for public services, with the service providers being made to compete, and with providers of public services being drawn from private and voluntary sectors as well as the public sector.

Osborne and Gaebler also proposed that governments should not assume that every public problem required a 'tax and spend' response in which tax revenue would be used to pay for new public services designed and delivered to solve the problem. They stressed that sometimes it might be more effective for the government to catalyse problem solving by others. They quoted approvingly the experiences of government in Indianapolis in Indiana (Osborne and Gaebler 1992: 28):

> In Indianapolis, Indiana, mayors Richard Lugar and Bill Hudnot worked with the Greater Indianapolis Progress Committee, formed by a group of civic and business leaders, to revitalise the city. Working together to develop a strategic vision and plan, they decided to make Indianapolis the amateur sports capital of America. They created partnerships, tapped foundations, and harnessed the energies of thousands of volunteers – stimulating more than $11 billion of new investment in building the 11 new sports facilities in a decade.

11

Throughout the book there are repeated references to 'entrepreneurial leadership'. The leaders are probably labelled as entrepreneurial leaders because their actions are meant to reinvent government, to bring in post-bureaucratic government, which they call an entrepreneurial government. On the whole, their book positions leaders in the public sector as the change agents who will bring in entrepreneurial government but mainly looks at what needs to change rather than how leaders would do it.

Shortly after the appearance of their ideas on reinventing government Kooiman (Kooiman 1993; Kooiman and van Vliet 1993) and others were also discussing how governments would address public problems through problem solving. From the ideas of Osborne and Gaebler and Kooiman we can see the kernel of the idea of a new public governance, in which governments lead society not by taxing, regulating and providing public services and welfare, but by working in partnerships with other stakeholders. Interestingly, Kooiman and van Vliet (1993) also pointed to another change in a post-bureaucratic world of government, which was that the traditional division of labour between elected politicians and appointed public administration officials would also evolve. It was thought that politicians might become more involved in implementation and the appointed officials might become more involved in clarifying public needs and priorities. With hindsight, this idea that the relationship between politicians and public administrators would evolve as a result of the reform of public governance is interesting; there has been some attention in recent times to the question of how this relationship can become more effective in order that the state might become more strategic.

PRACTICAL AND THEORETICAL CONSEQUENCES

There have been high hopes for the consequences of developing and improving leadership in the public sector. It was expected that leaders would produce more engaged and motivated government employees, changed cultures, improved organizational performance, more effective public service systems, greater responsiveness to citizens and reformed public governance institutions. An OECD report on public sector leadership commented (2001: 7):

> A common complaint is lack of dedication to the underlying values of public service interests of the citizens served. A common response seems to be the attempt to promote a certain kind of leadership.
>
> Leadership is a critical component of good public governance . . . This [public governance] has formal aspects such as separated powers, checks and balances, means of transferring power, transparency, and accountability. However, for these values to be actualized, they must guide the actions of public officials throughout the system. They must be embedded in culture.

In this regard 'leadership' is the flesh on the bones of the Constitution. It is at the heart of good governance.

... When we say we want more leadership in the public sector, what we are really looking for is people who will promote institutional adaptations in the public interest. [...]

Leadership is an important and crucial variable that leads to enhanced management capacity, as well as organizational performance.

The point in the OECD quote above about leaders promoting institutional adaptations can be elaborated in a theoretical way. It may be argued that as well as an expected practical consequence of leadership, there is a theoretical consequence of making leadership an important variable in the reform situation. Specifically, building leadership into a model of public governance reform has the consequence of identifying 'human agency' as a counterweight to a tendency towards structural understandings of society or of politics.

Structural understandings may start with ideas of the social or political whole and propose how individuals are fitted into them. As far back as Aristotle we can find an analysis that breaks down 'wholes' into their parts and identifies various 'roles' within the whole and the parts (Aristotle 1981). He analysed the state (the whole, in this case) as having rulers and ruled. The state could be subdivided into villages and the villages into households. The latter (the smallest part) had the roles of husband and wife, as well as the roles of master of slaves and slaves. The parts might be re-described today as institutions, meaning habitualized ways of acting and interacting. We might now say, therefore, that the roles of husband, wife, master and slave were to be found in the institution known as a household in the city-states of Aristotle's time.

In the 1950s and 1960s sociologists often employed or debated a concept of an institution in which it is implied that people were controlled (Berger and Luckmann 1966: 72–3):

Institutions also, by the very fact of their existence, control human conduct by setting up predefined patterns of conduct, which channel it in one direction as against the many other directions that would theoretically be possible. It is important to stress that this controlling character is inherent in institutionalization as such, prior to or apart from any mechanisms of sanctions specifically set up to support an institution. These mechanisms (the sum of which constitute what is generally called a system of social control) do, of course, exist in many institutions and in all the agglomerations of institutions that we call societies.

Expectations of how each other will act build up quickly between people who are interacting over some period of time. Actions are repeated and expectations become taken for granted. The patterns and the taken for granted expectations are transmitted to new generations through what sociologists call socialization.

13

In the 1960s and 1970s some sociologists stressed that the patterns had been made by people and were sustained by people. In principle, therefore, people could change and evolve the patterns of action and interaction (Berger and Luckmann 1966: 76): 'Although the routines, once established, carry within them a tendency to persist, the possibility of changing them or even abolishing them remains at hand in consciousness'.

So, while people generally may operate for much of their time on the auto-pilot of habit, and may have consigned some of their conscious and purposeful thinking into the taken for granted category, it is always a possibility that they will query what they are doing and think purposefully and consciously about continuing to do what they do. It is possible to imagine the control embedded in public sector institutions being resisted by an individual. It is possible to imagine an evolution in an institution caused by a widespread and simultaneous view by many individuals that the routines and patterns need to change.

> However elaborate and complex the institutional fabric of government is and, however overwhelming the situational pressures and contextual (historical, international, legal) constraints, at the end of the day it is down to individuals and groups taking up the strategic challenges and dilemmas of 'managing the public's business' (Lynn 1981) to give direction to governing. They do so by devising, deliberating, interpreting, challenging and changing the institutional rules and practices of government (and, increasingly, 'governance,' Rhodes 1997), which exist to deal predictably, reliably and efficiently with the much greater number and variety of routine tasks that day-to-day governance entails.
>
> ('t Hart and Uhr 2008: 3)

The interesting proposition found in more recent comments on public sector leadership is that leaders have a special role to play in changing institutions, including those of public governance. Levi (2006: 10) made the case for leaders partly in terms of their ability to change institutions:

> Leadership aligns incentives, helps design and redesign institutions, provides the learning environment that enables individuals to transform or revise beliefs, and plays a major role in inducing preferences. Most importantly, leadership – both of government and within civil society – provides the human agency that coordinates the efforts of others. This is not a question of a Machiavellian Prince, who manipulates the populace to achieve his ends, but of a leadership that combines some of the strategic and other competences Machiavelli describes with the Weberian 'ethics of responsibility.'

While leaders are also individuals, they are leaders because they organize collective action and mobilize others to act in a joint manner. Leaders turn individuals into collectivities. According to this argument, purposeful and conscious action by people becomes effective in redesigning and changing institutions when leaders organize it.

WHAT IS EXPECTED OF LEADERS?

Back in the 1980s Kouzes and Posner (2007) began researching what people look for and admire in a leader whose direction they would follow willingly. They initially began by surveying business and government executives, and by 2007 had surveyed the views of 75,000 people around the world. It seems that the same four characteristics tended to head the list of 20 qualities (see Table 1.1). They conclude that people look for leaders who are honest, forward-looking, inspiring and competent (Kouzes and Posner 2007: 29).

They comment on the significance of the leader having been perceived as honest (Kouzes and Posner 2007: 32):

> It's clear that if people anywhere are to willingly follow someone – whether it's into battle or into the boardroom, the front office or the front lines – they

Table 1.1 Kouzes and Posner's surveys of admired leaders (2007)

Characteristic	%
Honest	89
Forward-looking	71
Inspiring	69
Competent	68
Intelligent	48
Fair minded	39
Straightforward	36
Broad minded	35
Supportive	35
Dependable	34
Co-operative	25
Courageous	25
Determined	25
Caring	22
Imaginative	17
Mature	15
Ambitious	16
Loyal	18
Self-controlled	10
Independent	4

Base: respondents from Africa, North America, South America, Asia, Europe and Australia. Respondents from the United States were in the majority.

Source: Table 2.1, page 30, Kouzes and Posner (2007).

15

first want to assure themselves that the person is worthy of their trust. They want to know that the person is truthful, ethical, and principled . . . We want to be told the truth. We want a leader who knows right from wrong.

They state that, in respect of being forward-looking, leaders must have a point of view about the future and they have to be able to imagine or discover a desired future towards which the organization should head. The key points they make, in respect of leaders being inspiring, is that leaders need to be enthusiastic, positive and upbeat. They connect this with the requirements of those being led to be hopeful about the future. Kouzes and Posner say (2007: 18):

> Leaders breathe life into the hopes and dreams of others and enable them to see the exciting possibilities that the future holds. Leaders forge a unity of purpose by showing constituents how the dream is for the common good. Leaders stir the fire of passion in others by expressing enthusiasm for the compelling vision of their group. Leaders communicate their passion through vivid language and expressive style.

The competence of the leader is defined as an ability to get things done and is believed to be founded on relevant experience and sound judgement. It is suggested that leaders need to put time into learning the business. But the required competence may also vary according to the leadership position occupied; for example, senior leaders need abilities in strategic planning and policymaking.

They put a very interesting construction on these findings about leadership characteristics. They suggest that three of them – honest, competent and inspiring – together form the basis of credibility; and then this, if combined with being forward-looking, is the essence of leadership. To paraphrase, leaders are people who are credible and forward-looking.

Having defined credibility as the basis of leadership, they provide examples of phrases used to describe credibility in a leader. Three examples are (Kouzes and Posner 2007):

- 'They do what they say they will do'
- 'They practice what they preach'
- 'They follow through on their promises'.

Remarkably similar findings were obtained from a survey of public sector managers in the UK. This was a survey of 1,890 mostly middle and junior level managers, carried out in late 2002 (Charlesworth et al. 2003). More than half of them reported that major reforms in the preceding three years had impacted service delivery. The respondents reported on the personal attributes they sought from leaders. The five top attributes were:

- Clarity of vision (66 per cent)
- Integrity (52 per cent)

16

- Sound judgement (50 per cent)
- Commitment to people development (49 per cent)
- Strategic (46 per cent).

If we assume that 'integrity' corresponds to being honest, 'clarity of vision' corresponds to being inspiring, 'sound judgement' corresponds to being competent, and 'strategic' to being forward-looking, then we might conclude that this sample of British public sector managers wanted public sector leaders to be credible and strategic.

In summary the argument is as follows: credible leaders are leaders who know how to build trust in their leadership and do this on the basis of their honesty, their competence and their ability to inspire. We trust leaders with this set of characteristics. Could leaders be credible if they were perceived as dishonest? Could they be credible if they were incompetent? Could they be credible leaders if they could not build hope among followers in the future direction they wanted to take?

THEY ARE NOT OMNISCIENT, OMNIPOTENT AND INFALLIBLE

If it was normally easy to plan actions and activities, fix timescales, allocate responsibilities and resources, and implement it all as planned, life would be easy. But it is usually not like that; change and activities cannot be easily programmed. Limits in both knowledge and power are the basis of many of the challenges leaders face. Because of the existence of these limits, a number of propositions can be suggested about leadership. First, leaders are always working in the context of limits to their knowledge and power, and therefore they sometimes get things wrong and sometimes cannot make things happen. Second, leaders must make decisions and act even though there are important things they do not know and have limited control over. Third, they need self-awareness of their limitations and thus need to have personal humility as well as a strong will to succeed. Collins (2006: 34), in his book on management in the social sectors, described a certain type of leader as one who 'displays a paradoxical blend of personal humility and professional will'. He believed such leaders were effective leaders of great organizations whether they were in the business or social sectors. They were leaders who people consented to follow. Fourth, they should recognize that they depend on others to help them in terms of knowledge and power. As Grint argued (2010: 105):

> ... leaders don't need to be perfect but, on the contrary, they do have to recognize that the limits of their knowledge and power will ultimately doom them to failure unless they rely on their subordinate leaders and followers to compensate for their own ignorance and impotence.

17

Fifth, because of the limits of knowledge and power, leaders need to be good at experimenting and learning (hopefully in a socially responsible way) and they need to be good at negotiating and managing conflicts.

Light (2014) researched failures by the US federal government, seeing them as indicators of government vulnerabilities and using them to think about government reform. He carried out an analysis of 41 highly visible failures in the period after 2001 until mid 2014. The failures were of two types: oversight failures, where government was responsible for monitoring and regulation, and operations failures, where government was involved as the provider of goods and services. Many of the 41 government failures were the subject of congressional or presidential investigation. They were also failures that attracted public attention and were heavily covered in the media. They included the terrorist attacks of September 2001, the slow government response to Hurricane Katrina in 2005, the 2008 banking system collapse, and the 2010 explosion on an offshore drilling platform in the Gulf of Mexico. Light commented that these four failures were likely to be remembered in the US for decades.

While he found multiple causes of every failure, in all but one of the 41 cases he identified a leadership issue. In about half the 41 cases this was judged by him to be ineffective decisions by leaders. For example, Light saw ineffective leadership decision making as an issue in the 9/11 terrorist attacks, the poor response to Hurricane Katrina, and the banking system collapse of 2008. He also saw poor decision making as an issue in the Secret Service Misconduct government failure in 2012 and in the Healthcare.gov launch of 2013. He found that ineffective decisions might be made before the failure event, during it and afterwards.

Light argued that most of the government failures were not caused by what the federal government did, but by what the federal government did not do. For example, he comments that the slow response to Hurricane Katrina in 2005 was a problem because the government did not have the leadership or plans to provide a quick response.

However, it is worth repeating that his analysis suggested multiple causes of government failure. We can illustrate this in Light's summing up of the 2013 Healthcare.gov website launch failure (Light 2014: 20):

> Designed as the portal for delivering a complex policy, healthcare.gov was highly dependent on a poorly coordinated collection of 55 outside vendors; delegated to an understaffed, underfunded agency; connected to antiquated information technology; embedded in a highly diffuse, over-layered, and poorly coordinated organizational structure; led by the first Senate-confirmed administrator in seven years; leashed to a deadline that required nearly flawless delivery; and aggressively monitored by a House of Representatives that wanted it to implode.

Elsewhere in his paper, Light argued that the impact of party politics within the federal government was partly to blame for problems in government effectiveness. (Arguably, the US Constitution – according to which Congress makes the laws and the president is responsible for their execution – is a factor in the functioning of US government, with gridlock occurring because of party politics.) One implication of this is that leadership in the federal government had to contend with a highly politicized environment and no doubt required considerable political shrewdness.

He clearly grounds his remarks about failure in a political context. For example, he suggests, looking back over an even longer period, that government failures increased in frequency in the last part of presidential terms. Also, with reference to the Bush and Obama presidencies after 2001, he noticed that failures were more frequent in the second term as compared to the first term of a presidency.

DEFINING STRATEGIC LEADERSHIP IN THE PUBLIC SECTOR

In the public sector, as elsewhere, there is a tendency to see strategic leadership as occurring only at the top levels of hierarchical structures. For example, some years ago the US government published a model of leadership with different types of leadership at different hierarchical levels. The model proposed that strategic leaders should be located at the higher levels (OECD 2001: 15): 'Strategic leadership is required at the higher levels for such components as strategic thinking, political savvy, vision, external awareness, influencing or negotiating, and cultural awareness'.

The US government model can be used to suggest a definition of strategic leaders in the public sector. Strategic leaders can be defined as public officials (elected or appointed) who ensure that actions taken by governments and public sector organizations are purposeful and conscious; who make decisions based on strategic thinking and external and cultural assessments; who make decisions that are politically shrewd; and who use influence and negotiation to increase their effectiveness.

This definition of strategic leaders is broadly consistent with Mulgan's view of strategy (Mulgan 2009: 7): 'Strategy translates wishes into results by mobilizing power and knowledge.' Strategic leaders are the people who, ultimately, mobilize power and knowledge. Knowledge is obtained and used through strategic thinking and political shrewdness. Power is mobilized using influence and negotiation. This suggested definition of strategic leaders is shown in Figure 1.4.

Strategic leaders can be defined as: public officials (elected or appointed) who (i) should ensure that actions taken by governments and public sector organizations are purposeful and conscious; (ii) make decisions based on strategic thinking and external and cultural assessments; (iii) make decisions that are politically shrewd; and (iv) use influence and negotiation to increase their effectiveness.

19

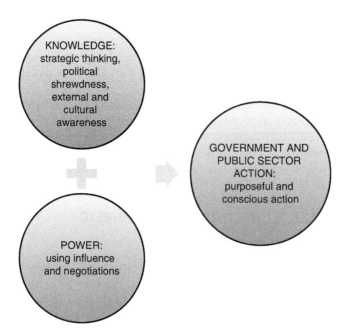

Figure 1.4 *Strategic leaders and public sector action*

It is still common to assume that strategic leaders are all top officials (as proposed in the US government leadership model). However, there are some strategic leaders at the higher levels of government or public sector organizations who are keen to see strategic thinking and leadership at all levels. They may not want people at middle and lower levels to develop formal strategic plans as such, but they recognize that agile and effective public sector organizations benefit from others apart from themselves acting as leaders and using strategic thinking. For example, they may say they want managers at middle levels to be good at strategic issue management and to provide leadership in taking actions to solve strategic issues. By identifying strategic issues, and planning and implementing feasible actions, this middle-level leadership shares in the responsibility shouldered by leaders at the higher levels to make government strategic and effective. They are removing the barriers and obstacles to the successful implementation of formal strategic plans emerging at the higher levels.

Where responsibility for strategic thinking has been spread to other levels, the leaders at lower levels are part of a network of strategic leaders within government (or within a public sector organization). We might hypothesize that such networks are especially valuable in more decentralized structures and in structures that allow more autonomy to management at lower levels.

Changes in the concept and practice of public governance probably means we should see strategic leadership as applicable beyond single public sector organizations (Osborne and Gaebler 1992; Kooiman 1993). We can explain this

20

point in the following way: It is common to stress that leaders are not individuals who achieve things by themselves. Strategic leaders work through people. They devise strategies, or ensure strategies are devised, and then use them to get effective joint action by people working in government or working in organizations in the wider public sector. They increasingly extend this joint action to people outside government and outside the wider public sector, including citizens and people in interest groups and private sector and voluntary organizations.

GUIDE TO THE REST OF THE BOOK

This book is an inquiry that sets out to discover as much as possible about the facts concerning strategic leadership in the public sector. The intention is to pay attention to both the theory and the practice. There are three overarching questions:

1 What are the actions of strategic leaders in the public sector?
2 What techniques do strategic leaders use?
3 What are the consequences of their actions?

SUMMARY

Strategic leadership became an important issue in the public sector after the 1990s; it is not certain why this happened. It might have been directly connected to the reforms and modernization of public governance, and the attempts by governments to develop strategic management capabilities. It might have just been that it took a few years for the ideas of leadership and strategic leadership to surface in the private sector and then spread to the public sector. It may be that the attention being given to leadership may wane and all the fuss made about leadership in the last 15 years will appear to have been just a passing fad. Perhaps all of this is true.

A pragmatic response (philosophically speaking) to the uncertainty about the causes of the rise of leadership as an issue in the public sector would be to say that understanding the causes is not a high priority. It is probably more useful to leave to one side the issue of why leadership became more important when it did, and instead concentrate on understanding the actions of leaders and their consequences in a public sector setting. Understanding how leaders act and what consequences flow from leadership action should have both theoretical and practical usefulness.

In reviewing some old but influential ideas we came across Tom Peters' propositions that there were dangers of strategic plans becoming rigid and bureaucratic and that strategic plans in themselves were of little use. He said the strategic planning process could be useful, but he saw its justification as mainly

21

that it might provoke thought. He believed that business success in the 1980s depended on organizations being fast and flexible so as to take advantage of short-lived opportunities. Before such ideas can be transplanted to the public sector, it is worth remembering that Tom Peters had an argument in which everything made sense on the basis that survival of a business had become problematic because the environment was fast changing, complex and volatile. And he assumed it was a time in which prediction was futile. The question has to be asked: does the public sector context present the same challenges? Or does a public sector situation make specific demands that were not considered by Tom Peters?

There are in fact a lot of special pressures and issues in a public sector context because leaders are inevitably involved in public governance. Hence, the World Bank (1997) was quoted above as saying that public sector leaders sought the public's ownership of reforms. Why was ownership important? Maybe it is because the public might provide support to the implementation of reforms if they felt some ownership of them. But it may also be because in modern public governance there may be an idea that government serves the public, and this involves both being responsive to the public and being accountable to it. So, the public is brought into the process of formulating reforms as a partner of the government, and because of this the public feels some ownership of the reforms. Likewise, in the public sector there are issues about open government and transparency and these no doubt have implications for leadership. Neither Tom Peters nor Bernard Bass were concerned with leaders facing distinctively public sector challenges. Neither were they concerned with accountability to the public. It is worth mentioning also that Tom Peters did not like hierarchical control but did like experiments and learning. But, in democratic countries, how is accountability to the public to be made real if there is no upward accountability of managers and employees to elected politicians? Therefore, accountability to the public and learning are both important in a democracy, not just learning.

Another question mark over the influential ideas from the 1980s concerns the view taken on conflicting interests. As was seen when looking at the ideas of Bernard Bass, transformational leaders are hypothesized to get individuals to put aside their self-interest and instead commit to pursuing the common good. Something similar can be inferred from the ideas of Tom Peters when he suggests that the organizational flexibility required in fast-changing business environments will only be obtained if there is more trust and less 'adversarial dealings' (Peters 1987: 392). How easily can individuals in an organization be persuaded to put their self-interests to one side and act in ways that are for the common good? In the rest of this book the assumption that leaders can get followers to suspend their self-interests will be treated as a proposition to be tested against evidence.

The ideas of Osborne and Gaebler were, and still are, important in suggesting reform agendas for strategic leadership in the public sector. For example, leaders might have to bring about and sustain: competition between public service providers; moving control out of the bureaucracy and into the community (public empowerment); and catalysing actions by all sectors (public, private and voluntary) to solve the public's problems.

Later in the book we will see that research on leadership in the public sector has been published that shows that leadership has consequences, it has effects. Sometimes the effects may be bad ones, as well as the hoped for good ones. In this book it will be assumed that leaders in the public sector are constrained by public opinion and behaviour even though leaders might also be able to influence what the public thinks and does. Likewise, in this book it will be assumed that leaders in the public sector are constrained by existing government institutions but are also able to change the institutions of government and the wider public sector.

Based on available empirical research it seems that others expect leaders in the public sector (and the private sector) to be both credible and strategic. It would seem, furthermore, that leadership credibility is perceived to exist when a leader is honest and has integrity, inspires, and is competent.

Light's study of failures by the US federal government is an important reminder of what we should already know: public sector leaders are fallible, may make poor decisions and may create poor outcomes for the public. This should not be surprising. Leaders to a greater or lesser extent act purposefully and consciously and this means we should expect mistakes, failures of will and so on.

Finally, we can suggest that strategic leaders should ensure that actions taken by governments and public sector organizations are purposeful and conscious; make decisions based on strategic thinking and external and cultural assessments; make decisions that are politically shrewd; and use influence and negotiation to increase their effectiveness.

Assignment

The assignments in this book are mostly for civil servants and other public services staff who have management experience. In this case, however, experienced managers can do the assignment based on their experiences of being a manager, and those without experience may want to try it on the basis of how they imagine they would answer it in the future or how they would like to be able to answer it in the future. For the latter group, this may be a difficult but still a worthwhile exercise.

The contents of Tables 1.2, 1.3 and 1.4 below have been modelled on or inspired by some of the items that have been used in the past to investigate transformational and transactional leadership. Please rate the items in each of the tables by ticking the appropriate column. In each case judge how frequently the statement fits you. If you find it impossible to rate an item, please rate it as 'not at all'.

When you have rated all the items, please study the patterns in your answers. Have you placed a lot of ticks in the 'fairly often' or 'frequently' columns for transformational leadership items? What about the transactional leadership

Table 1.2 *Transformational leadership: items for rating*

		How frequently did you do this?				
		Not at all	Once in a while	Sometimes	Fairly often	Frequently, or always
1	I ensure the people I lead feel pride in what we do					
2	I put the good of the department/section above my own self-interest					
3	I conduct myself in a manner that earns the respect of those I lead					
4	I present myself as both confident and capable of getting things done					
5	I discuss my core personal values and attitudes with the people I lead					
6	I stress to the people I lead that it is essential that we have clarity and strength of purpose					
7	I assess the moral and ethical implications of decisions before deciding what to do					
8	I stress to the people I lead that we need a collective view of our mission or purpose					
9	I discuss the future optimistically with the people I lead					
10	I discuss our goals and targets in an enthusiastic manner with the people I lead					
11	I present in writing and verbally a convincing vision of the future					
12	I make it clear to the people that I lead that I am confident that we will deliver the goals that have been set					
13	When making decisions about future direction and choice of options I carefully check the assumptions I have made					
14	I encourage the people I lead to consider a range of perspectives when we have to address problems					

Table 1.2. *(Continued)*

	How frequently did you do this?				
	Not at all	Once in a while	Sometimes	Fairly often	Frequently, or always
15 I ask the people I lead to analyse and assess problems from a range of different points of view					
16 I propose options and new ideas when discussing with the people I lead how we will do a project or how we will meet a performance target					
17 I invest my personal time in coaching and mentoring the people I lead					
18 I make sure I interact with the people I lead as individuals as well as treating them as part of the whole group					
19 I assess the needs, skills, career goals and hopes of the people I lead on an individual basis					
20 I put time into supporting the people I lead to develop their strengths and reduce their weaknesses					

items: are there lots of ticks in 'fairly often' and 'frequently'? Therefore, do you seem to be a transformational leader or a transactional leader – or both or neither? It is common for individuals to be both transformational and transactional to some extent. And how do you seem in terms of the third table in which there are items looking at some possible consequences of leadership?

You can use this assignment to make a contribution to a class discussion or an online forum discussion. The discussion might address the following questions:

1 How easy is to apply the ideas of transformational and transactional leadership to practical experiences as leaders?
2 Is the transformational style equally effective in all situations? What, based on your experience, acts as a constraint on the use of a transformational style? Does it work as well in a public sector as in a private sector context?
3 Is the transformational style of leadership socially oriented and does it result in moral uplifting of followers?

Table 1.3 *Leadership using contingent rewards: items for rating*

	How frequently did you do this?				
	Not at all	Once in a while	Sometimes	Fairly often	Frequently, or always
1 I support the people I lead and they know I have a clear expectation that they will work hard in return for the support I give					
2 I make clear who is responsible and accountable for the things we have to do – including the delivery of goals and performance targets					
3 I am very clear with the people I lead what rewards they will get if we are successful (e.g. if we deliver our goals and targets)					
4 I always let the people I lead know that I am satisfied and appreciative when they do what has been required					

Table 1.4 *Leadership consequences: items for rating*

	How frequently did you do this?				
	Not at all	Once in a while	Sometimes	Fairly often	Frequently, or always
1 I am effective in meeting organizational requirements					
2 The people I lead are seen in the organization generally as being an effective group					
3 I increase the desire of the people I lead to succeed					
4 The people I lead think my style of leadership is satisfactory and they are satisfied with how well I lead					

DISCUSSION QUESTIONS

1   The idea of leadership in the public sector seemed to become popular in the late 1990s and during the 2000s. What was the cause of public sector leadership's emergence as a 'hot issue'? Can its rise be attributed mainly to the diffusion of the concept of leadership from the US private sector oriented writing of the 1980s (e.g. Tom Peters and Bernard Bass) and its diffusion into the European public sector a little bit later?
2   The reform and modernization of public sector institutions (including the state) requires effective leadership. Do you agree? Why do you agree/disagree?
3   What should be expected of leaders in the public sector?
4   Based on your reading of newspapers and journals, what was the worst government or public sector failure that occurred in the last two years? What part did poor public sector leadership play in the failure? What are the lessons for making leadership more effective in the future?

FURTHER READING

Kouzes, J. M. and Posner, B. Z. (2007) *The Leadership Challenge*. 4th edition. San Francisco, CA: Jossey-Bass. Chapters 1 and 2.

Chapter 1 provides a fairly typical example of the sort of leadership model that emerged from various writers in the US in the mid to late 1980s. In Chapter 1 it is argued that exemplary leadership practices include: model the way (set values and set the example), inspire a shared vision, challenge the process (experiment and take risks), enable others to act (this includes building trust and developing competence) and encourage the heart (appreciate individual excellence, celebrate victories, etc.). In Chapter 2 the evidence from a number of countries on what people expect of leaders is reviewed and the suggestion is made that expectations tend to focus on leaders having credibility (i.e. being honest, inspiring and competent) and being forward-looking (i.e. leaders should have a point of view about the future).

REFERENCE LIST

Aristotle (1981) *The Politics*. London: Penguin Books.
Bass, B. M. (1997) Does the transactional–transformational leadership paradigm transcend organizational and national boundaries? *American Psychologist*, 52(2): 130–9.
Bass, B. M. (1999) Two decades of research and development in transformational leadership. *European Journal of Work and Organizational Psychology*, 8(1): 9–32.

Berger, P. L. and Luckmann, T. (1966) *The Social Construction of Reality*. Harmondsworth, Middlesex: Penguin Books.

Bichard, M. (2000) Creativity, leadership and change. *Public Money and Management*, April–June: 41–6.

Bryson, J. M. (1988) *Strategic Planning for Public and Nonprofit Organizations*, 1st edition. San Francisco, CA: Jossey-Bass.

Burns, J. M. (1978) *Leadership*. New York: Harper & Row.

Charlesworth, K., Cook, P. and Crozier G. (2003) *Leading Change in the Public Sector: Making the Difference*. London: Chartered Management Institute.

Collins, J. (2006) *Good to Great and the Social Sectors*. UK: Random House Business Books.

Davis, D. D., Guan, P. L., Luo, J. J. and Maahs, C. J. (1996) 'Need for continuous improvement, organizational citizenship, transformational leadership and service climate in a Chinese enterprise'. Unpublished manuscript.

Grint, K. (2010) *Leadership: A Very Short Introduction*. Oxford: Oxford University Press.

Hamel, G. and C. K. Prahalad (1994) *Competing for the Future*. Boston, MA: Harvard Business School Press.

Kooiman, J. (ed.) (1993) *Modern Governance: New Government–Society Interactions*. London: Sage.

Kooiman, J. and van Vliet, M. (1993) 'Governance and public management', in K. A. Eliassen and J. Kooiman (eds) *Managing Public Organizations*. London: Sage.

Kouzes, J. M. and Posner, B. Z. (2007) *The Leadership Challenge*. 4th edition. San Francisco, CA: Jossey-Bass.

Levi, M. (2006) Why we need a new theory of government. *Perspectives on Politics*, 4(1): 5–19.

Light P. C. (2014) *A Cascade of Failures: Why Government Fails, and How to Stop It. Center for Effective Public Management at Brookings*. [Online]. Available from: www.brookings.edu/research/papers/2014/07/14-cascade-failures-why-government-fails-light [Accessed: 4 January 2016].

Lynn, L. (1981) *Managing the Public's Business: The Job of the Government Executive*. New York: Basic Books.

Mulgan, G. (2009) *The Art of Public Strategy: Mobilizing Power and Knowledge For the Common Good*. Oxford: Oxford University Press.

OECD (2001) *Public Sector Leadership for the 21ˢᵗ Century*. Paris: OECD Publications.

Osborne, D. and Gaebler, T. (1992) *Reinventing Government: How the Entrepreneurial Spirit is Transforming the Public Sector*. Reading, MA: Addison Wesley.

Pereira, D. (1986) Transactional and transformational leadership scores of executives in a large Indian engineering firm. Paper presented at the meeting of the International Congress of Applied Psychology, Jerusalem.

Peters, T. (1987) *Thriving on Chaos: Handbook for a Management Revolution*. London: Pan Books.

PUMA (1996) *Focus*, Number 1 (June). Paris: OECD.

Rhodes, R. A. W. (1997) *Understanding Governance*. Buckingham and Philadelphia: Open University Press.

Steyrer, J. and Mende, M. (1994) *Transformational leadership: The local market success of Austrian branch bank managers and training applications*. Paper presented at the meeting of the International Congress of Applied Psychology, Madrid, Spain.

't Hart, P. and Uhr, J. (2008) 'Understanding public leadership: an introduction', in P. 't Hart and J. Uhr (eds) *Public Leadership: Perspectives and Practices*. Canberra: ANU E Press, pp. 1–22.

Waldman, D., Bass, B. M. and Einstein, W. O. (1986) *Effort, performance and transformational leadership in industrial and military settings*. Working Paper 84–78). Binghampton: State University of New York.

World Bank. (1997) *World Development Report 1997: The State in a Changing World*. New York: Oxford University Press.

Yokochi, N. (1989) 'Leadership styles of Japanese business executives and managers: Transformational and transactional'. Unpublished doctoral dissertation. United States International University, San Diego, CA.

Chapter 2

The competent leader

LEARNING OBJECTIVES

- To consider the nature of competencies and to understand the context in which competency frameworks have developed in the public sector
- To examine some case studies on competency frameworks at national level of government
- To review relevant research findings on the consequences of strategic leadership competencies

INTRODUCTION

What do public sector leaders think makes a great public sector leader? The following are some judgements of three UK public sector leaders (Smith 2015). (See Figure 2.1.)

Sir Richard Leese, political leader of Manchester City Council since the mid 1990s, said the best leaders have analytical skills and understand their situation. He also said 'a leader needs to articulate a vision; set a direction . . . to take people with you – to articulate a vision that people share'.

Sir Bob Kerslake, who became head of the UK Civil Service in 2010, said,

> I don't think it's innate, but there has to be an appetite to take control. The most important trait of leadership is being self-aware, and recognising what your own strengths and weaknesses are. You can't necessarily alter them, but you can build up a team around you that can compensate for your weaknesses and complement your strengths.

Joanne Roney, Chief Executive of Wakefield Council, suggested, 'It's vital to have an awareness of the culture of the organisation and build a strong and effective leadership around that'.

In this chapter we explore the idea of leadership competencies. They have been put forward as the basis of frameworks for recruiting, evaluating and

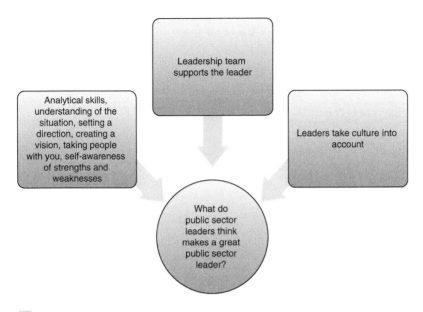

Figure 2.1 *What some public sector leaders think about good leadership*

developing leaders. The competency approach has been popular with governments and public sector organizations for 20 years or more.

LEADERSHIP GENERALLY

Brian Tracy (2015) argued that leaders are very good at planning and strategic thinking:

> Leaders are good strategists and planners. Again, what I've found in working with successful men and women in business is that they're very, very good planners. They have taken the time to learn or been taught how to do strategic thinking. Strategic thinking means taking the long view. It means engaging in what is called "big-picture thinking." Leaders look at everything they are doing and at all the different things that can have an impact on them. They look upon themselves as part of a bigger world. They think in terms of "If I do this, what is likely to happen? How will my competition respond; how will friends and enemies respond; what will the market do?"

A global survey carried out by the American Management Association in 2005 discovered that the most important leadership competencies in the USA and elsewhere were strategy development and communication skills (American Management Association 2005). The judgements of nearly 1,600 respondents, mainly from the USA, Canada and Western Europe, are shown in Table 2.1.

Table 2.1 Global survey of leadership by American Management Association (2005)

Leadership competencies	Average points allocated out of 100							
	Total sample (n = 1573)	USA	Western Europe	Eastern Europe	Middle East	Canada	Asia	Latin America
Strategy development	11.05	10.96	12.02	11.53	10.58	10.58	11.01	10.07
Communication skills	10.24	10.06	11.07	7.66	7.95	10.97	10.37	7.85
Development leaders	6.79	6.96	5.60	6.31	6.37	7.92	7.29	4.93
Hiring talent	6.10	5.52	5.72	5.49	5.74	5.83	5.29	7.26
Fostering creativity and innovation	6.06	5.73	6.61	5.57	6.11	6.21	5.62	5.56
Driving for results	6.02	5.34	6.89	6.51	8.21	5.56	7.42	6.26
Know the business	5.71	5.59	6.47	6.88	3.79	4.59	5.28	8.48
Role model for organization's values	5.53	5.52	5.35	5.47	7.32	5.54	5.88	3.89
Business ethics	5.43	6.19	4.18	4.31	6.00	5.44	5.11	7.44
Know the industry	4.42	4.69	4.17	4.66	3.26	4.27	3.96	3.63

Note: 1 Respondents were asked: What do you think are the leadership competencies needed to function effectively today? Each respondent had 100 points to allocate across 20 items according to what they saw as most relevant. 2 The survey was emailed to respondents in 2005 and 1,573 usable responses were obtained. Most of the respondents were from the USA (42.4 per cent), Canada (18.1 per cent) and Western Europe (20.9 per cent). Many (42.2 per cent) of the respondents had jobs at the corporate level or the divisional level (22.4 per cent). Many had jobs in Human Resources/Administration (27.1 per cent) and General Management (24.2 per cent).

So, it seems, leadership and strategy are seen by many people to go together. Leaders are responsible for the development of strategy for their organizations, and it seems that linked to this is the importance of leaders being good at planning and communicating. See Figure 2.2.

WHAT ARE COMPETENCIES?

In some countries regarded as at the forefront of management practice in the public sector, the idea of management in the public sector only started to become important in the 1980s. The name 'managers' started to displace that of 'administrators'. Management development seemed to grow in importance alongside the early 1990s' movement to improve the quality of public services. HR professionals began to design management competency frameworks.

We should note that these frameworks were originally for managers, not strategic leaders. Management competency frameworks spread widely. As Wilkins (2015) put it, in relation to Canada:

> A generation of public managers has been raised in a counter culture vested in claims of competence. A cottage industry of HR specialists and consultants feasts on the spoils, with mixed results. Competency frameworks cascade standardized roles, attributes, behaviours, and measures across the performance landscape.

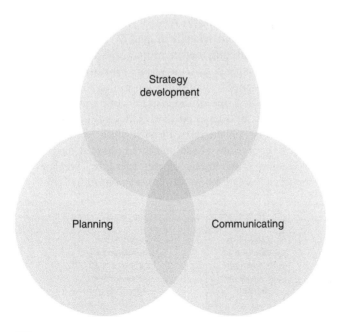

Figure 2.2 *Conventional wisdom on what business leaders need to be good at*

In essence, it seemed to be assumed that training and development of individuals to give them the right strategic leadership competencies would improve the performance and results of public sector organizations. See Figure 2.3.

The relevant competencies could be identified using functional analysis. The essence of this type of analysis is a logical and hierarchical analysis of the functions of a job (Holmes and Joyce 1993: 42):

> The methodology for analyzing work performance is a relatively new approach, functional analysis. This involves the identification or definition of the key purpose/function to establish the purposes or outcomes which must be met for the key purpose to be achieved. So the overall competence is analysed first into units of competence, then each unit is analysed into elements of competence . . . For each element a number of performance criteria are specified, presented in the form of required outcomes. Thus the overall disaggregation process leads to statements of outcomes to be achieved.

To illustrate this, here is a possible functional analysis for the job of strategic leader. We start by identifying the purpose of a strategic leader job; for example, it might be suggested that their function or purpose is to help organizations to manage change so as to bring about a good future. This purpose could be broken down into units of competence such as creating a vision and strategy, mobilizing people, demonstrating integrity and respect, collaborating with partners and stakeholders, promoting innovation and guiding change, and achieving results. These can each be considered in turn and broken down further into more detailed activities. Creating vision and strategy might be sub-divided into elements of competence such as analysing the situation, analysing the interests and power of stakeholders, articulating a strategic vision, formulating strategic goals, identifying issues and constraints, identifying and evaluating alternative courses of action, and so on. Taking one of the elements of competence, say 'analysing the situation', it might be suggested that there could be two performance criteria (outcomes): first, producing a PEST analysis of the external situation (including political, economic, social and technological events and trends) and second, producing a statement of the strengths, weaknesses, opportunities and threats (i.e. a SWOT analysis) of the organization.

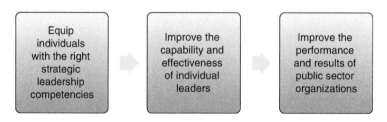

Figure 2.3 Strategic leadership competencies and their effects

It is important to be clear that the two performance criteria (outcomes) developed in this made-up illustration of functional analysis relate to an outcome defined in a special sense, and that defining the performance criteria in this way is significant for the implications of the use of functional analysis. We are not considering here some overall outcome, such as more effective public service delivery by an organization over the long-term, or a successful transformation of a public sector organization over a period of several years. The outcomes are instead of specific elements of competence and could be seen as immediate products of the performance of the units of competence (e.g. a SWOT analysis resulting from a person analysing the situation). To use this approach to functional analysis as the basis of assessments of the overall competence of a strategic leader, requires assessment of a large number of very specific outcomes of the numerous elements of competence. While an individual may demonstrate an ability to deliver the many outcomes of all the elements of competence, this type of assessment does not show that such a person has been effective in strategic leadership in terms of some con-sequential effects, such as successful strategic change by the organization and long-term success of the organization in terms of public support and public satisfaction.

When such a hierarchy of behaviours (performances) has been produced it can be tested for acceptability. Research can be carried out into the opinions of key users of competency frameworks for strategic leadership. Do the users agree with the results of the functional analysis? Do they think anything is missing? This research may be used to modify or refine the functional analysis so that acceptability of the competency framework is increased.

Such competency frameworks may be used to recruit, evaluate, promote, train and develop individuals. For example, interviewers may use the elements of competence or performance criteria to frame questions to put to job appli-cants. One tendency in practice is for the evaluation of the competence of individuals using such a framework to become superficial and a 'tick box' exercise. During selection interviews, job candidates may be asked if they have ever displayed the behaviour specified in an element of competence or per-formance criterion. Often interviewers take a report of prior experience of such required behaviour as evidence of the person being competent in it. There is no attempt to judge how well it was done and whether it was successful in terms of the consequences that resulted from the behaviour.

Making comparisons between strategic leaders who vary in effectiveness can also be used to identify competencies. Data can be collected on effective and ineffective leaders using a variety of methods. A comparison of the two groups might yield differences that become the basis for identifying competencies that are believed to cause strategic leaders to be effective. This option is not without its problems and is not foolproof, but it does have the virtue of enabling us to argue that there is some evidence for a link between strategic leadership com-petencies and the consequences in terms of leadership effectiveness. The functional analysis option, when it is ultimately justified on the grounds that it is

35

acceptable to stakeholders, does not directly address the issue of the effects of strategic leadership competencies.

There are probably many other possible ways in which competencies might be identified. The following example is taken from a large government department in the UK in 2004. The trainers in the civil service department used an interviewing technique based on Kelly's repertory grid, which essentially involved them asking civil servants to consider sets of three people they knew. For each set of three, they were asked to decide in what way two of them differed from the third. This interviewing provided data from which the departmental trainers created a list of competencies for senior civil servants. Finally, they designed a range of courses to which individuals were matched based on an evaluation of their competencies. It seems likely that this method, used on its own, might result in cloning senior civil servants but it did not appear capable of showing that the identified competencies would produce effective strategic leaders.

It is possible to define strategic leadership competencies in two entirely different ways. First, they can be defined in terms of personal skills and qualities. Second, when using functional analysis, they can be specified as required behaviours (performances) of a role or a job. Defining strategic leadership competencies as personal skills and qualities might produce more versatile leaders who can operate successfully in a range of situations. Defining them in terms of required behaviours might help with establishing and stabilizing role definitions in a specific organization. But could it also reinforce or encourage a mechanistic view of organizational capacity and lead to rigidity and a compliance mentality in organizations?

It has often seemed in practice that the distinction between personal skills and characteristics on one hand, and required behaviours on the other, can become blurred. This blurring might occur because of the complementary nature of these two conceptions of competencies. The existence of personal skills and qualities is important for the successful accomplishment of required behaviours, and required behaviours influence the valuing and development of personal skills and qualities. See Figure 2.4.

COMPETENCIES AND TALENT MANAGEMENT

Management development programmes were often redesigned to provide leadership as well as management development, or even just leadership development. As early as 2001, the OECD was reporting (OECD 2001: 8): 'Many countries are expanding their existing management development programmes to encompass leadership development'. These changes can be seen as an indication that a cultural shift was underway in the public sector and (indirectly) as a sign that agility, flexibility and innovation had moved up the agenda of government and the public sector.

Public sector and civil service reform has been occurring in many countries both before and just after the arrival of the new millennium. Civil service reform

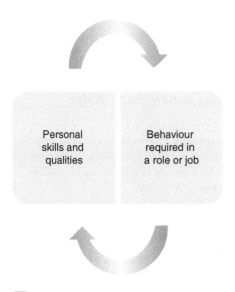

Figure 2.4 *What are competencies?*

seems to have been co-occurring with increased attention to leadership and strategy, and also with increased interest in performance management, career management and people development generally. There were signs of a shift towards thinking of people development in terms of talent management, high potential schemes and succession planning.

Talent management in relation to leadership can involve creating talent pipelines and pools. Linking together and integrating various activities may do this: workplace planning, assessments of the leadership potential of individuals, training programmes, and recruitment and selection of individuals.

The idea of talent management also represented (potentially at least) a significant break in the development of thinking about the very essence of training and development interventions. The following may be a slight caricature, but late 1980s' and early 1990s' management development approaches might be seen as largely about training people to fit roles, to make them into competent managers, meaning that they should be trained to perform required behaviours as laid out in functional analysis and as linked to formal job descriptions. In contrast, talent management entailed, to some degree, the idea that the development of effective leaders was more than training people to perform actions as required by a standard set of job requirements. Leaders were expected to make a more personality-based contribution, to act in a more personally authentic way, making more use of their values and personal qualities. For example, much was made of the need for leaders to act honestly and with integrity to earn the trust of their workforce. The performance of leaders was seen in some sense as more dependent on their personal skills and qualities than those of managers. Talent management, again to some degree, might lead those

37

doing the development to think in terms of supporting people with a raw talent for leadership to develop this talent further.

Vignette: Talent management plans in New South Wales (Australia)

The Government of New South Wales in Australia undertook various reforms to improve its managerial leadership and its workforce from 2012 onwards. A survey carried out in 2014 provided evidence on the extent of talent management plans (Public Service Commission, NSW Government 2015: 22):

> NSW public sector agencies increasingly see talent management as a necessary part of their workforce management practices.
>
> The inaugural agency survey shows 40 per cent of agencies have a talent management plan at some stage of implementation for identifying, developing and retaining high-performing or high-potential employees [. . .]. This is a relatively new concept in the NSW public sector, reflected in the results that show that many (32 per cent) of these agencies are at a basic stage of use while only 8 per cent of agencies described their plans as developed or highly developed.
>
> The survey also showed that agencies were most likely to have actively identified senior managers (31 per cent) and managers (31 per cent) as high-performing or high-potential employees compared to other employee groups (22 per cent) or graduates (15 per cent). The focus on the management level is consistent with talent management principles that emphasise the need for succession planning and growing the leadership pipeline. [. . .]
>
> It is also notable that the majority of agencies (57 per cent) are incorporating talent management and succession planning for future leadership roles into their workforce planning processes.

CASE STUDY

United States: competencies of the Senior Executive Service

The federal government of the US spends huge sums of public money and operates through federal agencies. The US policy on strategic planning by federal agencies was established through the Government Performance and Results Act (GPRA) of 1993. As a consequence, a system of producing strategic plans for each federal agency was institutionalized and agencies have been producing strategic plans since the late 1990s. In 2010 the GPRA Modernization Act (GPRAMA) was passed. This was intended, in part, to prompt a more 'joined-up' approach to government. A General Accounting Office (GAO) representative made this point in a report to a US Senate Committee (Dodaro 2011: 2):

> The federal government faces a series of challenges that in many instances are not possible for any single agency to address alone. Many federal program efforts, including those related to ensuring food safety, providing homeland security, monitoring incidence of infectious diseases, or improving response to natural disasters, transcend more than one agency. Agencies face a range of challenges and barriers when they attempt to work collaboratively. GPRAMA establishes a new framework aimed at taking a more crosscutting and integrated approach to focusing on results and improving government performance.

In the US the Senior Executive Service has operated at just below the level of presidential appointees and has been responsible for providing leadership to the workforce of the federal agencies. The members of the Senior Executive Service, comprising some 7,000 career senior executives, have been identified as strategic leaders within the federal government (United States Office of Personnel Management 2012: 1):

> The law requires that the executive qualifications of each new career appointee to the Senior Executive Service (SES) be certified by an independent Qualifications Review Board based on criteria established by the Office of Personnel Management (OPM). The Executive Core Qualifications (ECQs) describe the leadership skills needed to succeed in the SES; they also reinforce the concept of an "SES corporate culture." This concept holds that the Government needs executives who can provide strategic leadership and whose commitment to public policy and administration transcends their commitment to a specific agency mission or an individual profession.

The members of the Senior Executive Service have been expected to operate as a coherent and cohesive leadership group that pursues a 'whole of government' approach.

In 2012 there were 28 Senior Executive Service competencies. Twenty-two of them were grouped into five ECQs and the remaining six were identified as fundamental competencies. These are shown in Figure 2.5.

The definitions of the competencies were normally relatively obvious. For example, the 'strategic thinking' competence was concerned with the formulation of objectives and priorities, the implementation of plans, taking advantage of opportunities and managing risks. The 'vision' competence included taking a long-term view, building a shared vision with others, catalysing organizational change and influencing others to turn vision into action. The 'political savvy' competence related to acting appropriately in line with organizational and political reality, and identifying pressures originating from internal and external politics.

Some of the competencies seemed to be closer to personal skills and qualities rather than being required behaviours. For example, the 'resilience' competence was defined as dealing effectively with pressure, remaining optimistic and persistent and recovering quickly from setbacks. 'Flexibility' was about being open to change and information, and rapidly adapting to new information, changing conditions or unexpected obstacles. The content of the 'integrity/honesty' competence included what might be called personal qualities rather than skills: behaving in an honest, fair and ethical manner. 'Public service motivation' included a reference to showing a commitment to serve the public. 'Interpersonal skills' was defined as including treating others with courtesy, sensitivity and respect. All of them could be seen as generally applicable to the tasks and activities of leading rather than as a specific functional task or activity of leadership.

Figure 2.5 *United States – competencies of Senior Executive Service (2012)*

The OPM reported that the ECQs were formulated in 1997 and were based on extensive research in both the private and public sectors; they were refined in 2006. It has been claimed (United States Office of Personnel Management 2012: Introduction), 'In their current form, ECQs represent the best thinking of organizational psychologists, human resources professionals both at OPM and other agencies and Senior Executives themselves'. This sounds like the competencies may reflect a combination of conventional wisdom and what is acceptable to the Senior Executives. It is not clear that the competencies have been validated by research into the consequences of the application of such competencies.

The competencies framework developed for the Senior Executive Service has been used for various things, including selecting who will enter it (United States Office of Personnel Management (2015): 'The Executive Core Qualifications are required for entry to the Senior Executive Service and are used by many departments and agencies in selection, performance management, and leadership development for management and executive positions'.

The focus of the Senior Executive Service Candidate Development Programs set up by individual agencies has been on developing candidates' competencies. The programmes have been required to last for a year, and involve at least 80 hours of formal training, mentoring and executive level developmental assignments.

According to a McKinsey report (McKinsey 2013: 7):

> ... OPM doesn't have the capacity, resources or authority to take charge of executive development government-wide. [...] because every agency independently develops its executive pipeline, quality varies markedly and little attention is given to government-wide needs. [...] Although many agencies have elements of a strong pipeline in place, such as workforce planning or training, we found that those elements often are disconnected from one another rather than functioning as parts of a cohesive strategy.

It seems that the US may have aspired to a whole of government approach by the Senior Executive Service but the agency-by-agency model of leadership development may have left individuals ill-prepared for tackling government-wide needs. The McKinsey report also made criticism of the talent pipelines for leadership: they were fragmented and not functioning as part of a cohesive strategy. Ideas for civil service development are one thing; how they are executed in practice is another. Despite 'pockets of excellence', the McKinsey report suggested more action was needed immediately to improve leadership pipelines.

The report also identified issues in terms of agency leadership support for leadership development (2013: 9):

> We found that senior agency leaders, for the most part, pay insufficient attention to ensuring that their agency identifies, develops, recruits and selects the best executives. "I'm struck by the inability of organizational leadership to look at their SES corps critically," said one senior agency leader, observing that most of his peers at other agencies don't think of developing SES

41

pipelines as their core responsibility. Our interviewees suggested that even while senior agency leaders see lack of SES 'bench strength' as an issue, they often treat development of talent for the SES as a process-oriented function rather than a strategic one.

Perhaps this criticism explains the poor execution alleged by McKinsey. Presumably, if existing top leaders do not realize that leadership talent development is their responsibility then the processes of leadership development will be unsatisfactory.

CASE STUDY

United Kingdom: leadership competencies of the Senior Civil Service

Strategic planning and business planning in the UK public sector over the last 20 to 30 years has been diverse and constantly evolving. In the 1990s local governments had corporate and strategic plans and a number of the pioneering local governments also tried community and joint strategic planning. The National Health Service (NHS), publicly funded since its inception in the late 1940s, had business planning in the 1990s, a ten-year plan for modernization and reform (in 2000) and a five-year strategic plan approved in 2004. Local governments were the main movers in Local Strategic Partnerships that were set up in the period 2002–5, and through them they developed community strategies (Joyce 2015). The national government in the period 2010–15 produced a long-term economic plan, a UK industrial strategy and a national infrastructure plan. Individual departments of central government first produced structural reform plans (from 2010 onwards) which later became business plans. The UK government was also a partner in the delivery of the Europe 2020 strategy approved by the European Council in 2010, and as a result prepared a National Reform Programme on an annual basis, which was considered each year within a European Union monitoring process known as the 'European Semester'. One sign of the level of acceptance of strategic planning in the UK public sector is the following statement made by the body monitoring English NHS foundation trust hospitals (Monitor 2013: 2):

> Strategic planning is the process of developing an organisation's purpose, aims and objectives. It includes the allocation of related resources and responsibilities, drawing on robust evidence and setting challenging but feasible timescales for achieving goals.
>
> Across business sectors, including health care, evidence shows that strong strategic planning delivers significant benefits for organisations, their stakeholders, their staff and the customers – or in the case of health care, the patients – that they serve. In particular, carrying out strategic planning at relevant points in the development of an organisation will guide it through decision-making about service provision and resource allocation, and help executives and non-executives to govern effectively.

It is important that NHS foundation trusts use strategic planning to guide and inform the development of their organisations so they are able to adapt to the changing and increasingly challenging English health care sector and continue to give patients high quality care.

The increasing belief in the value of strategic planning in the public sector has been accompanied by an interest in civil service reform and the idea that civil servants need to develop strategic thinking skills and other strategic abilities. Capability reviews of government departments were carried out in 2006–7, including an assessment of departmental capabilities in relation to leadership, strategy and delivery. Civil service reform continued to be of interest in the period 2010–15. The UK government introduced a new civil service competency framework in 2013. It had ten competencies, as shown in Figure 2.6.

The competency framework, explained as setting out how the government wanted civil servants to work, was for use in recruitment, performance management and development. Not all competencies were assumed to apply to every civil servant: it was expected that six out of ten competencies would be relevant to an individual and would be identified through a discussion of the individual and their line manager. Competencies were defined as 'the skills, knowledge and behaviours that lead to successful performance' (Civil Service Human Resources 2015: 1).

The first three competencies – seeing the big picture, changing and improving, and making effective decisions – were defined as forming a cluster of strategic competencies. This list of competencies was backed up by specific explanations of what they meant for leaders. See Table 2.2.

People in director general and director positions were expected to act as strategic leaders. For example, they should: create long-term strategies; take

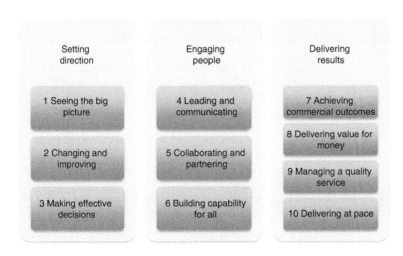

Figure 2.6 *UK Civil Service competency framework (2013)*

account of political and other pressures when setting strategy and priorities; assess and understand external dynamics and issues (political, economic, social, environmental and technological); appreciate effects of change on organizational culture; and negotiate with and influence external partners, stakeholders and customers.

Table 2.2 *Leaders and the competencies (UK, 2013)*

Competency	For leaders this competency is about . . .
1 Seeing the big picture	scanning the political context and taking account of wider impacts to develop long-term implementation strategies that maximise opportunities to add value to the citizen and support economic, sustainable growth.
2 Changing and improving	creating and encouraging a culture of innovation and allowing people to consider and take informed decisions.
3 Making effective decisions	reaching evidence based strategies, evaluating options, impacts, risks and solutions.
4 Leading and communicating	being visible, establishing a strong direction and persuasive future vision; managing and engaging with people in a straightforward, truthful and candid way.
5 Collaborating and partnering	being approachable, delivering business objectives through creating an inclusive environment, welcoming challenge however uncomfortable.
6 Building capability for all	investing in the capabilities of our people, to be effective now and in the future as well as giving clear, honest feedback and supporting teams to succeed. It's also about creating a learning and knowledge culture across the organization to inform future plans and transformational change.
7 Achieving commercial outcomes	identifying economic, market and customer issues and using these to promote innovative business models, commercial partnerships and agreements to deliver greatest value; and ensuring tight commercial controls of finances, resources and contracts to meet strategic priorities.
8 Delivering value for money	embedding a culture of value for money within their area/function. Leaders work collaboratively across boundaries to ensure that the Civil Service maximises its strategic outcomes within the resources available.
9 Managing a quality service	creating an environment to deliver operational excellence and creating the most appropriate and cost effective delivery models for public services.
10 Delivering at pace	keeping a firm focus on priorities and addressing performance issues resolutely, fairly and promptly.

CASE STUDY

Canada: leadership competencies in the Canadian Government (2015)

The policy on Management, Resources and Results Structures (MRRS), which came into effect in 2010, was aimed at strengthening management and accountability. According to the Treasury Board of Canada Secretariat (2015), 'The objective of this policy is to ensure that the government and Parliament receive integrated financial and non-financial program performance information for use to support improved allocation and reallocation decisions in individual departments and across the government'. This policy was aimed at creating capacity for performance budgeting. The deputy heads of government departments were responsible for ensuring clearly defined strategic outcomes aligned to the government's priorities and intended results, as well as reflecting the department's mandate and vision. These strategic outcomes were to provide the basis for linkages with other government departments that had overlapping strategic outcomes. The deputy heads were to develop and update strategic outcomes as necessary with direction from the minister.

The Canadian Federal Government also had a Management Accountability Framework that was used to assess executive and other senior leaders. According to a government website in July 2015 (Government of Canada 2015), 'The Key Leadership Competencies define the behaviours expected of leaders in Canada's Public Service. These leaders play a pivotal role in creating and sustaining a modern, connected and high-performing public service that is ethical, professional and non-partisan'.

Table 2.3 shows the six key leadership competencies (as they were in the middle of 2015), brief comments on each and a selection of examples of effective behaviour for deputy ministers – the civil servants who reported to a minister and the top civil servants in the Canadian federal system.

This leadership competency framework was intended to be relevant to decisions on selection, learning and development, performance management and talent management.

CASE STUDY

Estonia: strategic leadership competencies

When Estonia became independent it set up a centre of government, which was established as essentially a source of technical support. As an OECD review (2015) put it, the centre of government (CoG) in Estonia had relatively limited capacity to lead government strategy setting and to coordinate strategy implementation (OECD 2015: 67–8):

> Thus, the early 1990s in Estonia could be characterised as a period with no CoG role in the overarching strategic management of the government's strategic direction; national development was being pursued through

Table 2.3 *Canada's key leadership competencies (2015)*

Competencies	Comments	Selection of examples of effective behaviour for Deputy Ministers
1 Create vision and strategy	Leaders define the future and chart a path forward. They build on diverse ideas and create consensus around visions.	Extracts key issues; engages others to develop a vision; defines and communicates the departmental vision and strategy; sets forward-looking long-term goals.
2 Mobilize people	Leaders inspire and motivate people. They also lead by example.	Invests time in managing and developing leaders; ensures rigorous performance management.
3 Uphold integrity and respect	Leaders exemplify ethical practices and personal integrity.	Holds self and the organization to the highest ethical standards.
4 Collaborate with partners and stakeholders	Leaders bring a whole of government perspective. They are open to alternative solutions and manage expectations.	Forms strategic alliances with partners and stakeholders to advance government priorities.
5 Promote innovation and guide change	Leaders challenge convention. They create an environment for experimentation and intelligent risk taking.	Encourages experimentation and evaluation of outcomes; manages the scope and pace of change.
6 Achieve results	Leaders mobilize and manage resources to deliver government priorities. They anticipate, plan, monitor progress and adjust as needed. Leaders take personal responsibility for their actions and for the outcomes of their decisions.	Sets direction and oversees the implementation of priorities; decisions based on sound understanding of context, data and evidence; makes challenging decisions and acts at opportune time.

uncoordinated and at times incoherent siloed line ministry decision making (Kasemets, 2014).

Public governance began to change later in the 1990s as Estonia moved through the European Union accession process (OECD 2015: 68):

> As a result of the government's preparations to adopt the *Acquis communautaire* and to comply with EU directives, a significant number of sector specific strategies were presented by ministers to parliament either to fulfill EU requirements or to align their own political priorities in specific policy fields with EU requirements thus enhancing their own sector's visibility, or both. Consequently, the absence of central co-ordination led to a proliferation of disconnected single-sector strategies. By the early 2000s, the number of sector-specific national development strategies adopted by the government or parliament had grown to over 120.

In the mid 2000s the government began to create more oversight and coordination. The Ministry of Finance prepared a decree on strategic planning in 2005 that appears to have had the intention of improving the links between development and budgeting. Its immediate effect seems to have been to increase the number of strategies. In 2006 the Prime Minister created a Strategy Unit within the Government Office and this Unit and the Ministry of Finance exercised oversight of government-wide strategies. Following this development, there was a reduction in the number of government strategies.

In the years that followed, strategic management within the Estonian government improved in a number of different respects. First, there was increasing coherence between the Government Programme, overarching national strategies, sector development plans, organizational development plans and the state budget. Second, work was done to improve the alignment of the overarching objectives of the Government Programme and development plans. Third, there were improvements in the quality of the development plans. Fourth, efforts were made to improve the design and use of performance targets and to improve the linking of strategic planning and the budget framework. The development of long-term thinking by the Estonian government was also reflected in new national strategies: the Estonia 2020 National Competitiveness Strategy, the National Sustainability Strategy and the National Security Strategy.

The OECD pointed out that Estonia had made much progress after 2009 in 'treating the senior civil service as a community of leaders who share a common value set and dedicate themselves to serving the state from a whole-of-government perspective' (OECD 2015: 168). A key change in leadership development for the top civil service began in 2005 when a competency-based approach to recruitment, selection and development was begun. A competency framework for top civil servants in Estonia was introduced in 2009 (see Figure 2.7). The framework listed four core competencies (leadership, corporate identity, citizen oriented and credibility) and ten competencies (strategic leadership, self-management, communication, cooperation, networking, policy making, awareness of law, process management, resource management and HR management). 'Under this model, senior managers ... work as a united team to achieve the strategic goals of the state whilst in different organisations' (OECD 2015: 168).

THE CONSEQUENCES OF STRATEGIC LEADERSHIP COMPETENCIES

Where is the hard evidence that leadership competencies work in the public sector? When we look for evidence and analysis of the facts, relatively few empirical studies have been published.

One of the exceptions is the outstanding study by Boyatzis (1982). The whole study was based on a sample of private and public sector managers, but we will concentrate here on a sub-sample comprising 154 public sector managers who were working in federal government organizations in the US. Using supervisory ratings or nominations, Boyatzis divided the public sector managers into three performance categories (poor, average and superior). Data on competencies was collected using a form of critical-incident interviewing. The transcripts or write-ups of the interviews were coded for frequency of occurrence of competencies, then frequencies were analysed by performance groups.

The sampling of individuals and organizations was not random and Boyatzis considered that his findings were exploratory in nature. So this study provides us with hypotheses rather than definitive conclusions regarding the contribution of competencies to superior performance. His data analysis of public sector managers in poor and superior performance groups is shown in Table 2.4.

As can be seen, the 39 managers judged to be superior performers were more likely than poor performers to have provided evidence of competence in six

Core competencies	Competencies
• Leadership • Citizen orientation • Corporate identity • Credibility	• Strategic leadership • Self-management • Communication • Cooperation • Networking • Policy making • Awareness of law • Process management • Resource management • HR management

Figure 2.7 Estonia – Competency Framework for top civil servants (2009)

Table 2.4 Boyatzis' study: frequencies analysed by skill level (poor and superior performing) for the public sector sample

Competencies	Poor performance group ($N = 63$)	Superior performance group ($N = 39$)	Significance level of T-Tests
Self-confidence	0.111	0.436	0.0001
Use of socialized power	0.286	0.846	0.002
Use of oral presentations	0.048	0.256	0.004
Diagnostic use of concepts	0.476	0.923	0.004
Proactivity	0.905	1.41	0.0053
Managing group process	0.302	0.513	0.037

Source: Table A-3, page 270, Boyatzis (1982).

competencies. The most significant difference was in the case of self-confidence, and the least significant difference was in the case of managing group process. Boyatzis provided definitions of all of these and explained them. A brief outline summarizing them follows:

Managers with self-confidence were said to have positive self-esteem and display self-presentation skills. They make decisions and live with them and believe they will be successful. There was a hierarchy of self-confidence in the public sector sample, with superior performers demonstrating more self-confidence than average performers, who in turn demonstrated more self-confidence than poor performers.

People who are good at using socialized power are able to build teams, networks, alliances and coalitions. Average performers as well as superior performers in the public sector demonstrated the use of socialized power more than did the poor performers.

Use of oral presentations relates to the use of effective verbal presentations in small meetings and to large audiences. People with this competency can make presentations that are clear and convincing. The superior managers in the public sector demonstrated more of this than both the average and poor performers.

Diagnostic use of concepts means that an individual 'brings' a concept to a situation to interpret it. Boyatzis suggests that when people who are competent in the diagnostic use of concepts do not have a relevant concept they move swiftly to get one. This skill in applying concepts may, he suggests, be helpful in sorting out what is and what is not relevant. As Table 2.4 shows, Boyatzis found that superior performing public sector managers demonstrated this skill level more than did their poor performing counterparts. His comment on this was (Boyatzis 1982: 85):

The observation that effective managers in the public sector utilize this competency more than do their less effective peers suggests that diagnostic use of concepts may be an important competency in effectively applying the standardized concepts that public sector managers are required to use.

This shows that there is an intellectual or thinking component to superior performance – it is not just about self-confidence, being good at speaking and being good at creating and sustaining teams, networks, etc.

Proactivity might be defined as a readiness to take action. Boyatzis linked it to a sense of efficacy, meaning that people have a belief in their ability to control their lives and to act and produce beneficial results. He mentioned people being masters of their life rather than pawns. He suggested, also, that such a competency is demonstrated in problem solving and information seeking skills. In the public sector sample, this competency was again a feature of the superior managers as against both the average and the poor managers.

The competency of managing group process differentiated the superior and poor managers in the public sector. The superior managers did not demonstrate this competence significantly more than the average ones, and the average managers did not demonstrate it significantly more than poor ones. In this sense, competency in managing group process was not as much a discriminator of differences in performance in the public sector than were the other competencies we have discussed.

The Boyatzis study was not focused on strategic leadership competencies; however, going back to some of the activities discussed in this chapter in relation to strategic leadership, such as strategy development, planning, communication and so on, we can try to link competencies to activities (see also Boyatzis 1982: 242). See Table 2.5.

Consequently, we might argue that superior performing managers in the public sector demonstrated that they had competencies that meant they were better equipped in terms of their individual characteristics to carry out strategic leadership than their counterparts who were poor performers.

Table 2.5 *Strategic leadership activities and competencies*

Strategic leadership activities	Findings from Boyatzis about superior performing compared to poor performing managers in the public sector
Strategy development	Diagnostic use of concepts (pattern identification, deductive reasoning)
Planning	Proactivity (problem solving, information seeking)
Influencing/Negotiating	Self-confidence (self-presentation skills)
	Use of socialized power (alliance formation)
	Managing group process (group process skills)
Communicating skills	Use of oral presentations (verbal presentation skills)

CASE STUDY

The gap between current competencies and desired ones

Limbach-Pirn (2014: 115), head of the Top Civil Service Excellence Centre in the Estonian Government Office, recently carried out a study of the competencies of the top strategic leaders in the Estonian government. She interviewed a small sample of civil servants and politicians whom she described as having strategic leader roles in the Estonian government. According to her (Limbach-Pirn 2014: 125):

> All respondents associated their role as a strategic leader foremost with the vision and goals of the organization. Their own capabilities and skills to communicate this vision to employees and involve them in achieving the vision were considered more important than the ability to create the vision, as well as its correctness.

This may be the result of the reality of how their time was divided between formulating visions and strategies and implementing them. One of the interviewees said (Limbach-Pirn 2014: 125):

> You cannot plan strategies every day. You draw up a strategy, and then you have it for the next four years. Developing it takes up to 10% of my time. Then it's the implementation part of it that I'm engaged in every day. In the end, implementing a strategy depends on how good and how motivated your people are . . . I invest a lot of time in communicating with people – for some it might seem that I am not working at all. And people trust me because they know that they can talk to me freely.

Implementation involved more than just communicating. It also involved changing the organization and redirecting resources to achieve the vision and strategic goals.

Limbach-Pirn's interviews also led her to the conclusion that both ministers (political leaders) and secretaries-general (administrative leadership) are strategic leaders together. While secretaries-general were very focused on their organizations and ministers paid attention to a wide variety of stakeholders and relationships, both had to provide coherent strategic leadership together, which she thought was easier if they had a relationship based on trust. In drawing conclusions from her findings she returned to the point that it was necessary for political leaders and administrative leaders to work together cooperatively as strategic leaders and referred to them as working on strategic leadership 'in tandem'. Her remarks also underlined the fact that ministers were the senior partners in this joint strategic leadership. She also said that the top civil servants understood this and appreciated that their role was one of supporting the leadership of the ministers.

Limbach-Pirn concluded that strategic leaders needed three competencies, which she labelled as inspiration, communication and working with information. She elaborated a little on each of these competencies. For example, inspiring followers may involve setting a personal example. In relation to a competence in communication she mentioned that it was an aspect of strategy implementation and that there was an expectation that strategic choices and decisions will be convincingly explained and justified. She also considered it possible that communication was a bridge between the ability to work with information and inspiration. In relation to working with information she pointed out that strategic leaders work with a great volume of information and that making sure they keep well informed is important for their success. It requires intellectual skills such as an ability to analyse and synthesize information, seeing connections and linking details and the 'big picture'.

She connected the competencies with characteristics relevant to recruitment and selection decisions. She also identified behaviours and skills relevant to leadership development programmes, which are shown in Figure 2.8.

To sum up, Limbach-Pirn used her interview data to argue that strategic leaders needed to be good at working with information, communicating and inspiring people. If they were good at these three things, she thought that leaders would succeed in delivering strategic visions, innovation and organizational transformation. Against this 'model pattern' of strategic leadership she reported that the annual evaluation of the competencies of Estonian top civil servants and research

Figure 2.8 Eve Limbach-Pirn: interviews with Estonian Government leaders – competencies and associated behaviours and skills for development programmes

into their expertise that was carried out in 2011 showed that their strongest competencies were actually knowledge of the law and management of finances. Their weakest competencies were in managing people and cooperation. In other words, there was a gap between what strategic leaders needed to be good at and their current competencies. Obviously, closing the gap could be seen as the purpose of leadership development in the public sector.

SUMMARY

The competencies of strategic leadership in the public sector may include personal skills and qualities as well as required behaviours. There appears to be relatively little controversy about the various competencies to be included in the competency frameworks for senior civil servants in countries such as the US, UK, Canada and so on. They may not all be exactly the same but they all clearly have 'family resemblances'. What also emerges is that there is no need to think about a competency framework for senior leaders and a distinct and specialist framework for strategic leaders. Senior civil servants are now expected to have strategic leadership competencies. And this expectation of civil servants seems to be little different from the expectation of senior private sector business leaders. Peter Drucker's foresight from the 1950s was that at some time in the future business management would understand and make strategic decisions and this he saw as an imperative and applicable to all levels and all management functions (Drucker 1954). It seems that his foresight has been coming true for both public and private sector management.

A second conclusion might be that countries that have developed competency frameworks for senior civil servants may be implicitly assuming that there is a 'model pattern' of what is a good leader. The competency framework is, in effect, a model pattern that has been made explicit by making a formal statement of the composition of leadership as a role. It is then put into practice through development programmes. The idea is that different individuals should be developed to fit the same model pattern. In other words, the widespread development of competency frameworks can be seen as a tendency to greater standardization of leaders (Wilkins 2015).

A third conclusion is that governments (and individual public sector organizations) publish little supporting material on how their competency frameworks were designed and the justification for them in terms of actual consequences of their use in government. The following is conjecture rather than fact: it may be that the main issue in practice has been to design competency frameworks that are acceptable to key stakeholders. Of course, acceptability is an important criterion when evaluating a competency framework but it is not more important than the criterion of efficacy. The latter criterion might be stated as: do leaders who are exemplars of practice as defined by competency frameworks get better outcomes? Ideally, it would be great to see the evidence that leaders who act in accord with the competency frameworks do actually achieve better consequences than others who act in ways that contradict the competency frameworks.

A fourth, and perhaps a less immediately obvious conclusion, is that our understanding of competency frameworks can be placed in an organizational or a public sector reform context. If we approach understanding of strategic leadership competencies as a phenomenon in an organization, it might seem obvious that every organization needs competent leaders who can make the organization efficient and innovative; and it might seem obvious that strategic leaders should be good at coming up with visions to inspire employees and at communicating the vision because of their communication skills. It may seem obvious that the HR department in the organization should integrate leadership competencies into existing HR systems, and thus get the organization's members to use a competency framework for selecting new employees, for performance appraisals, for designing training and development and for making promotion decisions. The competencies (especially if they are written as required behaviours rather than personal skills or qualities) could almost be seen as core elements of a job or role description within the organization.

Trying to understand strategic leaders and their competencies in a public sector reform context leads to some very specific issues not encountered when considering the same things as organizational phenomena. For example, can the competency frameworks be used as a tool of civil service reform, which itself is needed for the overall reform and modernization of government? Can the competency frameworks be used to develop the strategic capabilities of governments (and individual public sector organizations) by creating 'whole of government' approaches (and more coherent strategic leadership in individual organizations)? Can senior civil servants and others develop the skills needed for better public governance, especially for becoming more responsive to citizens, and for working in partnership with citizens to develop government strategies and reform programmes? Is the pace of government reform fast enough and are more leaders needed to carry out the critical role of changing the institutions of government? Therefore, can the pool of talented leaders be increased and can talent pipelines be made more effective?

Assignment

Bennis and Nanus (1985) emphasized the importance to leaders of learning (Bennis and Nanus 1985: 59 and 188): 'It's the capacity to develop and improve their skills that distinguished leaders from followers ... Leaders are perpetual learners'. Their research suggested that leaders know their strengths and weaknesses. Such self-knowledge is partly important for guiding the personal learning and development that leaders undertake. It is also an important factor in their thinking as they go about building their team.

This is a good moment to remember the views of Sir Bob Kerslake on leaders and self-awareness (Smith 2015). He pointed out that a leader who recognized their own strengths and weaknesses could develop a team around them to compensate for their weaknesses and complement their strengths.

What follows is an exercise for people who have some leadership experience. It involves reflecting on your leadership experience, reviewing the chapter and making a self-assessment.

Step one

Please reflect on your experiences as a leader and identify things you have done well and things you have done badly. Make a note of some 'critical incidents' – maybe one in which you acted as a leader and it was successful, and one in which you now think that your actions as a leader failed. Reflecting on the critical incidents, are you aware of any personal strengths or weaknesses revealed by them?

Step two

Review the chapter and the different competency frameworks and research on leadership competencies. Select six competencies that you think are the most important. These may be competencies mentioned in the chapter, or may be mentioned in any further reading that you have done. Write the six competencies in the first column of Table 2.6 below. In the second column provide a brief definition of each.

Step three

Complete the table by making self-assessments for each leadership competency. Indicate by ticking the appropriate column whether you feel that each

Table 2.6 Basing competency framework on personal experience

Leadership competencies	Short definition of leadership competency	Self-assessment		
		This is a strength	This is a weakness	High priority for my development as a leader
1				
2				
3				
4				
5				
6				

competency is a 'strength', 'weakness' or 'high priority' area for your development as a leader in the public sector.

DISCUSSION QUESTIONS

1 Are all good leaders also strategic leaders? Should they be? Can managers at middle and lower levels actually act as strategic leaders?
2 What is the nature of the competencies of strategic leadership? Are the competencies personal skills and qualities or are they required behaviours? Which is the best way of defining strategic leadership competencies – as personal skills and qualities or as required behaviours?
3 What are the most important competencies of strategic leaders?
4 Should we evaluate strategic leadership competencies in terms of their acceptability to key stakeholders or in terms of their consequences?

FURTHER READING

Limbach-Pirn, E. (2014) 'What are the competencies for effective strategic leadership in Estonia?', in P. Joyce and A. Drumaux (eds) *Strategic Management in Public Organizations: European Practices and Perspectives*. London: Routledge, pp. 115–32.

Eve Limbach-Pirn is a senior practitioner. A short case study in this chapter was taken from this suggested reading. Eve reviews academic ideas and looks at the competencies thought to be important for politicians and civil servants in high level roles. Then she briefly examines the competencies that actually exist.

REFERENCE LIST

American Management Association (2005) *Leading into the Future: A Global Study of Leadership 2005–2015*. New York: American Management Association. [Online]. Available from: www.amajapan.co.jp/j/pdf/HRI_Leading_into_the_Future_E.pdf [Accessed 26 December 2015].

Bennis, W. and Nanus, B. (1985) *Leaders: The Strategies for Taking Charge*. New York: Harper & Row.

Boyatzis, R. E. (1982) *The Competent Manager*. New York: John Wiley.

Civil Service Human Resources (UK Government) (2015) *Civil Service Competency Framework 2012–2017* (2015 update).

Dodaro, G. L. (2011) 'Government Performance: GPRA Modernization Act Provides Opportunities to Help Address Fiscal, Performance, and Management Challenges' (Testimony Before the Committee on the Budget, US Senate). GAO-11-466T. Washington: United States General Accountability Office.

Drucker, P. (1954) *The Practice of Management*. New York: Harper & Brothers.

Government of Canada (2015) *The New Key Leadership Competencies*. [Online] Available from: www.tbs-sct.gc.ca/psm-fpfm/learning-apprentissage/pdps-ppfp/klc-ccl/klcp-pccl-eng.asp [Accessed: 28 December 2015].

Holmes, L. and Joyce, P. (1993) Rescuing the useful concept of managerial competence: From outcomes back to process. *Personnel Review*, 22(6): 37–52.

Joyce, P. (2015) *Strategic Management in the Public Sector*. London: Routledge.

Kasemets, L. (2014) 'Background report for the Integrated Public Governance Review of Estonia and Finland'. Unpublished.

Limbach-Pirn, E. (2014) 'What are the competencies for effective strategic leadership in Estonia?', in P. Joyce and A. Drumaux (eds) *Strategic Management in Public Organizations: European Practices and Perspectives*. London: Routledge, pp. 115–32.

McKinsey & Company (2013) *Building the Leadership Bench: Developing a Talent Pipeline for the Senior Executive Service*. Washington: McKinsey & Company.

Monitor (2013) *Meeting the Needs Of Patients: Improving Strategic Planning in NHS Foundation Trusts*. London: Monitor.

NSW Public Service Commission (2015) *A Better Picture: State of the NSW Public Sector Report 2014*. Sydney: NSW Public Service Commission. [Online]. Available from: www.psc.nsw.gov.au/about-the-public-sector/state-of-the-nsw-public-sector-reports/state-of-the-sector-report-2014 [Accessed: 9 June 2015].

OECD (2001) *Public Sector Leadership for the 21st Century*. Paris: OECD Publications.

OECD (2015) *OECD Public Governance Reviews: Estonia and Finland: Fostering Strategic Capacity across Governments and Digital Services across Borders*, OECD Public Governance Reviews. Paris: OECD Publishing.

Tracy, B. (2015) *The Leader as Strategist*. [Online]. Available from: www.amanet.org/training/articles/The-Leader-as-Strategist.aspx [Accessed: 26 December 2015].

Treasury Board of Canada Secretariat (2015) *Policy on Management, Resources and Results Structures*. [Online]. Available from: www.tbs-sct.gc.ca/pol/doc-eng.aspx?id=18218&section=HTML [Accessed: 30 December 2015].

Smith, M. (2015) *What Makes a Great Public Sector Leader?* [Online]. Available from: www.theguardian.com/public-leaders-network/2012/feb/21/what-great-public-sector-leader [Accessed: 24 June 2015].

United States Office of Personnel Management (2012) *Guide to Senior Executive Service Qualifications*. [Online]. Available from: www.opm.gov/policy-data-oversight/senior-executive-service/reference-materials/guidetosesquals_2012.pdf [Accessed: 28 December 2015].

United States Office of Personnel Management (2015) *Senior Executive Service*. [Online]. Available from: www.opm.gov/policy-data-oversight/senior-executive-service/executive-core-qualifications/ [Accessed: 28 December 2015].

Wilkins, J. (2015) *The Right Stuff: Competency Framework*. [Online]. Available from: www.canadiangovernmentexecutive.com/leadership/item/1619-the-right-stuff-competency-frameworks.html [Accessed 30 March 2016].

Chapter 3

Leaders and followers

LEARNING OBJECTIVES

- To consider what types of leaders get the best results
- To explain the meaning of strong leadership
- To examine social constructionist accounts of leaders in the public sector
- To explore the theory of leadership credibility

INTRODUCTION

It has almost become a maxim of modern management that command and control leadership no longer works. It is now often said that, instead of using command and control techniques, leaders should seek to empower followers (Kouzes and Posner 2007: 21):

> Leaders understand that the command-and-control techniques of traditional management no longer apply. Instead, leaders work to make people feel strong, capable, and committed. Leaders enable others to act not by hoarding the power they have but by giving it away.

Others have gone even further and suggested that leaders generally (not just command and control leaders) have become less important and followers more important. If we judge by a growing number of books on the topic of followership, the change seems to have been accelerating since around 2007–8. As recently as 2006, it was possible to claim that researchers had neglected followers; for example Benjamin and Flynn (2006: 217) referred to the limited research into the characteristics of followers:

> In the past, research on individual differences and leadership has tended to concentrate on the behaviors and traits of the leader ... Answering the question, "what characteristics define successful leaders?" is, of course,

important. However, relatively little research has examined how the characteristics of the follower might affect their reactions to a particular leader . . .

Keith Grint (2010) in a book on leadership suggested that followers were part of a range of elements that make a difference between success and failure but were not presently understood. He said (2010: 111), 'Perhaps the least under-stood or evaluated of these other elements is the role of followers'.

So, from 2008 onwards, many academic commentators have woken up to the need to understand followers better. One of the first was Kellerman (2008), who proposed a typology of followers comprising five types: isolates, bystanders, participants, activists and diehards. The isolates are completely detached. Bystanders are non-participant observers. Participants are followers who may support or oppose their leaders. Activists feel strongly and may be working to support their leaders or may be trying to get them ousted. Diehards, the most intense category, are prepared to die for their leader.

The approach taken in this chapter is to keep the focus on leaders and not shift it to followers, but to try to understand leaders in relation to their followers. Collins (2006) defined true leadership as when people have the freedom to choose and decide whether or not they will follow the leader. On this basis, true followers may be defined as people who consent to the leadership of someone. All the approaches that we look at here bring the followers into the picture, one way or another. One of the approaches presents the followers as victims of the misuse of unconstrained leader power, another sees followers as consumers of leader ideology, and another sees the behaviour of followers as simply a dependent variable in relation to leadership characteristics and style. Arguably, there is still a long way to go to really understand leader–follower relationships.

All the approaches are distinct in their focus and purpose. There are some fundamental differences between them in how they imagine the role of fol-lowers. One approach looks for a style of leadership that produces leadership effectiveness and the satisfaction of the followers; this is transformational leadership theory. Bass and others are focused on the essential behaviours and characteristics of a leader and implicitly assume that research should be describing the leaders and what they do as objectively as possible. He argued that transformational leaders moved their followers to transcend their self-interests (Bass 1997: 130): 'The transaction-transformational paradigm views leaders as either a matter of contingent reinforcement of followers by a transactional leader or the moving of followers beyond their self-interests for the good of the group, organization, or society by a transformational leader'. Bass saw this change in followers as a moral transcendence; he claimed, 'the socially oriented transformational leader engages in moral uplifting of fol-lowers' (Bass 1997: 131). Followers change from pursuing their self-interest to pursuing what Bass said were transcendental goals. As a result, for the fol-lowers, 'What is right and good to do becomes important' (*ibid.*: 133). This paradigm's intended relationship to practice appears to be one of providing direct guidance. Bass and others present a model pattern for practitioners to follow if they want to be good leaders.

A second approach also attempts to describe the essence of a specific type of leadership – 'strong leadership'. It might be seen as the antithesis of trans-formational leadership in that, although it is attempting to describe behaviours and characteristics of real leaders, it is interested in leadership results that are bad and not good. As a theory it positions followers as 'victims' of a misuse of power by leaders who think they know better than everybody else. It too, like trans-formational leadership theory, assumes a theoretical position of addressing an objective reality. It might be suggested that its service to practitioners is to warn them against behaving in a harmful way and to point out the types of leadership practices they should avoid.

A third approach, the social construction of reality, is in principle not con-cerned with portraying leaders as a force for either good or bad. Berger and Luckmann (1966: 15) explained the study of the social construction of reality as follows:

> And in so far as all human 'knowledge' is developed, transmitted and maintained in social situations, the sociology of knowledge must seek to understand the processes by which this is done in such a way that a taken-for-granted 'reality' congeals for the man in the street.

In fact, in the case of public sector theorizing and research, a particular variant of social constructionism has been developed. This is a variant that is concerned with how leaders (and not followers) communicate meanings and interpretations of situations (conceived as problems) and how they do so in order to legitimize the style of authority they would like to exercise. Arguably, therefore, it positions the followers as 'consumers' of the ideology of leaders, since their communications and interpretations appear not have any weight in the resultant legitimization of authority. The usefulness of this theory to practitioners must be in terms of providing a new meaning, a new interpretation, for them of what it means to be engaging in leadership. It says, in effect, that what you are doing as a leader when communicating to your followers is trying to convince them to consent to the authority (or the type of authority) that you are claiming. It could be seen as debunking the role of public sector leaders and their sense of responsibility for leading their part of the public sector in the service of the public. It is possible that practitioners who are leaders might conclude from this variant of social con-structionism that leaders' attempts to communicate about making public services better in the interests of the public are really just self-serving communications (i.e. ideology) being aimed at maintaining their leadership rather than making things better for the public. Alternatively, the lesson for practitioners might be that they should pay attention to their leadership legitimacy while at the same time trying to make things better for the public.

Finally, there is an approach to leadership in the public sector that is arguably an interesting mix of transformational leadership theory and social constructionism.

It is also searching for a style of leadership that produces good outcomes and assumes that this can be objectively measured. However, the approach assumes that successful leadership depends on the 'believability' of the leader. The leader, according to this theory, is successful not simply because their behaviour and characteristics fit the model pattern of leadership in the public sector but because the followers believe the leader's communications. This believing is not a simple act of faith in the leader; believing the leader has several parts to it. There is a part that has its transformational or charismatic element: the followers believe because the leader is a good communicator in the sense of being inspiring or convincing. But it is not just about this – there are also judgements to be made. The followers believe in a leader because they judge the leader is honest and has integrity, and has sound or competent judgement. If the followers ever begin to judge the honesty and competence of the leader as being doubtful, the credibility of the leader begins to fragment. The decision to trust the leader and judge them to be credible is a decision of the followers. This approach to leadership theory identifies the followers as 'judges' of the leaders, that is, judging leaders' credibility as a factor in their decision about how to respond to leaders. The usefulness of this theory of leadership credibility is to sharpen the practitioners' understanding of how they can earn and sustain the trust of followers, what they have to do in order to maintain credibility in the eyes of their followers.

This introductory overview of leader–follower theory in the public sector can be summarized as in Figure 3.1, which shows four theoretical approaches.

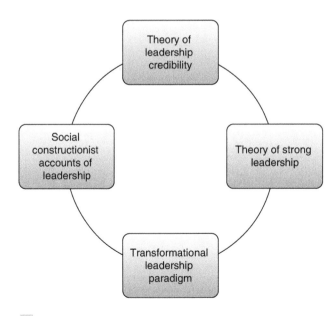

Figure 3.1 *Leaders and followers in the public sector – four theoretical approaches*

Four different roles for followers implicit in the four approaches are shown in Figure 3.2.

It is not necessary to choose one of the four approaches as correct and suggest all the rest are wrong. All four approaches must have a degree of basis in reality and all have valuable lessons for leaders in the public sector. The transformational approach has lessons for practitioners in terms of the importance of communicating and inspiring people through missions, visions and strategic goals and the importance of recognizing and rewarding the positive contributions of followers. The strong leadership theory warns leaders against having too much self-confidence and will to lead and direct others. The social constructionist approach is a reminder that leaders have to maintain their power base and legitimacy while getting things done and making things better. The theory of leadership credibility reminds leaders that competence in making the right decisions and their personal honesty and integrity will affect their ability to lead based on the consent of followers.

TRANSFORMATIONAL LEADERS

Transformational leadership sounds like it should be of great relevance to strategic leaders. The emphasis is on charisma and visions of a better future and then inspiring and motivating employees to pursue collective goals.

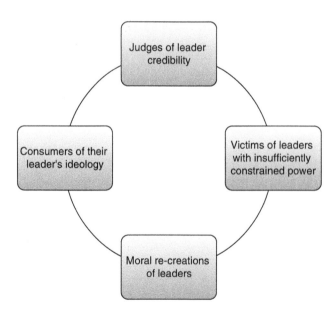

Figure 3.2 The roles of followers implicit in approaches to theorizing leaders and followers in the public sector

Bernard Bass (1997) was aware that his paradigm of transactional and trans-formational leadership was part of a cluster of leadership theories that could be described as similar, all more or less linked to some idea of the charismatic leader. He wrote (1997: 130):

> Although I focus here on the transactional–transformational conceptualiz-ation derived from Burns (1978) and elaborated by Bass (1985), it is one among a number of neocharismatic conceptualizations built around similar leader behaviors and perceptions with slight variations in emphases (House, 1995). Referred to as the "New Leadership" (Bryman, 1992), these conceptualizations include the 1976 theory of charisma (House, 1977), the attributional theory of charisma (Conger and Kanungo, 1987), the leadership challenge (Kouzes and Posner, 1987), and visionary leadership (Sashkin, 1988).

The Bass model has been tested with public sector samples. We look at three studies of transactional–transformational styles in the public sector: Gellis (2001), Trottier, Van Wart and Wang (2008) and Alban-Metcalfe and Alimo-Metcalfe (2000).

Gellis (2001) carried out a study of social work managers based on data collected from the social workers they managed. The social workers were asked to judge how frequently their managers exhibited various transformational leader behaviours using items from the Multifactor Leadership Questionnaire (designed by Bass and a colleague). It is worth recalling here the key themes in transactional and transformational leadership. Gellis used four subscales for transactional leadership in this study. The one that turned out to be important was 'contingent reward', which was operationalized using items that included one in which the manager pointed out what the employee would receive if the employee did what needed to be done. There were four factors or dimensions for transformational leadership (Gellis 2001: 18):

> Bass described transformational leadership as comprising four conceptually distinct factors: (1) charisma (idealized influence attributes and behaviors), (2) intellectual stimulation, (3) individual consideration, and (4) inspira-tional motivation. Charisma refers to the leader's ability to arouse devotion and articulate a vision through personal dynamics such as self-confidence and emotional appeal, for subordinates to identify with and develop higher order goals, and instill respect and loyalty for the leader. The charisma factor is separated into idealized behaviors and attributes (Bass and Avolio 1997). Intellectual stimulation refers to the leader's ability to understand and solve problems in novel ways, to "break with the past." Individual consideration refers to the leader's ability to treat each subordinate with care and concern (Bass 1985). Inspirational motivation orients subordinates toward action, building confidence, and inspiring belief in a cause.

63

Outcome variables were measured using multiple items. For example, leader effectiveness was measured by four items that included contributing to organizational effectiveness, meeting the job-related needs of social workers, representing social work needs to managers at higher levels, and performance by the work group. Two items were used for leader satisfaction and three for extra effort. The operationalization of these variables using multiple items is obviously of great significance when we attempt to compare the findings of different studies.

The responses of the social workers were analysed according to the subscales linked to the dimensions of transformational and transactional leadership. As can be seen in Table 3.1, all four of the transformational leadership dimensions and the contingent reward dimension of transactional leadership were positively related, statistically speaking, to outcome variables. In the case of perceived leader effectiveness the two leadership factors that had the highest correlations were individual consideration (0.81) and idealized attributes (0.80).

Gellis reported that the social work managers who were scored highly on the transformational dimensions appeared to get better results (as measured by extra effort, rating of leadership effectiveness and satisfaction with the leader). Statistical analysis of the questionnaire data suggested, first, that transformational dimensions as a set of factors helped to explain the scores on outcome variables significantly better than the transactional ones by themselves. For example, the R^2 for a regression to explain leader effectiveness using just transactional factors was 0.47 ($p < 0.001$) but it increased to 0.79 when transformational factors were added. Second, analysis showed that the 'idealized influence attributed' and 'individual consideration' were the key factors in explaining the social workers' satisfaction with their managers. And in the case of the perceptions of leader effectiveness, the key factors were 'individual consideration', 'idealized influence attributed' and 'contingent reward' (see Table 3.2).

In fact, as can be seen, individual consideration by itself produced an R^2 of 0.66 and the addition of idealized attributes and contingent reward increased the

Table 3.1 Gellis (2001) Pearson product–moment correlations between leadership subscales and outcome variables (N = 187 social workers)

	Extra effort by social workers	Satisfaction with the leader	Perceived leader effectiveness
Idealized attributes	0.73*	0.80*	0.80*
Idealized behaviours	0.69*	0.71*	0.74*
Individual consideration	0.80*	0.77*	0.81*
Intellectual stimulation	0.70*	0.69*	0.72*
Inspirational motivation	0.64*	0.67*	0.70*
Contingent reward	0.66*	0.67*	0.74*

Note: *denotes $p < 0.01$.

Table 3.2 Regression analysis, Multifactor Leadership Questionnaire factors and leader effectiveness – Gellis 2001

Step	Variable entered	β	t	p	Model R^2
1	Individual consideration	81	18.78	0.001	0.66
2	Individual consideration	46	8.07	0.001	
	Idealized attributes	45	7.89	0.001	0.74
3	Individual consideration	31	5.09	0.001	
	Idealized attributes	29	4.71	0.001	
	Contingent reward	19	3.18	0.01	
	Laissez-faire	−18	−3.15	0.01	0.78

model's R^2 to 0.78. So this suggests that individual consideration is the most important factor in leadership effectiveness.

Gellis also found that contingent reward was correlated with all five of the transformational dimensions. So, the study by Gellis indicated that contingent reward mattered – a factor associated with transactional leadership. The overall summary might be stated as: transformational variables plus contingent rewards explain positive leadership outcomes. This is represented in Figure 3.3. To this may be added, for later consideration, the finding that individual consideration was an important factor in explaining variations in leadership effectiveness.

Gellis commented (2001: 24):

> This article provides some evidence that transformational leaders can be found in social work practice fields. . . . Therefore, encouraging staff to reflect on new goals and to champion new ideas were essential components of transformational leadership, according to the study participants.

Another study that set out to test Bass's leadership theory was by Trottier and colleagues (2008). They had access to a very large US dataset based on a survey of US federal government employees, from a 2002 survey carried out by the US Office of Personnel Management. The researchers concluded that both transactional and transformational leadership were important in the US federal government. One point of interest in how this study was carried out was the researchers' decision to conceptualize individualized consideration as an aspect of transactional rather than transformational leadership.

In this study rather than just emphasizing the contribution of Bass's model as being the distinction between just two types of leadership – transformational and transactional – the researchers underlined that Bass had distinguished eight types: laissez-faire, passive management by exception, active management by exception, contingent rewards, individualized consideration, idealized influence, intellectual stimulation and inspirational motivation. They also emphasized that Bass did not treat transformational and transactional leadership as rival or

Figure 3.3 Gellis (2001) – contingent reward matters plus transformational leadership

alternative styles of leadership. He had considered that both might be combined together to produce effective leadership.

They made some changes to Bass's model. First, they reduced eight types of leadership down to six styles. They dropped laissez-faire on the grounds that it was not really leadership at all, and they combined into one type Bass's two types of leadership based on management by exception. More significantly, in their framework individualized consideration was treated as a transactional dimension, not a factor in transformational leadership. They explained their alteration of the framework as follows (Trottier *et al.* 2008: 332):

> Although we adopt Bass's factor analysis as a given here... we place individualized consideration among the transactional factors... Nearly all the transactional theorists include individual consideration as one of the elements of leadership... Although individual consideration enhances transformational leadership, in which change is prominent (Kouzes and Posner 1987), we nonetheless feel a more balanced approach can be achieved by placing it with the transactional cluster.

Arguably, this was their most significant deviation from Bass's model; and also arguably, what Trottier *et al.* were proposing was quite plausible. How might its plausibility be argued? It might be suggested that individualized consideration is transactional because it could be seen as an exchange or bargain between leader and led. The leader might be treating each subordinate with care and concern in exchange for the support of the subordinate.

The database they had to work with was huge. The survey had been sent to over 200,000 federal government employees and the response rate was 51 per cent, meaning the database contained responses from over 100,000 people. A key part of the study was the selection of survey items for use in testing the Bass model; this was a critical part of their research design. They had to select and group items from the survey to act as indicators of the six leadership styles and the two outcome variables they decided to use. The items were measured on five-point scales, usually running from strongly disagree to strongly agree. The survey contained 118 question items and they managed to find 24 of them that they thought could be used as indicators of leadership styles (see Figure 3.4). So, the big issue might be the validity of their measures, with validity in this case meaning: were they able to get good proxies for the concepts Bass was using?

There is a degree of plausibility about the selection and grouping of the items from the survey, and their linking to Bass's different leadership styles. This, however, does not mean that there could not be arguments about the validity and robustness of the re-use of the survey data to test the Bass model.

The study employed two dependent variables: perceived leadership effectiveness and satisfaction of followers. Again, the selection of survey items to operationalize these two variables could have been quite critical to the validity of the variables for the purposes of testing the Bass model of leadership. In fact, two items were selected for perceived leadership effectiveness – first, the individual's feeling about how well their immediate supervisor or team leader was doing their job and, second, whether an individual held the organization's leaders in

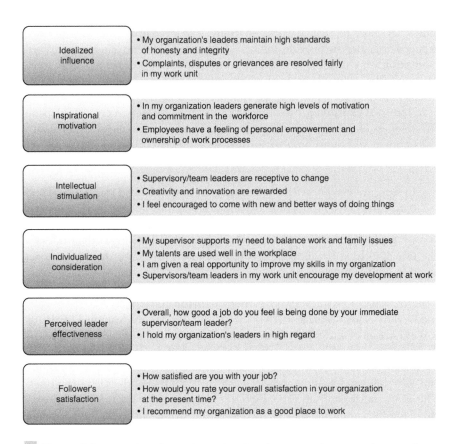

Figure 3.4 *Examples of transformational and outcome factors and survey items selected to act as indicators of them – Trottier et al. (2008)*

high regard. To operationalize follower satisfaction they used three survey items. These were concerned with the individual's job satisfaction, their overall satisfaction with the organization and whether individuals would recommend their organization as a good place to work. As can be seen, perceived leadership effectiveness was operationalized in a reasonably convincing way by the first of the items. But was the second item really valid? Does holding someone in high regard necessarily imply you think they are effective? It is also difficult to see that the operationalization of follower satisfaction really provided a valid measure of satisfaction with the leader. It might be argued that the research, on such a large sample, was very useful but some caution might be needed in terms of the validity of the measures constructed using the survey items.

Their operationalization of the six leadership factors and two outcome variables may or may not have been valid, but they did check the internal consistency of their measures, and their findings and statistical analysis were definitely very interesting. First, the federal employees were most in agreement with the items grouped together as an index of individualized consideration. The highest agreement of all was with the item that addressed supervisor support for the individual's need to balance work and family. The levels of agreement with items grouped together to provide indices of idealized influence and inspirational motivation were much lower. Trottier *et al.* (2008: 326) comment: 'One competency seems to stand out as the best: individual consideration . . . However, federal managers are weakest at inspirational motivation'.

In terms of explaining variations in their measures of perceived leadership effectiveness and follower satisfaction, their indices of transformational and transactional leadership both performed well. Their conclusion was (Trottier *et al.* 2008: 330):

> In sum, we can say with confidence that Bass's blended transactional and transformational model of leadership does capture well the major elements of what followers perceive to be important and that very good leadership seems to depend even more on transformational elements than transactional, even when individual consideration is placed on the transactional side of the model.

Both the previous studies were carried out in the US. Robert Alban-Metcalfe and Beverly Alimo-Metcalfe (2000) carried out the next study in the UK. It was part of a stream of research work by them on leadership. Their research study was designed to explore 'nearby' or close leadership in local government. In introducing their study they noted that a number of writers had questioned the generalizability of US findings on leadership to countries with different cultures. This is, of course, only an issue if US thinking on leadership is actually generalized to other countries; they seemed to assume that it had been. They certainly pointed to all the writing on leadership that had emerged from the US and impacted on management education and development (texts and practices). This writing had, they said, contributed significantly to received wisdom on leadership. For good measure they quoted one opinion, that of Hunt (1999), who claimed, 'many scholars outside the USA saw [leadership research] as a virtual US hegemony' (Alban-Metcalfe and Alimo-Metcalfe 2000: 280).

They set out to develop a leadership questionnaire for use in the UK, one based on qualitiative, grounded theory. They did not want to start the research with preconceived ideas. They also wanted to pay attention to gender as an important factor. In the first instance they researched the constructs of leadership held by men and women at different levels in the public sector (local governments and public health services). They did this by interviewing 92 managers and collecting data using focus groups. The constructs of leadership they investigated were perceptions of immediate line managers. They identified about 2,000 constructs and these were used in designing a questionnaire survey of managers in local government. The questionanire had 176 items on leadership and five criterion variables (outcomes). Four of the criterion variables were taken from the Multifactor Leadership Questionnaire designed by Bass and a colleague, which they saw as offering the advantage of facilitating cross-cultural comparisons. They described the questionnaire as measuring transformational leadership.

They sampled organizations in local government on a random basis and arranged for questionnaires to be distributed to a random sample of managers within each one. Each manager surveyed was asked to rate a manager (boss). This could be someone they worked with currently or someone they had worked with previously for at least six months. They achieved a national sample of 1,464 local government managers (and a credible 46 per cent response rate).

Their quantitative analysis of the data from the questionnaires led them to propose nine factors (scales) and their use of correlational analysis and multiple regression led them to conclude that the scales were generally correlated with the five criterion variables. Table 3.3 shows some of their findings from the correlational analysis as an illustration; it has only two outcome variables – 'enables me to achieve more than I expected' and 'leads in a way that I find satisfying'. For the cases shown in the table, the highest correlations for male and female managers at two levels involved 'genuine concern for others' and the lowest correlations were with 'political sensitivity and skills'. It may also be noticed that for the female respondents the correlations between 'political sensitivity and skills' and both outcome variables was much lower than for males at the same organizational level.

Their multiple regression analysis of the data suggested that 'genuine concern for others' explained a lot of the variation in the achievement variable (enables me to achieve more than I expected). This was the case for respondents of both genders. See Table 3.4.

The multiple regression analysis shown in Table 3.4 produced high multiple Rs, and the highest beta coefficients were found for 'genuine concern for others', 'encourages critical and strategic thinking' and 'decisiveness, determination, self-confidence'. Their analysis led them to conclude that 'encourages critical and strategic thinking' was mainly relevant to the cases of lower-level

69

Table 3.3 Product–moment correlation coefficients between scales and two criterion variables (analysed by level of respondent and gender) – Alban-Metcalfe and Alimo-Metcalfe (2000)

Scale label	Level and gender of survey respondent					
	Enables me to achieve more than I expected			Leads in a way that I find satisfying		
	Board, chief executive, directorate, director – male respondents	Middle level/section-unit head – female respondents	Middle level/section-unit head – female respondents	Board, chief executive, directorate, director – male respondents	Middle level/section-unit head – male respondents	Middle level/section-unit head – female respondents
1 Genuine concern for others	0.78	0.81	0.82	0.81	0.84	0.84
2 Political sensitivity and skills	0.53	0.55	0.22	0.51	0.60	0.35
3 Decisiveness, determination, self-confidence	0.56	0.65	0.62	0.61	0.71	0.70
4 Integrity, trustworthiness, honest and open	0.66	0.71	0.72	0.82	0.79	0.81
5 Empowering, develops potential	0.62	0.65	0.72	0.70	0.71	0.74
6 Inspirational networker and promoter	0.59	0.66	0.61	0.73	0.75	0.68
7 Accessibility, approachability	0.50	0.67	0.65	0.66	0.72	0.75
8 Clarifies boundaries, involves others in decisions	0.52	0.67	0.71	0.65	0.73	0.78
9 Encourages critical and strategic thinking	0.67	0.72	0.72	0.76	0.76	0.74

Note: Data for 681 respondents: 126 males at level of board, chief executive, directorate and director; 393 males at middle level and section-unit head; and 162 females at middle level and section-unit head. All the correlations in the table were significant ($p < 0.01$).

Table 3.4 *Multiple correlations between leadership scales and achievement outcomes variable (analysed by gender of respondent) – Alban-Metcalfe and Alimo-Metcalfe (2000)*

Leadership scales	Enables me to achieve more than I expected	
	Male respondents	Female respondents
Genuine concern for others	0.359	0.368
Political sensitivity and skills	0.060	−0.094
Decisiveness, determination, self-confidence	0.135	0.202
Integrity, trustworthiness, honesty and openness	—	—
Empowering, develops potential	0.074	0.171
Networker, promoter, communicator	—	—
Accessibility, approachability	—	—
Clarifies boundaries	0.106	—
Encourages critical and strategic thinking	0.168	0.237
Multiple R	0.77	0.81

Note: The table shows beta coefficients and multiple Rs. Based on data for 1,144 respondents: 855 males and 289 females.

managers and not to managers at the top levels. In the case of 'decisiveness, determination, self-confidence' this seemed to be more relevant to the achievement outcome ('enables me to achieve more than I expected') and increasing motivation to achieve than to the satisfaction and stress variables. These detailed observations make the point that their leadership variables were not seen by them as equally applicable to all outcome variables.

The importance of the first of their scales – 'genuine concern for others' – was underlined by Alban-Metcalfe and Alimo-Metcalfe in relation to other outcome variables in this 2000 study and in their subsequent research. They described this scale as the single best predictor of the various outcomes and characterized it as being concerned with 'sensitivity to the feelings of others, and to offering personal support and communicating positive expectations' (Alban-Metcalfe and Alimo-Metcalfe 2000: 290). Two years later, in another paper (Alimo-Metcalfe and Alban-Metcalfe 2002: 32), now drawing on evidence from the health service and the private sector as well, they were still highlighting the same factors they had found in the local government study: 'Leadership is not about being a wonder-man or wonder-woman. It is about being someone who values the individuality of their staff, who encourages individuals to challenge the status quo and who has integrity and humility'.

In subsequent research they continued to develop their analysis using UK data and focusing on a UK model of leadership. The dimensions of leadership

71

evolved but 'showing genuine concern for others' continued to be singled out as especially important. Its importance and meaning were clarified as follows (Alimo-Metcalfe and Alban-Metcalfe 2001: 300):

> The first, and single most important dimension of the TLQ [Transformational Leadership Questionnaire], undoubtedly makes the greatest contribution to understanding what staff perceive to be the characteristics of individuals who have a powerful positive impact on staff's motivation, satisfaction, self-efficacy (sense of personal effectiveness), morale and performance. It explains around 60 per cent of the variance explained by the total TLQ. It has been named "Showing genuine concern for others". This scale reflects a variety of individual-focused behaviours, and attitudes, which include showing a genuine interest in staff as individuals, being interested in their needs and aspirations, and how they feel about working in the organization; valuing their contributions, developing their strengths; coaching, mentoring; and having positive expectations of what staff can achieve.

In 2006 they were still expressing concerns about the validity of the US models of leadership in relation to the UK public sector. They comment on their findings in the UK as follows (Alimo-Metcalfe and Alban-Metcalfe 2006: 302):

> The most obvious implication of these findings, is the staggeringly [sic] complexity of the role of leadership in the UK public sector. [...] ... existing US models of leadership do not encapsulate this complexity. Perhaps of even greater importance, is the nature of leadership as perceived by US versus these UK perspectives. Typically, the US models place an overwhelming emphasis on charisma and vision, that is, on the leader as primarily acting as the role model for his/her followers. [...] the results that emerge from asking the recipients and ultimate arbitrators of leadership effectiveness, namely, the staff who work in the NHS and local government, how they perceive leadership, presents a very different model. They are stating clearly that the most important prerequisite role for the leader, is what he/she can do for their staff. This is far more reminiscent of Greenleaf (1970) notion of leader as servant.

In the end they leave open the possibility that the UK and US difference they believe to exist might be due to differences in research methodologies.

To sum up this section, it is evidently quite challenging to evaluate the findings of public sector research spurred by Bass's work on transformational leadership. Nothing shows this more than trying to think about 'individual consideration' in the Gellis and the Trottier *et al.* studies, and 'showing genuine concern for others' in the Alimo-Metcalfe and Alban-Metcalfe series of studies. The concepts are presumably quite closely related in meaning, but they are operationalized in three different ways. Gellis used the Multifactor Leadership

Questionnaire, Trottier *et al.* selected items from a survey and tried to link them to leadership variables, and Alimo-Metcalfe and Alban-Metcalfe used qualitative work to develop constructs and then used them in a questionnaire that they designed. All three studies used data from respondents making judgements about their managers. In their conclusions, we find Trottier *et al.* supporting the orthodoxy that transformational factors matter more for effective leadership than transactional factors. They also say this is true even though individual consideration is included in the transactional factors. Alimo-Metcalfe and Alban-Metcalfe arrive at a very different destination: they report that their UK model puts 'showing genuine concern for others' as the single most important factor and identify this as a major difference with US models of leadership, where pride of place is said to be given to charisma and vision. Gellis provided more support for the importance of transformational leadership, but coupled this conclusion with finding that contingent reward also mattered. An examination of the regression analysis of leadership effectiveness carried out by Gellis suggests that the most important factor is 'individual consideration', which could be seen as aligned to the UK findings of Alimo-Metcalfe and Alban-Metcalfe!

What should a practitioner make of this? One answer would be that the practitioner could build on the conclusion from the UK study and suggest the public sector needs leaders to be servants to public sector employees and make doing what they can do for them as their first priority. Is this counter-instinctive as a conclusion? It seems to be saying something quite paradoxical: leaders in the public sector can serve the public best by putting the employees and professionals they manage first. Surely, public sector leaders should put the public first and try to look after the people who work in the public sector as well?

Perhaps these paradoxical results are a product of a methodology based on asking people to rate their managers. (But Trottier *et al.* were also using a survey that asked people about their managers.) In an effort to cast more light on this paradox, it might be worth referring back to a Boyatzis 1982 study covered in the previous chapter. Buried away in that study was a particular finding regarding a management competency in developing others. People who demonstrate this competency apparently 'adopt the role of coach or helper' and 'demonstrate feedback skills in facilitating self-development of others' (Boyatzis 1982: 143). Arguably, this might correlate quite well with individual consideration and showing genuine concern for others. Boyatzis found that it was the average performers among managers who demonstrated more of this competency than did the superior managers or the poor managers! In Boyatzis's study, this was much more pronounced in the public sector than it was in the private sector. Boyatzis speculated on why this competency was a feature of the average managers (Boyatzis 1982: 147): 'If developing others becomes a primary objective, decisions may be made and actions taken that help others develop but which do not result in maximum current productivity or performance'. This surprising finding, and the associated speculation by Boyatzis, can be put alongside the key finding of the Alimo-Metcalfe and Alban-Metcalfe study of transformational leadership in local government. Of course, it could be that

73

'showing genuine concern for others' is quite unrelated to skills in 'developing others' or that the UK local government situation was very different from the situation of US federal managers some 20 years earlier. But it is an interesting finding to end this rather inconclusive section of the chapter.

THINK PIECE: Did this leader have charisma?

When I think about good leadership one person immediately springs to mind. He led the non-departmental government body [NDPB] I work for through rapid growth and big challenges using his effective people management and impressive relationship building skills.

Even as the organization reached hundreds of employees he still welcomed every new starter, congratulated every promotion and thanked every leaver in his fortnightly 'stand up'. His lively performance brought every staff member together to hear headline news, understand recent successes and challenges, hear key updates and then see and hear from everyone across the organization.

He just 'got' people. I remember introducing him to two new starters on their first day. He was walking to his office with a bowl of cereal and stopped to meet the two new faces. He stood there, CEO of a huge NDPB, talking to them about their first day while holding a bowl of breakfast cereal.

His meetings gave everyone a voice. While he could (and would!) make crucial decisions quickly, he would also use the team of people around him. He would utilize people's experience and skills to inform his decisions. Don't get me wrong, he could make very strategic decisions very quickly and he seemed to always get it right but his ability to welcome, motivate and draw on the skills of his team made him one of the best leaders I have ever worked with.

Source: A manager at a UK non-departmental public body (31 January 2016).

STRONG LEADERS

Jay Conger (1990) wrote an essay on 'dark leadership' that warned of the dangers of leadership and especially leadership based on charisma. He suggested that people tend to think only of the positive side of leaders, but he considered that there were also risks and liabilities. In fact, he believed not only that the behaviours of leaders and managers were different but also that leaders were capable of behaviours that could have problematic consequences. For example, leaders might take decisions that were unrealistic or self-interested. He illustrated some of his arguments by reference to prominent US business leaders of the past, such as John DeLorean and Steve Jobs. John DeLorean's business was famous for manufacturing a highly innovative looking car, but the firm was short-lived and soon went bankrupt. He referred to the way that DeLorean had increased production targets even though there was market research saying that the targets were massively ambitious. He used Steve Jobs to illustrate several points about dark leadership. Steve Jobs had been at the Macintosh division of Apple Inc. and Conger said there were reports that he was very dictatorial. He was described as making random and impulsive suggestions outside the management line – an example of using informality in a way that undermined the authority of others.

Conger's arguments are full of references to charismatic and visionary leaders. He warned that leaders might not have good judgement or sufficient realism when putting forward a vision. He said that visionary leaders might focus on the 'big picture' and pay no heed to details. He quotes a DeLorean executive as criticizing John Delorean for not having time for the details of a project. Leaders might be so committed to their vision that they overlook relevant information. They may fail to test their strategic ideas (e.g. new products). They may ignore advisers who tell them things they do not want to hear or signals from the business environment because they do not support their vision. And when a mistaken vision is implemented and the results are unsatisfactory, instead of reviewing things, the dark leaders persevere with their vision.

Some of the problems created by leaders might be made worse by the behaviour of people around them. For example, the leader may have appointed 'yes-men' or the people might idealize the leader and be reluctant to question their orders. They may be encouraged to behave like this by the leader themselves. Then there might be dangers of 'groupthink' when the leader and their circle of advisers all see things in the same way and are so committed to the course of action they are taking that there is a failure to consider alternatives and to objectively review what is being done and how it is working. In other words, there is no proper evaluation and learning.

Archie Brown (2014) began his book on political leadership with more or less the same proposition as Jay Conger. In his first paragraph he set out the argument against what he referred to as 'strong leadership'. He wrote (Brown 2014: 1):

> In democracies there is quite broad agreement that a 'strong leader' is a good thing. Although the term is open to more than one interpretation, it is generally taken to mean a leader who concentrates a lot of power in his or her hands, dominates both a wide swath of public policy and the political party to which he or she belongs, and takes the big decisions . . . But process matters. When corners are cut because one leader is sure he knows best, problems follow, and they can be on a disastrous scale.

His book is mainly based on a large collection of biographies of political leaders and his analysis takes in many different types of political system, not just parliamentary ones. Brown, like Conger, seemed to have doubts about charismatic leadership. He said (Brown 2014: 5), 'Charismatic leadership can be won and lost, and is not generally a lifetime endowment. It is often dangerous, and frequently overrated'. Arguing more generally, he states that there have been leaders who have had power but did not have wisdom. Perhaps we can reformulate what Brown is saying: leaders may have limited knowledge combined with insufficiently limited power. He writes about the myth of the strong leader as follows (Brown 2014: 359–60):

> A myth may contain an element of truth, and yet be greatly misleading . . . an element of truth, and yet be greatly misleading. Some of the people who have been thought of as strong leaders – Hitler, Stalin, Mao Zedong, Kim Il Sung or Saddam Hussein – did indeed wield enormous power. In that sense they were strong leaders. The myth here consists of the idea, sedulously promoted by these leaders and their propagandists, that each of them was singularly wise, gifted and farseeing. Vast resources are devoted in many totalitarian and authoritarian states to spreading the message of the people's good fortune to have such a great leader. In the absence of alternative sources of information and criticism, the regime's narrative can be, and often has been, widely believed for a time. The fabrication lies also in the idea that concentrating enormous power in the hands of an individual leader brought great benefits to their countries. In reality, their tyrannical rule had disastrous consequences.

In Brown's view the possibility of strong leaders having such disastrous effects is reduced but not impossible within a democracy in which leaders and governments are ultimately accountable to an electorate. He does point out that in party politics in democracies it has become common for parties to attach the label of 'weak' to the leader of other parties to undermine them. Two of the recent examples he provided were in the UK in the run up to the 2015 general election when the Prime Minister of the coalition government tried to make the label of weak stick to the leader of the Labour Party; and in Canada in 2006 when the Conservative Party tried to label the newly elected leader of the Liberal Party as weak. Brown suggests (2014: 2), 'It is evident that politicians believe that if they can pin the "weak" label on the principal opponent, this will work to their advantage with voters'.

It is possible that there is a constituency in all types of country for a strong leader who will solve the problems that concern the public. Presumably, the worse and the more intractable the problems, the bigger will be the constituency in favour of strong leadership, even in democracies that genuinely have very transparent and accountable systems of public government. Brown quotes a 2007 survey of 13 countries that were in transition from a communist system. He reports that in eight of the countries more than a third of respondents supported the idea of a strong leader who could solve the problems facing the country today even if the leader overthrew democracy. The support was the greatest in Bulgaria and Ukraine, where support stood at over 50 per cent. In Hungary, Russia and Latvia it stood at over 40 per cent. It would seem possible from this that public attitudes might reflect past experience, and it may also reflect an instrumental attitude towards democracy. The public may be more inclined to support democracy if they believe it will help to solve the problems of the public.

Because Brown is concerned with political leadership rather than leadership of private sector businesses some of the detail of his thesis differs from Conger's analysis. For example, he is concerned with how prime ministers relate to ministers in their cabinet, the rule of law and democratic accountability to parliament and the public. But despite such differences, there are some echoes of Conger's arguments about dark leadership in the business world.

Just like Conger, Brown points to the issue of the behaviour of people around the leader. A tendency of advisers to defer to the leader is one problem. He says (Brown 2014: 19):

> Too much deference, however, makes for bad policy. A leader needs colleagues of political stature who will stand their ground and not hesitate to disagree with the judgement of the person who formally or informally presides over their deliberations. . . . Only leaders of autocratic temperament, too sure of the superiority of their own judgement, will attempt to railroad a policy through against the wishes of the majority of their colleagues.

Brown points out that the heads of government usually have some influence in deciding on the promotions and demotions of cabinet ministers and that this causes the conformity of people to the leader's wishes. He believes that even this power has its limits and that a political leader who loses the confidence of a large proportion of their cabinet will not survive.

He discusses bad foreign policy decisions and suggests that they can arise because strong individual leaders 'are more prone to serious error because of their willingness to discount the accumulated knowledge of people with expertise on the part of the world in question' (Brown 2014: 294). He basically argues that such leaders stifle proper debate and examination of issues in cabinet prior to a decision being made. And he quotes the idea of a 'hubris syndrome' (Brown 2014: 295):

> Leaders who pride themselves on being 'strong', or who are anxious to appear strong, may be especially tempted by military intervention in another country . . . Among the symptoms [of leaders suffering the hubris syndrome], to which such leaders are prone, are 'a narcissistic propensity to see the world primarily as an arena in which they can exercise power and seek glory rather than as a place with problems that need approaching in a pragmatic and non-self-referential manner'; a belief that they need not feel accountable to mere colleagues but to something higher, 'History or God'; and a lack of curiosity about what might go wrong, which amounts to a 'hubristic incompetence', since excessive self-confidence 'has led the leader not to bother about the nuts and bolts of a policy'.

77

In the quote above Brown makes the same point as Conger about disregard or indifference to detail (nuts and bolts). In the case of a leader, the detail matters because this is where the difficulties may lie – the devil is in the detail. To ignore the detail is to be careless at best and maybe, as suggested by the hubris syndrome, might indicate the leader is a narcissist.

Conger saw leaders as failing to take account of all the information about a problem. Brown believed that the leaders' beliefs screened what information they took in (Brown 2014: 341):

> Beliefs simplify reality and mould the way in which information is processed. They screen out inconvenient facts and are systematically more receptive to information consonant with prior beliefs than to information that runs contrary to those convictions.

The process of information informing decision making is reversed so that a decision (belief) filters the way in which information is understood. Leaders make an early commitment to those beliefs and look for confirmation that they are right and then become victims of self-deception.

So, are leaders in politics a bad thing? Brown argues against the myth of the strong leader and in favour of leaders being constrained by due process, by people surrounding the leader and by democratic accountability to the public. In the case of heads of government, he thought it was important that ministers be independent minded and able to engage in argument with the leader. Just as Conger suggested that yes-men were a problem, so Brown argued the need for ministers not to be 'placemen'. Ministers who surrounded the prime minister needed to take responsibility for giving independent advice and challenging the judgement of the leader. He also wanted to see party leaders constrained by the political parties they led. He thought leadership in other political systems – such as Stalin's Soviet Union – could wreak more damage because they were not constrained by accountability to the public. Perhaps we might say he was arguing for the importance of constraint on political leaders by democratic institutions that include cabinet government, effective party organizations and ultimately accountability to the public.

SOCIAL CONSTRUCTIONISM

The third approach to understanding leaders and followers is social constructionist. The way social constructionism developed originally was to some extent to define itself against the theories of society that said the behaviour of individuals was determined by social roles and institutions. According to this preexisting theory, institutions (such as the family) were made up of roles (wife and husband, mother and father, son and daughter and so on) and individuals learnt to play the roles. The roles could be analysed in terms of role expectations and learning to play the role involved socialization into acting in line with those expectations. Social constructionists were not very interested in doing research to arrive at an objective description of reality. They were interested in what people said and thought in order to maintain or change reality. Social constructionists were interested in the everyday and subjective side of life. Berger and Luckmann (1966: 172) explained some of this as follows:

> The most important vehicle of reality-maintenance is conversation. One may view the individual's everyday life in terms of the working away of a conversational apparatus that ongoingly maintains, modifies and reconstructs his social reality. Conversation means mainly, of course, that people speak with one another . . . Most conversation does not in so many words define the nature of the world. Rather, it takes place against the background of a world that is silently taken for granted . . . If this is understood, one will readily see that the great part, if not all, of everyday conversation maintains subjective reality.

Through discussion people produce accounts of what has happened; they produce and reaffirm their expectations of what will happen. Changes in the interpretations, accounts and the expectations that are produced through speech and social interaction can lead to changes in patterns that are, in effect, the social structures people inhabit.

If social constructionism is applied to the study of leaders in the public sector then we might expect that there would be research into the discussions and inter-communications of leaders and followers as they make subjective interpretations of the public sector situations they find themselves in and as they try to make subjective sense of the future choices that they expect to have. The discussions, interpretations and communicative interactions generally, when they are strategic in nature, may touch on issues of risk and future vision. The accounts produced of current performance, of pressures, of crises and much more, can be expected to create a weighing of means and ends and risks and rewards through strategic conversations. The research might also look at the social stock of knowledge shared and used by leaders and followers. Social constructionism, when applied to leadership in the public sector, might focus on life as subjectively experienced and would not focus on it as objective reality.

Grint (2005) took as the point of departure for his social constructionist approach to leadership the idea that successful leaders do not make decisions in response to a situation, but construct a definition of the situation to legitimate their exercise of authority. As we explain shortly, Grint was interested in situations defined as crisis situations. The successful leader uses the crisis to justify becoming decisive and ignoring sceptics and cynics. The key thing here is that leaders define situations to persuade followers that some specific kind of leader is required.

This approach to understanding leadership is summed up as follows (Grint 2005: 1470–1):

> In effect, leadership involves the social construction of the context that both legitimates a particular form of action and constitutes the world in the

79

process. If that rendering of the context is successful – for there are usually contending and competing renditions – the newly constituted context then limits the alternatives available such that those involved begin to act differently.

So Grint believed that leaders determine or shape what followers do through their process of defining the nature of the situation; this is not a new idea in itself. Long ago Boyatzis (1982) analysed data on managers working in the US federal government and showed that those rated as having superior performance were significantly more likely than poor performing managers to have provided evidence of competence in 'diagnostic use of concepts'. Boyatzis (1982: 79) provided the following definition of this competence: 'Diagnostic use of concepts is a way of thinking in which the person identifies or recognizes patterns from an assortment of information, by bringing a concept to the situation and attempting to interpret events through that concept . . .'.

For Boyatzis this management activity of using a concept to understand a situation involved using a personal competency in applying concepts to situations in order to understand them. For Grint it was a process through which leaders legitimize their authority and get followers to behave in a certain way. Grint, as a social constructionist, argued that there was a choice of either seeing reality as objective, which might be described as an 'essentialist' perspective, or paying attention to the processes through which leaders construct contexts. There is a third possibility, derived from the tradition of pragmatist philosophy, which presumes neither that the interpretation and definition of the situation by the leader is objective reality nor that many interpretations/definitions are possible; instead, it suggests that the way leaders deal with the complexity and uncertainties in a situation is through an experimental approach, testing the correctness of their understanding by putting their ideas into practice.

Arguably, the issue at stake here is whether the definition of the situation by the leader normally reflects the reality of the situation *to a substantial extent* or whether the defining of a situation is often so wide open that a leader is able to pick from a whole range of different interpretations and sell to followers the one that enables the leader to manipulate them.

Grint placed his arguments in a conceptual framework of roles and problems. He began with tame and wicked problems. Tame problems were defined as complicated but resolvable. He linked this type of problem to the manager's role and argued that this was to put in place processes to solve the problem. In contrast a wicked problem was defined as complex and intractable. The solutions being considered appeared to just generate new problems. He said that with this second type of problem there was no right or wrong answer; there were instead alternatives that were better or worse. The wicked problems he linked with the role of leaders.

Concern with complexity and wicked problems has been a feature of much academic writing in recent years. The distinction between management roles

80

and leadership roles has also been much popularized by Kotter (1990). (Kotter was talking about leadership and management in general, not specifically in public administration.) So, Grint was making use of very familiar ideas when he linked one pair of concepts (tame and wicked problems) with another pair of concepts (management and leadership).

Grint then built on this. He identified a third type of problem, which he named a 'critical problem'. This type of problem, he suggested, appears self-evident and might be linked with authoritarianism. He said that the critical problem is one that is seen as allowing very little time for decision making. In other words, urgent action is required in the face of crisis. He links this type of problem to the role of 'commander'. We then have a final formulation: managers organize a process to address a situation they have defined as tame, leaders ask questions to address a situation they have defined as wicked, and commanders provide answers to a situation they have defined as a crisis. See Figure 3.5.

It is important to remind ourselves that these three types of problems, which Grint advanced as, in effect, definitions of situations, were seen by him as not objectively existing but as definitions of the situation that had been actively constructed by the leader. So, a crisis is not a crisis objectively speaking, but a crisis in a subjective reality since people have been persuaded by a leader to perceive the situation to be a crisis.

Grint and Holt (2011) used the typology of problems to contribute to a debate about leadership in health services that was hosted by the King's Fund. They suggested that tame problems required technical followership, wicked problems

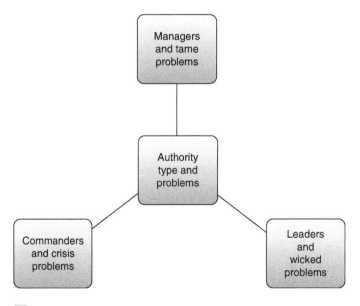

Figure 3.5 Keith Grint – managers, leaders and commanders

required responsible followers and critical problems required compliant followers. In line with Grint's earlier arguments, they suggested that those in
authority needed to provide a persuasive account of the situation for it to work
out in that way and that they did so in line with their access to, or preferences for,
particular forms of power. They said (2011: 12): '...we are suggesting that
decision makers tend to legitimize their actions on the basis of a persuasive
account of the situation. In short, the social construction of the problem
legitimizes the deployment of a particular form of authority'.

Having set up the conceptual framework of leaders providing a persuasive
account of situations that lead to three types of socially constructed problems and
three types of corresponding followership, Grint and Holt then try to apply this
social constructionist model to an anticipated reality created by health service
reforms introduced by the secretary of state. For example, they speculated that
introducing price competition would create a wicked problem but produce a
commander response (2011: 17):

> Conventional competitive behavior – another tame problem for those used
> to working in the private sector – may well be perceived as a crisis by many
> unused to such an approach, and that will encourage the rise of command
> not leadership, as we define it. Yet command is also deeply problematic in
> terms of encouraging innovative behavior on the part of followers –
> precisely what is necessary when facing wicked problems.

In these remarks it feels like a shift from social constructionism to a belief that
problems are not just social constructions. It is not clear that their discussion of
the problem created by competition is a social constructionst analysis. They
seem to be talking about how problems might appear to followers, not about
problems that leaders have socially constructed. They concluded (2011: 18): 'In
effect, the transition period between the old and the new NHS may generate a
crisis during which many followers will seek a commander to relieve them of
anxiety and to command the answer'. Their model seems to have flipped from
the original one of situations being constructed by leaders for reasons of legit-
imation. Now it seems they are proposing that government reforms create a new
situation and on the basis of this new situation, as defined by followers, followers
want a certain type of authority.

So, what was to be done? Grint and Holt (2011: 19) are not in favour of heroic
leaders and instead turn to the NHS professionals, who they encourage to
'become more engaged and allow the NHS to become a network of effective
leadership teams, rather than a bureaucratic institution of chronic followers and
refuseniks'.

What does this all mean in practice for leadership in public services? If we go
back to Grint's basic model of leaders–problems–followers, he was claiming that
successful leaders are successful because they are skilful in persuasive rhetoric. He
suggested we should focus on looking at how leaders persuade followers
to accept the leaders' formal authority (manager, leader and commander).

The obvious issue with this social constructionist position is that it might be of interest to sociologists and others who are trying to understand leadership, but how does it help leaders to better discharge their responsibility to the public? How does this approach help public services leaders be more responsive to the public and provide better governance and better public services? In the end, we would say, Grint's social constructionism seems to be an exercise in debunking public services leadership, rather than providing useful evidence on how leaders can become better.

LEADERSHIP CREDIBILITY

As we saw in Chapter 1, Kouzes and Posner's (2007) concept of leadership credibility contained three elements: leaders who scored high on leadership credibility were honest, competent and inspiring. Gabris and his colleagues (2000) investigated the applicability of this concept to the public sector through a study of 11 local governments in the Chicago metropolitan area. Respondents to their surveys included board members (elected officials), chief administrative officers (i.e. chief executives) and departmental heads in the local governments concerned. They devised a leadership credibility (LC) index that consisted of the following eight survey items:

1 The chief administrative officer clearly communicates the purpose and rationale behind new programmes and reforms.
2 The chief administrative officer actively works to communicate the organization's vision and mission to employees.
3 The development of a shared vision and set of core values is a fundamental objective of the chief administrative officer.
4 Employees believe they can trust the chief administrative officer and put their fate in his or her hands.
5 The chief administrative officer makes sure employees have sufficient power and authority to accomplish assigned objectives.
6 The chief administrative officer practises what he/she preaches in terms of values, work effort and reform. The chief administrative officer sets a good example.
7 The chief administrative officer follows through on promises regarding changes others are expected to carry out.
8 The chief administrative officer actively seeks to reward, praise and recognize high performance.

They analysed the survey data they obtained and discovered a number of significant correlations. These included the following:

i '... respondents who perceive that their organizational CAOs [chief administrative officers] have high LC are also more likely to perceive the use of increased levels of strategic planning, mission statements, and environmental scans' (Gabris *et al.* 2000: 99).

ii 'LC seems to be reasonably associated with enhanced perceptions about the local government's strategic capacity' (Gabris *et al.* 2000: 99).

iii Correlations between LC and the following variables were also found (Table 3.5): 'City utilizes more advanced strategic planning techniques', 'This organization adapts well to its environment', 'Strategic change is constantly a priority' and 'The overall effectiveness of this local government organisation as a service and program provider' (Gabris *et al.* 2000).

As noted already, Gabris *et al.* found that leadership credibility was correlated with the use of advanced strategic planning techniques, mission statements, stakeholder analysis and environmental scanning. Perhaps this was because the credible leaders were strategic in their behaviour and expected others in the local government to be strategic and use strategic planning techniques. Perhaps, therefore, we can speculate that credible leaders encourage capabilities for strategic leadership among the managers of public sector organizations. See Figure 3.6.

This study by Gabris and his colleagues has provided evidence that effective leadership is strategic leadership: it connects leadership credibility and strategic planning as well as leadership credibility and strategic change and adaptability. It also connects leadership credibility and service and programme delivery

Table 3.5 Product–moment correlations between leadership credibility and other variables (Gabris et al. 2000)

Variable	Elected officials	Chief administrative officer	Department heads	Overall
City utilizes more advanced strategic planning techniques	0.46*	0.42	0.69*	0.56*
City has a clear, updated mission statement	0.27*	0.52*	0.39*	0.34*
City has conducted a stakeholder analysis and environmental scan	0.39*	0.45	0.15	0.29*
Strategic change is constantly a priority	0.28	0.85*	0.74*	0.56*
Rate the overall effectiveness of this local government organization as a service and programme provider	0.26	0.78*	0.75*	0.60*
This organization adapts well to its environment	0.60*	0.71*	0.57*	0.59*

Note: Significance levels: * indicates significance at 0.1 level, one-tailed test. Sample size: n = total of 108 respondents.

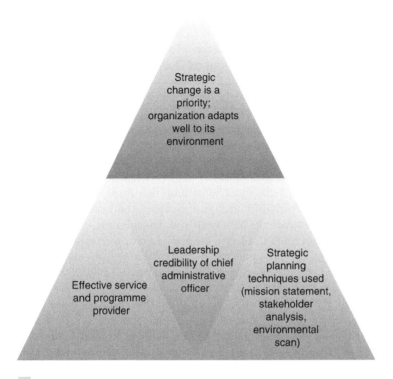

Figure 3.6 *Selected findings of the Gabris et al. study (2000)*

effectiveness. Implicit in this theory of leadership is the importance of followers. The data suggests that leaders who orient themselves to their followers by demonstrating integrity and trustworthiness are successful. Moreover this is a type of leadership that pays attention to ensuring that followers have power and authority to do the job and that will respond with reward, praise and recognition for high performing employees. These findings do not support the traditional command and control leadership model. Nor do they seem to support the idea of the leader full of hubris or being narcissistic. They are leaders that are leading – since employees put their trust in them and place their fate in their hands. And they are leaders that provide intellectual leadership in relation to change – since the credible leader clearly communicates the purpose and rationale behind new programmes and reforms.

SUMMARY

Reflecting back on the theories and approaches we have explored in this chapter it is a reasonable judgement to make that they are all useful and worthy in their own right. Each one gives us a glimpse of an aspect of the phenomenon of leadership in the public sector. To leave any of the four approaches out would be a serious impoverishment of a total understanding of leadership in the public sector. And to a significant degree some of them are focused on strategic leadership and not just leadership (i.e. transformational leadership and leadership credibility).

But they are all so focused on leaders and followers that somehow we lose sight of the context of public sector leadership, not least the public governance context, including democratic arrangements and accountability systems to the public. Leaders operating in effective public governance systems have also to be concerned about issues of public ownership of strategies, transparency of government decision making and actions, and open government generally. Nor do any of them really help us think about something that is the whole point of leadership – that is, joint action by groups of people. The joint action is, of course, what mediates between the behaviour and characteristics of leaders and the consequences of leadership. Leaders in the public sector who cannot rely on command and control techniques have to steer joint action, maintain its momentum, guard against it becoming dysfunctional and out of control and so on. Joint action is not led by pulling a lever. Consequently, in the next chapter and the rest of the book, every opportunity should be taken to understand leadership in relation to joint action and its public sector context – which is not a uniform context when we think of central government, the executive, the civil service, local government, regulatory bodies and public service providers. Surely leadership and joint action will have its own specificities according to their exact location within the public sector? See Figure 3.7.

Work-based assignment: assessing readiness for change

The work-based assignments in this book are for civil servants and other public services staff who have some years of management experience.

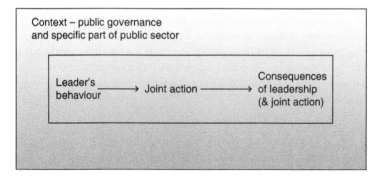

Figure 3.7 *Leaders, joint action, consequences and context*

Please prepare an importance and readiness chart (see Table 3.6) for a specific organization based on your understanding of how the stakeholders would react to a specific case of reinvention, modernization or reform. Also, outline the specific case of modernization or reform and identify some implications of the assessments in the chart.

This assignment is focused on assessing readiness for change. It is concerned with whether individuals, groups and organizations are willing, supportive or enthusiastic about a proposed change and, if so, to what extent they are willing, supportive or enthusiastic. For example, there may be individuals who are supportive, but for whom the change is of marginal importance and so their readiness would be assessed as less than someone who is highly enthusiastic and keen to make the change a success.

Table 3.6 *Importance and readiness chart*

Stakeholders	Importance of stakeholders (low, medium, high)	Readiness for change		
		Low	Medium	High
1				
2				
3				
4				
5				
6				

Note: Adapted from Beckhard and Harris (1987) page 63. An individual, group or organization is rated as 'high' in terms of state of readiness if it sees a specific change as a top priority for them and tends to welcome the change and support its implementation. Importance ratings of stakeholders may be based on an assessment of their power, influence, degree of need, etc., or combinations of things.

Table 3.7 *Commitment chart*

Individuals or groups or organizations	Commitment rating			
	No commitment	Let it happen	Help it happen	Make it happen
1		O		X
2		O	X	
3		O	X	
4	O		X	
5		O		
6	OX			

Note: Adapted from Beckhard and Harris (1987). Current commitment might be shown by O and amount of commitment required by X.

Work-based assignment: commitment chart

Please consider a current or recent change that you know well and prepare a commitment chart as a way of capturing your judgements about the amount of commitment that is needed (or was needed) from the stakeholders in order for the change to be a success (see Table 3.7). You may judge that some groups are unimportant and that no commitment is required from them. For other groups you may make the judgement that it is important that they are committed even if it is merely to the extent that they are prepared to let the change happen. From others you may want them to help it happen, or to take responsibility for making it happen. Such a commitment chart, when completed for all or for the most important stakeholders, demonstrates a meticulous approach to the assessment of the initial conditions for a change. This chart may be further developed by also showing the ratings of the current amounts of commitment for each of the stakeholders.

DISCUSSION QUESTIONS

1 Are followers morally uplifted by transformational leaders?
2 Does leadership effectiveness depend to a large extent on leaders showing genuine concern for others? Does it depend on leaders showing individualized consideration? Or does collecting data from individuals on their managers as leaders produce such results because that is what followers want to believe? Has leadership effectiveness been measured correctly in the studies reviewed in this chapter?
3 How serious are the problems of 'strong leaders' in the public sector? Are 'strong leaders' found among civil servants and appointed public sector managers as well as among politicians? How can the problems and the disasters created by strong leaders be minimized and managed? Are robust democratic institutions the answer?
4 Do situations select leaders or do leaders socially construct situations to suit their purposes? Can social constructionism offer any useful practical insights to responsible leaders in the public sector? What are they?
5 Is the research on 'leadership credibility' convincing? What are the lessons it offers for improving leadership in public sector organizations?

FURTHER READING

Heifetz, R. A., Grashow, A. and Linsky, M. (2009) *The Practice of Adaptive Leadership.* Boston, Massachusetts: Harvard Business School Press. Chapter 21: Inspire People, pp. 263–75.

> The idea of inspiring followers is perhaps one of the most challenging leadership ideas there are. Ronald Heifetz and his colleagues provide a discussion of this topic that

does not base it in a charismatic individual. The focus of the chapter (and the book) is practice so it is likely to be of particular interest to people who have leadership responsibility.

REFERENCE LIST

Alban-Metcalfe R. J. and Alimo-Metcalfe B. (2000) The transformational leadership questionnaire (TLQ-LGV): a convergent and discriminant validation study. *Leadership & Organization Development Journal*, 21(6): 280–96.

Alimo-Metcalfe, B. and Alban-Metcalfe, R. J. (2001) The development of a new Transformational Leadership Questionnaire. *Journal of Occupational and Organizational Psychology*, 74(1): 1–27.

Alimo-Metcalfe, B. and Alban-Metcalfe, R. J. (2002) The great and the good. *People Management*, 8(1): 32–4.

Alimo-Metcalfe, B. and Alban-Metcalfe, R. J. (2006) More (good) leaders for the public sector. *International Journal of Public Sector Management*, 19(4): 293–315.

Bass, B. M. (1985) *Leadership and Performance Beyond Expectations*. New York: Free Press.

Bass, B. (1997) Does the transactional-transformational leadership paradigm transcend organizational and national boundaries. *American Psychologist*, 52(2): 130–9.

Bass, B. M. and Avolio, B. J. (1997) *Full range of leadership: Manual for the Multifactor Leadership Questionnaire*. Palo Alto, CA: Mind Garden.

Beckhard, R. and Harris, R. T. (1987) *Organizational Transitions*. Reading, MA: Addison-Wesley.

Benjamin, L. and Flynn, F. J. (2006) Leadership style and regulatory mode: Value from fit? *Organizational Behavior and Human Decision Processes*, 100(2): 216–30.

Berger, P. L. and Luckmann, T. (1966) *The Social Construction of Reality: A Treatise in the Sociology of Knowledge*. London: Penguin Books.

Boyatzis, R. E. (1982) *The Competent Manager*. New York: John Wiley.

Brown, A. (2014) *The Myth of the Strong Leader: Political Leadership in the Modern Age*. London: The Bodley Head.

Bryman, A. (1992) *Charisma and Leadership in Organizations*. London: Sage.

Burns, J. M. (1978) *Leadership*. New York: Harper and Row.

Collins, J. (2006) *Good to Great and the Social Sectors*. UK: Random House Business Books.

Conger, J. A. (1990) The Dark Side of Leadership. *Organizational Dynamics*, 19(2): 44–55.

Conger, J. A. and Kanungo, R. N. (1987) Toward a behavioral theory of charismatic leadership in organizational settings. *Academy of Management Review*, 12: 637–47.

Gabris, G. T., Golembiewski, R. T. and Ihrke, D. M. (2000) Leadership credibility, board relations, and administrative innovation at the local government level. *Journal of Public Administration Research and Theory*, 11(1): 89–108.

Gellis, Z. D. (2001) Social work perceptions of transformational and transactional leadership in health care. *Social Work Research*, 25(1): 17–25.

Greenleaf, R. K. (1970) *The Servant as Leader*. San Francisco, CA: Jossey-Bass.

Grint, K. (2005) Problems, problems, problems: The social construction of 'leadership'. *Human Relations*, 58(11): 1467–94.

Grint, K. (2010) *Leadership: A Very Short Introduction*. Oxford: Oxford University Press.

Grint, K. and Holt, C. (2011) *Followership in the NHS*. London: The King's Fund.

House, R. J. (1977) 'A 1976 theory of charismatic leadership', in J. G. Hunt and J. L. Larson (eds) *Leadership: The Cutting Edge*. Carbondale, IL: Southern Illinois University Press. pp.199–272.

House, R. J. (1995) 'Leadership in the twenty-first century: A speculative inquiry', in A. Howard (ed.) *The Changing Nature of Work*. San Francisco, CA: Jossey-Bass. pp. 411–50.

Hunt, J. G. (1999) Transformational/charismatic leadership's transformation of the field: an historical essay. *Leadership Quarterly*, 10(2): 129–44.

Kellerman, B. (2008) *Followership: How Followers Are Creating Change and Changing Leaders*. Boston, MA: Harvard Business School Press.

Kotter, J. (1990) What leaders really do. *Harvard Business Review*, 68(3): 103–11.

Kouzes, J. M. and Posner, B. Z. (1987) *The Leadership Challenge: How to Get Extraordinary Things Done in Organizations*. San Francisco, CA: Jossey-Bass.

Kouzes, J. M. and Posner, B. Z. (2007) *The Leadership Challenge*. 4th edition. San Francisco, CA: Jossey-Bass.

Sashkin, M. (1988) 'The visionary leader', in J. A. Conger and R. N. Kanungo (eds) *Charismatic Leadership: The Elusive Factor in Organizational Effectiveness*. San Francisco, CA: Jossey-Bass. pp. 122–60.

Trottier, T., Van Wart, M. and Wang, X. (2008) Examining the nature and significance of leadership in government organizations. *Public Administration Review*, 68(2): 319–33.

Chapter 4

Pragmatic strategic leaders

LEARNING OBJECTIVES

- To consider the key characteristics of pragmatic strategic leadership
- To examine ideas about strategic leadership during the process of change
- To examine the issue of conflict management as part of the role of strategic leadership

INTRODUCTION

After three chapters, is it time to do an interim stock take? So far we have seen that the ideas that emerged on leadership in the business sector in the 1980s and early 1990s included ideas about the potency of charismatic, visionary and transformational leaders (who could be morally uplifting for their followers). These were all models of heroic leadership. Side by side with this, in the same years, there were also ideas that leadership in company headquarters could not be trusted to know enough to set long-term directions and strategies for companies because the pace of change was too great and the business world too chaotic; so the initiative should be placed with front-line managers. These ideas, linked to Tom Peters, meant that leaders at the centre should support the moves of front-line managers, who were not to be constrained by corporate strategic plans, although the top leaders were to provide visions.

Meanwhile, in the public sector in the mid-1990s a major rethink of the role of the state was underway. The 1980s' ideas of neoliberalism – rolling back the state, privatizing, deregulating and cutting income taxes – was no longer in vogue. There was now a call for the state to be more effective; this meant being more effective in supporting national economic and social development, with the state being more strategic, more focused and more frequently taking on the role of catalyst for societal problem solving. Leadership became a 'hot issue'. In recent years, right up to the present day, governments responded by creating competency frameworks and talent management to create the leaders needed in the new public sector.

While government practitioners were focusing on leadership competencies and the organization of HR systems to produce more leaders in the public sector, academic research examined the applicability of leadership theories to the public sector, notably the theories of charisma and transformational leadership. As we have seen, this research has led to questions about cross-societal differences in public sector leadership that have yet to be resolved. There has also been a little research into leadership credibility in the public sector, which seemed to confirm that effective leadership is strategic and trustworthy.

The academic research of recent years has also included some work that looks more critically at leadership in the public sector and also looks at the social construction of legitimacy for different types of authority. From 2008 onwards theorizing by some academics has entertained notions that leadership no longer matters as much as it did, and that followership is becoming more important. The latter is also implicit in the theory of leadership credibility, which views effective leaders from the point of view of their credibility to followers. To all this might be added ideas of distributed leadership that suggest leadership should become a popular thing, with anyone who takes an initiative, whatever their rank or formal authority in the organization, being seen as a leader. In essence the ideas of distributed leadership see (or would like to see) leadership as unconnected to formal positions in an organizational hierarchy.

The doubts about heroic leaders (charismatic and transformational) may be seen to relate to both their feasibility and their desirability (Kellerman 2008; Brown 2014). In fact, there is no real evidence that the public sector (or the business sector) have been reinvented as non-hierarchical systems. There are still levels of responsibility and authority, and associated differentials of income and status, within public sector organizations. So, the question facing us is, arguably, what is the best way for people in positions of responsibility and authority to provide leadership in a world where they have to do this with limits to their knowledge and their power? This is an important question when an increasing number of commentators are pinning their hope on dispersing leadership across everybody. As Grint (2010: 113) put it: 'In attempting to escape from the clutches of heroic leadership, we now seem enthralled by its apparent opposite – distributed leadership: in this post-heroic era we will all be leaders so that none are'. He took the view that this distributed leadership would not be viable in large-scale organizations and that some form of institutionalized leadership was needed.

Being in a position of responsibility and authority in a public sector organization provides leaders with resources, but attached to the resources are also expectations (Heifetz 1994). Whether fair or not, these expectations include that those in authority will provide direction to those on lower responsibility and pay grades. So, for as long as the public sector continues to have hierarchies of officials employed in large-scale public administration organizations (bureaucratic structures), we *should* be expecting that they will be leaders, and we should expect that they will be leaders acting in the public interest and for the good of the public. In which case, the search for the best kind of leadership continues, a search that should avoid the extremes of heroic and distributed leadership.

In the first chapter we noted the idea of Mulgan (2009), that strategy mobilizes knowledge and power to turn wishes into results. We also noted that there were limits to the leader's knowledge and their power. A leader cannot just design a strategy and expect it to be implemented, and know the strategy is perfectly right and that its implementation will be perfectly under their control. What does this mean for strategic leaders in the public sector? The proposition of this chapter is that they should be pragmatic. Pragmatic leaders use strategy to guide actions and then look at the consequences to work out if the strategy needs revising. This involves them learning from putting the strategy into operation. They also have to use their political skills to handle the conflict created by strategic change and to manage stakeholders to give the strategy the best chance of success.

Heifetz, Grashow and Linsky (2009) recommended the development of something they defined as a continuous-learning mind-set. This meant, among other things, that people in an organization should 'view the latest strategic plan as today's best guess rather than a sacred text' and should 'expect to constantly refine it as new information comes in' (Heifetz *et al.* 2009: 107). In other words, strategic planning may be seen as combined with continuous learning.

The experimental mind-set is needed not just because of the limits of knowledge but also because of the limits of power and control. Bryson (1995: 183–4) emphasized that designing strategic implementation processes requires leaders to assess both technical difficulties (knowledge) and political difficulties (resistance to change). There is also an interaction between them. For example, the nature and extent of resistance may be anticipated as carefully as possible but it may only be in the process of implementation that resistance from a specific stakeholder develops and can be better understood and assessed reasonably accurately.

This experimental mind-set can be linked to the characterization of leaders as pioneers and sponsors of change and innovation. According to Kouzes and Posner (2007: 18–19):

> Leaders are pioneers. They are willing to step out into the unknown. They search for opportunities to innovate, grow, and improve. [. . .] Leaders know well that innovation and change involve experimenting and taking risks. Despite the inevitability of mistakes and failures leaders proceed anyway.

The reason for doing experiments is the need for learning. Leaders learn from their experiments; leaders are learners (Bennis and Nanus 1985; Kouzes and Posner 2007).

THE THEORY OF ADAPTIVE LEADERSHIP

Ronald Heifetz and colleagues (2009) put together a position on leadership that distances their ideas from both the heroic leadership model and from the idea

93

that leaders do not matter – they called it adaptive leadership. One of their important ideas was that leaders have to run the risk of the displeasure of others. Why? Heifetz *et al.* (2009: 17) state:

> There is a myth that drives many change initiatives into the ground: that the organization needs to change because it is broken. The reality is that any social system (including an organization or a country or a family) is the way it is because the people in that system (at least those individuals and factions with the most leverage) want it that way. In that sense, on the whole, on balance, the system is working fine, even though it may appear to be "dysfunctional" in some respects to some members and outside observers, and even though it faces danger just over the horizon. As our colleague Jeff Lawrence poignantly says, "There is no such thing as a dysfunctional organization, because every organization is perfectly aligned to achieve the results it currently gets."

In the case of public services, the outside 'observers' may be the public for whom the public service has been created and who pay for the service through their taxes. We also know that members of the public often expect their elected politicians to keep the promises they make during elections, get the best value for tax-payers, take decisions about the long-term direction of the country and run the government professionally. At the same time we have survey evidence that shows that members of the public often fear the public services are badly run and providing extra tax revenue to services will be wasted by poor management. In these circumstances we can imagine many members of the public thinking that some public services are dysfunctional and could be better led and managed.

Take a hypothetical example of the public wanting better access to public services (without paying higher taxes) and the service providers being reluctant to extend access hours because of the impact of a change on the quality of life. Arguably, this is a case where the system is seen to work fine by the service providers but the service users (outsiders) would like to see the system change. It is not obvious in this hypothetical example whether the access should be improved or kept the same. There are probably quite difficult issues for leaders in judging feasibility, fairness and so on. The point is, however, that leaders in a public service are meant to be leading in a way that is responsive to public needs so that they do what is right for the public, and at the same time they need to lead in a way that is fair to the employees and professionals in the public service ('showing genuine concern for others'). If it turns out that the system needs to be changed, it is difficult to see how this can be done without some sense of loss by employees who feel that the system was already right as it was.

An interesting by-product of seeing leaders as in a relationship with followers, but not recognizing or giving due attention to the leaders' relationship with the public, is the sense in which the mediating role of public sector leaders is neglected. This mediating role is profoundly important. When pressures for change arise from the public and this is experienced inside a public sector organization, it is a problem if it is experienced as something that is just the leaders imposing change on followers. (The leaders, it might be said, are the phenomenal appearance of public pressures in the eyes of employees.) Likewise, when the public observe the public sector organization from the outside and see an organizational reluctance to change and adapt, they may only see poor leadership, even if it is the professionals and other employees that are resisting changes. Arguably, this mediating role has never received the attention it deserves in attempts to understand public sector leaders. See Figure 4.1.

Another important idea, first developed by Ronald Heifetz in his 1994 book, was the idea of two types of problems and two types of work. He used these distinctions to characterize different types of situations. In one case, he suggested, there was a need to rethink our expectations of leaders in authority positions who were not able to simply direct others in what to do. He labelled these situations technical and adaptive. The first he explained as follows (Heifetz 1994: 125):

> In technical situations, adequate preparations for the current problem have been made already. Procedures, lines of authority, role placements, and norms of operation have been established. People have a sufficiently clear idea about what needs to be done and how to go about doing it. Creativity and ingenuity may be needed, but only to devise variations on known themes, not new themes altogether.

In technical situations, expecting leaders to direct is realistic. In adaptive situations the leader is not able to simply direct others. The solution is not known and learning needs to occur before a solution will be found. In the adaptive situation, more is needed from followers and the whole process can be a lot more difficult, even dangerous, for leaders in positions of authority (Heifetz 1994: 126):

> Exercising leadership from a position of authority in adaptive situations means going against the grain. Rather than fulfilling the expectations for answers, one provides questions; rather than protecting people from outside threat, one lets people feel the threat in order to stimulate adaptation; instead of orienting people to their current roles, one distorts people so the new role relationships develop; rather than quelling conflict, one generates it; instead of maintaining norms, one challenges them.

Leaders in adaptive situations may be attacked in a variety of ways by people who want things to stay as they are. If a leader comes through in one piece they must be pretty resilient and highly motivated. Leading adaptive change is not a recipe for an easy life – there is no simple set of rules to follow that will guarantee success. It is also a highly skilled and highly political process of learning and adaptation. 'Everything you do in leading adaptive change is an experiment'

95

Figure 4.1 *The mediating role of public sector leaders – in a relationship with the public and with employees and professionals*

(Heifetz *et al.* 2009: 277). Heifetz likens leading to walking a razor's edge (Heifetz 1994: 126–7):

> In adaptive situations, fulfilling the social functions of authority requires walking a razor's edge. Challenge people too fast, and they will push the authority figure over for failing their expectations for stability. But challenge people too slowly, and they will throw him down when they discover that no progress has been made. Ultimately, they will blame him for lack of progress. To stay balanced on the edge, one needs a strategic understanding of the specific tools and constraints that come with one's authority.

Table 4.1 summarizes Heifetz's ideas, which come across as very empathetic to the leader in an authority position who takes on the challenge of adaptive work.

The idea of the razor's edge that the leader walks is given a diagrammatic form in Heifetz *et al.* (2009), where the edge becomes a 'productive zone of disequilibrium' (see Figure 4.2).

According to Heifetz *et al.* (2009), when people in the organization are at a low level of stress they are below the threshold of change. This is what

Table 4.1 *Technical and adaptive situations – leaders in positions of authority (Heifetz 1994)*

	Type of situation	
	Technical	Adaptive
Who provides solution?	Leader provides problem definition and solution	Leader identifies the adaptive challenge, diagnoses conditions and asks questions about problem definition and solutions
Are employees protected from threats?	Leader protects employees from external threats	Leader lets employees feel the external threat in order to stimulate adaptation
Current roles	Employees are oriented to their current roles	Employees are disoriented so that new role relationships develop
Management of conflict	Leaders quell conflict to maintain order	Leaders generate conflict or let it emerge
Norms	Leaders maintain norms	Leaders challenge norms or allow them to be challenged

Source: Adapted from Table 2 in Heifetz (1994) page 127.

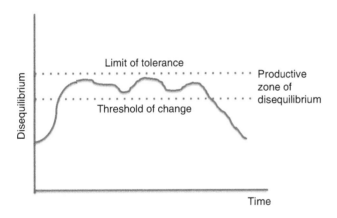

Figure 4.2 *The disequilibrium diagram and the productive zone of disequilibrium*

management consultants sometimes call a 'comfort zone'; they are comfortable and satisfied. When they are above the limit of tolerance the tensions in the organization are dysfunctional. Between the threshold of change and the limit of tolerance lies the productive zone of disequilibrium. In this zone the stress level is high enough that people can be mobilized to focus on and engage with the problems they do not wish to tackle. In other words, Heifetz and his colleagues imagine there is a level of internal stress that is optimum, not too high and not

97

too low. The adaptive work of the leader is to keep the organization in the productive zone over a period of time. If the leader does not do this work, the stress level falls back below the threshold of change. The leader also needs to get the stress level down if it goes too high and above the limit of tolerance. The change process needs continuous attention as the leader observes events and patterns, interprets them, intervenes and then goes back to observing again, when a new cycle starts. The leader, they say, needs a plan. But the plan needs to be flexible, as new discoveries are made and new forms of resistance develop. They warn that leaders will encounter people using tactics to avoid adaptive work. The challenges are not only ones of learning but also of handling the politics of change. And to think politically leaders have to look at their organization as a web of stakeholders (each with values, loyalties, fears of losses and hidden alliances). The interventions leaders make are experiments. They warn leaders that they need patience and persistence. They say (Heifetz *et al.* 2009: 37): '. . . adaptive leadership is about will plus skill'.

In 1994 Heifetz offered five strategic principles of strategic leadership that clearly relate to the adaptive work of the leader intent on getting people into, and keeping them in, the productive zone. These were:

1 Identify the adaptive challenge.
2 Keep the level of distress within a tolerable range for doing adaptive work.
3 Focus attention on ripening issues and not on stress-reducing distractions.
4 Give the work back to people, but at a rate they can stand.
5 Protect voices of leadership without authority.

One of the reasons Heifetz mentioned (1994) protecting voices of leadership without authority, was that these were people who asked hard questions, generated distress and who pointed to the internal contradictions of society. The idea of contradiction also appeared as a suggestion for a question proposed for use in diagnosing adaptive challenges (Heifetz *et al.* 2009: 75):

> Are there internal contradictions, breaks in the linkage that ideally should coherently connect the orienting values and mission of the organization through its strategy, goals, objectives, and action plans down to the concrete level of its operations close to the ground?

Heifetz and colleagues did not say much explicitly about strategies and strategic planning. The most important thing they did say was that the experimental approach had for periods been at the heart of government strategy-making in the US, both during the time of Franklin Roosevelt and more recently during the Obama administration (Heifetz *et al.* 2009: 277–8):

> Experiments involve testing hypotheses, looking for contrary data, and making midcourse corrections as you generate new knowledge. Indeed, this was central to Franklin Roosevelt's crisis strategy during his first term in

office: multiple overlapping experiments that both reduced panic (because activism spoke even louder than reassuring words) and tested an array of programs to provide economic relief, some of which worked. The lessons learned informed not only his next set of initiatives, but also the economic policy experiments run more than seventy years later by the Obama administration.

Heifetz and his colleagues have neatly summarized the implications of an experimental mind-set for leaders (2009: 36–7):

> When you adopt an experimental mind-set, you actively commit to an intervention you have designed while also not letting yourself become wedded to it. That way, if it misses the mark, you do not feel compelled to defend it. This mind-set also opens you to other, unanticipated possibilities. [. . .] Thinking experimentally also opens you to learning: you stay open to the possibility that you might be wrong. Finally, an experimental mind-set facilitates the iterative nature of the adaptive leadership process: you make an intervention based on your interpretation of the situation, and you see what happens. You use the results of your experiment to take the next steps or to make a midcourse correction.

They also make a point about strategy that is not made sufficiently – this is the possibility that an organization may not be ready to have a strategy. In such a situation, they suggest that the leader build allies and ask questions in the decision making team that draws them eventually towards recognition that a new strategy is needed. They emphasize the importance of timing and the risk of trying to rush people into a commitment to a strategy before the time is ripe.

In summary, it seems that while strategic management as a formal technique or system of management was not uppermost in Heifetz and his colleagues' thoughts, nevertheless their suggestions for adaptive work might be the closest thing there is to guidance on to how to make strategic plans effective. However, the implication of this is to recognize that strategic plans are tools of experimental joint action in situations that contain serious barriers to change, and that they require leaders to have political as well as analytical skills.

LINKING ADAPTIVE LEADERSHIP TO CONCEPTS FROM STRATEGIC MANAGEMENT THINKING

It is difficult to think of many mainstream writers on strategic management who have emphasized that strategic management should be informed by experimenting and learning. But there have been two attempts to develop the idea of learning and even experimenting as part of strategic thinking and planning, which are worth noting.

99

Quinn (1980) was someone who developed an idea of learning as an aspect of an 'incremental approach to strategic change'. Based on his analysis of case studies of ten major corporations, he found strategy did not appear at the end of a formal analytical process but would crystallize as a 'widely-shared consensus for action among key members of the top management team' (Quinn 1980: 34). He found that strategy was developed in a way that was 'typically fragmented, evolutionary and largely intuitive' (Quinn 1980: 34). He explained the existence of incremental logic as partly an issue of power (leaders deciding it would be best to keep some of their intentions a secret) and partly a matter of seeking and gaining extra knowledge as the strategy was pursued. The learning aspect was explained as a response to precipitating events as follows (Quinn 1980: 38):

> Recognizing this, top executives usually consciously try to deal with precipitating events in an incremental fashion. Early commitments were kept broadly formative, tentative and subject to later review. In some cases neither the company nor the external players could understand the full implications of alternative actions. All parties wanted to test assumptions and have an opportunity to learn from and adapt to the others' responses.

This model of decision making, labelled by Quinn as logical incrementalism, saw leaders as acting in a conscious and purposeful manner. Arguably, this analysis of Quinn's, of precipitating events and companies not fully understanding the implications of alternative courses of action, might be seen as in some respect like an adaptive problem – at least it was not a technical problem in the sense we have been discussing.

Ansoff and McDonnell (1990) tried to develop a logical framework for selecting strategic learning and suggested that the nature of the strategic challenges facing an organization were important. Strategic learning was more appropriate when strategic challenges were low in terms of predictability, and had high novelty and complexity. They thought predictability might be low if information was partial, alternative actions were not clear and the consequences of actions were unclear. Novelty was defined as high when it was difficult to extrapolate from past experience information that might be used to understand new strategic challenges. The frequency and pervasiveness of challenges combined to define complexity.

Ansoff and McDonnell suggest that in the face of these conditions learning could take place through a process of 'progressive commitment'. Their explanation of this did sound like Quinn's findings of learning that occurred as a result of precipitating events, but also it sounds more like a formal experimental approach. Each commitment decision was to be designed both to keep options open and to maximize the learning that occurred. This learning was then to be used in a subsequent commitment decision. Presumably, this would imply acting when not quite knowing how it might turn out, hoping for good results, but being prepared to learn from results and use them for future decisions.

100

CASE STUDY

Leigh Lewis at Jobcentre Plus

Jobcentre Plus was created in 2002 by integrating two UK government services, one that had provided benefits to unemployed people and one that had assisted job seekers. The change was described by a Jobcentre Plus manager based in one of the regions as follows:

> ... about two or three years ago we had a network of Social Security Offices run by the Benefits Agency, and we had a network of Job Centres run through the Employment Service ... September/October 2001 it would have been now, we had 56 Employment Jobcentre Plus offices. And that would have been the essence, the merging of both those services, so actually you [i.e. the public] had one office to go through, so you didn't go into one office to [look for] jobs, and another office to get your benefit. You actually merged the two together.
>
> (Interview with the author in 2003)

The then Prime Minister, Tony Blair, provided the political formulation of a vision in a statement to the House of Commons:

> In a sense there was a vision, the Prime Minister in I think March 2000 set out the vision, the Government's vision, there was a statement in the House of Commons as to why the Government was doing this and what it wanted to achieve.
>
> (Milner and Joyce 2005: 118)

Leigh Lewis, the first Chief Executive of Jobcentre Plus, had the responsibility of making the vision meaningful:

> ... out of a whole set of discussions came gradually more detailed iterations of the Prime Minister's vision and they started to be drawn down to a lower level. I had a lot of influence in that process, but it was not my process to control in its entirety. I had to ensure that a lot of other stakeholders were alongside me, that Ministers were comfortable with the way we were articulating the Prime Minister's vision and so on. And there were a lot of people involved; first of all you have government departments with interests quite rightly to pursue and defend, so the interests of the Treasury is 'Is this going to cost a lot of money, what are we going to get from it, how are we going to know we are succeeding, what are the outcomes going to be, what are the targets going to be, were they stretching enough, were they tough enough?' You had the Secretaries of State most directly concerned wanting to be sure that the policy outcomes and objectives were the ones they wanted to achieve and not some group of objectives that belonged to somebody else, and it's not impossible of course in any government system, that different departments have different competing priorities. And then you had a set of other stakeholders,

stakeholders representing the staff, stakeholders representing the customers, stakeholders representing employers, etc., and again part of the challenge is to try and emerge with a vision and a way ahead and structures which command the confidence of the widest possible group of the people you are trying to work with, and it's not an easy process.

(Milner and Joyce 2005: 118–9)

A new network of 1,000 merged offices was planned, and each of these was intended to offer an entirely new quality of service to the public who were to be treated like valued customers. Leigh Lewis commented on the offices of the past:

Former Social Security Offices that had not been lavished with investment were pretty grim places in many cases. They were not places you would want to stay in for any length of time. A single parent with a child would not have wanted to go into that environment.

(Interview with the author in 2003)

New offices were rolled out across the whole country, beginning with 56 in 2001–2. Resistance to the change began at the pilot stage. A strike was called by the Public and Commercial Services Union (PCSU) on the day the pilot offices opened, and the members called out were in the new offices. It was called because of what the Union said was a safety issue – the absence of screens to protect their members from the public. Leigh Lewis saw the screens as an impediment to offering a high quality service to the clients of Jobcentre Plus. Putting up large screens in the new offices to keep the public separate from the staff working there was not the kind of service environment that he wanted. He wanted it to be predominantly open plan and unscreened. In December 2001 there was a national strike on this issue with the Union leader on record as saying that the new offices were unsafe; it lasted six months. However, the new agency, Jobcentre Plus, remained a largely unscreened environment.

When asked, Leigh Lewis said this about leadership:

Leadership is about painting a picture. Leadership is about standing up at the front. Leadership is about saying we're here today, but we want to be there tomorrow. Leadership is about giving people the belief and confidence that they can get there. Leadership is saying I'm not going to ask you to do anything that I wouldn't do myself. Leadership is saying that I'll back you on the bad days as well as the good days if you are doing your best. Leadership is about saying I'm hugely demanding but I'm hugely supportive. I used to say that I was the organization's proudest champion and its fiercest critic, and in some ways that's what you've got to be in a leadership role, I think.

(Interview with the author in 2003)

A 2008 report by the UK Comptroller and Auditor General described the introduction of the new office network in Jobcentre Plus as relatively well done and said that it provided lessons to others. The development was described as a 'profound change in the way the largest government agency does business with its five million customers' (Comptroller and Auditor General 2008: 5). The Comptroller and Auditor's report concluded that the roll-out of the new offices had contributed to improvements in customer service while at the same time delivering savings against the agreed budget. The savings were estimated to be about £135 million per year by 2006–7.

The 2008 report on Jobcentre Plus identified six sets of lessons:

■ Communicating a vision of improvement

    ☐ Senior management had provided leadership and communicated the vision and this resulted in staff buy-in to the roll-out process.

■ Consistent leadership, strong governance and close monitoring by a central project management team

    ☐ The experiences of the early stages of the change had led to an effective project management structure being set up (which included the formation of a stable core project management team and senior management assuming ownership and accountability for the change programme).

■ Planning in detail and developing a replicable process

    ☐ Among other things, going for a single design for the new office allowed costs to be closely controlled.

■ Change was managed well at sites that learnt from previous experience

    ☐ Experienced implementation managers supported local managers in the set-up of the new design offices.

■ Using partnering to incentivize contractors to innovate and reduce costs

    ☐ Target pricing and performance management was combined with a partnering approach in 2003 to create a positive relationship with contractors.

■ Being prepared to learn as the roll-out progressed

    ☐ The review of the initial phase of the roll-out led to the appointment of someone from the private sector as a works programme manager to make various adjustments to the change programme, including the adoption of a single design for the offices and changes to procurement arrangements.

Case questions:

1   Who was the strategic leader in this case and who created the vision for Jobcentre Plus?

2   What were the biggest leadership challenges in this change?
3   How did Leigh Lewis manage the key stakeholders?
4   Was the Union being unreasonable? Could Jobcentre Plus have done something to avoid strike action?
5   Was there any evidence of an experimental mind-set in the case study?

SUMMARY

One of the interesting points to emerge from this chapter is the way that the approach to studying leadership using a pragmatic model and in which leaders experiment and learn is that it opens up fairly readily a discussion of leadership actions during the change process. In hindsight some of the theories we looked at in previous chapters treat the change process as a 'black box'. But with Heifetz and his colleagues we see that there is much to be understood about how leaders steer and negotiate change through an implementation process.

Heifetz and colleagues also seem quite different from many others who have addressed the issue of leadership, in that they seem to have a real empathy for the situation of leaders and all the challenges they face in carrying out their role responsibly.

Work-based assignment: self-assessment

The assignments in this book are mostly for civil servants and other public services staff who have management experience.

Experienced managers can do the assignment based on a recent organization for which they have worked or are still working. For those without experience

Table 4.2 *Stakeholder analysis*

Stakeholder (individual person, organization, etc.)	How will the stakeholder be affected by the proposed action?	What would the stakeholder like to see come of the strategic issue being addressed?	What are the most important values and beliefs of the stakeholder?	What obligations or loyalties does the stakeholder have to any person or organization outside of the stakeholder?	What does the stakeholder fear losing as a result of the proposed strategic action? (resources, power, etc.)

you may want to try the assignment using an organization that will give you access to ask questions about strategic issues and stakeholders.

Identify a strategic issue that you would like to see addressed in your organization and identify a proposed action to solve it. Perform a stakeholder analysis based on this issue and action and write it up in Table 4.2. Then reflect on how the action might need to be modified to make it more acceptable or how acceptability of the action could be increased.

DISCUSSION QUESTIONS

1 Keith Grint (2005) used a typology of problems comprising tame, wicked and critical. Heifetz and colleagues only use two types of problem: technical and adaptive. What can we learn from comparing the two sets of problems and from comparing the models of Grint and Heifetz and colleagues?
2 What are the benefits of applying an experimental mind-set to strategic planning?
3 If a plan for implementation involves the use of pilots, is this an example of an experimental mind-set being applied to strategic action? Why don't strategic leaders always use pilots before full-scale implementation?
4 Was the change at Jobcentre Plus a technical or an adaptive change?

FURTHER READING

Heifetz, R. A. and Laurie, D. L. (2001) The work of leadership. *Harvard Business Review*, December: 131–40.

   This article provides a very useful summary of the ideas of adaptive leadership and offers an accessible way into this perspective.

REFERENCE LIST

Ansoff, I. and McDonnell, E. (1990) *Implanting Strategic Management*. 2nd edition. Hemel Hempstead, UK: Prentice Hall International.
Bennis, W. and Nanus, B. (1985) *Leaders: The Strategies for Taking Charge*. New York: Harper & Row.
Brown, A. (2014) *The Myth of the Strong Leader: Political Leadership in the Modern Age*. London: The Bodley Head.
Bryson, J. (1995) *Strategic Planning for Public and Nonprofit Organizations: A Guide to Strengthening and Sustaining Organizational Achievement*. Revised edition. San Francisco, CA: Jossey-Bass.

Comptroller and Auditor General (2008) *Department for Work and Pensions: The Rollout of the Jobcentre Plus Office Network*, HC 346 Session 2007–08. London: The Stationery Office.

Grint, K. (2005) Problems, problems, problems: The social construction of 'leadership'. *Human Relations*, 58(11): 1467–94.

Grint, K. (2010) *Leadership: A Very Short Introduction*. Oxford: Oxford University Press.

Heifetz, R. (1994) *Leadership without Easy Answers*. Cambridge, MA and London, England: The Belknap Press of Harvard University Press.

Heifetz, R., Grashow, A. and Linsky, M. (2009) *The Practice of Adaptive Leadership*. Boston, MA: Harvard Business Press.

Kellerman, B. (2008) *Followership: How Followers Are Creating Change and Changing Leaders*. Boston, MA: Harvard Business School Press.

Kouzes, J. M. and Posner, B. Z. (2007) *The Leadership Challenge*. San Francisco, CA: Jossey-Bass.

Milner, E. and Joyce, P. (2005) *Lessons in Leadership: Meeting the Challenges of Public Services Management*. London: Routledge.

Mulgan, G. (2009) *The Art of Public Strategy*. Oxford: Oxford University Press.

Quinn, J. B. (1980) An incremental approach to strategic change. *The McKinsey Quarterly*, Winter: 34–52.

Part 2

Techniques

INTRODUCTION

Strategic leadership in the public sector is a conscious and purposeful activity. Practitioners have a choice of numerous techniques to help them do the work of strategic planning and strategic implementation. These techniques complement the personal skills of leaders in strategic analysis, in analysing strategic issues, in generating ideas for strategic action, in evaluating options and in planning the implementation of action. Strategic leaders use techniques in the hope and anticipation that they will help them make more competent strategic decisions.

Some people refer to the techniques used in strategic thinking and planning as 'tools'. It may sound a bit strange to use a word that we might tend to associate with physical work rather than intellectual activity, but the word has the advantage of underlining the fact that strategic thinking and planning are hard work. Rumelt (2011), in a very influential book on how strategic thinking should be done, castigated lazy and superficial thinking. He claimed that bad strategy is not the result of miscalculations but the 'active avoidance of the hard work of crafting a good strategy' (Rumelt 2011: 58). While strategic leaders have to expect that their thinking will always contain some errors, the assumption made here is that it is important to do the best you can in developing strategic thinking, and, as Rumelt said, it is important to do the hard work of strategic thinking.

Of course, no amount of hard work will guarantee the right outcome. The 'correctness' of strategic plans always has to be tested by being put into practice. The philosophical position taken here is, very crudely, a 'critical realist' perspective. This means that the models or understandings of the reality that we construct when doing strategic thinking and planning are imperfect representations of reality. The analysis and synthesis work that we do, unfortunately, just does not produce perfect representations. Consequently, we should not accept the models or understandings we produce at face value – we have to check the objectivity of our strategic thinking through putting plans into action. When we implement strategic plans and the result is good, meaning that the consequences are generally good, then we tend to think that on the whole our understanding of the situation was approximately correct.

This attitude to the need to test our strategic understanding of situations is based on accepting that the world is normally rich in its detail, can appear very confusing and contradictory, and there is generally just too much to be completely understood adequately by any one person. The understanding that is achieved by a person is always partial. The importance of testing our understanding also reflects the fact that the world is a social place and that people are constantly taking the world (or bits of it) and changing it. Hence we are trying to hit a constantly moving target when we try to use strategic thinking. All in all, it is not surprising that there is no such thing as infallibility as a result of following a strategic planning process.

We can define strategic thinking and planning techniques, or tools, as being intellectual instruments used by strategic management practitioners to accomplish strategic management. You may notice that the tools of strategic management can be coming into, or going out of, fashion at any particular time. For example, a number of techniques have been developed to help with strategic thinking about the future and for anticipating future possibilities; these have included: extrapolation of trends, econometric modelling, PEST, SWOT, scenario planning and long-term visioning. Some of the earlier ones on the list were popular when it was assumed that future situations could be forecast using calculations and data (1960s and 1970s). Scenario planning seems to have grown in popularity from the 1970s onwards.

Various techniques have been developed for the work of framing and evaluating strategic choices. They have included: investment appraisal, cost–benefit analysis, risk–reward calculations, the balanced scorecard, and consulting citizens and stakeholders in workshops. Survey evidence suggests that cost–benefit analysis was a well-known technique in the 1980s and early 1990s. The use of the balanced scorecard dates from the early 1990s and spread ferociously in the public sector in the 1990s. The use of formal monitoring and evaluation techniques (including the flourishing 'science' of performance targets) developed very visibly in the early to mid 2000s in a number of different national governments. It seems probable that the popularity of techniques may be linked to developments in how strategies are created and evaluated.

REFERENCE LIST

Rumelt, R. (2011) *Good Strategy Bad Strategy: The Difference and Why It Matters*. London: Profile.

Chapter 5

Strategic planning in the public sector

LEARNING OBJECTIVES

- To consider the nature and context of strategic planning as a decision-making system within the public sector
- To review some relevant research findings on the role of formal strategic planning in the public sector and on the problem of integration
- To analyse the rejection of formal strategic planning by Henry Mintzberg

INTRODUCTION

Alan Budd mentioned the idea of governments making use of strategic planning back in 1978. In a book on the politics of economic planning, he suggested that parliament (in the UK) tended to be preoccupied with the immediate in its decision making rather than the long-term and then turned to consider the possible benefits of governments using strategic planning. He quoted the ideas of Lindblom who favoured strategic planning by government because it was selective (it did not try to plan everything in society and in the economy) and made much use of interaction (presumably a reference to the interactions of planners and stakeholders). Budd (1978: 153) commented:

> Strategic planning resembles the style of planning undertaken by companies in competitive markets. They recognize that their control over the environment is limited, and develop a system for responding to market forces. They are negotiating with the environment rather than seeking to control it.

If the idea of government using strategic planning was a prescient thought back in 1978, by 2012, when Martin Sorrell, Chief Executive of WPP, a global advertising company, was asked his opinion, he was being far from contro-versial with his view on what the UK government should do to help business.

His answer was, 'Develop a strategic plan for growth and jobs and implement it' (Gribbin 2015).

This chapter sets the scene for the following chapters when various techniques for strategic thinking and strategic planning are examined, and processes and stages of strategic planning are reviewed. In this chapter it will be important to place all the observations and analysis in the context of the public sector, its parties and processes (see Figure 5.1). Public sector organizations inhabit the public sector and we should not lightly assume that private sector organizations and public sector organizations are almost identical.

In the paragraphs below we review the nature of the public and the nature of politicians and priorities. This is followed by looking at strategic planning in the public sector, including its increasing significance in the national life of the leading countries of the world. We make an important digression to examine in some detail the idea of emergent strategies and informal learning in the work of Henry Mintzberg, someone who has had much influence on the thinking of public sector practitioners and academics. Finally, we look at probably the biggest issue today in terms of strategic planning systems – integration – which we approach by means of a study of the Belgian government by Anne Drumaux. More and more governments want further integration in terms of strategic planning across government ministries as well as up and down levels of governance.

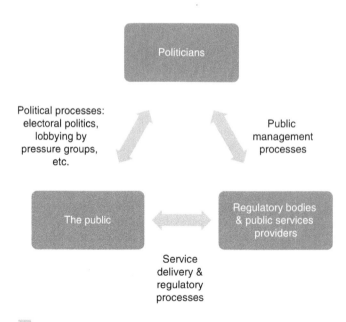

Figure 5.1 *The public sector – parties and processes*

THE PUBLIC

In the 1990s Mark Moore (1995) popularized the notion of public value in his book on strategic management in government. He suggested that public value is activity by government organizations that satisfies the desires of citizens and clients (Moore 1995: 53). How can this public value be measured? There are many options; he said one approach was to measure customer satisfaction (Moore 1995: 22), but however it is measured, ultimately, judging public value is down to politics (Moore 1995: 38). This seems to mean that public value in a democratic society has to be judged by politicians and not by market forces.

A recurrent aspiration in many countries has been to empower the public in relation to the design and reshaping of public services. Essentially, there is often a concern that voting in elections every few years is not enough power for the public, and that other channels for 'empowerment' of the public are also desirable. These other channels include involving members of the public in policy making, in strategic planning and in choice systems when service users make a choice of the providers of public services they will use (e.g. schools, hospitals).

Taking the involvement in policy making first, Geoff Mulgan, previously head of the UK government's Policy Unit and Forward Strategy Unit, drew attention to the importance of involving the public for purposes of building support for reforms and made the following negative appraisal of success so far in attempts to be inclusive in the formulation of policy on illegal drugs:

> ... there have been many expert commissions and reviews, but not ones which actually have involved large sections of the public who remain quite resistant to many reforms which otherwise rational people who study the issues in detail support and that therefore creates a blockage in terms of political possibilities and creates a rationale for the media often to take up very knee-jerk positions on drugs. That is probably an example of the sort of issue where we need to think much more radically about ways of involving large sections of the public in the policy process and not just officials, ministers and experts.
>
> (Mulgan 2007: Ev6)

Attempts to engage the public with strategy and long-term thinking have been conducted by individual government departments. The UK's Department for Education and Skills (DfES), for example, planned regional events in late 2006 to find out the views of partners and service users on a strategy document. The Department also invited comments to be sent direct to the Strategy Unit of the DfES.

It has been argued many times that younger generations of the population in society expect greater ability to make choices according to their own individual priorities and that the public generally has learnt from experiences of being a consumer in the private sector that it wants greater choice. A policy review

111

process by the UK government a few years ago covered the public services and presented some evidence on the popularity of the choice approach to public empowerment (Prime Minister's Strategy Unit, Cabinet Office 2007: 34):

> Citizens want to have a greater ability to take important decisions that directly affect their lives. For example, 63 per cent of people believe that they should have 'a great deal' or 'quite a lot' of choice over which hospital they go to for treatment. People from lower socio-economic groups are the most in favour of more choice. A MORI poll in 2004 found that people in social classes D and E were most likely to consider choice 'absolutely essential' . . . This finding is supported by the British Social Attitudes Survey.

The degree of public empowerment through public channels may still be modest, but the public is not without power and some of its power is that of public opinion. Politicians may encounter the power of public opinion when attempts are being made to design and implement programmes based on government's official political priorities. Government has to have an expectation that it can deliver improvements in its performance in the priority area in question and also maintain public support for it as a priority. When this is not the case, a priority may get sidelined. This conclusion seems consistent with developments in the UK over the period 2000–5 specifically in respect of transport as a key performance area of government. So, it looks as though doubts about the feasibility and public acceptability of ideas for strategic actions to make improvements (e.g. road pricing), and disappointing delivery results against performance targets (e.g. road congestion), may cause politicians to downgrade an area as a priority.

POLITICIANS AND PRIORITIES

If the government of a country wishes to act on the basis of strategic thinking, where is the correct starting point? One possible answer is that it needs to start with a strategic vision. The centrality and usefulness of a vision is made clear in the following statement (OECD 2000: 13):

> A common vision serves to unify political leaders, senior officials, front-line workers and the general public. It also provides a guideline for choosing goals, for developing strategies to achieve those goals and for measuring results. In order to articulate a common vision, government should learn to consult with stakeholders and bring together their many, varied visions.

While it may be tempting to begin strategic planning and management with the formulation of a strategic vision, political leaders in the public services seem to be more comfortable in using priorities as a starting point. For example, the Indian

Government set up the National Institution for Transforming India (NITI) in 2015 and described some of its tasks as follows (Indian Government 2016):

[The NITI will seek to] put an end to slow and tardy implementation of policy, by fostering better Inter-Ministry coordination. It will help evolve a shared vision of *national development priorities*, and foster cooperative federalism, recognizing that strong states make a stronger Nation. [Emphasis added]

As can be seen, the Indian Government was talking about the delivery of a shared vision of priorities.

For elected politicians, it seems, 'priorities' carries the weight that 'visions' and 'missions' do in the private sector. 'In any government you need to ensure there are ways of setting the overall strategy, what you are trying to achieve, why and what is a priority and what is not' (Mulgan 2007: Ev11). Politicians often use the word priority; they may arrive at their overall priorities through consideration of the findings of surveys and focus groups. Some priorities may come from more direct interaction with the public, for instance it has been said that public concern about anti-social behaviour came to the notice of MPs in the UK through their constituency work. MPs were told of this problem directly and face to face by citizens whom they met in their constituencies.

Setting priorities is, arguably, inevitably a very political process in which both values and interests are involved. Politicians who espouse a democratic relationship to society or a community may see in priority-setting an opportunity to draw on the values of the society or the community, and we often look to politicians to resolve issues of priority-setting created by the existence of competing interest groups. Moreover, it is sometimes obvious that elected politicians at local government level adopt, or are influenced in their priorities by, those priorities established by elected politicians at national level, perhaps reflecting an assumption about the mandates of local and national politicians.

Priorities may be seen as equivalent to the concept of key performance areas as used in strategic management. Duncan, Ginter and Swayne (1995: 198) define key performance areas as a few key areas of activity necessary for an organization to achieve its purpose. Textbooks might suggest that key performance areas can be best identified after a mission statement has been clarified. But as used by contemporary politicians, key performance areas are priorities that represent a focused expression of their political values.

Obviously, it is important that once the overall priorities are set by a government or an organization that they are actually the basis for strategic planning. Conversely, because strategic planning will involve situational analysis, there is potential for strategic planning to generate an implicit set of priorities that are in conflict with those of the politicians. This means that politicians may worry that their support for strategic planning by senior civil servants or top managers may backfire and produce goals that are not aligned to their political priorities. In effect, there is a danger that strategic thinking in the civil service or by top managers may lead to rival strategic agendas. Presumably, politicians will be happier about supporting strategic planning if they believe that it will advance achievement of their political priorities and not get in the way of them.

The problem of linking political priorities to strategic thinking and planning may be part of what Mulgan had in mind when giving evidence to a House of Commons Public Administration Select Committee (Mulgan 2007: Ev3):

> What has happened in the last eight years is some basic bits of machinery which make government more inherently long term . . . They include the creation of strategic capacity . . . We have seen a big improvement in the methods being used to think about the future . . . None of this is easy. It is bound to clash often with political priorities. It only works if the top politicians really want it to happen . . .

As Figure 5.2 shows, overall political priorities are potentially influenced by the electorate, senior civil servants, political parties, pressure groups, public service users and many more groups and organizations.

Geoff Mulgan, in evidence to the UK's House of Commons Public Administration Select Committee in 2005, also pointed out the need for government departments to understand such priorities, and how special advisers could help with this (Mulgan 2007: Ev3): 'Where special advisers are doing their job well, they generally oil the wheels, getting things done, or helping departments

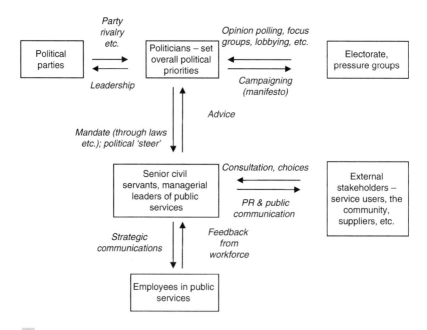

Figure 5.2 Influences on the formation and impact of political priorities

understand ministers' priorities and so on'. In the UK, the special advisers have played a crucial role in relaying and interpreting political priorities to senior civil servants (Mulgan 2007: Ev3).

THINK POINT: Why is setting priorities so important?

Setting priorities is about making choices. Governments and individual public service organizations confront situations that appear to offer a multitude of problems and opportunities. Strategic management is about making changes to achieve better futures, but what problems and what opportunities should be addressed? So many different lines of action seem possible, so where should government or the individual organization make a start?

Choices have to be made because of resource rationing. This is true of all sectors – public, private and voluntary – but perhaps this is more challenging for government organizations because their activity is funded from tax, and thus they are always faced by pressures from citizens and interest groups wanting a larger share of public spending. There is a general appreciation nowadays that there will be a constant search in government services for savings and efficiency gains. We can support this contention with some findings of the OECD. After two decades of public services reforms, the OECD (2005) found that, although governments had a larger not a smaller role, general government primary outlays had remained broadly the same when looked at in cyclically adjusted terms and that upward pressure on expenditure remained. The OECD (2005: 21) concluded:

> For OECD countries, improving the cost-effectiveness and performance of their public sectors will help to reduce pressure on spending. As the past decade has shown, however, this in itself is unlikely to stem the continued upward pressure on expenditure generated by social entitlement programmes and social transfers. Public sector reform is not a substitute for the hard and, in many cases, unpopular choices that politicians have to make in some countries if long-term difficulties are to be avoided.

Summing up, setting overall priorities is made essential because there is a limit to the availability of a range of critical resources, not just money, but also management attention, public support, expertise, etc. 'If resources were unlimited, priorities would not need to be set because all needs could be met' (York 1982: 92).

The picture so far is only one possible way in which politicians and civil servants may operate in relation to public management (see Figure 5.3). First, there are examples in which the strategic planning is led by the politicians and it is fully justified to describe the role of civil servants as delivering the strategic plans of government ministers. Second, it is arguable that because of their role in

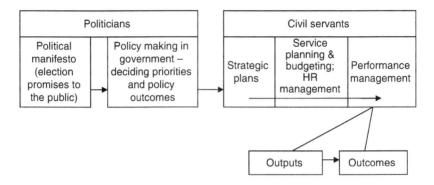

Figure 5.3 *Politicians and civil servants: oversight model*

implementation civil servants are becoming more political. Kooiman and van Vliet (1993: 65) see this as a trend in a number of societies:

> In modern society with all its new problems and opportunities (due to complexity, dynamics and diversity), the traditional Weberian distinction between the political system and the administrative apparatus can no longer be contained. In societies where policy making and policy implementation are interactive and can be seen as co-products of governmental agencies and their clientele groups, public managing is more and more 'political' in the traditional sense. Also the civil servant sets the agenda, promotes or hampers consensus, wins social support and makes bargains.

Third, the activities of politicians and civil servants in policy making is a much more negotiated, confusing and even chaotic experience than might be suggested by some of the models of it as a linear or cyclical process. These are just models representing reality and not the reality itself.

The following morphological box (Table 5.1) suggests the many permutations in the institutionalization of strategic planning within government.

THE USE OF FORMAL STRATEGIC PLANNING IN PUBLIC SECTOR ORGANIZATIONS

Depending on how we define strategic planning, it is possible to argue that some of the earliest uses of formal strategic planning systems in the public sector occurred in the US and the UK in the 1960s and 1970s. In these early days the systems were known as planning–programming–budgeting systems (PPBS) and corporate thinking. These early appearances of strategic planning in the public sector preceded the spread of strategic plans in subnational governments in the 1980s and 1990s (for example in the United States). Surveys suggested that management practitioners in subnational governments were using strategic

Table 5.1 Morphological box – politicians and the public in strategic planning

Component	Possible options (may be combined)		
	1	2	3
Focus of strategy process	Influencing or steering budget decisions	Ensuring agreed purpose (mission) of organization (or community) is realized	Solving strategic issues
Role of politicians	Setting major objectives and choosing between competing objectives	To provide political oversight and hold managerial leadership accountable	To provide strategic leadership and negotiate trade-offs within the planning process
Status of the public	Citizens (voters, pressure groups)	Service users ('customers')	Partners (empowerment of the public)
Role of management	To provide politicians with data on the needs of the public, costs of activities and likely results	To develop strategic plans and seek support for them by politicians	To facilitate strategic decision making by politicians, partners and the involvement of the community in the strategic planning process
Analytical and planning activities	Cost–benefit analysis	Performance planning	Problem solving and creative techniques, scenarios, simulations
Focus of efforts in managing implementation	Ensuring strategies and budget decisions are integrated	Culture management – ensuring staff are motivated to deliver the mission statement	Maintaining support of partners and the public
Results sought	'Objective' and efficient allocation of budgets (possibly analysed by programme area)	High levels of satisfaction reported by service users (an organizational achievement)	Solution of community problems (a community achievement)
Achievement orientation	Administrative achievement	Organizational achievement	Community achievement

planning, often on a voluntary basis, and finding it useful (Berry and Wechsler 1995; Flynn and Talbot 1996; Poister and Streib 2005).

The growth of strategic planning at national level occurred in most of the leading countries of the world over the period 1993 to 2014, beginning with legislation in the US requiring federal agencies to prepare strategic plans on a regular basis and ending in the summer of 2014 when the President of the Russian Federation signed a new federal law establishing strategic planning systems at federal, regional and local government levels. Some very notable developments towards strategic planning systems at national level occurred in this period, such as the Chinese government and the Saudi government both making improvements in their five-year planning systems to deliberately base them more closely on strategic planning. Turkey, which had been overhauling its public financial management systems, brought in legally required strategic planning by government departments, municipal governments and universities. The most recent development of significance occurred in India in early 2015 when India's Planning Commission, which had been responsible for India's Five-Year Plans, was scrapped and a Cabinet Resolution created a new body, the NITI. The vice-chairman of the new body said that India would complete its 12th Five-Year Plan (2012–17) but was likely to switch over to strategic planning, under which efforts would be made to achieve long-term goals.

At supranational level there have been important developments as well. In late 2015 the United Nations General Assembly formally adopted the 2030 Agenda for Sustainable Development. The Secretary-General described this agenda as a universal, integrated and transformative vision for a better world. It established 17 new long-term Global Goals which should be pursued by the United Nations, its various organizations and national governments. It was intended that the United Nations would not only be working to deliver the development goals, it would also be supporting national governments to deliver the goals. According to the Secretary-General of the United Nations (United Nations 2015: 43):

> ... the UN system is committed to working more collaboratively to leverage the expertise and capacities of all its organizations in support of sustainable development. At the country level, UN Country Teams will provide coherent support to national stakeholders to implement their new post-2015 development strategies while accelerating implementation of the standard operating procedures for "delivering as one" in order to achieve greater results for sustainable development.

The expectation is, of course, that individual countries will incorporate the development goals into their national strategies and then implement them through their national strategic planning systems.

Despite all this evidence of the rise of strategic planning in national, subnational and supranational governance systems, there are sometimes doubts about the depth and impact of strategic planning. Are public sector organizations really engaging in formal strategic planning and are they really using strategic thinking to guide action to bring about change?

Aage Johnsen (2014) investigated the state of strategic planning and thinking in Norway's public sector; his study was quite small scale. Using teams of students, he obtained data on what was happening in a diverse set of 12 public sector

118

organizations. The sample included the Directorate of the Police, the Norwegian Directorate for Children, Youth and Family Affairs, Directorate of Integration and Diversity, the Norwegian Labour and Welfare Administration, Oslo University Hospital, Norwegian Railway, National Library of Norway, Oslo and Akershus University College of Applied Sciences and three municipal bodies. As can be seen, it was a very diverse sample.

The spur to this study was Aage Johnsen's interest in Mintzberg, Ahlstrand and Lampel's (2009) description of ten strategic management schools of thought. Each school had at its heart a specific conception of strategic thinking and therefore a specific conception of strategy. For example, according to the planning school and the design school a strategy was a plan. For the power school a strategy was a plot. For the learning school a strategy was a pattern in a stream of actions. For the positioning school (e.g. see the work of Michael Porter) a strategy was choosing a market position in an industry (e.g. low cost, differentiation).

Johnsen (2014) analysed the data and found that all of the 12 organizations used some form of strategic planning approach to strategic thinking. He discovered that types of strategic thinking he associated with the design school, learning school and power school were also present in the organizations. Six of the case study organizations used thinking corresponding to the design school (e.g. a SWOT analysis in strategy formulation). For six cases there were indications of the use of thinking of the type associated with the power school. Finally, in five cases there appeared to be use of organizational learning in their strategy processes. Other types of strategic thinking were rarely present. He concluded that the planning school was the dominant type of strategic thinking in the Norwegian sample of public sector organizations.

Johnsen also mentioned the existence of important expectations about transparency and accountability in Norway. Such expectations are not unusual all over the world – governments now frequently express a desire to set up governance systems that are not only responsive to citizens and participative but also are transparent. Take for example the following statement made by the Indian Government in early 2015 as part of a Cabinet Resolution (Indian Government 2016):

> Transparency is now a sine qua non for good reason. We are in a digital age where the tools and modes of communication, like social media, are powerful instruments to share and explain the thoughts and actions of government. This trend will only increase with time. *Government and governance have to be conducted in an environment of total transparency* – using technology to reduce opacity and thereby, the potential for misadventures in governing. [Emphasis added]

Furthermore, transparency in government strategic planning matters for the governance system at both the formulation and monitoring stages. In China, after a mid-term review of the Tenth Five-Year Plan in 2003, changes were made to the planning system to enhance levels of monitoring and evaluation

119

in time for the mid-course evaluation of the Eleventh Five-Year Plan in 2008. The improved monitoring and evaluation was used to provide better reporting to the public and to increase transparency (Wang and Lin 2014: 33):

> The introduction of the output/outcome indicators with targets and implementation measures adopted by the central government has helped to strengthen the accountability and improve the transparency of the government's work. Already, the monitoring information on the energy consumption per unit GDP and the total COD [chemical oxygen demand] and SO_2 emission volume during the first six months of the Eleventh FYP [Five-Year Plan] has been made public: none of the levels have decreased as outlined in the Plan, instead amounts have increased due to economic growth. Such a level of transparency on Plan implementation is historically unprecedented in China.

Perhaps, therefore, we should not be surprised that the Norway sample of public sector organizations all used a strategic planning approach to strategic thinking. It seems likely that it is this approach that is most likely to meet modern requirements for transparency and accountability. This obviously creates a problem for any strategic leaders in the public sector who prefer their strategy formulation processes to be emergent, messy and informal.

A DIGRESSION – MINTZBERG'S CRITIQUE OF FORMAL STRATEGIC PLANNING

It can be surprising the number of times that public sector practitioners and academics express an opinion that strategic plans do not matter even if there is some value in the experience of doing strategic planning. This same idea was encountered in the brief review of Tom Peters' 1980s' thinking on private sector leadership and management. A linked, and equally influential, idea is that formal strategic planning is impossible to do effectively and is undesirable for various reasons. A third idea, less frequently mentioned, is that a process of evaluation is good for reasons of strategic learning rather than because of an emphasis on monitoring and accountability processes. As explained above, in the public sector the drive for good governance has led to the stress on the need for responsiveness and accountability to the public and transparency. So, for the public sector, some of this thinking derived from the 1980s and early 1990s, and mainly with the private sector in mind, is problematic because it runs contrary to important public sector concerns for the requirements of a good public governance system.

This section of the chapter is a short digression to check out just how solid the basis is for the arguments in favour of informal and emergent strategy and for suspicion about the feasibility and desirability of formal strategic planning. Is there much evidence for, and merit in the arguments for, informal and

120

emergent strategy rather than formal strategic planning? We will come back to the arguments about evaluating processes for strategic learning versus accountability processes in a later chapter.

The big name in relation to emergent strategies is a Canadian management and organization theorist, Henry Mintzberg. He is now well known for the book he wrote with colleagues on ten schools of strategic thinking (Mintzberg *et al.* 2009). In this section we take a look at an article he wrote by himself back in 1987 (Mintzberg 1987) in which he sets out earlier work done by him on classifying different meanings of the word strategy and which leads into his thinking on planning and emergent strategy.

His starting point is not really a study of strategy but the development of some definitions of strategy that he hopes he can use to dispel confusion in the field (Mintzberg 1987: 24):

> To conclude, a good deal of the confusion in this field stems from contradictory and ill-defined uses of the term strategy, . . . By explicating and using five definitions, we may be able to remove some of this confusion, and thereby enrich our ability to understand and manage the processes by which strategies form.

In this paper he presents his five definitions; they are summarized in Table 5.2 below. His commentary on the relationships between the definitions appears to make two of them the most significant – Strategy as Plan and Strategy as Pattern. We say this because they are woven into his discussion of deliberate and emergent strategy.

In the article the definitions are the springboard for a discussion of deliberate, emergent and realized strategies. In the following quote he begins by referring to the definitions of both Strategy as Plan and Strategy as Pattern and then proposes that strategies may be realized or unrealized and may be deliberate or emergent (Mintzberg 1987: 13):

> Thus, the definitions of strategy as plan and pattern can be quite independent of each other: plans may go unrealized, while patterns may appear without preconception. To paraphrase Hume, strategies may result from human actions but not human designs. If we label the first definition intended strategy and the second realized strategy, as shown in Figure 5.4, then we can distinguish deliberate strategies, where intentions that existed previously were realized, from *emergent strategies, where patterns developed in the absence of intentions, or despite them* (which went unrealized). [Emphasis added]

In Mintzberg's diagram of the interrelationship between the intended and emergent strategies, the emergent strategy feeds into the realized strategy. There is no arrow showing intended strategy feeding into emergent strategy. Mintzberg's diagram seems to be saying that emergent strategy is not intended. This is also consistent with his written explanation quoted above, 'we can distinguish

Table 5.2 Mintzberg's five definitions of strategy (1987)

Name of definition	Mintzberg's definition
Strategy as Plan	'To almost anyone you care to ask, strategy is a plan – some sort of consciously intended course of action, a guideline (or set of guidelines) to deal with a situation... By this definition, strategies have two essential characteristics: they are made in advance of the actions to which they apply, and they are developed consciously and purposefully.' (Mintzberg 1987: 11)
Strategy as Ploy	A ploy is a specific type of plan – one that is intended to outwit an opponent.
Strategy as Pattern	'... a third definition is proposed: strategy is a pattern – specifically, a pattern in a stream of actions. By this definition, when Picasso painted blue for a time, that was a strategy, just as was the behavior of the Ford Motor Company when Henry Ford offered his Model T only in black. In other words, by this definition, strategy is consistency in behavior, whether or not intended.' (Mintzberg 1987: 12)
Strategy as Position	'The fourth definition is that strategy is a position – specifically, a means of locating an organization in what organization theorists like to call an "environment". [...] in management terms, formally, a product-market "domain," ...' (Mintzberg 1987: 15)
Strategy as Perspective	'... the fifth [definition] looks inside the organization, indeed inside the heads of the collective strategist. Here, strategy is a perspective, its content consisting not just of a chosen position, but of an ingrained way of perceiving the world. Some organizations, for example, are aggressive pacesetters, creating new technologies and exploiting new markets; others perceive the world as set and stable, and so sit back in long established markets and build protective shells around themselves, relying more on political influence than economic efficiency.' (Mintzberg 1987: 16)

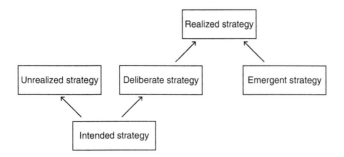

Figure 5.4 Mintzberg's concepts of emergent and intended strategies (1987)
Source: adapted from a diagram by Mintzberg (1987: 14).

deliberate strategies, where intentions that existed previously were realized, from emergent strategies, where patterns developed in the absence of intentions, or despite them (which went unrealized)'.

The impression in the article is that Mintzberg is playing around with definitions. He makes assertions (propositions) such as 'realized strategy' as a mixture of 'deliberate strategy' and 'emergent strategy'. But the only ground for his argument (as so far presented) was the definitions he had made up for the purpose of the paper.

What happens when Mintzberg confronts his propositions with evidence? In this article the main attempt to connect his definitions with reality consists of a very brief account of Honda in the US. The key part of this is presented in the following quote in which he seems to be arguing that a pattern evoked a plan and that an unexpected success *presumably* became a plan (Mintzberg 1987: 19):

> But a closer look at Honda's actual behavior suggests a very different story: it did not go to America with the main intention of selling small, family motorcycles at all; rather, the company seemed to fall into that market almost inadvertently. But once it was clear to the Honda executives that they had wandered into such a lucrative strategic position, *that presumably became their plan*. In other words, their strategy emerged, step by step, but once recognized, was made deliberate. Honda, if you like, developed its intentions through its actions, another way of saying that *pattern evoked plan*. [Emphasis added]

If we present his conclusions as a diagram, we find the model as shown in Figure 5.5.

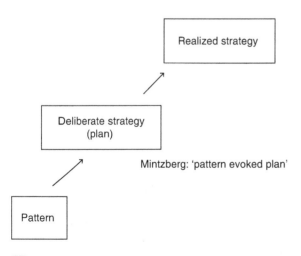

Figure 5.5 *Mintzberg's Honda case (1987)*

If Honda actually did develop a plan, or a deliberate strategy, based on the unexpected success (i.e. pattern), this seems like a smart strategic move. An organization preparing a formal strategic plan (strategy) could usefully examine the organization's current and recent experiences and evaluate what has been successful and what has failed. In other words, surprising successes should be studied by leaders and evaluated for their implications for strategy formulation. How does the Honda case invalidate Strategy as a Plan? And why shouldn't strategic leaders try to learn from unintended patterns?

Later on, in the 1990s, Mintzberg became famous for his criticisms of formal strategic planning on a variety of grounds. Equally, however, in an argument with Igor Ansoff, Mintzberg (1991: 495) seemed to concede that learning and deliberate planning might be in some sort of interactive relationship, with learning and deliberate planning alternating:

> We both know that we shall get nowhere without emergent learning along-side deliberate planning. If we have discovered anything at all these many years, it is, first, that the conception of a novel strategy is a creative process (of synthesis), for which there are no formal techniques (analysis), and second, that to program these strategies throughout complex organizations, and out to assenting environments, we often require a good deal of formal analysis. So the two processes can intertwine. I'll use your words: "cognition-trial-cognition-trial, etc." We may differ on where to begin, but once it has gone on for a while, who cares? (Does it matter if the chicken or the egg came first?) You call it "strategic learning." I have no problem with that so long as you don't pretend it can be formalized. And in return I'll promise never to claim that planning shouldn't be formalized. [. . .] And so it is with planning and learning. BCG's [Boston Consulting Group] mistake was not in what it did describe so much as in what it left out; the critical period of emergent learning that had to inform the deliberate planning process. In other words, strategy had to be conceived informally before it could be programed formally.

Mintzberg's framing of these matters seemed to have evolved from just a few years earlier. He was no longer talking about Strategy as Pattern (defined by Mintzberg as consistency in behaviour, intended or not) but 'emergent learn-ing'. In Mintzberg's Honda case example, we saw that the emergent pattern did not feed directly into realized strategy but was mediated by a plan. It would appear that something has shifted in Mintzberg's argument. It seems as though 'unintended consistency in behavior' and 'emergent strategy' have disappeared to be replaced by 'emergent learning'. Furthermore, logically speaking, it is only by implicitly dropping unintended consistency in behaviour from his emergent strategy definition that Mintzberg can equate his 'emergent learning' with Ansoff's 'strategic learning', which is clearly set out as a form of conscious and purposeful learning.

124

Despite the sentences in which he appeared to be reconciling his and Ansoff's positions, Mintzberg also preserved some sense of tension between their positions by insisting emergent learning has to be informal. But does it? Does all learning have to be informal? Just as we might ask, does all planning have to be formal?

Mintzberg did something valuable by arguing for the importance of emergent strategies and the importance of learning. Whatever criticisms might be made about his methods of arguing, Mintzberg provided a powerful reminder to researchers and practitioners in strategic management that strategy does not always turn out as planned and that along the way certain parts of a strategic plan might be dropped or fail and other new aspects might be introduced. In his discussion of patterns evoking plans (the Honda case) we get the basis for encouraging strategic leaders to learn and refine their strategy (i.e. recognize patterns and exploit them). All this is important. It only becomes a problem when practitioners take up the idea that strategy should be emergent and informal and that formal strategic planning is a bad idea.

INTEGRATION ISSUES

Anne Drumaux's detailed exploration of strategic plans in the Belgian government warns us that politics and policies are not always aligned and that plans are not necessarily integrated with budgetary resources. In the end she seems to suggest that strategic planning is not necessarily a strong system or framework for action because of the effects of emergent developments, but that strategic planning may play a part in clarifying ideas and influencing conditions in which action takes place (see Research Box 5.1).

RESEARCH BOX 5.1   STRATEGIC MANAGEMENT AS A REFORM IN THE BELGIAN FEDERAL ADMINISTRATION

By Anne Drumaux, Solvay Brussels School of Economics and Management, Université Libre de Bruxelles, Belgium.

Strategic management was introduced in 2000 into the Belgian Federal Administration within the framework of a larger reform, called the 'Copernicus Reform'. The federal reform aimed at introducing new dynamics into administration by a redefinition of the status, selection and role of top civil servants. Enrolled through a new assessment with a term mandate of six years, so called 'top-managers' were asked to define administration strategy into true management plans. In this vision, strategic plans were key elements in order to elaborate and to implement public action priorities as well to evaluate top civil servants' actions. Nowadays, even if the Copernicus Reform is not sustained anymore at the political level, strategic plans still exist, as well as the 'virtual' matrix organization introduced by the reform.

Intentions cartography

Using a typology proposed by Poister and Streib (1999), three models characterize the intentional strategic management in the Belgian Federal Administration (Drumaux and Goethals 2007a) (see also Figure 5.6):

■ The first is a strategic management turned outwards: a high relative proportion of objectives focus on external relations, and programmes and services, to be delivered to external customers. This model is found in the horizontal ministries' (ICT, Personnel & Organization, Budget & Control), which is logical due to their role turned towards the development of programmes and services for the use of the vertical ones. The same tendency can be seen both in the Economy and the Scientific Policy plans, which is related to their prompting role.

■ The second model is a strategic management turned inwards. Human relations and the internal management system represent, proportionally, the highest concerns in this management plan; the Defence plan belongs to this category, while the Finances and the Public Health plans are also strongly polarized towards the internal management system.

■ The third model is a strategic model equally polarized towards all four dimensions (external relations, programmes & services, human resources, internal management system); the Justice, Foreign Affairs, Mobility, and the Social Integration plans belong to it; the Home Affairs plan is polarized towards three dimensions and, to a lesser extent, towards human relations.

Strategic plans processes

Strategic management is not only a question of intentions; the processes through which actions are decided and implemented are equally important (Mintzberg 1978). How are politics and policies related? Do we find top-down hierarchy, or eventually bottom-up relations between objectives, activities, and projects? How are strategic management plans and operational plans coordinated? A detailed analysis (Drumaux and Goethals 2007b) allows several conclusions:

■ First, as presented in Figure 5.7, there is not always a clear top-down hierarchy between the view of the minister (politics level) and the design of policies (policy level). This is shown, for example, by the unbundling between the orientation note of the Minister of Justice based, even in operational details, on a bottom-up approach, and the justice management plan prepared by the Ministry President with the help of consultants. Both documents were prepared in 2003.

126

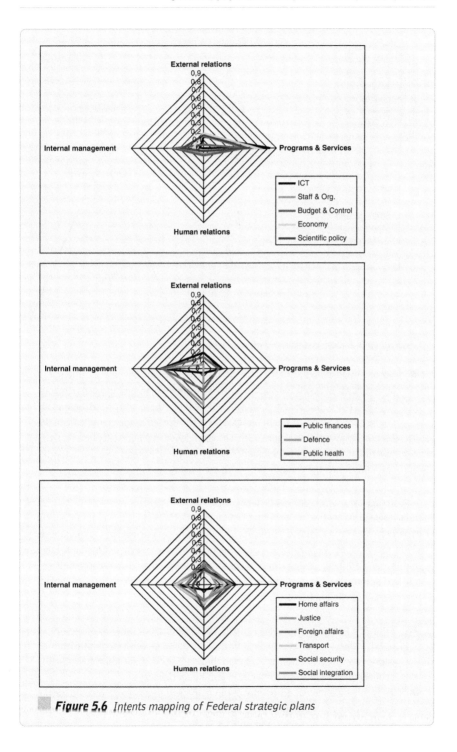

Figure 5.6 *Intents mapping of Federal strategic plans*

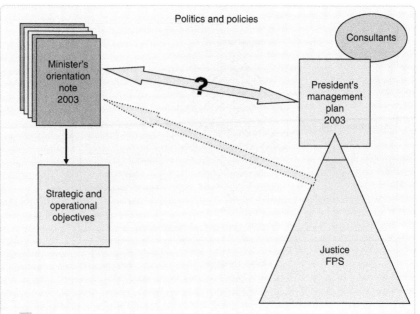

Figure 5.7 *Justice strategic plan process*

- Second, regarding the internal hierarchy between plans, the relationship might be top-down between the top manager's strategic plan and the departments' strategic plans, but becomes nonexistent between those and operational plans on the core business of the ministry. This is illustrated by an example from the Mobility Ministry (see Figure 5.8). The President's management plans focus on functional objectives (Personnel & Organization) instead of core activities (Mobility), and the chain is broken at the level of operational plans.

Similarities and differences with other experiences
Largely inspired by the 'New Public Management' thinking, the Belgian Federal experience has been focusing merely on accountability at the level of top managers. From this perspective, strategic management is more a by-product of the reform than an aim in itself. Using Joyce's typology (1999), the strategic plans of the federal administration are in fact a kind of hybrid between an unfinished 'traditional/classic' model and a formal 'business-like' model:

- They are partially top-down in their conception from mission definition to operational objectives, nevertheless with some process irregularities as previously shown. Moreover, the plans have not been really and systematically connected to results or to resources and budget process.
- They rely on a formal autonomy of top managers that are responsible for the elaboration of plans, but the autonomy is not systematic due to unclear relations between politics and policies levels.

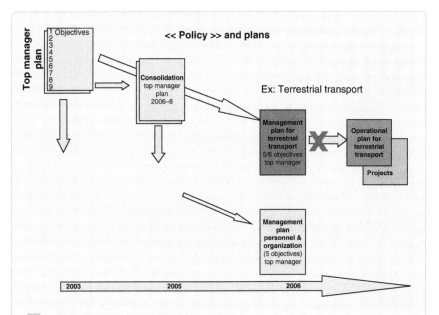

Figure 5.8 *Mobility strategic plan process*

What factors influence the specific forms of strategic management?
Different factors might influence models of strategic management. Some are obviously of an institutional nature: (non)involvement of parliament in performance assessment, respective roles of budget authority and ministries in policies definition, role of cabinets versus top civil servants, and (in)sufficient stability of political intent. Others are cultural, or, at least, more organizational: elite selection modes for top civil servants, effective empowerment, and accountability culture.

What are the potential benefits of strategic management for top civil servants and politicians?
A survey among top managers of the Federal Belgian Administration (Drumaux and Goethals 2007a) confirms the existence of some 'effective behaviours' of public top managers, during the strategic process, that have already been documented by Ring and Perry (1985) in another context. Indeed public decision makers are burdened by the specific constraints of the political, institutional, and administrative system. To be effective, their behaviour has to be incremental and adaptive, allowing flexibility, searching and binding in multiple stakeholders' interests, and be based on influence rather than authority. In this perspective, strategic plans allow top civil servants to clarify constraints, but, despite the plans, effectiveness forces them to stay open to emergent strategies because of their position. At least, this is the condition to make the best out of them. From the politicians' point of view, strategic management has the advantage to seem compatible with the primacy of intention over action, that is, the dominant paradigm in the ideas sphere, and in

129

their professional practice. Provided that one remains aware that this a heuristic short-cut, intentional strategy may contribute to clarify strategic and operational objectives, and create conditions for action since the sole rhetoric on intentions would not be sufficient from the citizens' point of view.

Has strategic management a future in federal administration?
Since the Copernicus Reform is not sustained any more at political level, the risk is high that strategic plans lose their main quality of being an interactive management tool between political and administrative levels, and join the 'club' of forgotten past reforms. Finally, it is difficult to predict the future of strategic management in federal administration since the existence of a federal state, and obviously those of the administration itself, are nowadays in question. It seems clear that strategic management cannot develop without any political vision.

SUMMARY

There are a number of issues that emerge from this chapter that are potentially worth keeping in mind when looking at strategic techniques and considering strategic leadership in a public governance context. First, as implied at the beginning of the chapter, strategic planning by government might be a much better option than either very short-term decision making or trying to plan everything through centralized state planning. This type of strategic planning would be selective and interactive. This type of strategic planning in the public sector would allow government to enable and negotiate change and progress rather than try to impose order on everything to achieve long-term goals.

A second issue is how the public can be enabled to participate in strategic planning by government and how they can be empowered through it. There are a lot of good intentions in respect of this issue but it is also a matter where there is often disappointment about the levels and extent of public participation achieved.

The chapter has also raised the issue of who are the strategic leaders in the public sector; it has been suggested that they might be political or administrative leaders. It should be expected that whether it is a politician or a public administrator will be very important in terms of the consequences and that there might be some significant differences in processes as well. A similar issue can be raised about whether the target for strategic planning is described in terms of a vision or a set of priorities. It should be expected that this might also be a very important distinction. It might be suggested that setting strategic direction in terms of priorities might be very pertinent where government is conscious of the need to be selective in where and how it intervenes, and where a government might be negotiating with powerful stakeholders over what its priorities are to be in relation to national, regional and community level development and investment.

130

There is an issue about how strategic planning in the public sector is designed and operated to suit the requirements of good governance. If governments are now aspiring to total transparency, to being responsive to and enabling citizens, then public sector leaders need to operate strategic planning in a way that is aligned to these aspirations. For example, in terms of the drive to greater transparency, formal strategic planning might be highly appropriate for the public sector.

The issue that emerges from debates about formal strategic planning and informal learning does not have to be resolved by coming down in favour of one or the other. The challenge for the public sector is managing to carry out formal and deliberate strategic planning and ensuring that formal and informal learning feeds into the improvement of results obtained from strategic planning.

Perhaps the issue discussed in this chapter that looms very large as we look forward in time is how the public sector can achieve more integration in its strategic planning practices, including between strategic plans where there are overlapping mandates between different government ministries or different public sector organizations, between higher and lower levels of governance, and between strategic plans and other management systems (e.g. budgeting, monitoring and evaluation, HRM, etc.).

Work-based assignment: assessment

Use the morphological box in Table 5.1 to create a short written appreciation of the respective roles of politicians, senior civil servants/appointed managers and the public in respect of your own public services organization or one that you know well. Comment on whether you think the roles should be changed and, again, relate this to the conceptual framework provided by the morphological box. Explain what advantages would be created by the changes you propose.

DISCUSSION QUESTIONS

1 Should elected politicians be the strategic leaders or is the strategic leadership role best carried out by civil servants and appointed public services managers? What are the advantages and disadvantages of elected politicians being strategic leaders and the actual authors of strategic plans for government departments?
2 Can the public be empowered in relation to their public services? Why should they be empowered?
3 Can strategic learning be seen as preferable to formal strategic planning or is it something that needs to be integrated into strategic planning?
4 Does the research by Anne Drumaux (presented in this chapter) show that strategic planning in government is impossible or that governments need to become more disciplined and integrated so that strategic planning could work more coherently?

FURTHER READING

Moore, M. (1995) *Creating Public Value: Strategic Management in Government*. London: Harvard University Press.

> This book is one of the classics of public sector strategic management. It provides a particular way of conceptualizing strategic management; its focus was the US. Although its case studies are now quite old, its arguments and concepts have been very influential. Its core proposition is that strategic management in the public sector should produce public value.

REFERENCE LIST

Berry, F. S. and Wechsler, B. (1995) State agencies' experience with strategic planning: findings from a national survey. *Public Administration Review*, 55: 159–68.

Budd, A. (1978) *The Politics of Economic Planning*. London: Fontana.

Drumaux, A. and Goethals, C. (2007a) Strategic management: a tool for public management? An overview of the Belgian federal experience. *International Journal of Public Sector Management*, 20(7): 638–54.

Drumaux, A. and Goethals, C. (2007b) De l'intention à la mise en œuvre stratégique dans l'administration fédérale belge. *Revue Politique et Management Public*, Paris, 25(4): 21–44.

Duncan, W. J., Ginter, P. M. and Swayne, L. E. (1995) *Strategic Management of Health Care Organisations*. Oxford: Blackwell Business.

Flynn, N. and Talbot, C. (1996) Strategy and strategists in UK local government. *Journal of Management Development*, 15: 24–37.

Gribbin, A. (2015) *Martin Sorrell: "Advice? Start your own business"*. [Online]. Available from: www.newstatesman.com/business/2012/04/martin-sorrell-advice-start-your-own-business [Accessed: 23 December 2015].

Indian Government (2016) *Government Establishes NITI Aayog (National Institution for Transforming India) to Replace Planning Commission*. [Online]. Available from: http://pmindia.gov.in/en/news_updates/government-establishes-niti-aayog-national-institution-for-transforming-india-to-replace-planning-commission/?comment=disable [Accessed: 31 January 2016].

Johnsen, A. (2014) 'Strategic management schools of thought and practices in the public sector in Norway', in P. Joyce and A. Drumaux (eds) *Strategic Management in Public Organizations: European Practices and Perspectives*. New York & London: Routledge. pp. 34–40.

Joyce, P. (1999) *Strategic Management for the Public Services*. Milton Keynes: Open University Press.

Kooiman, J. and van Vliet, M. (1993) 'Governance and public management', in K. A. Eliassen and J. Kooiman (eds) *Managing Public Organizations*. London: Sage.

Mintzberg, H. (1978) Patterns in strategy formulation. *Management Science*, 24: 934–48.

Mintzberg, H. (1987) The strategy concept I: Five Ps for strategy. *California Management Review*, 30(1): 11–24.

Mintzberg, H. (1991) Learning 1, Planning 0: Reply to Igor Ansoff. *Strategic Management Journal*, 12(6): 463–6.

Mintzberg, H., Ahlstrand, B. and Lampel, J. (2009) *Strategy Safari*. London: Financial Times/Prentice Hall.

Moore, M. (1995) *Creating Public Value: Strategic Management in Government*. London: Harvard University Press.

Mulgan, G. (2007) 'Oral evidence', in *House of Commons Public Administration Select Committee: Governing the Future, Second Report of Session 2006–07*, Volume II, HC123-II. London: The Stationery Office Limited.

OECD (2000) *Government of the Future*. Paris: OECD.

OECD (2005) *Modernising Government: The Way Forward*. Paris: OECD.

Poister, T. H. and Streib, G. D. (1999) Strategic management in the public sector: concepts, models and processes. *Public Productivity & Management Review*, 22(3): 308–25.

Poister, T. H. and Streib, G. D. (2005) Elements of strategic planning and management in municipal government: status after two decades. *Public Administration Review*, 65(1): 45–56.

Prime Minister's Strategy Unit, Cabinet Office (2007) *Building on Progress: Public Services*. London.

Ring, P. S. and Perry, J. L. (1985) Strategic management in public and private organizations: implications of distinctive contexts and constraints. *The Academy of Management Review*, 10(2): 276–86.

United Nations (2015) *The Road to Dignity by 2030: Ending Poverty, Transforming All Lives and Protecting the Planet*. [Online]. Available from: www.un.org/disabilities/documents/reports/SG_Synthesis_Report_Road_to_Dignity_by_2030.pdf [Accessed: 28 September 2015].

Wang, M. and Lin, X. (2014) 'China: towards results-based strategic planning', in *Emerging Good Practice in Managing for Development Results*. 2nd edition. [Online]. Available from: www.mfdr.org/%5c/Sourcebook.html [Accessed: 2 April 2014].

York, R. O. (1982) *Human Service Planning: Concepts, Tools, and Methods*. Chapel Hill, NC: The University of North Carolina Press.

Chapter 6

Linear strategic thinking

LEARNING OBJECTIVES

- To appreciate the steps in a conventional model of strategic thinking as a linear process
- To outline some of the techniques that can be used as part of a strategic thinking process
- To consider the fact that strategic thinking occurs within organizational processes and structures

I should say that what we are saying is that some strategic thinking – horrible phrase – needs to be going on across the democratic process, which of course involves political parties, involves Parliament and, in terms of them giving advice, involves the Civil Service too.
Sir Michael Bichard (former permanent secretary in the UK)

(*Source:* evidence given to House of Commons Public Administration Select Committee 'Governing the Future', second report of session 2006–07, volume 2, Ev15)

INTRODUCTION

A few years ago a UK initiative, Professional Skills for Government (PSG), made strategic thinking a core skill that was important for the senior civil service. What is meant by 'strategic thinking'? One definition is that it is thinking ahead. This is a surprisingly rare activity in many public and private organizations with very many leaders focusing on the here and now and on short-term matters. In contrast, strategic thinking pays a lot of attention to the future and thinking about long-term developments. This definition of strategic thinking is often implicit in the comments of politicians and civil servants. Arguably, it is a definition that has become more important over the last 20 years. There are also other definitions of strategic thinking. Strategic thinking may be defined as thinking clearly about goals, situations, alternative options, resources, costs, benefits and the feasibility of the actions under consideration. In effect, this can be seen as a specific form of thinking ahead, one in which goals figure very prominently. If strategic thinking is thorough when looking at alternative options and feasibility, time and resources are not wasted on actions that make little difference; in this sense, strategic thinking can also be defined as thinking which finds good 'leverage points' for bringing about change. Strategic thinking may also be defined as thinking which pays attention to strategic issues, which are issues vital to the overall success or even survival of the public services organization. This type of strategic thinking means, first, posing questions about fundamental issues in the right way to facilitate the search for solutions and, second, thinking 'out of the box' to create new and novel solutions. Both of these steps in thinking are essential for strategic issue management (which we discuss in the next chapter). This view of strategic thinking, when the importance of clarifying the issues is stressed, may lead on to a concern to understand the interrelations between strategic issues. Strategic issue management is also endorsed by people who prize creativity in strategic thinking and the pursuit of innovation rather than simple efficiency.

The elaboration of what strategic thinking means in relation to a senior civil servant or top public manager is not just going into more detail about the thinking involved; the thinking has to be embedded in behaviour. So civil servants and public managers are encouraged to become more concerned with advising the politicians on strategic choices, addressing trade-offs and tensions, and communicating on strategy. They are encouraged to become more involved in long-term direction, working on strategic agendas across boundaries and solving strategic issues or suggesting possible solutions. So, they are seen as having a role in increasing the responsiveness of the government, anticipating issues, risk management and problem solving. (We return to this point later in the chapter.)

In this chapter we start off with a simple view of strategic thinking and then add some layers of complexity. We begin, in fact, with a linear model of strategic thinking. We then add some complexity by looking at techniques that may be used to inform strategic thinking. Finally, we acknowledge more complexity for other reasons, such as the way the real world of pluralism can muddy the clarity of the simple linear process, and as a result of the thinking being based within organizations that have levels of authority within them.

TYPES OF STRATEGIC THINKING

There is not just one type of strategic thinking. While not claiming there are no others, we can identify the following three types. First, there is the kind which may involve mission statements or vision statements, but which is essentially intended to produce improvements in performance. This is very much what was intended in the United States when a legal requirement for strategic management in federal agencies was developed in the early 1990s. Second, there is strategic issue management. This may be seen as requiring definite and formal management processes, but may also be seen as an individual capability and thus as requiring the personal development of senior civil servants or public service managers. This, arguably, is reflected in the call that we need more of our senior civil servants and public managers to be strategic thinkers. We can guess that lying behind this idea is a belief that having more resourceful and creative people heading up the management of the public services would result in more issues or dilemmas being tackled successfully. Third, there is a type that is multi-organizational and even multi-sector in nature. The English example of Local Strategic Partnerships illustrates this. These different types address different outcomes, including performance, issue resolution and community well-being, and they may be found at different levels of government.

In the next section we look at a linear model of strategic thinking which probably is most easily associated with the type of strategic thinking that is meant to produce improvements in performance. The linear model may also be used as a platform for creativity in strategic thinking and may help to produce innovations, but in practice it may be more conducive to a focus on performance improvements.

THE LINEAR STRATEGIC THINKING MODEL

According to John Kay (1993) there was a rationalist model of strategy that had, as a first stage, the analysis of an organization's environment. The second stage was when the executives of an organization decided on a strategy based on that analysis. The third stage involved implementation of the strategy. He highlighted the many criticisms of the rationalist model, but noted that 'few firms, or their advisers, approach the strategy process in any different way' (Kay 1993: 336). Of course, while organizations may approach strategy in a rationalist way, how it turns out as a process could be very varied because of differing skills and circumstances.

The representation of the strategic planning process, consisting of three steps, more or less corresponds with the three component approach proposed by Johnson and Scholes (1989), which they labelled as involving strategic analysis, strategic choice and strategic implementation (see Figure 6.1). They warned, however, that in practice the three components do not take a simple linear form (Johnson and Scholes 1989: 10): 'It is very likely that, far from being separate, the stages are very much involved with each other'.

Such simple overviews of a linear strategic planning process can be useful as a way of presenting ideas about strategy formulation and implementation, even if they are problematic in the presentation of stages as sequential.

For the time being, let us stick with the simplification of the process as a sequential one, but elaborate it by looking in more detail at what is involved in analysis, making strategic decisions and implementation. The linear strategic planning process presented in the flow chart in Figure 6.2 displays it as a series of steps that are followed in a linear sequence. Of course, we recognize that in

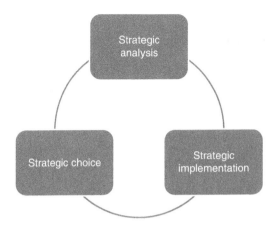

Figure 6.1 *The Johnson and Scholes (1989) model of strategic management*

practice an organization may deal with different stages more than once in producing a final draft of the strategic plan, and that, often, a sense of a clear sequence becomes compromised.

The process begins with the creation of a mission statement for the organization. This statement may prescribe who the intended beneficiaries of the activities of the organization are, and what activities the organization will carry out in order to provide the desired benefits. The next step is to carry out a situational analysis, which can be composed of an external and an internal analysis. The external analysis may identify and evaluate external trends and events, and assess the opportunities and threats for the organization posed by such developments. The internal analysis may focus on the capacity of the organization, mapping its values and capabilities. The data produced by the internal analysis may be critically evaluated, and strengths and weaknesses identified. Following on from this analysis there can be an assessment of the organization's performance and of the programmes and services it delivers. In the light of the mission statement and the analysis of external and internal situations, as well as the assessment of organizational performance and programmes and services, there can be a decision on the strategic objectives of the organization. Subsequently, the various strategic options available to the organization are identified. These options are evaluated in some systematic way, looking perhaps at feasibility of proposed actions, the risks and rewards of the actions, and perhaps the trade-off between risks and rewards. Following agreement on strategic action, work is carried out on planning the implementation of the strategic action. This may entail identifying and agreeing which individuals are responsible for managing actionable elements of the strategy, timescales, reporting arrangements and resource plans. A key part of the resource plan will be decisions which have implications for budgetary allocations. A strategic plan that does not have budgetary proposals in the implementation

137

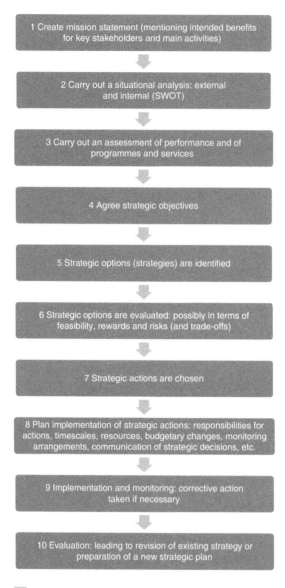

Figure 6.2 Linear strategic thinking process

section probably should be considered inadequate. The planning of implementation should also cover how the strategic decisions will be communicated to key stakeholders. Next, the strategic decisions are implemented and monitoring is carried out to determine if corrective action is necessary to ensure the strategic objectives are achieved. Finally, at some point there needs to be a thorough evaluation of the strategy – has it been fully implemented and

138

has it been successful? This enables either a revision of the strategy or the preparation of a completely new strategy. The evaluation may be scheduled, but may occur sooner if circumstances change or there is an obvious failure of the existing strategy.

This simple linear process needs some revisions to make it more applicable to a public services situation. Some obvious additions include:

- Review of the organization's current mandate (e.g. legislation which has to be taken into account)
- Taking account of performance budgeting frameworks maintained by, for example, a ministry of finance or finance department
- Consulting and researching stakeholders, especially the public (service users, clients), on their expectations of the public service in question.

The last of these, involving stakeholder identification and analysis, is very important in the public services and is probably needed prior to clarifying either a mission statement or a strategic vision.

USE OF TECHNIQUES

What do we normally find in strategic plans in the public sector? They may include mission statements, vision statements, values statements, strategic goals and strategic actions (or programmes comprising strategic actions).

One recent study of the use of strategic techniques was carried out in the public sector of the United Arab Emirates (UAE). The strategic planning techniques used most extensively in the public sector organizations surveyed were: SWOT analysis, benchmarking, stakeholder analysis, balanced scorecard and gap analysis (Elbanna 2013).

Table 6.1 shows only a selection of the concepts and techniques available. We will look at some of these below; some we will look at in the next chapter.

Mission statements

A mission statement is a short statement of the aims of the organization. It should have been strongly influenced, shaped, directed or mandated by elected politicians. The core components of an understanding of organizational mission may be set out in legislation passed by the elected politicians.

At the very least, a mission statement should spell out the intended beneficiaries of the organization's activities, what the intended benefits are, and the main categories of activities that will be used to deliver the intended benefits. The beneficiaries may be a specified group or section of the public who will receive a public service of some kind. (But not all activities will take the form of service provision and nor will all the stakeholders of a strategic plan be service users in an obvious sense).

Table 6.1 Extent of use of strategic planning techniques (Elbanna 2013)

	Use of strategic planning techniques	
	Mean	% saying not familiar
SWOT analysis	3.8	4
Benchmarking	3.4	12
Stakeholder analysis	3.4	7
Balanced scorecard	3.3	10
Gap analysis	3.2	13
PEST(EL) analysis	3.1	12
EFQM excellence model	3.1	10
Strategic planning software	2.7	9
Scenario planning	2.4	15
Value chain analysis	2.1	19

Note: 1 The mean scores were calculated using Five-point Likert Scales. Respondents to the survey could score each technique from 1 to 5. A score of 1 meant that their organization did not currently use the technique. A score of 5 meant the organization currently used the technique to a very great extent. Respondents were asked to rate a total of 12 strategic planning techniques.
2 The sample comprised 67 public sector organizations in the UAE.
3 The survey was carried out in 2011.

It is also possible to include in the mission statement other important information that helps to amplify the three core components. For example, the statement may indicate the geographical extent and location of its activities; for instance, it may say that a service will be provided in a specific locality, a specific country, or internationally. The statement may also elaborate on the beneficiaries, benefits or the main activities of the organization in some way so as to draw attention to important principles it intends to follow in its operations and future developments. For example, a statement may say something about service user choice, or funding, or attitude to use of the latest technology (see Figure 6.3).

Perhaps the best preparation for answering the key questions used in drawing up a mission statement is a stakeholder analysis (a variant of which can also be used in thinking about and planning implementation). A study of stakeholders can help with identifying and understanding the intended beneficiaries of the organization's activities. It can be thought-provoking to consider not only who the powerful stakeholders are, but also who the important stakeholders are. There may need to be an appreciation in a public services organization that these two groups of stakeholders – the powerful and the important ones – may overlap but may not be identical. Some public services organizations are set up to serve groups of people who are not good at pressurizing or lobbying for what they want. The stakeholder analysis also needs to explore the values and interests of the important stakeholders and how they might make judgements (including

Figure 6.3 *Writing mission statements*

their criteria) about the public services organization. The conclusions from these types of considerations of stakeholders can directly inform what is written in a mission statement, as well as prompting ideas about whom the leaders of the organization ought to consider involving or consulting when preparing strategic plans.

Strategic goals may be drawn from the mission statement. While the mission statement is a declaration of the purpose of the organization, and, in that sense, will be setting out a positive and desirable agenda for a public service organization, the strategic goals are framed in the light of circumstances for the foreseeable future. In consequence, strategic goals are influenced by both aspiration and reality: 'Goals combine judgments about what is desirable and estimates about what is possible. It is generally wise to begin with an analysis of what is possible' (Heymann 1987: 19).

Mission statements also need to be written in a way that facilitates monitoring and evaluation of the strategic effectiveness of an organization.

Vision statements

Vision statements are not to be confused with predictions that claim to be based on objective knowledge of the future. Vision statements are more like targets – something to be aimed at (Nutt and Backoff 1992). They should be based on possibilities but cannot be certainties (Kouzes and Posner 2007: 17):

> Leaders gaze across the horizon of time, imagining the attractive opportunities that are in store when they and their constituents arrive at a distant destination. They envision exciting and ennobling possibilities.

141

Leaders have a desire to make something happen, to change the way things are, to create something that no one has ever created before. In some ways, leaders live their lives backwards. They see pictures in their mind's eye of what the results will look like even before they've started their project, much as an artist draws blueprint or an engineer builds a model. Their clear image of the future pulls them forward.

We can define a vision statement as a foresight or intention about the organization's future activities and achievements. Defined in this way, it is possible to have a situation in which a mission statement is kept the same, but a vision statement is changed to reflect new circumstances. Of course, in some circumstances, an organization may want to change both mission and vision statement.

The strategic vision sets a target for moving the organization's capabilities, values, activities, etc. forward in time to, say, a future destination identified as five or maybe ten years ahead. Therefore, writing a strategic vision is the same as developing a point of view about the future. We would expect that the overall direction in which the public service organization is travelling has in some way been defined for the managerial leadership by elected politicians.

Three different techniques for developing ideas for writing a vision statement are set out briefly below.

Technique 1: Empathy with service users and other stakeholders

This involves appreciating how the future could create more value for service users and other stakeholders. Having identified the powerful and the important stakeholders, having better understood their interests and values, the strategic leaders can ask: what would we need to be doing and achieving in the future to deliver the expectations and values of the most important stakeholders? What would our activities and accomplishments look like if we really met what they want from us? What capabilities would we have developed as an organization that would make these activities and accomplishments possible? What would be the delivery channels we would use?

The first step is therefore to carry out a stakeholder analysis. The leaders identify the key stakeholders of the organization by considering who is affected by the organization and who affects the organization. Next, they identify the top criteria by which each of the key stakeholders evaluates the organization. For example, service users might judge the organization favourably mainly on the basis of the reliability of the service. Finally, strategic leaders place themselves in the shoes of the most important stakeholder groups and consider the top criteria they have identified, and answer the question: what should the organization be doing in five years that would cause this stakeholder group to rate the organization more positively? The implication behind this technique is that the vision is a future scenario in which key stakeholders are more positive about the organization.

142

Technique 2: Challenging 'industry' assumptions

The first step is to identify all the current assumptions of how successful public service organizations in a particular part of the public sector operate, and then to imagine each one of the core assumptions no longer being true. If a core assumption was not true, what might be possible?

Technique 3: Exploring strategic issues

In this technique the strategic leader begins by listing the top strategic issues for the organization and then they identify those that have been issues for a considerable period of time. The next step is to answer the following questions: Why is this issue a concern? What is it making difficult for us, as an organization, to do? What might we do if we could solve this issue? The last question is obviously the one that gets to the heart of what might be a strategic vision for the organization.

How is vision used to produce strategy? There are at least two methods. You can brainstorm actions that move the organization from where it is currently to where it must be to deliver the vision. The actions comprise the strategy. Another method is to identify the issues that stand in the way of moving towards the vision and then carry out creative problem solving to identify strategic actions to solve the issues and realize the vision. I suspect that more people have used the first method. The second method is quite challenging, although it should be quite motivating. If an organization's leaders are optimistic, then identifying and resolving issues can be seen as an interesting and energizing experience. However, if the leaders are pessimistic or cynical, then dwelling on strategic issues that are difficult to resolve can dissipate energy. (There is more on the creative approach to strategy formulation in the next chapter).

Values statements

Values statements were probably in their heyday in the late 1980s and early 1990s. They were seen by some leaders as a list of explicit values that could be communicated to people who worked in a public services organization so as to influence their behaviour. For example, the values might relate to how the public were to be treated by staff during service interactions, the quality of the service, and the importance of equal opportunities both in relation to employment matters and the delivery of services.

The values could be identified by the top leadership team of an organization reflecting on their experiences in the organization and on the values in society (e.g. the rise of equal opportunities as an important value in society and as demonstrated through legislation). Sometimes it was considered possible to design training courses to instil these values throughout a public service organization.

These values statements can be seen as important to back up strategic developments, but at times have also served in some way as statements of political priorities.

Forecasting

In the past, strategic management was often associated with forecasting. The strategist would attempt to model the future in some way, and then adjust the organization's trajectory to the outcomes of the forecast. Some years ago, organizations were inclined to favour forecasts based on past trends. A major problem with this type of analysis is that discontinuities may arise that throw out the existing trend. A good example of this is the 1973 oil crisis when OPEC (Organization of Petroleum Exporting Countries) managed to engineer a steep rise in oil prices by restricting supply.

There is still a place for trend projection despite the now evident limitations of forecasting – providing we do not assume that we can use trend projection to predict the future scientifically. Strategic leaders should look at history and at trends. They do, however, need to ask the question: will this trend continue as in the past or will there be a change in the future – are we approaching a turning point in this particular phenomenon?

Scenario planning

Scenario planning was a response to the rise of unpredictability in the 1970s that created severe problems for forecasting techniques. It is logically best suited to a situation where there would be confusion about what to do because of a small number of factors that are unpredictable. It would not be much use where there were a large number of important but unpredictable factors; this would over-whelm anyone trying to use scenario planning because there would be lots of possible scenarios. The point of scenario planning is to allow focused strategic thinking in the context of a *modest* degree of confusion.

Scenario planning creates scenarios of two or more different futures. It allows leaders to consider the 'best' way forward that maximizes the organization's future irrespective of which actual future occurs. For each scenario, leaders ask: If the future is going to be such and such, what do we need to put in place because of this? Through scenario planning the organization would start with a confused and unclear situation, but by identifying different possible futures and then describing them as scenarios it would have a way of conversing about the future.

Scenarios are usually written as reports as if they had been written at a future time. The reports are produced using both analysis and imagination. Leaders can develop worst case, best case and most likely case scenarios, continually testing their assumptions about the future. They can use past data to extrapolate into the future, while being aware of the difficulties inherent in this.

Leaders could involve others through meetings and workshops. Where this happens, it is possible that leaders will find it easier to build understanding about the future and adaptability in the organization, and thus greater receptivity to change.

Scenarios are written in one or two paragraphs by encompassing the vari-ables, assumptions and the dependent variables within an appreciation of the

144

organization's environment and how it had developed, written as if it is at the end of the selected planning horizon. One way of creating scenarios is to combine 'assumptions' and 'uncertainties' and then add supplementary detail. The following 'analytical' approach is reasonably logical:

1 Select a planning horizon for the scenarios.
2 Identify a set of assumptions for the scenarios.
3 Identify a list of critical variables that feel very unpredictable (e.g. public expenditure plans).
4 Review the list of variables and eliminate those that (i) are thought to have a low potential impact *and* a low probability of occurrence, (ii) may not happen within the planning horizon and (iii) are events which would be a total disaster.
5 Distinguish the variables which are dependent on other variables in the list – use these to enrich the scenarios, but not to define them.
6 Aggregate variables on the list into broader variables, aiming to end up with two to five key variables.
7 Assign two or three realistic values to each of the key variables (e.g. change of government, no change of government).
8 List all possible combinations of the key variables (e.g. three key variables each with two values would generate eight scenarios).
9 Reject scenarios which are implausible and those scenarios which vary very little from other scenarios.
10 End up with a final list of three scenarios, including the scenario that is the most probable case and a worst case scenario.

Performance measurement

Performance measurement techniques include benchmarking, tracking and the balanced scorecard.

Benchmarking has become a very popular technique worldwide in recent years. Public sector organizations have been using benchmarking for many years as part of the drive to modernize the management of services and increase performance. A few years ago, Poister and Streib (2005) reported that a third of city councils in their sample in the US, that had made strategic planning efforts in the preceding five years, were also benchmarking their performance against others to judge the effectiveness of their strategic initiatives. Benchmarking can be defined simply as comparisons of performance and other matters. It can also be defined more narrowly as a process where the managers of an organization measure their performance against the best performing organizations in an industry and make other comparisons (e.g. with internal processes, competencies and costs) to explain the causes of the superior performance of the industry leaders. The purpose is often to arrive at an analysis of how the organization might improve its performance and catch up with industry leaders. Financial (and non-financial) data can be used to benchmark the organization's position and performance against its competitors.

Organizations can cooperate directly for the purposes of benchmarking studies. Public sector organizations have been cooperating extensively to generate more valid data for performance comparisons. Benchmarking can involve making observations on the performance of rival organizations where the services are delivered publicly (e.g. refuse collection).

Another approach to performance measurement is to start with the organization's vision and mission statements and the associated strategic goals. Then the organization can track results against strategic goals using specially selected or designed measures. In practice this means setting up reporting systems so that results are reported on a regular basis to a strategic management group (see Figure 6.4).

The final technique considered here is that of the balanced scorecard. Kaplan and Norton (1992) argued that financial indicators of performance were more attuned to the needs of the industrial age, but today non-financial indicators (NFIs) are needed. They argued that performance should be evaluated using a combination of both kinds of indicators – financial and non-financial. The evaluation framework they proposed – the balanced scorecard – contains four categories of performance indicators; these have been adapted for use in the public sector by many organizations:

1 Customer perspective: how do customers see us?
2 Internal perspective: what must we excel at?
3 Innovation and learning perspective: can we continue to improve and create value?
4 Financial perspective: how do we look to shareholders?

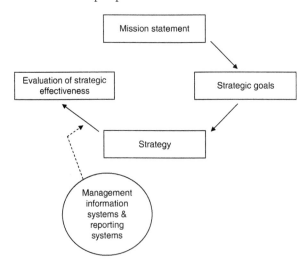

Figure 6.4 *Reporting systems*

Occasionally, organizations have spotted that there is an opportunity to study relationships between different performance indicators. For instance, a rise or fall in customer satisfaction may tend to precede a corresponding rise or fall in financial performance indicators, and improvements in performance on innovation may be followed in due course by improvements in financial indicators. It does not take much imagination to see how valuable it could be for strategic leaders to have a better understanding of such relationships – if they exist – and then how this could be the basis for continuous improvement as the organization learns more and more about how to achieve better results.

Situational analysis

A situational analysis is a major ingredient in strategic decision making. This type of analysis is an assessment of the current and the future situation of the organization. Such an assessment could involve studying:

1   current or future opportunities and threats;
2   organizational capabilities, values and resources (including those resources owned by partner organizations); and
3   achievements and failures of the organization.

The strategic situation can be defined in a broad way to include internal and external environments, organizational values as well as capabilities, and recent performance of the organization. Analysis means breaking something up into its parts. It can be useful for understanding not only the composition of something, but also how something works by studying the ways in which various parts interrelate.

Commonly, strategic analysis is focused on the analysis of the situation of an organization, meaning both its external and internal environment. In private sector management courses, managers are taught PEST analysis – political, economic, social and technological factors – and they are taught to use Michael Porter's five forces analysis, which examines five types of competitive force in relation to a specific industry (Porter 1980). It can also be useful in the public services to analyse the external environment and to examine the social, economic, political and technological trends. Among the social trends will be, importantly, changes in lifestyle and changes in values held by people in society. As we have noted, an analysis of the strategic environment of a private business can include the competitive structure of its specific industry. In the public services there can also be competitive forces, but, in addition, thought needs to be given to the possibilities and consequences of partnership and cooperation with external organizations.

As long ago as the mid 1980s, Philip Heymann (1987) was writing about public services organizations having overlapping mandates and, therefore, in the process of developing a strategic plan, he considered it important that there were some explorations of those overlaps of mandate in order to produce a good

147

strategic plan. The same idea was followed up in the United States in the 1990s when evaluation criteria for the strategic plans produced under the GPRA 1993 were being devised for Congress – evaluation frameworks were created that included looking at what kind of consultation had taken place with other organizations where there were overlapping mandates.

The analysis of the internal environment will include reviewing assets, resources, strengths and weaknesses of the organization. Assets, resources and strengths can be used in taking successful strategic action; they need to be considered when choosing courses of action. It is important to know the weaknesses of an organization – it would be foolish to take strategic action where the critical resource needed for a successful strategic action was missing, or which depended on an organizational activity that was currently weak. Of course, identifying a weakness relevant to an otherwise attractive strategic action might trigger a decision by the organization's top managers to develop the organization and overcome the weakness. So weaknesses can be a constraint on action, or have to be remedied.

There is not much discussion in strategic management textbooks of how to carry out strategic analysis of the values of the organization, and yet values are important. Values, just like capabilities, determine the capacity of an organization for taking strategic action.

Finally, some analysis of the organization's current or recent performance would be important as part of the overall strategic analysis of the current situation. This may be important in the sense of identifying any potential threat to the future survival of the organization. A downward trend in the numbers of service users, a downward trend in income, or a deteriorating quality of service are just some examples of performance indicators that could spell future problems for the survival of the organization. Also a review of performance could be useful for setting ambitious, but realistic, performance targets.

Situation analysis is not restricted just to analyses of the current situation. Situation analysis can, for example, be useful in the selection of a course of action. The analysis in this case may involve risk assessments as well as an analysis of expected rewards from taking a course of action. Finally, situation analysis might also be useful in the planning of a strategic action. In order to make success more likely, situation analysis may be used to identify the resources that will be needed in strategic action, and to anticipate and manage the reactions of stakeholders to strategic action.

TREND ANALYSIS – HISTORY IS IMPORTANT IN MAKING CHOICES ABOUT THE FUTURE

Trend analysis may be seen as part of the analysis of the external environment. We can carry out a trend analysis using the PEST analysis as a starting point. This means looking at political, economic, social and technological factors. It can be useful to think about these external factors not simply as factors but as events, trends and turning points. Public services managers can list all the events, trends and turning points over, say, the last five years. This can be done through managers drawing on their personal experience. While this is subjective, it may also be argued that managers experience the trends, events and turning points and they do think about these things and assess the evidence for their existence and seriousness. So we can argue that it is not unreasonable to ask managers to use their experience and judgement to identify and even rate them in terms of their importance for the organization.

As part of a strategic planning process, managers can then be asked to consider the possible future course of each of the top rated trends, events and turning points over, say, the next five years. Will an important trend continue much as it has been continuing in the past, or will the trend accelerate or slow down? Will the trend go through a major turning point in the next 3–7 years? Will an event be completed or will it still be in progress?

Some kind of a consideration of what might happen to trends, events and turning points is very important. The manager drawing up strategic plans needs to make sense of the history of their organization, and this is largely a pragmatic process rather than a totally scientific one. We can usefully stress that making sense of the history of an organization by studying the trends occurring in its environment is even valued where strategic thinkers are exhorted to be very creative and imaginative in describing ideal futures for the organization. When thinking about the future it seems that it is good preparation to think about past trends. Although not concerned with the public services, Gary Hamel and C. K. Prahalad (1994) accepted that it could be useful to do trend analysis even when the intention is not to simply extrapolate the past, but to come up with something imaginative that will create entirely new strategic futures.

The anticipation of turning points in trends must be very important in the public services area. Take, for example, trends in public concerns; just because a specific concern has been growing year by year it should not be assumed that this concern will continue to grow. There is a degree of volatility in public concerns (Nutt and Backoff 1992) partly explained by the changing circumstances of society and partly, hopefully, explained by the successes of government organizations. For example, public concerns about unemployment will, no doubt, increase during periods in which global economic activity is sluggish; and successful reforms of major public services may decrease public concerns over, for example, health and education.

CORE COMPETENCIES

Core competence became popular as a concept in the 1990s. Very broadly, as a first approximation, we can say that a core competence is something the organization is good at doing. A core competence is sometimes seen in strategic management as an advantage. An advantage can be defined as a competitive strength that allows one organization to triumph over rivals. We can also define core competence as something that makes it more likely that an organization will be successful in a strategic challenge – this may or may not involve beating competitor organizations.

So, core competencies are activities that the organization is very good at. Core competence is also something that creates relatively high levels of satisfaction with the products or services the organization produces – we say it creates 'customer value'. In the private sector context we might restrict the term core competence to those activities that are not only done well and create relatively high levels of satisfaction for customers, but are also difficult for other companies to acquire or develop – not easily imitated. This last requirement reflects the definition of core competence as a competitive advantage as opposed to its definition as a strength in relation to a strategic challenge.

Klein and Hiscocks (1994) provided a way of identifying 'skills' which might be seen as components of core competencies. Skills might be identified by asking the following questions:

1 What clues as to the skills of the company may be obtained by looking at the organization structure? Are there specialist units, for example, and what are their names?
2 What do members of the organization perceive to be the skills?
3 What will an examination of the products or services of the organization tell us about its skills?
4 What do customers and market watchers think the skills of the organization are?

The skills are thought to be woven or 'bundled' together to form core competencies.

Lewis and Gregory (1996) outlined an approach to identifying core competencies that involves reviewing and evaluating all the activities of the organization, and doing this in a way that requires working down through a hierarchy of activities and sub-activities. The main steps of a simplified version of their method are as follows:

Step 1: Top managers identify the main activities of the organization and then map their interdependencies and linkages.
Step 2: Each of the main activities is rated: how well is the activity done, how much does it contribute to customer satisfaction, and how easy is it to acquire or develop excellence in this activity?
Step 3: The top rated main activities are broken down into their constituent activities and then the latter are rated (using the same questions as in Step 2).
Step 4: The requirements of the top rated activities (as rated in Step 3) are identified in terms of equipment, machines, software, people skills, technology skills and management.

150

SWOT ANALYSIS

The SWOT analysis may be the most commonly taught technique within short management courses or postgraduate manager education. Probably any sample of managers will include quite a few who have at some point in their careers used SWOT analysis. Very often SWOT analysis is thought of as being nothing more than a simple listing of strengths, weaknesses, opportunities and threats facing an organization. But it may be better to think of the SWOT analysis as a way of summing up the work of situational analysis that has been based on the application of a whole set of techniques – trend analysis, core competence analysis, values analysis, etc.

Let us begin by providing a simple definition of each of the four key terms.

- Strengths – enhance the performance of the organization
- Weaknesses – constrain performance
- Opportunities – are external events or trends that can be made to produce benefits if the organization takes action
- Threats – are also external events, developments or trends, but these are ones that can damage the organization unless some action is taken.

It might also be useful to make clear whether strengths and weaknesses are defined in absolute or relative terms. If defined in relative terms, relative to what? Is strength, for example, relative to other organizations or to a goal?

There is a need to think carefully about the items listed in a SWOT analysis. It is very easy, for example, to confuse an opportunity with an action. Sometimes people list an idea such as the launch of a new product or new service as an opportunity. Strictly speaking this is an action that is taken by the organization, possibly in response to an opportunity that has occurred. Sometimes people confuse performance with strength or weakness. So, sometimes a high level of customer satisfaction is taken as strength. Strictly speaking this could be taken as a performance variable and we should look for the cause of the customer satisfaction because it is the causal factor that should be listed as a strength.

Lists supplied as part of a SWOT analysis should also be scrutinized for duplication. This can occur where an idea is expressed in different ways but is essentially the same idea. It can therefore be useful to go through the lists, grouping together all the items which are actually the same idea, but which are just expressed using different words.

Finally it can be useful to use a process of ranking all the strengths, weaknesses, opportunities and threats. The justification for this procedure of ranking is that, with limited managerial attention and capacity, management should be concentrating on the organization's most important strength, its most important weakness, etc., when trying to formulate strategic plans; and it may be argued that it is a mistake to be paying attention to less important strengths etc.

151

STRATEGIC CHOICES

There are at least two ways of deciding strategic actions. The first involves making a selection from a pre-determined and fairly familiar list of strategic options. Strategic decisions can be embedded in a more creative process so that it is not merely a matter of choosing from a pre-determined set of strategic options, but first involves creating a unique set of strategic options. Either way, there comes a point in the strategic planning process when strategic leaders decide to implement some options and reject others. In order to do this, they need to carry out an appraisal of the strategic options.

In practice, strategic choices may be made in a conversational way without great clarity about the criteria being used and with much being left as unspoken assumptions. Arguably, there is scope for more systematic approaches to evaluation, in which the options are laid out in detail and the criteria to be used are agreed in advance of the evaluation (see Bryson 2004: 218–19).

One of the most widely used frameworks for choosing action is based around the application of three criteria: suitability, feasibility and acceptability. Suitable strategic action can be defined as action that looks like it offers a good fit between the action and the circumstances of the organization, and between the action and the desired outcome. So some strategic options may not be judged suitable because they are not suitable in the circumstances, or not suitable in the sense of being likely to produce the desired outcomes.

Feasible strategic action is action that looks capable of being carried out. This is not to be confused with the previous criterion. It is not a matter of whether the action will have positive consequences – it is a matter of whether we can complete the action at all. One aspect of judging feasibility is assessing whether we have or can get the resources needed to implement the proposed strategic action. Strategic actions may be judged to lack feasibility because the organization lacks the money needed to take the course of action or because it requires certain skills not currently found in the organization and not easily obtained by recruiting people from the labour market.

Acceptable strategic action is action that looks as though it will be favoured or supported by all the powerful or important stakeholders. Stakeholders may react positively or negatively to a proposal to take a specific strategic action for a variety of reasons, including their perception of the impact on their interests. However, they may find an action acceptable or unacceptable because of their values, their ethical standards or because of their concern for its impact on a third party and so on.

Two further comments might be made about the use of these three criteria. First, we could stretch the concept of feasibility to also take on the issue of political feasibility. One interpretation of politically feasible action might be action that is acceptable to powerful stakeholder groups. On this basis, there is an overlap between feasibility and acceptability. Second, it does seem sensible to judge proposed action by its timeliness. An organization should think about timescales and about how long it will take to carry out proposed courses of action. For example, strategic leaders may worry about a development that could threaten the organization and may have estimated that the organization has only, say, two years to take action to counter the threat. Or, alternatively, there may be a political judgement that powerful stakeholders will allow the current leadership of the organization only so long to bring about an overall improvement in the performance of the organization. So, sensible leaders will assess options for action in terms of how long they will take to implement and produce their positive effects. Will the benefits flow within six months, two years, five years or ten years? In some cases strategic options may be rejected because the benefits will take too long to flow. While it is possible that there may be some proposed strategic actions that are not timely, because they will take too long to work, there may also be some actions that will impact too quickly. This seems less likely, but should not be ruled out as a possibility.

HOW SOUND IS THE INTELLECTUAL PROCESS FOR PRODUCING A STRATEGIC PLAN? THE ISSUE OF FEASIBILITY

Nutt and Backoff (1992) stressed the importance of feasibility as a key concept in strategic thinking for public sector and third sector organizations. There is evidence from research into local government in the USA that feasibility assessment of proposed strategies is a very important element of a strategic planning process (Poister and Streib 2005). So, civil servants and public services managers should build into their strategic thinking a strong concern for the feasibility of the strategies they are thinking of adopting. How can this concern be acted upon?

It will be suggested here that civil servants and public services managers can do at least three things as part of their strategic thinking to show concern for feasibility:

1 Look at trends over previous years and consider their likely future development.
2 Evaluate the feasibility of alternative courses of action before selecting the best course of action.
3 Check out proposed actions in terms of resource availability and acceptability to powerful stakeholders.

So, we can ask if strategic thinking has included a trend analysis, if the best course of action has been selected after evaluation of the feasibility of alternatives, and if alternatives have been evaluated in terms of resource availability and acceptability to powerful stakeholders. If the answer in all three cases is yes, then we may guess that the selected strategic action is more likely to be successful.

153

The importance of examining trends prior to the selection of action can be argued in terms of an understanding of freedom to act. Any organization, in practice, has some choice about what it will do. But, in practice, an organization makes its choices in a set of circumstances. What someone can do nowadays is very different from what someone could do 2,000 years ago. The difference is only partly explained by different inclinations on the part of the individual; it is also because of very different circumstances then and now. Anyone can choose to travel halfway around the world, but the experience will be entirely different in a world in which travelling by plane is commonplace from a world in which there are no planes. Therefore, specific action is a function of will and circumstances. To make decisions purely on the basis of will, ignoring the circumstances that prevail, surely must increase the likelihood of failure.

The circumstances of an organization can be examined by analysing the key trends. As suggested earlier, there need be no presumption that trends can be always extrapolated. When examining trends, managers should ask themselves whether the trends will continue as in the past, or whether there is any reason for suspecting that the trend will pass through a turning point.

The benefit of considering the feasibility of alternative courses of action before selecting the best course of action may seem so obvious that it warrants no further discussion. Surely, choosing to take some action simply because it is the first action thought of must lead (on average) to poorer results than tending to choose action only after the feasibility of alternatives have been considered and evaluated? If feasibility is not checked out in advance, we can guess that attempts to implement action will run into obstacles and there will be an implementation failure. This occurs quite often and it is widely accepted that implementation of strategic plans is very difficult.

Finally, we can simply assert the obvious point that managers can usefully look at the resources that are required, and how they can be obtained, and look at the likely reactions of various stakeholders (Nutt and Backoff 1992). These are both very important for planning the implementation of strategies.

RISK ASSESSMENT

A basic proposition we could make is that it is very hard for many people in public services to agree on the right goals for their organization, and then to think creatively about courses of action to pursue those goals. But it seems to be even more difficult to get people in public services to manage the risks of strategic action. In other words, risk assessment and then risk management does not necessarily come naturally or easily to public service leaders and others in the public services.

How can you conduct a risk assessment in relation to proposed strategic action in a reasonably coherent manner? One approach, outlined here, is to begin by identifying a number of environmental and organizational factors that might create barriers to successful implementation of strategic action.

One example might be a sudden announcement by national government that it is having budgetary problems and it has to implement, very rapidly, a series of spending cuts throughout the public services. An unexpected change of government as a result of a general election could herald changes of policy and funding part way through planned strategic change. An example of an internal development might be the sudden departure of a chief executive half way through the planned strategic change. It is often thought very difficult to maintain the momentum of strategic change when there is little continuity in who leads the organization – so the departure of a chief executive could be quite a blow to radical strategic action (Osborne and Gaebler 1992). If not the departure of the chief executive, it might be that there are two or three key managers or key professionals in a public service organization who might suddenly decide to take early retirement, and their departure could have quite devastating effects on the organization's ability to implement a planned strategic action. Another possible factor could be a scandal about a public service in the media that makes a particular service suddenly become less popular.

Once the factors are identified, what then? The next thing to do is to calculate the probability of these various factors occurring during a specified time period. For example, how probable is it that there will be a change of government at a general election? The probability could be scored using a scale of zero to ten, with ten meaning that the factor is 'very probable' and with zero meaning that the occurrence of the factor is 'very improbable'.

The third step is to estimate the impact of the factor on the strategic action. You consider: What would be the impact should this thing happen? Would the impact of this factor on the proposed strategic action be disastrous, would it block its realization? Or would it be less serious, possibly merely a minor effect, perhaps just slowing down the implementation of the strategic action? Impact could also be assessed using a points system. We could use a scale of zero to ten points, where ten points means that the impact is very likely to cause complete failure of the strategic action and a score of zero means the impact is negligible.

To determine the relative risk of each factor we multiply the probability by the impact. So we define risk specifically as the probability of an event occurring multiplied by the magnitude of its negative impact. If we add up all the risk figures for all the factors considered we can come up with a total risk score for each course of action.

The best public services leaders will encourage an entrepreneurial approach to strategic action. They will be ambitious for the improvement of the public services and be prepared to take risks to bring about radical improvements, but they will not want to take foolish and unnecessary risks. They will, therefore, want to remove as much risk as possible from strategic action so that only the unavoidable risks are left. They would use risk analysis and risk management to eliminate strategic actions that are dangerously risky and cannot be de-risked to acceptable levels of risk.

155

POINTS SYSTEMS FOR EVALUATING STRATEGIC OPTIONS

While they may be scientifically dubious, a good case can be made for the value of points-based systems for promoting a thorough conversation about the strategic options among the strategic leadership.

The method of constructing a points-based evaluation system is very simple. First, the strategic leadership decides on the number and nature of the criteria it wishes to use to evaluate the various strategic actions being actively considered. For example, they might select some of the following ten criteria:

1 Acceptability to key stakeholders
2 Acceptability to service users
3 Acceptability to the general public
4 User benefits
5 Consistency with mission
6 Technical feasibility
7 Cost of financing
8 Cost-effectiveness
9 Risk
10 Timeliness.

Next, the leadership decides if all the criteria are to be equally weighted, or whether some are considered of more importance in making a choice of which actions to implement and therefore need to be weighted accordingly. Proposed actions are then rated on each of the criteria on, say, a scale of zero to ten points. A course of action rated as zero points on one of the criteria would be judged to be totally unsatisfactory in this respect. Action rated ten points for a criterion would be judged to be highly satisfactory in that respect. The raw scores would then be adjusted according to the weightings and an aggregate score calculated for each course of action. If two or more courses of action are scored using this point system they can then be compared, both in terms of the overall score, and in terms of the scoring against specific criteria.

It is sometimes said to be a mistake for managers to simply decide on a course of action based upon the one which achieved the highest score under such a points-based system. Instead it is suggested that strategic leaders and their teams might better debate the scoring and argue through their disagreements, and then take the score into account when making their final decision. So, the total scores are considered but do not determine in a simple way the judgement made.

To repeat the point made at the beginning of this section, the process of scoring the different criteria, and deciding on weightings, should not be taken as a completely scientific process (in the sense of being completely 'objective'). It is a process that can help strategic leaders make sure there is a thorough and detailed consideration of all the alternative actions that might be approved.

USING A MATRIX TO DISPLAY TRADE-OFFS

If there is broad agreement between those involved in assessing the strategic actions that have been generated, and there are two – and only two – criteria, perhaps a matrix provides a good way of displaying trade-offs when selecting action.

Consider the case of a trade-off between selecting actions that are popular with elected politicians that have a political oversight role, and actions that seem to offer more public value in the eyes of service users. If proposed strategic actions can be rated as low, medium or high in these terms we can draw up a three by three matrix (see Figure 6.5). The strategic options then can be placed in the matrix to facilitate the conversation among strategic leaders trying to choose between them.

There are two obvious decision zones in the matrix. Actions which are unlikely to be popular with the elected politicians, and create little value for service users, can be seen as an obvious rejection, whereas strategic actions that are highly popular with elected politicians, and would be perceived as very valuable by service users, can be seen as an obvious choice. The interesting cases occur where action is thought likely to be very popular with the elected politicians, but is expected to create little public value for service users, and the opposite situation where there is a clear case in terms of value for service users, but the politicians are not interested. It is more likely that cases will be clustered in the remaining cells of the matrix where actions are judged to be medium in popularity and/or value to service users.

STRATEGIC PROCESSES INVOLVE MORE THAN THINKING AND TAKE PLACE IN ORGANIZATIONAL STRUCTURES

According to Dyson (1990: 3) a strategic planning process is a 'management process involving consultation, negotiation and analysis which is aimed at ensuring effective strategic decision-making'. In this chapter we have largely

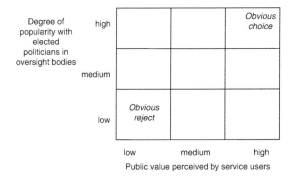

Figure 6.5 *Matrix to judge trade-offs*

addressed strategic thinking as a process involving analysis. This is the conception of the strategic thinking process that is most frequently assumed in formal education courses about strategic management. Students are largely taught that strategic planning is an analytical process aimed at producing rational decisions. Concerns that strategic management is not reducible to an analytical, or technical, process are rarely given much consideration in courses.

However, we should not assume thinking precedes communication. Sometimes we only clarify our own strategic thinking as we explain our ideas to others – our own implicit ideas suddenly come into mind as we talk. The implicit thinking can then become explicit. We sometimes only clarify our implicit strategic thinking as we react against other people's spoken ideas. So listening to others as part of strategic thinking processes and consultation, in which we explain proposals and seek the opinions of others, can be very important in the development of strategic thinking.

A consultation process may entail formal meetings between managers and others within organizations, but there can be consultation even when there is no formal process. As a low-key and informal process, consultation may be found in everyday and ordinary conversations. Moreover, such conversations may be interwoven with many other types of conversations – so we should not assume that consultation is always an explicit and discrete activity. It may be, but in some organizations it may be occurring in a very 'natural way'.

It may not be just consultation that occurs through an informal conversational process – so may analysis and negotiation. In fact, the idea of strategic management taking place conversationally has been remarked on in recent years by Gary Hamel (2002). Although his book on strategy appears to be written primarily for the private sector reader, he provides food for thought about the strategic management process in any organization when he presents it as an ordinary conversational process rather than as a highly technical or analytical process based on using a whole set of techniques. This suggests we should look out for a fairly fluid strategic thinking process occurring through lots of conversations, including formal conversations in management meetings, casual conversations over tea, in fact, conversations taking place in a whole range of settings. Out of this, according to Hamel, we get strategic decisions. We may also get forward looking and strategic ideas about the future of an organization, and ideas about how the organization can get to the future.

When Dyson writes about the planning of strategy involving negotiation, this can serve to remind us that strategic management is partly about bringing about change, and we may then recall the discussion from an earlier chapter that change can affect many interest groups inside and outside the organization. Some groups may hope to gain an advantage from change, but some groups may stand to lose from a strategic change. Consequently we can think about groups that favour the status quo and other groups that form – or could form – a coalition for change around any specific strategic decision. So, strategic processes are fundamentally political in the sense of being laced with conflicts between groups with differential and fluctuating amounts of power. We might,

158

here, think of organizations, therefore, as pluralistic coalitions of groups, some coalitions trying to impede changes and some trying to advance changes.

The various interest groups, and their perspectives and interests that form the organization and its environment, may be well understood. If an interest group has 'clout', this is a very important dimension to the nature of strategic thinking. Take the tendency of a ministry of finance (in a national government), or a finance department (in a single public services organization), to be a powerful voice in strategic conversations. They will have a lot of say in decisions not only on strategic investments, but also in what is a strategic priority because of the grip they have on the budgetary process. This can produce tensions between different parts of government or of a public service organization. This came out very clearly in the United States when the federal budgetary process began to be seen as undermining the strategic planning of government agencies acting under the Government and Performance Results Act 1993.

This view of strategic management as a political process underlines the reality that the arguments that go on about strategy are often not really arguments about what is in the best interests of the organization or the public, but rather arguments about how the interests of different groups are being affected. There is an important point here for strategic leaders in public services. While it is important to listen carefully to what different groups say in response to strategic ideas, it not wise to take what is said at face value (Heifetz and Linsky 2002).

Dyson's conception of strategic planning as having three elements (consultation, negotiation and analysis) is important for a realistic view of what happens in practice, but it is difficult to keep all three elements in mind when we talk about strategic processes, and we may find ourselves drifting into focusing on, say, the analytical element.

What else is there to say about strategic thinking processes? By looking at real examples we can see that thinking processes have an organizational aspect. For example, Smith (1994) reported on the corporate planning process used by the Countryside Commission in the 1990s (UK). In this case the strategic planning process had six stages. The first stage was the initial analysis; the second was top-down guidelines; the third was bottom-up proposals; the fourth was finalization of the plan; the fifth was submission of the plan to, and discussion with, government; and the sixth was monitoring of the plan. In the outline of the Countryside Commission's process there is an obvious element not found in the flow chart presented earlier in this chapter – this is an indication of how strategic planning works organizationally and how it works between the organization and government. Specifically, the outline draws attention to the different roles or contributions of top management, more junior management, and government. So, the value of the description of the Countryside Commission's process provided by Smith (1994) is that it underlines the need to see strategic thinking as not merely a set of analytical steps, but also as being structured into relationships within and beyond public service organizations.

If we look again at the flow chart at Figure 6.2 we can imagine the whole process being conducted in various ways organizationally. For example, a centralized organization might have the whole plan being produced by a small group of top managers, but, in a more decentralized organization, we can imagine top management providing the managers of departments or parts of the organization with a mission statement and a written briefing setting out a strategic analysis and stating the corporate objectives. The top managers may then require lower levels of management to carry out strategic thinking to identify, evaluate and propose actions to top management for approval. Once proposals have been approved by top managers, then lower level managers may be required to think about and produce implementation plans, which may then have to be referred up to top managers for approval especially in relation to changes in budgetary allocations. Monitoring may involve both top managers and lower level managers through reporting systems which allow the top managers to judge the success of implementation and the meeting of key milestones in the implementation of strategic decisions.

Even in a decentralized organization, we can expect variations in how the process works in practice, meaning that the distribution of power within the organization may affect how tightly or loosely bottom-up thinking and planning is controlled from above. The difference between centralized and decentralized systems also emerges in terms of the role of government in the approval of strategic plans of individual public services organizations. If finalized strategic plans have to be submitted to government, this might suggest a centralized system. Again, it is quite likely that the degree of centralization may vary even if strategic plans have to be submitted. Where public services organizations are very independent, then the submitted plans might be merely rubber-stamped. If government has a high degree of centralized control, then the submitted plans may be modified through serious bargaining between government and public service organizations.

Once we locate strategic thinking in organizational processes and organizational structures, and do not see it as a process that takes place as pure intellectual thought and contemplation, then strategic thinking becomes a skill involving communication and political skills. This is illustrated in the development of the concept of strategic thinking within the Professional Skills for Government (PSG) framework in the UK (see Concept Box 6.1).

CONCEPT BOX 6.1   A PRACTICAL VIEW OF STRATEGIC THINKING IN THE UK CIVIL SERVICE

PSG was developed in the UK after 2003. One of the core skills needed at a senior level in this framework was strategic thinking.

In 2010 strategic thinking was defined as:

1   Able to shape and set the long-term vision and direction for the department, taking into account both wider government priorities and delivery systems

2   Knows how to identify tensions, set priorities and make trade-offs between different policy areas and over different timescales (short, medium and long-term)

3   Able to present ministers and colleagues with key choices based on robust evidence and facilitate the strategic development process

4   Knows how to take a corporate perspective across government, pro-actively working as a team with Whitehall peers, influencing and shaping their strategic agendas and understanding key strategy and decision processes

5   Champions the role of strategic thinking in the organization, working effectively with relevant internal and external experts.

Some of the behaviours entailed in this strategic thinking included:

- Understanding and explaining the long-term vision and direction for the government department
- Using the government's wider priorities to develop the long-term vision and direction for the department
- Consideration of the trends relevant to the development of the long-term vision and direction of the department
- Using focus groups, formal surveys, etc. to include views of people in department
- Understanding and explaining strategic choices and the likely implications from pursuing the various strategic choices
- Presenting ministers and colleagues with key strategic choices
- Using trends, scenarios, etc. to make judgements about strategic choices
- Working across departmental boundaries on strategic agendas
- Making use of internal strategy experts in strategic thinking.

DO TECHNIQUES MATTER?

Hopefully the techniques we have been reviewing in this chapter look plausible, but if strategic processes involve more than thinking, and they involve communication and negotiation, do we have an exaggerated sense of the value of techniques for strategic thinking? Surprisingly, few studies have been carried out to evaluate the use of strategic thinking techniques in a public services context. Of course, as we saw in Chapter 3, there is some evidence that effective leaders are linked to the use of strategic planning techniques (Gabris, Golembiewski and Ihrke 2000). As John Bryson and a colleague (Bryson and Anderson 2000) remarked specifically about large-scale interactive methods of strategic planning, there are some very good descriptions of techniques, but very little systematic evaluation of the benefits of using them. This is generally true of strategic thinking techniques in the private and public sectors. There is little systematic evaluation of their benefits and advantages in practice.

SUMMARY

This chapter has mainly concentrated on strategic thinking as a rational process consisting of a sequence of steps. Despite objections that are frequently voiced about representing strategic thinking as a rational and linear process, it is worth remembering the point made by John Kay, who claimed that organizations generally do approach strategic thinking as a rational process.

Techniques were presented as additions to the process of strategic thinking, additions that provided structured ways of carrying out thinking as part of the overall strategy process. If we think of strategic thinking as akin to a craft, then the techniques are intellectual tools that can be selected and used to fashion ideas as a skilled accomplishment. In a sense, they are available to be used, not used or used in a modified way. One example of this is the way the stakeholder analysis can be used to corroborate and refine ideas about the mission of a public services organization; and it can be used again for the purpose of thinking about how strategies can be implemented to minimize resistance to change. The specific form of the stakeholder analysis will probably change slightly depending on how it is to be used within strategic thinking.

Another view of strategic thinking is to consider it as embedded in organizational processes and structures. Reference was made to the ideas of Dyson, who referred to strategic planning as being a management process involving analysis, consultation and negotiation. A key point about situating strategic thinking within consultation and negotiation processes, as well as within analytical processes, is to recognize that strategy is also subject to the effects of conflicting perspectives and interests.

Work-based assignment: core competencies analysis

The work-based assignments in this book are for civil servants and other public services staff who have management experience.

Either use your own organization or select another organization you know very well and use the approach suggested by Klein and Hiscocks to identify its top skills. Use what you discover to make an assessment of the core competencies of the organization.

Work-based assignment: feasibility assessment of strategies

Interview one or two people who were closely involved in writing your organization's current strategic plan, and ask them whether proposed strategies were assessed carefully for feasibility before they were chosen. Ask them if any strategies were dropped at the choice stage because they were not feasible. Ask them for their views on the importance of assessing feasibility before choosing between strategic options.

DISCUSSION QUESTIONS

1   Even though it may be hard to follow it exactly, should leaders in public services follow a linear model of strategic thinking and try to be as rational as possible?
2   Are there any techniques that you think are especially important in strategic thinking in the public services? What two or three techniques do you think are most useful?
3   What criteria should be used in making strategic choices and how important are assessments of feasibility?
4   Does strategic thinking in public services need to be developed in some way to cope better with the negotiation processes that may occur?

FURTHER READING

Nutt, P. (2008) Investigating the success of decision making processes. *Journal of Management Studies*, 45(2): 425–55.
Prime Minister's Strategy Unit, Cabinet Office (2003) *Strategy Survival Guide*. London: Strategy Unit.

The article by Paul Nutt is quite thought provoking. It might be useful for reflecting on how you make decisions. The *Strategy Survival Guide* was written for civil servants; it approaches the whole issue of strategic planning quite differently from this book and thus might be useful if you wanted to read something very different.

REFERENCE LIST

Bichard, M. (2007) 'Oral evidence', in *House of Commons Public Administration Select Committee, Governing the Future, Second Report of Session 2006–07*, Volume II, HC123-II. London: The Stationery Office Limited.
Bryson, J. M. (2004) *Strategic Planning for Public and Nonprofit Organizations: A Guide to Strengthening and Sustaining Organizational Achievement*. 3rd edition. San Francisco, CA: Jossey-Bass.
Bryson, J. M. and Anderson, S. R. (2000) Applying large-group interaction methods in the planning and implementation of major change efforts. *Public Administration Review*, 60(2): 143–62.
Dyson, R. G. (1990) *Strategic Planning: Models and Analytical Techniques*. Chichester: Wiley.
Elbanna, S. (2013) Processes and impacts of strategic management: evidence from the public sector in the United Arab Emirates. *International Journal of Public Administration*, 36(6): 426–39.

Gabris, G. T., Golembiewski, R. T. and Ihrke, D. M. (2000) Leadership credibility, board relations, and administrative innovation at the local government level. *Journal of Public Administration Research and Theory*, 11(1): 89–108.

Hamel, G. (2002) *Leading the Revolution*. Boston, MA: Harvard Business School Press.

Hamel, G. and C. K. Prahalad (1994) *Competing for the Future*. Boston, MA: Harvard Business School Press.

Heifetz, R. A. and Linsky, M. (2002) *Leadership on the Line*. Boston, MA: Harvard Business School Press.

Heymann, P. B. (1987) *The Politics of Public Management*. London: Yale University Press.

Johnson, G. and Scholes, K. (1989) *Exploring Corporate Strategy: Text and Cases*. London: Prentice Hall.

Kaplan, R. S. and Norton, D. P. (1992) The Balanced Scorecard – measures that drive performance. *Harvard Business Review*, January–February: 71–9.

Kay, J. (1993) *Foundations of Corporate Success*. Oxford: Oxford University Press.

Klein, J. A. and Hiscocks, P. G. (1994) 'Competence-based competition: a practical toolkit', in G. Hamel and A. Heine (eds) *Competence-Based Competition*. Chichester: Wiley.

Kouzes, J. M. and Posner, B. Z. (2007) *The Leadership Challenge*. 4th edition. San Francisco, CA: Jossey-Bass.

Lewis, M. A. and Gregory, M. J. (1996) 'Developing and applying a process approach to competence analysis', in R. Sanchez, A. Heene and H. Thomas (eds) *Dynamics of Competence-Based Competition: Theory and Practice in the New Strategic Management*. Kidlington/Oxford: Pergamon.

Nutt, P. C. and Backoff, R. W. (1992) *Strategic Management of Public and Third Sector Organizations*. San Francisco, CA: Jossey-Bass.

Osborne, D. and Gaebler, T. (1992) *Reinventing Government: How the Entrepreneurial Spirit is Transforming the Public Sector*. Reading, MA: Addison-Wesley.

Poister, T. H. and Streib, G. (2005) Elements of strategic planning and management in municipal government: status after two decades. *Public Administration Review*, 65(1): 45–56.

Porter, M. (1980) *Competitive Strategy: Techniques for Analyzing Industries and Companies*. London: Free Press.

Smith, R. J. (1994) *Strategic Management and Planning in the Public Sector*. Harlow: Longman.

Chapter 7

Strategic issue management

LEARNING OBJECTIVES

- To understand the concept of strategic issues
- To explore strategic thinking used to identify and address strategic issues
- To appreciate methods that may be used to probe strategic issues and to generate ideas for action to solve issues

INTRODUCTION

The point has already been made that strategic thinking should normally be hard work. One reason for this is the existence of strategic issues. Some guides on how to do strategic planning spell out that strategic issues need to be identified and managed. Some organizations set up fast-track systems to manage strategic issues alongside their normal system for producing long-term strategic plans. Such a fast-track system could be conceptualized as in Figure 7.1 below.

The most direct way to uncover strategic issues is to ask two questions:

- What will make it difficult for this organization to achieve its top goals, its mission or its strategic vision?
- What would make it much easier for this organization to achieve its top goals, its mission or its strategic vision?

The answers we give to these questions can be called strategic issues. It is because an issue includes something that makes achieving a strategic vision easier, such as an opportunity or strength, that it is probably better to talk about 'addressing' a strategic issue rather than the more obvious phrase of 'solving' an issue, which implies an issue is always a problem (e.g. a threat or weakness). Sometimes issues might also be identified by observing and analysing conflicts or tensions between different stakeholder or interest groups.

By definition, a strategic issue is a development or event that has serious consequences for the likelihood that an organization (or a consortium) will

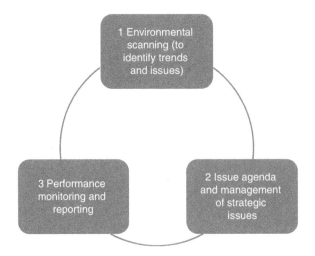

Figure 7.1 *Fast-track for strategic issues*

achieve its strategic goals (or strategic vision, strategic mission, etc.). Strategic issue management is a process in which such issues are first identified, and then action is taken to address them.

As long ago as 1983, Douglas Eadie in the United States was writing about the need for strategic issue management to be used in the public sector. His version of strategic issue management was very concerned with fostering creativity in strategic management, and innovation in terms of action. Overall, he was less concerned with efficiency and performance as such. Other leading American scholars gave their attention to strategic issue management in the 1980s and onwards; for example, Nutt and Backoff (1992, 1993) and John Bryson (1988, 1995, 2004 and 2011). (See Concept Box 7.1).

CONCEPT BOX 7.1   ISSUE MANAGEMENT

Nutt and Backoff (1993: 311) defined issue management as an approach that concentrates on issues, and involves thinking about the situation (through a SWOT analysis) in order to develop ideas for the organization's strategic development:

> Issues are treated as emergent developments that are apt to influence the organization's ability to meet its goals. Issues can arise internally or externally and may have beneficial or negative effects. Issues are used to fill the gap between a SWOT analysis and strategic development. This approach allows for the continuous revision of SWOTs, suggesting a process that periodically updates strategy with the insights drawn from recent developments. Annual strategy sessions are planned to resolve a few pivotal issues,

with SWOT review and revision done every five years. Using issues as the focus of inquiry allows strategic managers to become more flexible and responsive to emergent developments.

Some of the leading ideas in strategic issue management are, first, that strategic management revolves around addressing strategic issues; second, that leaders need to think about how to overcome barriers to action and use opportunities for the realization of strategic goals; and third, that leaders need to pay attention to implementation (see Figure 7.2). The third idea is linked to an awareness of the importance of conflict management, and stakeholder analysis and management. Nutt and Backoff (1992), for example, highlight the need to look at how various stakeholders will respond to proposals for new strategic actions.

Despite the focus on strategic issue management by influential leading scholars in the United States, when it came to reforming the public services in the US federal government in the early 1990s the reforms did not emphasize strategic issue management, but instead focused on performance management and getting results. It is worth underlining the contrast between strategic issue management, with its concerns for solutions and creativity, and the federal government reforms focused on strategic planning and performance measurement and management. As federal agencies moved towards the implementation of strategic planning linked to performance management, they worked on performance measurement and identifying performance indicators and targets linked to strategic goals. This seems diametrically opposed to the creative problem solving and coalition building efforts of strategic issue management. Of course, there is no logical reason why individual organizations should not design strategic management processes that attempt to do both – both concern themselves with long-term strategic goals and managing performance towards

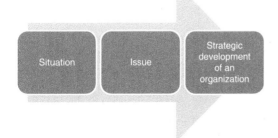

Figure 7.2 *Strategic thinking using issues (based on explanation of issue management by Nutt and Backoff (1993))*

the achievement of those long-term goals and, at the same time, the identification and management of strategic issues involving the handling and management of stakeholders and coalitions of interest groups.

STRATEGIC ISSUES

Some experts identify issues with developments or events that are threats or opportunities. Some imply that a strategic issue is not easy to resolve. In part, this might be because a solution is not immediately obvious and it takes some intellectual effort to work out what a solution might entail. Alternatively, as Nutt and Backoff (1992) argue, a strategic issue can be seen as a 'tension' that is formed by opposing forces pushing the organization in different directions. At one point (Nutt and Backoff 1992: 181) they suggest that strategic management groups who formulate issues as tensions 'begin to appreciate the need to reconcile contradictory pressures'.

Nutt and Backoff were not the first to think about strategic management in terms of contending forces and strategic issues. They outlined some of the antecedent ideas as follows (Nutt and Backoff 1992: 129):

> Treating issues as tensions is consistent with several schools of thought pertinent to strategy formation. Jantsch (1975) contends that strategic management should balance opposing forces, such as budget cuts and the treatment of the disadvantaged needing care in a mental health centre. Tensions are similar to the dialectical ideas used by Mitroff and Emshoff (1979) and Mason and Mitroff (1981) to frame needs in policy making as opposites. The opposing ideas produce strong claims and counterclaims that create tensions for which a response is devised. Cobb and Elder (1972) identify issues as conflicts between interest groups. Both Mason (1969) and Sussman and Herden (1985) found that exploring these opposing forces led to superior results in policy making. Strategic managers that deal with one of two opposing forces and ignore the other create potentially dangerous situations in which the barriers to action or opportunities posed by the unrecognized forces may be overlooked.

Perhaps an example will make this conception of a strategic issue as a tension clearer. Nutt and Backoff (1992: 127) provided the example of a hospital that had a low bed occupancy rate, was suffering a decline in revenue and wanted to cut back on the numbers of employees, but at the time had a contract with a trade union that constrained its ability to do this. So, one implication of this idea of a strategic issue as a tension is that solving a strategic issue (low occupancy causing reductions in revenue) in an obvious way can cause side-effects which are serious and unwelcome (e.g. resistance to layoffs by the union). In this case, we can use the word dilemma to understand the subjective problems caused for leaders by a strategic issue. The resolution of the dilemma involves finding actions that solve the problem and avoid unwelcome side-effects (or take advantage of opportunities). This suggests that the definition of strategic issue can be formulated as being a special type of problem which exists when it is not easy to know immediately what the best solution might be, or a problem when it is difficult to see how to resolve it without creating further serious problems (or missing good opportunities). In addition, we can sometimes recognize this type of problem by the fact that leaders face fairly clear problems of mobilizing sufficient support behind obvious solutions and of dealing with resistance and opposition – and this can be both within and outside the organization. This may be the case when a strategic issue manifests itself as the site of a major conflict of interest.

One point stressed by some experts is that strategic issues often require urgent responses by leaders. On this basis, they point out the danger of trying to delay handling strategic issues caused by only considering them within an annual strategic planning cycle. If strategic issues tend to be very urgent in nature because they emerge suddenly, and require a very rapid response, then it may be necessary for an organization to develop a strategic management process for issue management that sits alongside the annual strategic planning process. On the other hand, perhaps there are some strategic issues that do not fit this pattern of sudden acute development, but are more chronic in nature and can be handled through the annual planning process.

There needs to be some clarity about how different types of problems – strategic issues and operational problems – are being processed. Where a problem is a strategic issue, then this should be considered by the leaders of the organization (or by the leaders of the relevant part of the organization). The strategic leaders need to ensure issues are analysed and action taken to resolve them. If the problem is not a strategic issue, then it needs to be referred elsewhere – say to middle or front-line management. So, the main practical justification for trying to be clear about what is and what is not a strategic issue is a matter of deciding who in management is responsible for dealing with which issues and problems.

If we assume that strategic leaders need to focus on the most important strategic issues otherwise their credibility as a leader will suffer, and they may find themselves being sacked and replaced (Nutt and Backoff 1992), there is a need for leaders to be good at distinguishing top priority strategic issues from those which are less important. One way to define the top strategic issues is to evaluate the consequences for the organization if they are ignored. All strategic issues are of interest (positive) or cause concern (negative) because of their consequence for the future success and future viability of an organization. But the top strategic issues will be those that offer the biggest opportunities or pose the biggest threats to achieving the top strategic goals, and the biggest opportunity for the success of the organization or the biggest threat to its survival. Therefore, perhaps every time a strategic issue comes along a leader should pose the question: What will be the consequence of us doing nothing about this issue? Will doing nothing mean we fail to achieve our long-term strategic goals (or, equivalently, will it mean that we fail to deliver our organizational mission,

169

or stop us moving towards a strategic vision of the future of the organization)? Will doing nothing about it mean we are significantly less successful or even threaten our survival?

MORE ABOUT THE NATURE OF STRATEGIC ISSUES

We have laboured in the preceding paragraphs to express an important idea about strategic issues – and it is worth underlining this point. Specifically, many but not all strategic issues are 'problems' in the usual sense of the word. It is very easy to assume that strategic issues are always problems. However, arguably, there are some issues that are not problems but, as we have been saying already, are opportunities. We can define an opportunity as something that we can use to better achieve strategic goals (or to better deliver the mission of the organization, or to move more swiftly to realizing a desirable strategic vision). The issue is then one of exploiting an opportunity. In this case, we could still say we have a problem – but in the distinctive sense we have the problem of not wasting an opportunity!

Some strategic issues may not actually be affecting current organizational results. Some could be issues because they will have an impact on the organization in five years' or ten years' time. This, of course, requires that leaders who are interested in using strategic issue management are on their guard against merely reacting to their experiences of what is happening now. Leaders must also use their imagination and develop their ability to anticipate issues, by looking at things that could impact on the organization in the future. Studying trends that are starting to emerge could be one way of strategic leaders sensitizing themselves to possible future strategic issues.

Perhaps most strategic issues concern the public services that the organization produces, and its success in meeting the needs of service users (or customers). If a public service is substantially failing to meet the needs of existing users, or if there is a key section of the public missing out on a service, for example, then this probably means the organization is failing in respect of its mission. And, of course, a failure in a serious way to deliver a mission is a strategic issue. But strategic issues may be found in other aspects of a public service organization – and not just in the public services it produces and whose needs it serves.

Some experts see strategic issues as originating in the external environment of the organization. Public services are continually faced with changing external environments. These changes may be economic and technological, and they may be political. Among the most important external developments are, however, changes in society, lifestyles and public attitudes. Leaders of public services who overlook such changes fail to keep their organizations adapting to new requirements. As we saw in an earlier chapter, at one point in time, for example, there may be public concerns about the quality of educational and health services, and leaders will need to respond to this. Within a matter of a few years – five or ten years, maybe – such concerns may have receded and the public attention has turned to new concerns, such as community safety, personal safety and the levels of immigration. It is a basic fact that society evolves all the time; lifestyles change continually and, in consequence, what the public wants from the public services also continues to change. Strategic issue management processes can, therefore, be useful in helping to adjust the organization, its values and capabilities to the new external realities.

Technological change is an important source of strategic issues. Governments all around the world have been coming to terms with the astonishing growth of the internet since the mid 1990s and the way in which more and more of the daily lives of citizens are influenced by the internet. People now frequently communicate by email. They often do their shopping online. They shop for holidays and book hotels and plane flights online. This technological development has also affected the business world. There are internet-based retail businesses. Banks now offer to conduct their interactions with their customers online. Manufacturing businesses are using the internet for procurement. Inevitably, with the public and businesses using the internet, questions arise about online access to government services and citizens being able to carry out transactions with government using the internet. Indeed governments all around the world made major efforts in the late 1990s and early years of the twenty-first century to migrate government services to the internet. This is an example of a technological change that was actually linked to lifestyle changes and economic changes, and posed a major challenge to government services.

So we could envisage strategic issues as emerging from the external environment of a public service organization and then, in a sense, there being an issue because the organization needs to adapt its strategy, its values and capabilities and its alliances so as to continue to be a successful provider of services. By adapting the organization and thus addressing the issue, the leaders of public services create or renew satisfaction among service users and politicians.

However, perhaps we should specify a second characteristic of strategic issues. They not only necessitate an ongoing 'dialectic' between the environment and the organization, but, in addition, they are determined by the strategic intent of those who lead the organization. This is because, in developing a strategic goal and thus a strategic intent, trends or events become issues by virtue of the fact that they impinge on this strategic intent. If, as a strategic leader, you have a clear strategic intent, then what is happening in the external environment may matter because it blocks or facilitates the realization of that intent. So there is a degree of relativism in a strategic issue. The significance of external developments depends in part on what it is the organization is trying to do in order to make the public services better in the future. But this relativism is limited by the public's experiences and judgements of the public services. A strategic issue cannot be reduced purely to a reflection of the intentions of strategic leaders within the public services. Issues are also partly a matter of what the public needs and wants.

171

STRATEGIC ISSUE AGENDA

Should public services organizations be systematic in considering the management of strategic issues? Some organizations may be in slow changing environments, and may feel able to deal with sporadic strategic issues on an ad-hoc basis. But if an environment is complex and dynamic, then an organization's strategic leaders have, at any point in time, to be concerned about its capacity to deliver its strategic vision if there is a stream of fairly tough or intractable strategic issues. Presumably that type of situation can overwhelm the capacity of many organizations to identify and resolve strategic issues. A key dimension of this capacity is the amount of attention strategic leaders can give. Leaders cannot give limitless attention to strategic issues.

The consideration of strategic issues is begun by the strategic leaders of an organization constantly monitoring their environment, reviewing their strategic goals and intentions, and therefore thinking about what strategic issues they are currently or will be facing. They evaluate these strategic issues in terms of their seriousness. They might be judged in terms of the consequences for their strategic goals or strategic visions of not solving the issues. They also need to evaluate their urgency. On this basis, strategic leaders form a ranking of the strategic issues, with serious and urgent issues being ranked most highly, and less serious and urgent issues being ranked lower. Such a ranking of strategic issues is the essence of the formulation of a strategic issue agenda.

The strategic issue agenda, which should be reviewed fairly frequently, is used for structuring discussions about what to do. Decisions need to be made about what issues on the strategic issue agenda require action now or in the future. Strategic leaders may review the ranking of the issues and then consider each issue in turn and decide whether it is an issue that needs attention now and what action needs to be taken, or whether it is an issue that is serious but that they should continue to monitor and keep under surveillance. They might also decide that an issue is becoming less serious and less urgent, but decide to continue monitoring it for the time being. There may be some issues that are fading away or are judged now to be of no importance and may be dropped from the strategic issue agenda.

KEY CHARACTERISTICS OF STRATEGIC ISSUE MANAGEMENT

The design of the thinking aspects of a strategic planning process that can be used to manage strategic issues has been explored by Eadie (1983), Nutt and Backoff (1992) and Bryson (2004).

Eadie (1983) provided an early encouragement to recognize 'issues' as relevant to strategic thinking and planning in the public sector. Whereas a process of budget preparation and operational planning could be useful for productivity improvements, and strategic planning techniques could be applied in a process of mission and goal formulation that might be useful for organizational cohesion, he argued that the techniques of strategic planning were needed to deal with issues.

> Often important issues cannot be dealt with through operational planning because they cross too many intra-organizational lines, or are heavily influenced by a complex, changing environment – or, frequently, both. In this instance, the need is for innovation and creativity, which calls for applying the techniques of strategic planning.
>
> (Eadie 1983: 450)

As well as some case material, Eadie offered what was, in effect, an eight step process for strategic planning in which environmental scanning and opportunities loomed large (see Figure 7.3). Implicitly, this suggested that environmental scanning was a key technique for identifying strategic issues, and that the issues took the form of opportunities.

Eadie (1983) suggested starting strategic planning on a limited basis and widening its use as an organization's capability in strategic planning developed. Perhaps an organization should start with one strategic issue, tackle that, learn from the experience, and thus establish the credibility of thinking strategically and not just operationally. Logically, of course, if you establish the credibility of strategic management through strategic issue management, you also establish the credibility of the strategic leaders who use strategic issue management. The implication of Eadie's views is that strategic issue management which is focused on one or two issues only will be particularly useful in an organization with no past history of strategic management. Likewise, the leader who is new and has no history with an organization can use strategic issue management to show that they can make things better and, therefore, they are worthy of the trust for which they are asking when they put forward an ambitious long-term strategic plan (Joyce 2000).

Writers who came after Eadie were to offer more detailed advice on how thinking within strategic planning could be applied to issues and their solutions. However, a constant theme, found in the writing of Nutt and Backoff (1992) and Bryson (2004), as well as Eadie (1983), is the idea that strategic issue management is aimed at creativity, and this involves searching for and creating less obvious solutions. It is also evident from the attention given to stakeholder management that Nutt and Backoff take the view that strategic issue management requires conflict handling and resolution skills. John Bryson and Nutt and Backoff have also described the processes for strategic issue management in ways that put a lot of stress on fairly participative approaches.

These remarks are consistent with a view of strategic issues as intrinsically difficult to address and resolve, partly because they involve analysing strategic situations in which the solutions are not immediately obvious and not to hand ready-made. This means that strategic leaders need to be creative and imaginative. Furthermore strategic issues are difficult to solve and manage because of

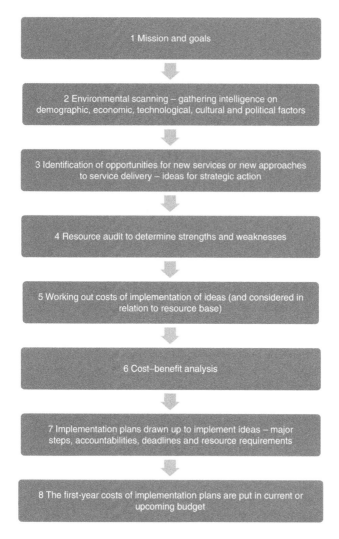

Figure 7.3 *Eadie (1983) – steps in strategic planning (to deal with issues)*

the multiplicity of interests present in the situation. Thus the need for strategic leaders to understand the impact of possible solutions on stakeholder groups, and the need to appreciate that these impacts will be different and thus produce different responses by stakeholders. Some responses will be ones of resistance to attempted solutions to strategic issues. Other responses will be ones of active or passive support for what strategic leaders are attempting. In other words, a strategic issue is difficult to resolve and requires some considerable effort – both intellectual and leadership – because it is a combination of intellectual challenge (of knowing what to do) and leadership challenge (of ensuring that enough interest groups are positive about the change and are mobilized to support the change).

The Nutt and Backoff view of strategic issue management sits very comfortably with a pluralist view of strategic management – the idea that inside and outside the organization there are a multiplicity of groups, and these groups are defined by their different interests. They may have related interests, but possibly we should stress the differences of interest they have about particular issues.

Why might a participative approach to strategic issue management be stressed? Strategic leaders may adopt a participative approach because they wish to engage people with the strategic management process, and the reason they want to engage people with the strategic management process is possibly based around a very simple idea that involving people in analysing issues and then coming up with solutions produces more support for change. So, it could be argued that a participative approach is intended to ease the problems of implementing strategic solutions. However, this probably does not mean that the process will be conflict-free. There will still be potential clashes between different interests, and thus the need for good conflict handling and resolution skills.

Finally, we should note here that strategic issue management, as described by Nutt and Backoff (1992) and by Bryson (2004), with an emphasis on participative approaches, also leads quite naturally to the design of large-scale planning events (including what are named whole systems development events). These large-scale events provide one way of creating a participative approach to strategic issue management. However, we should note the findings of an evaluation by Bryson and Anderson (2000) of these large-scale events. Their overall conclusion is that, while there are some good descriptions about what these large-scale approaches are, there is a lack of evidence about the consequences of using these methods.

A METHOD FOR IDENTIFYING AND UNDERSTANDING ISSUES

It was suggested above that leaders can experience strategic issues as dilemmas. Other, similar, words that come to mind are paradox and contradiction. All of these words suggest the need for creativity. Apart from an injunction to be creative, or possibly to think intuitively, is it possible to think of a way of developing creative solutions that overcome the dilemmas of strategic issues?

We can distinguish between methods of deepening an understanding of an issue and methods of finding a creative solution to that issue. Nutt and Backoff (1992) provide some interesting ideas for both of these – identifying and clarifying the nature of a strategic issue, and then structuring the use of a creative imagination. In this section we concentrate on some ideas for identifying and appreciating strategic issues.

Nutt and Backoff say that developments that signal the need for strategic action (i.e. one part of a strategic issue) can be classified into one of four types.

175

These include both internal and external developments, and are labelled by them as follows: equity, preservation, transition and productivity (see Figure 7.4). Equity developments include human resource developments within the organization that raise questions about the fairness with which people are treated. (Of course, there are also fairness questions about who is receiving a service and what benefits are being delivered to service recipients.) Developments which are classified as preservation ones could be internal to the organization, and these are ones that serve to maintain traditions by preserving cultures, practices or agreements. Transition developments might occur in the external environment and can be illustrated by the emergence of new needs and opportunities. In response to the development of new needs, a public service organization may consider developing new services. Other external developments may pressurize the organization to improve its productivity.

Nutt and Backoff suggest using this framework of four types of developments to specify issues as tensions. This involves first of all identifying the development signalling the need for action (e.g. the emergence of a new need) as a particular type of development (e.g. a transition development), and then trying to see if it can be paired with one of the remaining three development types. If the triggering development was 'transition', this step would yield the following three tensions:

- Transition–equity
- Transition–preservation
- Transition–productivity.

The point would be to describe each of the tensions using data from the situation under consideration. To explain this, let us consider a development triggered by, say, a new need. This may be paired with a pressure to increase

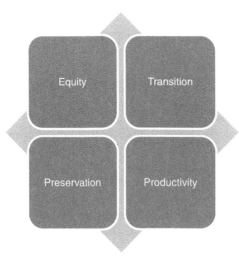

Figure 7.4 *Specifying issues as tensions*

productivity. This is labelled a 'transition–productivity tension'. Nutt and Backoff give as an example of this the continuing need by a hospital to produce cash flow (which will depend on productivity), while implementing a planned expansion of services (which is a response to a transition development). As this example seems to indicate, a pole of the tension may be described in terms of an organizational action (such as planned expansion) rather than in terms of the development that signals the need for organizational action (such as a growth of external demand for the service). We could say that the immediately obvious action in the face of increased external demand is to expand the service, but this could be a problem if we concentrate too much on change management and neglect the need to manage delivery to existing service users while the change is being implemented. Thus, the framework can be used to guide the search for tensions in actual situations.

The next step in using the framework, having already paired the triggering development with the three other development types, is to consider the remaining combinations of development types. So, if the triggering develop-ment was the emergence of a new need (a transition development), then the remaining combinations of developments would be:

- Equity–preservation
- Equity–productivity
- Tradition–productivity.

In this second step, the three tensions, according to Nutt and Backoff, are examined with the triggering development regarded as a 'moderator', which they define as relaxing an issue or stressing the issue further.

Logically, given four types of development, these two steps suggest six types of tension. In fact, Nutt and Backoff (1992: 134) suggest that 'an issue is con-nected or implicated in all six tensions'. The six issue tensions, which emerge from their exploration of the framework, are all plausible in the context of the modernization of public services. These are paraphrased as follows:

1 Continuing to meet service user demands during a change programme
2 Ensuring there is some fairness (between and among winners and losers) as a result of a planned change
3 Respecting traditional cultures/practices/agreements while ensuring fairness
4 Getting a productivity increase from a public service that is already feeling under a great deal of stress and is resisting pressure to abandon its traditional cultures/practices/agreements
5 Dealing with inertia during a change programme
6 Having regard to fairness within the system while making changes to increase productivity.

The value of using this framework is, in part, the production of fresh insights that might occur as a result of trying to reframe known facts and experiences in

177

terms of these fairly abstract categorizations of developments. It is important, however, that the strategic leader feels comfortable moving backwards and forwards between 'data' about the real strategic situation and the more abstract schema offered by Nutt and Backoff. It is no use thinking only at the level of the more abstract schema. By moving from situational data to the framework and then back to the situational data, the strategic leader gains a more considered (and hopefully more complete and balanced) appreciation of the situation.

It is probably important at this point to stress again the integral nature of conflicts of interest to this process. On one hand, what we have described is an intellectual technique and may give the impression that issue identification is an intellectual or even analytical process. But the framework also potentially highlights the range of interest groups that may be contending for influence in the definition of issues. This is obvious in the case of looking at equity developments and traditional developments. Consideration of equity (and thus who are the winners and losers) in planned change, or in action to improve productivity, should highlight some of the key stakeholder groups. Likewise, consideration of who is opposing or resisting change or productivity improvements again will highlight key stakeholder groups.

There are conflicts between the providers and service users and between different groups of service providers about both the issues and the data to show there is an issue. We can illustrate both of these with examples from the public services.

An example of a modest service issue relates to pressure to improve swimming pools in public leisure services. The providers may stress the use of 'scientific data' to judge the adequacy of water cleanliness. Based on professionally or technically excellent standards the water may be judged to be clean. The situation may appear quite different to members of the public using the swimming pool. They may say there is too much chlorine in the water, or the water looks cloudy and could be dirty. This shows the potential conflict between those providing the service and those using it.

An example of conflicts between providers can be taken from public art galleries where the public has free admission because the galleries are funded out of taxation. There can be an argument between different groups of professional employees within the art galleries about the issues that need addressing. One simple distinction is between professionals involved in acquiring and looking after the art collection, and those involved in engaging the public with the consumption of the services of the galleries. The former group may work in rooms not open to public, and rooms where the art collection is stored until it is put on public display. They include art historians and those involved in the preservation and protection of the paintings, and who, therefore, have scientific-technical skills to do with looking after paintings. The latter group includes people employed in art galleries who are concerned with, for example, the design and running of exhibitions and shows. They are interested in putting together paintings in a particular way, and advertising the exhibitions and shows to the public. They may think about featuring a particular painter or perhaps a particular theme. They are mostly concerned with how the paintings are being experienced by the public – how to put on a good exhibition. Those involved in the marketing function within the art galleries are also thinking about how they can perhaps draw in sections of the public to the art gallery, including types of people who are rare visitors, so that the art gallery becomes busier than in the past. But if the public come in larger numbers to view the paintings, some of the professionals who are responsible for preserving and protecting the collection may worry about the increased threat to the paintings because people may touch them more. So, perhaps those who are more concerned with the technical side of the art gallery may have mixed feelings about increasing the numbers of the members of public attending the art gallery, whereas those involved in exhibition work and marketing may feel that is a really good thing. Similarly, the professionals who want to make the art galleries more popular to wider sections of the population may think they can make exhibitions and shows even more interesting by borrowing paintings from other galleries in other countries. They will support the idea of forming a set of alliances with other major art galleries around the world, so that they can draw on a bigger collection than that owned by their own gallery. For others, such alliances would potentially be a problem since the paintings in their collection would have to be sent to other galleries, and might be damaged when being moved around the world.

However appealing the analytical framework offered by Nutt and Backoff, it is also important to remember their continual point that the tensions can be materialized in conflicts between different parties and interest groups. Strategic issue management is never a purely analytical exercise.

A METHOD FOR FORMULATING ACTION IN RESPONSE TO STRATEGIC ISSUES

We turn again to Nutt and Backoff (1992), this time for a method to formulate strategic action. They suggest a useful set of steps for structuring the use of imagination and intuition to identify suitable strategic actions to address strategic issues. First, they recommend the use of SWOT analysis to identify strengths, weaknesses, opportunities and threats. Second, they suggest stating issues as tensions and then assessing the significance of issues for the organization. In outlining a recommended strategic management process, Nutt and Backoff (1992: 434) suggest that issues are recognized by their effect on organizational functioning or ability to achieve a desired future, and they suggest looking for the 'most significant factor pulling in the opposite direction and pair the issue with this factor'. They go on (ibid.: 435) to advise the use of a discursive approach to establish an issue's significance: this involves 'identifying its important features and why it merits the organization's attention'. Third, they say that the top priority issue can be selected for the process of issue management. Fourth, they propose that the results of the SWOT analysis are used to identify actions that will address the top priority strategic issue in such a way as to move the organization towards its strategic vision. For example, proposals for action that use a top strength of the organization to address an issue, and that moves the organization closer to a desired future state (strategic vision), would be noted for subsequent evaluation of feasibility. But ideas for action do not have to make use of a single strength or address a single opportunity. The ideas may address a combination of strengths or a mix of strengths, weaknesses, etc. Indeed, Nutt and Backoff suggest that there may be proposals for action that address a strength, a weakness, an opportunity and a threat all at the same time! Fifth, ideas for action that have a common theme are grouped and labelled as a strategy (see Figure 7.5).

Their framework of six types of tensions, which was outlined in the previous section of this chapter, can be used in step two as a way of checking that all relevant tensions have been identified. This would be done before the discursive assessment of the significance of issues. One approach to the discursive assessment of an issue might be to consider two questions (Eadie 1983):

■ What would be the perceived cost of not dealing with the issue?
■ Will addressing the issue be complex because of the likely reactions of powerful stakeholders to obvious actions that might be taken to address it?

The fourth step in this process involves a 'sensitized' brainstorming that can be represented by Figure 7.6. This means that you remind yourself of all the top items in the SWOT, the strategic vision and the issue immediately prior to brainstorming, and if all these elements are in your mind then they may automatically inform the brainstorming. The brainstorming might be 'cued' using the following type of question in respect of each of the top issues:

■ What action using our top strength can we take to address the issue in order that the organization moves closer towards its strategic vision?

The question can be altered to make use of other items in the SWOT – for example the top weakness, the top opportunity and the top threat. The wording

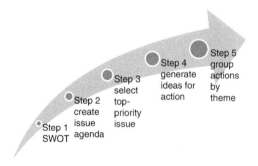

Figure 7.5 Formulation process

has to be altered to make the question read correctly with these other items. So the question might be rephrased, for example, what action overcoming or mitigating the top weakness can we take to address the issue in order that the organization moves closer towards its strategic vision? What action taking advantage of our top opportunity can we take to address the issue in order that the organization moves closer towards its strategic vision? What action blocking or avoiding the top threat can we take to address the issue in order that the organization moves closer towards its strategic vision?

Cued brainstorming is definitely not easy to do and can quickly produce a lot of ideas for action that will not stand scrutiny in terms of their feasibility. However, the best thing to do is to generate as many ideas as possible without being critical of any of them until all the ideas are expressed and captured, and only afterwards should you begin the process of sifting through them for their feasibility.

This process sounds easy to follow, but the idea of treating the issue as a tension makes it more difficult than it sounds. This is so even if we try to create a strategy for an issue analysed as a tension made up of a contradiction between two developments, which is one way that Nutt and Backoff see the task of strategy formulation. Nutt and Backoff (1992: 145) say: 'Strategy is sought that attempts to balance the opposing forces in a high-priority issue tension so that strategic action is taken to deal with one development in the tension while being cognizant of the other.' Above we noted their view that an issue is connected or implicated in all six types of tension. Trying to develop a single strategy that consciously dealt with all six types of tensions implicated in an issue would be very complex!

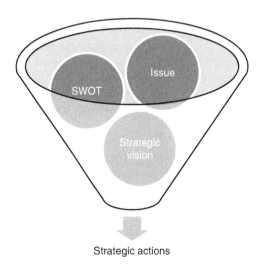

Strategic actions

Figure 7.6 *Cued brainstorming*

Table 7.1 *Issue brief*

Issue brief
1 Definition and explanation of the strategic issue
2 The cost of not addressing the strategic issue
3 Options
4 The interests and power of relevant stakeholders

Nutt and Backoff have many useful ideas for checking out the ideas and strategies produced in the process described above and then planning their implementation, but steps one to five above contain the essence of their method for strategy formulation.

A final practical point concerns how to document the results of strategic thinking about issues. One approach is to use 'issue briefs' and 'issue position papers' (Heath 1997). The issue brief can be used to record thinking which defines and explains a strategic issue, establishes the cost of not addressing the issue (the consequences and timescales of the consequences of doing nothing about the issue), discusses options and analyses the interests and power of stakeholders in respect of the issue. The issue brief is, more than anything else, a summary of strategic thinking on the issue and options. It is, therefore, preparation for evaluating and selecting strategic actions to address the issue, which is set out in a position paper (see Table 7.1).

SUMMARY

Strategic issues may be positive or negative events, or developments that can be identified by scanning internal and external environments. They may be identified as issues on the basis that they have important consequences for the mission or vision, or strategic goals of a public service organization. It is often suggested that strategic issue management requires creativity and innovation by strategic leaders, but it is also critical to remember that such management needs effective conflict handling and resolution skills, and may be usefully enhanced through stakeholder analysis and management.

Nutt and Backoff (1992) have provided some useful ideas and frameworks for understanding strategic issues and the underlying nature of strategic issues, and for using them to generate ideas for strategic action.

Work-based assignment: formulating an issue agenda

The work-based assignments in this book are for civil servants and other public services staff who have management experience.

This assignment is designed to enable you to practice thinking about strategic issues. Please carry this out on your own organization or select an organization that you know well. This could be an organization from which you receive a service. It could be an organization that you have researched.

First, think about any concerns you might have about the future success of this organization. If you can, list up to eight concerns.

Second, remind yourself of the definition of a strategic issue and then evaluate each of the concerns you have listed. Check that they are actually strategic issues. Remember, a strategic issue is one that should be referred to the leaders of the organization for solution. Other kinds of management problems that are not strategic issues need to be referred elsewhere. Only keep strategic issues in your list. Delete the others.

Third, have a go at ranking them in order of importance. Do this by asking what would be the consequence of not solving this issue? What would be the consequence for strategic goals? What would be the consequence for the future success or survival of the organization? Try if you can to justify your judgement of the seriousness of the consequences with some evidence.

Fourth, rate the urgency of each of the issues on the list (which should now be in rank order of importance). You could rate each issue on a scale of zero to ten, where you would rate an issue as ten if you think that it is very urgent and action should be taken immediately, and as zero if it is something that does not require action now but should be kept under surveillance.

Finally, identify the strategic issues that are both important and urgent.

Work-based assignment: assessing issues

Identify six strategic issues in your own organization or an organization you know well. Then choose one of them as the top strategic issue based on the consideration of the following criteria:

- What would be the perceived cost of not dealing with the issue?
- The complex consequences of likely reactions from powerful stakeholders to obvious actions that might be taken to solve the issue.

Prepare a one-page issue brief (see Table 7.1 for format).

Work-based assignment: creative ideas

This assignment is based on the method of Nutt and Backoff for generating ideas for strategic action. First, carry this out in your own organization, or select a public service organization you know reasonably well because you were employed by it, or now use its services, or have researched it. Second, carry out a SWOT analysis and rank all the strengths, weaknesses, opportunities and threats so you can identify the organization's top strength, the top weakness, the top opportunity, and top threat. Third, pick the top strength and generate a number of ideas for action in which this strength would be exploited. Try to generate ideas for action that simultaneously address the top strategic issue, and move

183

the organization towards achieving its strategic goals or vision. Repeat this but using the top weakness/top opportunity/top threat. Try to generate a large number of ideas and do not be disappointed if many of them prove, on further consideration, to be either not feasible or not suitable. This methodology is bound to create a large number of ideas that are not good enough, but if there is at least one really good idea then the whole exercise proves to be very worthwhile.

DISCUSSION QUESTIONS

1   In what circumstances should strategic leaders use strategic issue management thinking?
2   What are the advantages and disadvantages of using the methods proposed by Nutt and Backoff to probe the nature of strategic issues and to generate ideas for action?
3   What is the essence of 'creativity' in strategic thinking and how important is it for a strategic leader to be creative?
4   What techniques can strategic leaders use to think about the conflicts and tensions between interest groups that are a manifestation of strategic issues?

FURTHER READING

Rumelt, R. (2011) *Good Strategy Bad Strategy: The Difference and Why It Matters.* London: Profile.

> This books sets out to persuade readers of the importance of there being a 'nugget' of thinking at the heart of strategic analysis and not to settle for a very poor second best imitation of strategic thinking. Maybe not so good on the techniques but very clear on how a strategic thinker needs to push himself or herself to create an analysis that has some depth and point to it.

REFERENCE LIST

Bryson, J. M. (1988) *Strategic Planning for Public and Nonprofit Organizations.* 1st edition. San Francisco, CA: Jossey-Bass.
Bryson, J. M. (1995) *Strategic Planning for Public and Nonprofit Organizations.* 2nd edition. San Francisco, CA: Jossey-Bass.

Bryson, J. M. (2004) *Strategic Planning for Public and Nonprofit Organizations: A Guide to Strengthening and Sustaining Organizational Achievement.* 3rd edition. San Francisco, CA: Jossey-Bass.

Bryson, J. M. (2011) *Strategic Planning for Public and Nonprofit Organizations: A Guide to Strengthening and Sustaining Organizational Achievement.* 4th edition. San Francisco, CA: Jossey-Bass.

Bryson, J. M. and Anderson, S. R. (2000) Applying large-group interaction methods in the planning and implementation of major change efforts. *Public Administration Review,* 60(2): 143–62.

Cobb, R. W. and Elder, C. D. (1972) *Participants in American Politics: The Dynamics of Agenda Building.* Newton, MA: Allyn & Bacon.

Eadie, D. C. (1983) Putting a powerful tool to practical use: the application of strategic planning in the public sector. *Public Administration Review,* 43: 447–52.

Heath, R. L. (1997) *Strategic Issues Management.* London: Sage.

Jantsch, E. (1975) *Design for Evolution: Self-Organizing and Planning in the Life of Systems.* New York: Braziller.

Joyce, P. (2000) *Strategy in the Public Sector: A Guide to Effective Change Management.* Chichester: Wiley.

Mason, R. (1969) A dialectic approach to strategic planning. *Management Science,* 15(8): B403–14.

Mason, R. O. and Mitroff, I. I. (1981) *Challenging Strategic Planning Assumptions.* New York: Wiley-Interscience.

Mitroff, I. I. and Emshoff, J. R. (1979) On strategic assumption-making: a dialectical approach to policy and planning. *Academy of Management Review,* 4(1): 1–12.

Nutt, P. C. and Backoff, R. W. (1992) *Strategic Management of Public and Third Sector Organizations.* San Francisco, MA: Jossey-Bass.

Nutt, P. C. and Backoff, R. W. (1993) Transforming public organizations with strategic management and strategic leadership. *Journal of Management,* 19: 299–347.

Sussman, L. and Herden, R. P. (1985) Dialectical problem solving. *Business Horizons,* Fall.

Chapter 8

Strategic planning and management

LEARNING OBJECTIVES

- To appreciate the nature of strategic planning and management in the public services
- To review the benefits of strategic planning
- To consider the issue of responsiveness to the public

INTRODUCTION

The public services in the United States and the United Kingdom experimented in the late 1960s and early 1970s with the idea of a planning-programming-budgeting system (PPBS), which can be seen as an ancestor of the strategic planning systems that were subsequently developed in the late 1980s and 1990s. There were also attempts by the United Nations during the 1970s to encourage the use of planning based on objective setting to produce improvements in performance. Again this can be seen as a precursor to contemporary strategic management practices in the public services.

In the early 1980s, the diffusion of strategic planning into government and public services was still limited. Douglas Eadie (1983: 447) wrote that 'there is ample evidence that strategic planning of some kind is widely practised by large business . . . Strategic planning has barely penetrated the collective consciousness of the public sector'. Over the next 20 years, the use of strategic planning spread, and more and more public services organizations wrote strategic plans. Berry and Wechsler (1995: 159) remarked, 'since the early 1980s, strategic planning has been one of the "hot" innovations in public administration, promising public agencies the benefits of a rational and highly structured, future-oriented management technique borrowed from the best run private sector companies'.

A strategic plan can be defined as a formal statement of strategy, that is, a written document setting out a strategy. A strategy for a public service organization (or a consortium of organizations) may be defined as comprising strategic goals and a plan of action to achieve those goals (Heymann 1987). Formulating a strategy tends to involve making decisions that affect who benefits from the organization's activities, and what these benefits are. A strategy tends to have effects that are wide-ranging in their impact across the organization. Also, in consequence, a strategy tends to involve decisions with significant resource (money, people etc.) implications.

Strategic plans come in a variety of shapes and sizes. They can be quite lengthy, comprising many pages. They can go into great detail on services and programmes. They can vary in the degree to which they are produced as working documents for the management team, or as public relations (PR) documents for external stakeholders. In fact, individual organizations may find it useful to produce several versions of the strategic plan for different stakeholders. For example, one version of a strategic plan may be in use as a working document by the management, another version may be distributed to the public, a third version may be distributed to employees, and a fourth version might contain suitable performance and financial data so that it can be used in reporting to oversight bodies. The different versions might have different functions – from reassuring the public to mobilizing support of politicians and employees, from an inspiring but real plan for future activity to a compulsory report to oversight bodies.

In this chapter we will look at types of strategic planning process in the public services and its benefits. We will also consider how strategic planning can be more responsive to the wishes and needs of the public. We finish the chapter with a brief discussion of the difference between strategic planning and management that, to some extent, acts as an introduction to the following chapter, which has a focus on implementation.

TYPES OF STRATEGIC PLANNING PROCESS IN PUBLIC SERVICES

There can be a variety of motives for producing strategic plans, and a whole variety of types of strategic planning in public services. In terms of motivation, for example, strategic planning can be initiated voluntarily (Berry and Wechsler 1995) and then the contents of strategic documents may be designed by the top management of the public service organization to meet its own purposes. Thus a strategic plan that contains objectives, identifies planned actions and allocates management responsibilities for these actions would be useful for those managing strategic action. Other strategic plans may be more like bilateral agreements between central government and the department or agency or a local authority. In such a case, the contents may focus on financial aspects and performance, which implicitly challenges the provider organization to deliver a required level of performance in return for the stated volume of revenue.

Evidence from the private sector suggests that some organizations are highly successful because they concentrate on efficient performance, whereas other organizations are highly successful because they concentrate on innovation

(Miles and Snow 1978). If we extrapolate this to the public services, it might be suggested that some organizations use strategic plans to achieve performance and results, and some to facilitate change and innovation. If the organization puts an emphasis on both performance and change, we can expect to find not only performance measures in strategic plans, but also strategic projects that are concerned with new developments.

The strategic planning that was fostered in US federal agencies by the Government Performance and Results Act (GPRA) of 1993 was, formally anyway, very focused on performance and results. The US General Accounting Office (1996) believed that its studies had shown that results-oriented public services did three things: define mission and desired outcomes, measure performance and use performance information (see Figure 8.1). The US General Accounting Office (GAO) suggested that the GPRA required these three steps of federal agencies. It argued that, as a result of the GPRA, federal agencies were required to create strategic plans that had mission statements, to create annual performance plans containing annual performance goals and indicators, and to write annual performance reports about the achievement of the annual performance goals.

Osborne and Gaebler (1992) summarized the strategic planning process in a way that is concerned with performance and results, but also mentions issues and vision. So this is a model that might be seen as applicable for those organizations interested in both performance and change.

> In essence, strategic planning is the process of examining an organization's or community's current situation and future trajectory, setting goals, developing a strategy to achieve those goals, and measuring the results. Different strategic planning processes have different wrinkles, but most involve a number of basic steps:
>
> ■ analysis of the situation, both internal and external;
> ■ diagnosis, or identification of the key issues facing the organization;
> ■ definition of the organization's fundamental mission;

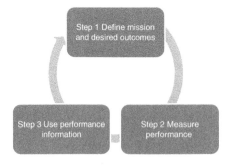

Figure 8.1 Key steps in implementing GPRA (based on a figure in US General Accounting Office (1996) p. 10)

- articulation of the organization's basic goals;
- creation of a vision: what success looks like;
- development of a strategy to realize the vision and goals;
- development of a timetable for that strategy;
- measurement and evaluation of results.

(Osborne and Gaebler 1992: 232–3)

It is not clear that there is anything distinctive to the public services about this summary of strategic planning by Osborne and Gaebler. There is another model of strategic planning which may be more tailored to suit the public sector environment. This was first outlined by Heymann (1987) and then again by Moore (1995) (see Figure 8.2). Arguably, it is more tailored to discussions of strategic change and innovation.

Heymann (1987) used his model of strategic planning to understand and analyse US government agencies. In what respect did his model suggest that strategic planning for these organizations was different from the private sector version? He argued that managers in public services needed the support of others outside the organization more than did their counterparts in the private sector.

> To a far greater extent in government than in a private corporation, the power to control major management decisions is shared not only with superiors, colleagues and subordinates but also with others outside the organization who also have power to shape its future and its goals. That is called democracy. Each of these outsiders has his own views of what should be done and how.
>
> (Heymann 1987: 13)

This suggests an important point about all organizations that are more exposed to the pressures of democratic processes – the strategic thinking of their leaders should benefit from expertise in stakeholder analysis, and implementation of their strategic plans may require more use of stakeholder management.

Figure 8.2 The Heymann–Moore model of strategy and strategic planning

So, arguably, stakeholder analysis and management may be more salient for leaders in public services than private sector business leaders.

Heymann put forward a series of propositions that have a great deal of plausibility. While he expressed these in relation to federal agencies, they are presented here as hypothetically relevant for all public services leaders. There are eight identified:

1 The strategic leader needs to get the support of others outside such as political bodies (for resources and authority), private businesses and individuals, special interest constituencies, the media, other public services organizations, etc.

2 The leader has to communicate and implement desirable goals that get the external support needed to secure the required authority, resources, and cooperation and collaboration.

3 The outside interests will support or oppose the organization's strategic statements and actions depending on their interests.

4 The strategic leader will not manage to satisfy all of the outside interests.

5 The strategic goals need to be credible in terms of the organization's capacities: 'The staff must include people able and willing to work for these goals, and the organizational structures, resources, and authority must be adequate to the task' (Heymann 1987: 14).

6 The strategic goals need to be aligned to organizational values (to ensure there is energy to deliver the goals).

7 The desirable goals must be defined by the strategic leader to meet social needs that superiors (including political superiors) see as important.

8 The leader needs a strategic plan containing actions to deliver the goals by ensuring there are the right amounts and types of capacity, and the right external support.

This model is summarized succinctly by Heymann (1987: 15): 'Thus the central challenge of strategy is to make desirable goals, external support, and organizational capacities fit together'.

The purpose of the strategic plan is, as we have seen, to identify the organizational steps needed to develop additional capacity and to generate external support to deliver desirable goals. But, according to Heymann, the strategic plan also indicates priorities and provides guidance on various matters. This guidance helps individuals frame their actions to support the overall goals and plan of actions. Logically, of course, when the leader of a public services organization articulates new strategic goals they will then need to develop a new strategic plan to develop new organizational capabilities and structures and new external support.

Moore (1995) included in his book an analysis of two case studies on Boston Housing Authority (BHA) and the Houston Police Department (HPD). Some echoes of the Heymann model of strategic planning can be found in his findings. First, the leaders studied by Moore paid a great deal of attention to getting external support. In these cases, it was external support from political management that they sought because they wanted resources and authorization. Second, they worked on organizational capacity in various ways. They took action to improve the effectiveness of the top management team (in one case bringing in new subordinates and in the other making responsibilities clearer); they addressed internal accountability; and they re-engineered operational procedures. Third, they were concerned with the fit between strategic purpose (desirable goals) and structure (organizational capacities). Fourth, they signalled priorities in respect of the important jobs that needed to be done.

Moore called the model of the organizational strategy 'the strategic triangle' and also suggested it was a model adapted for the public sector. He did evolve the concepts, but they were recognizably the same as Heymann's. Most notably, whereas Heymann suggested that the desirable goals not only needed to be consistent with organizational values, but also meet social needs that superiors (including political superiors) saw as important, Moore suggested (1995: 71): '. . . the strategy must be substantively valuable in the sense that the organization produces things of value to overseers, clients, and beneficiaries at low cost in terms of money and authority'. This nuancing of the nature of desirable goals brings us to the concept of 'public value'. Moore's discussion of public value has been widely noticed and appreciated (see Concept Box 8.1).

CONCEPT BOX 8.1   PUBLIC VALUE

First, an axiom: value is rooted in the desires and perceptions of individuals. . . . [Some desires] are for things produced by public organizations and are (more or less imperfect) reflections of the desires that citizens express through institutions of representative government. Citizens' aspirations, expressed through representative government, are the central concerns of public managers.

. . . managers can create value (in the sense of satisfying the desires of citizens and clients) through two different activities. . . [First] to produce things of value to particular clients and beneficiaries: they can establish clean parks to be used by families; they can provide treatment to heroin addicts; they can deploy military forces to make individuals secure and confident in the future. We can call this creating value through public sector production . . .

Public managers can also create value by establishing and operating an institution that meets citizens' (and their representatives') desire for properly ordered and productive public institutions.

. . . the world in which a public manager operates will change. Citizens' aspirations will change . . . new problems may crop up . . . It is not enough,

> then, that managers simply maintain the continuity of their organizations, or even that the organizations become efficient in current tasks. It is also important that the enterprise is adaptable to new purposes and that it be innovative and experimental.
>
> (Moore 1995: 52–5)

Both Heymann and Moore put forward their ideas on strategy in the public sector with an appreciation that things change. The concept of public value was an element of Moore's model, and so he emphasized the usefulness of the 'strategic triangle' for helping public managers to cope with change and continue to create public value.

> In short, the concept [of the strategic triangle] focuses managerial attention outward, to the value of the organization's production, upward, toward the political definition of value, and downward and inward, to the organization's current performance. To the extent that this review reveals important incongruities in the position of an organization, then the manager of that organization would be encouraged to rethink his or her basic strategy until it was once more properly aligned.
>
> (Moore 1995: 73)

For many years there was a problem for many public sector academics and for some public services practitioners. They were suspicious of anything that was copied from the private sector, but it is not necessary to either simply copy private sector strategic management, or flatly reject it in total. The Heymann and Moore model of strategy in the public services shows how the general idea of strategic planning, as developed in the private sector, can be adjusted to make it useful for strategic leaders in public services. Strikingly, both Heymann and Moore ultimately ground their adjustments to organizational strategy in assumptions about the public services situation created by democracy. These assumptions include the nature of power relationships in public services (which lead to an emphasis on the strategic leader's need for external support), and the nature of value created by public services (and thus the importance of receptivity to strategic change).

ACADEMIC STUDIES OF STRATEGIC PLANNING

Academics have produced some important insights into the nature of strategic planning processes and how they can be made more effective.

At least one study has found that there are many commonalities between the public and private sectors in how strategy is developed; this is by Collier,

Fishwick and Johnson (2001). Their study makes use of survey data from over 1,000 respondents in the public sector and over 4,000 in the private sector. They used their data to characterize the strategic development processes used by public and private sector managers, and found evidence in both sectors of the use of a command style of process. This is where a single senior individual, such as the chief executive, determines the vision of the future, is associated with the strategy and makes the strategic decisions. They comment (2001: 19): 'The strategy can become so intrinsically linked with the senior figure that he or she is often perceived as the embodiment of the strategy'. Collier and colleagues also found the use of a planning approach in both sectors. This is where strategy development is a rational and analytical process that involves making an analysis of the environment, evaluating options against strategic objectives and expressing the strategy in plans. A third approach, named an incremental approach, was also widely found and involved experimental, small steps with strategy emerging as an adaptive response to the need to change. Both sectors contained strategy development with a political dimension, where strategy emerges from the interplay of power, bargaining, compromise, blocking and so on, and where there are internal interest groups who compete for influence over strategy. Finally, they report two other approaches, which they named a cultural one and an enforced choice one. In the case of the cultural approach, a strategy is developed in line with the taken-for-granted beliefs, assumptions, etc. They defined enforced choice as strategy development processes that are constrained by external forces. It should be noted that these six different approaches to strategy development were not mutually exclusive; individual organizations could have varying amounts of each approach. (They refer to these different approaches as dimensions of the strategy development process.)

They did find some variations, however, in terms of the prevalence of these different approaches to strategy development. They said that public sector managers were less likely than private sector managers to use a command style development process, more likely to report a political process, and almost as likely to use a planning development process. These differences were less startling, however, than the findings in respect of which sector's respondents experienced strategy development as being most constrained. This particular difference is, arguably, consistent with Heymann's case study conclusions in the US, which were that public sector leaders were more dependent on external support than their private sector counterparts. Those dependent on an external group had to make compromises or adjustments to get their support, which could be seen as, in effect, an experience of being constrained.

While the findings of Collier and colleagues did suggest that the public sector managers were substantially more likely to report external constraint, meaning that forces outside the organization determined their strategic direction and strategy, overall this research showed a big overlap in the management experience of strategy development in the two sectors. Arguably, the key finding is that much of what happens around strategy development appears to be the same in both the public and private sectors.

Quite a different approach to the study of strategic processes was taken by Frost-Kumpf, Wechsler, Ishiyama and Backoff (1993). Their study was essentially a case study using qualitative data and inductive analysis of strategic change in a state agency in the United States. In their research they identified three streams of strategic actions. One stream concerned the leadership's use of strategic language to set out a new strategic direction for the agency. This action appears to have stimulated action by those working in the agency, and the action aggregated into a strategic transformation of the agency. A second stream of strategic actions was concerned with the capability of the agency, and included the development of management, participatory and planning abilities through collaborative planning efforts, and training. This second stream involved other stakeholders outside the agency, including the consumers. A third stream of actions was made up of actions creating cooperative ventures with other government agencies. In some ways, these findings reflect those of Heymann (1987) on strategic planning in government, and his isolation of the importance of planning to integrate changes in the strategic direction of a public services organization with its organizational capacity and external support.

The inductive analysis of Frost-Kumpf and his colleagues also identified nine thematic patterns among the strategic actions. These patterns were:

1 taking symbolic actions
2 developing new programme thrusts
3 empowering key constituencies
4 developing alternative sources of revenue
5 responding to opposition
6 building internal capacity
7 developing technical expertise
8 utilizing training, and
9 gaining external cooperation.

These seem to provide a finer grain view of the three streams of action, but at the same time provide a checklist of the elements of a strategic process that can be usefully compared and contrasted to the evaluation worksheet developed for the US Congress, which we will look at in a later chapter.

The two empirical research studies reviewed above have both been descriptive and analytical; they have been aimed at understanding strategic processes. Empirical research that can tell us about what strategic processes work best in what circumstances appears to be very unusual.

A recent empirical study has gone further than most studies in trying to use quantitative methods to establish the causal factors in the effectiveness of strategic planning processes. This is a study we will make use of several times in this book. It is the study by Poister and Streib (2005) of strategic

194

planning in municipal government in the United States. They carried out a postal survey of senior officials in cities with populations of over 25,000 people – getting over 500 completed surveys and producing, in their judgement, a highly representative sample of US cities. They note that 44 per cent of those surveyed reported the use of strategic planning on a citywide basis, which they suggest indicated a modest spread in strategic planning when compared to earlier studies. Most of the strategic plans contained a review of the mission of the organization, a vision for the future, strategic goals and action plans.

Were the strategic plans working? Most of the respondents in cities with strategic planning appeared to be satisfied with the results being achieved. This did not mean that all the municipal authorities with strategic plans were achieving all their strategic goals, but more than 40 per cent of the strategic goals were being achieved. Interestingly, there were some lessons from the Poister and Streib study about how to increase the impact of strategic planning. These are some of the lessons (we will repeat some of these points elsewhere):

1 Involve citizens and other stakeholders in developing the strategic plan.
2 Carry out feasibility assessments of proposed strategic actions.
3 Set annual objectives for managers (for example, department heads) based on the strategic plan.
4 Make sure new money in the budget is targeted on strategic goals and objectives.
5 Report performance measures to the public on a regular basis.
6 Use annual reviews of managers to check that they are accomplishing the strategic plan.
7 When evaluating strategic effectiveness, organizations should track performance data over time. It is not enough just to compare the actual performance against target performance.

Some of these lessons can be summarized as indicating that strategic planning should be integrated with performance management and budgetary systems. It is, therefore, also interesting to note observations made by Gordon (2005) about developments in strategic planning in US local government. Specifically, Gordon referred to the following developments: performance measurement (checking performance over time), performance management (linking individual objective setting and performance review for managers to the strategic plan), and also making the connection between strategic plans and budgetary decisions (making sure new money is targeted on strategic goals).

The final verdict of Poister and Streib (2005: 54) is quite upbeat: '... our study does show continuing growth and development in the field – a raising of the bar – with leading-edge jurisdictions that are broadening their strategic planning efforts into more sophisticated and comprehensive, and reportedly more effective, strategic management approaches'.

BENEFITS OF STRATEGIC PLANNING IN PRACTICE

Much time, effort and expense can go into the production of a formal and written strategic plan for a public service organization. One worry that is sometimes expressed by senior managers in the public services is that they will go to all the trouble of creating a strategic plan only for it to be ignored, for it to gather dust on a shelf. So, what is the evidence that strategic planning in the public services is worthwhile? This is the question being considered in this section.

Berry and Wechsler (1995) reported survey findings showing that US state agencies had begun to use strategic planning for a variety of reasons. The chief benefits intended by the state agencies in using strategic planning appear to have been to set a direction for policies and programmes, and to help them manage pressures to reduce spending and resolve competing resource allocation priorities. So, strategic planning is a process that supports management decision making. The planning process helps managers think about where they are trying to get to, know what warrants most attention, and make policy and budget decisions. It would seem likely from this that strategic planning would be most attractive to managers in times that were characterized by change and discontinuity. If there were no changes or discontinuities – and no prospects of them occurring – and organizations were in a steady state, then perhaps strategic planning would be less attractive because managers would operate on the basis of habit rather than purposeful decision making. So, providing there were not excessive costs or disadvantages involved in carrying out strategic planning, it would seem likely that it would be most used in periods of change and uncertainty. (See Research Box 8.1.)

RESEARCH BOX 8.1   BERRY AND WECHSLER (1995)

Strategic planning in government organizations emerged and spread in some countries as a voluntary innovation. This is illustrated by the case of state government in the US. A national study of strategic planning carried out in the spring of 1992 found most state agencies had introduced it in the preceding eight years (Berry and Wechsler 1995).

They noticed, as a result of their survey of state government in North America, that a minority of agencies had initiated it because of some top-down process such as a statutory requirement or a mandate from the state governor. Instead, the survey found that 88 per cent of the cases were the result of a leadership decision (Berry and Wechsler 1995: 160). Common factors in the introduction of strategic planning were the chief executive's experience in another agency and the recommendation of an internal planning officer. In fact, a quarter of agencies said that these were the most important factors in the decision to introduce strategic planning. Another one in ten said that the most important factor was the desire of agency leaders to have a framework for setting priorities, and a further set of responses – nearly a tenth – said the most important factor was to improve management and performance. So it was often a voluntary decision of management to adopt strategic planning; this presumably meant that leaders thought it helped them do their job and deliver on their responsibilities.

A UK study of public services managers also suggested that strategic planning supports management decision making. Very many of the respondents claimed that strategic planning helped with achieving goals, helped with setting milestones, allowed better use of resources and gave staff a unified vision (Flynn and Talbot 1996). Helping with setting milestones and using resources better both seem to suggest that strategic planning supports management decision making.

Flynn and Talbot's finding that strategic planning helped by giving staff a unified vision, and in achieving goals, is very interesting. Not all forms of strategic planning and management entail a step of preparing a formal strategic vision, which may be defined as a representation of a desired future state that acts as a goal for strategic action. However, when a public services organization is under pressure to make radical changes, then the idea of an explicit strategic vision becomes more and more useful. The usefulness is not restricted to helping leaders of the organization to make decisions about strategic actions and investments, but also potentially as a basis for mobilizing commitment and initiative throughout the organization. It could be assumed that the top leaders of the organization would spend time communicating this vision to managers and other employees and explaining the rationale for the vision. If successful, and if managers and others had authority to make decisions and take action, it might be claimed that using strategic planning for the purpose of 'giving staff a unified vision' would be part of a process of empowering people within the organization.

We return again to the survey of strategic planning in municipal authorities in the US by Poister and Streib (2005). The respondents in cities with strategic planning were generally satisfied with the implementation and achievement of strategic goals. Respondents that had one strategic plan had accomplished on average about 40 per cent of their goals, and those that had completed more than one round of strategic planning were reporting 60 per cent of their goals being accomplished. The vast majority said that the time and effort put into strategic planning had been worthwhile.

Most of the respondents said strategic planning had a positive impact on producing high-quality public services. There were also impacts in terms of focus and mission, improved decision making, organizational culture and employee focus, and external communications with the public and others (see Table 8.1). The reports of negative impacts of strategic planning were insignificant.

Table 8.1 *Impacts of strategic planning*

Rank	Impact	%
1	Delivering high-quality public services	89
2	Defining clear program priorities	86
3	Focusing the city council's agenda on the important issues	85
4	Orienting the city to a genuine sense of mission	85
5	Making sound decisions regarding programs, systems and resources	83
6	Enhancing employees' focus on organizational goals	80
7	Communicating with citizen groups and other external stakeholders	79
8	Building a positive organizational culture in the city	75

Note: $N = 225$ respondents in municipalities with strategic planning efforts in the last 5 years.

Source: Table of 'Top Ranked Impacts of Strategic Planning in US Municipal Authorities' (Poister and Streib 2005: 52).

The Poister and Streib survey suggests, therefore, that the experience of strategic planning was very positive in US cities. The satisfaction levels with the implementation of strategic goals is high, the proportion of goals accomplished is very respectable, and the positive impacts of strategic planning are extremely widely reported, with benefits for service delivery and the internal management and functioning of public services organizations.

DESIGNING A STRATEGY PROCESS IN PRACTICE

An early model of a public strategic planning process specified the first step as 'organization' (Sorkin, Ferris and Hudak 1985). Toft (2000: 8) justified this on the basis that public organizations at the time were new to strategic planning and needed a first step, which was a 'plan to plan'. He explained that the plan to carry out strategic planning was critical to the effectiveness of the whole process, and suggested the formation of a steering committee consisting of both staff and external stakeholders.

Even though strategic planning is no longer so new in the public services, there is still an argument for making the first step one in which the design of strategic planning process is agreed. Bryson (2004: 35) advises:

> Obviously, some person or group must initiate the process. One of the initiator's first tasks is to identify exactly who the key decision makers are. The next task is to identify which persons, groups, units or organizations should be involved in the effort.

Bryson also supports the idea of a policy-making body to oversee the effort, which is similar to Toft's suggestion of a steering committee.

198

How might such a policy making body or steering committee proceed in preparing a plan for carrying out strategic planning? First, the body or committee could carry out a stakeholder analysis and use the results to decide who needs to be involved in the strategy process and decide how they need to be involved. There are several different ways to involve stakeholders or their representatives in the strategic planning process, for example they could be part of the decision making, they could be consulted or, perhaps, they could be just kept informed. One possible result of the stakeholder analysis could be a decision to redefine the membership of the policy body or steering committee with a view to building wider sponsorship or commitment to the idea of carrying out a strategic planning cycle.

Second, the body or group could assess organizational readiness to engage in strategic planning. This assessment may even trigger some organizational development before strategic planning can be feasible (Joyce 2000: 82):

> So, a chief executive with a healthily functioning organization, which is running smoothly, may still need to develop strategic foresight, set a strategic direction, and bring about strategic changes. On the other hand, a poorly functioning organization may be in such bad shape that attempts to introduce strategic management processes would get nowhere. Thus, we are making the point that individual organizations in the public sector may need organizational development plans if they are to stand a reasonable chance of successful strategic management.

Bryson (2004: 82) recommends the assessment of organizational readiness should cover 'current mission; its budget, financial management, human resource, information technology, and communications systems; its leadership and management capabilities; the expected costs and benefits of a strategic planning process; and ways of overcoming any expected barriers'. He also suggests three possible options at the end of the assessment – proceed with strategic planning, improve the organization's readiness, or choose to give up on the idea of strategic planning.

Third, the body or committee should consider, in general terms, what type of strategic planning process it thinks will suit the circumstances. It could, for example, consider emphasizing strategic performance management or strategic issue management. It could consider some form of inter-organizational strategic planning. For a public services organization that is relatively inexperienced in the use of strategic processes, it may be unwise to go immediately to a process involving scenario planning and comprehensive corporate planning. It may be better to start off with strategic issue management, use it to solve a visible strategic issue successfully, and thereby build the credibility of strategic processes in the eyes of organizational members. At the same time, of course, success in strategic issue management builds the credibility of the strategic leaders of the organization, so that when they say they want to engage in some longer term, more comprehensive, strategic planning there is some confidence built up within the organization that these leaders are capable of successfully leading a strategy process.

RESPONSIVE STRATEGIC PLANNING

As a result of public services reforms, more and more strategic leaders want to ensure that what their organization delivers is not only important to politicians, but also creates public value in the eyes of those who use the services. Strategic planning needs to be adapted to suit this more responsive posture for the public services. How can more account be taken of service users for strategic planning in public services? First, there are lessons from private sector approaches that are customer centred. Second, there is expeditionary marketing. Third, there is a programme planning model. Fourth, there is the use of a whole systems development model. Each of these is described in a little more detail below.

LESSONS FROM THE PRIVATE SECTOR

One lesson is to make more use of data on service users. Public services organizations are often poor at using data on service users even if the data actually exists and even if public services managers say they understand the importance of collecting and using it. It is not clear why it is so difficult to get public services managers to use data on those who use the service for strategic planning purposes. Perhaps it is because, in practice, many of them see the service primarily from the perspective of the provider, do this as a matter of habit and simply forget to empathize with the service user.

Asking the right questions is the key in getting the right data and making the most of it. So what questions should be asked about service users? Osborne and Gaebler (1992: 174) present a set of questions which they attributed to an American police service chief called David Coupar. His questions have been generalized for use by any strategic leader in the public services.

1 What important service user needs are there in your area?
2 How do you find out what they are?
3 What methods can you use to find out?
4 What are you going to do to address problems identified by service users?
5 How successful have you been in solving the problems and meeting the needs?

When looking at service user needs it is important not to take at face value what the public say they want (or do not want) of a service. When the analysis of the data produces an answer on what the public wants, the next step in strategic thinking is to ask 'why?'. This will produce an answer in the form of 'the public wants this in order to . . .'. The next step is to repeat the 'why?' question, but now in respect of the new answer. Again, this produces yet another statement of what it is the public wants (the public want this in order to . . .). The process is repeated until no more new answers can be generated. As a result, the strategic leader will have a more complex view of the structure of what the public wants. For example, members of the public may object to planning permission being given to replace a single family home on a large plot of land by a block of flats. In this case we know what the public does not want, but why do they feel like this? It may be that the public who are objecting are worrying about the extra traffic congestion it will produce. By eliciting the underlying concern, the public service authority then has an additional range of possibilities for handling this situation. For example, perhaps there needs to be action to reduce traffic congestion.

It is also useful to think about what the private sector calls customer segmentation. It is useful because it helps those doing strategic planning to avoid unwarranted assumptions that each public service satisfies an obvious and single standard need. A customer segment is a group of customers who are of the same type. The type may be defined using personal characteristics that are familiar to planners of public services (gender, age, disability), but perhaps identifying customer segments should be approached with more of an open mind about the relevant characteristics. Having identified groups of customers the next step is to check out the distinct needs of each group in relation to a specific service. For example, it is sometimes said that women have a different interest in good street lighting than do men because of women's frequent concerns about their safety in using the streets of cities at night. People using a free public library, to take another example, might have very different motives depending on the type of person they are. Some library users may be students who need a quiet place to study, whereas retired people may want to borrow books to entertain themselves.

It is possible to build on customer segmentation to develop a 'customer service matrix'. This matrix cross-tabulates customer segments and public services; customer segments may form the columns and services form the rows. This can be used in a range of ways, for example it is possible to map which services are delivered to which customer segments. It will then be obvious if there are gaps in the services that are provided to some of the segments. The obvious follow up questions are: (1) would a specific type of customer benefit from having a service that it does not currently receive, and (2) is it feasible to extend this service to this group of customers?

This focus on the needs of the service users can be built into strategic planning in the following way. The process of strategic planning can start off by a search which involves market research and includes looking at what customer needs and the future social trends are. In this model of strategic planning, market research is really the first step. This is followed by a visioning step. At the third step the leaders involve employees. Then the planning turns to the creation of new standards and new services. Fifth, implementation planning is carried out in respect of roles, skills, organizational structures etc. When the change has been implemented, the final step is the evaluation of the results. This is a fairly logical and straightforward approach to strategic planning, but it begins with getting and analysing data on customer needs (Thurley and Wirdenius 1989).

EXPEDITIONARY MARKETING

The expeditionary marketing approach is based on trying out a strategic action that has not had the benefit of market research, but has been through a strategic planning process to identify feasible strategic action. After the strategic plan has been implemented, the organization carries out research into the reactions of the users of the public services affected by the strategic action. This is a simple reversal of the conventional model where the research is done first and then comes the strategic plan. This approach is potentially useful where the services are innovative ones and the service users find it difficult to articulate their needs and yet are able to give an opinion based on experiences of actual services. For example, the approach might be tried for services aimed at some specific groups such as people with learning disabilities.

PROGRAMME PLANNING MODEL

The programme planning model was used in the 1970s. In this approach, the public service begins with a step in which service users are helped in a workshop to identify and rank the problems that they are having with a service. The next step is to present the problems to the professionals who deliver the services. Importantly, sessions in which the professionals try to find solutions are attended by some external experts to bring a more detached view to the process of trying to identify solutions. The solutions generated by the professionals are then tested for their acceptability to the top decision makers who are responsible for the policies, strategies and budgetary decisions of the organization. If the solutions are not acceptable to these resource controllers, because of clashes with policies and strategies of the organization, these are dropped from further consideration. If any of the solutions are considered good ones, this process makes it possible for the organization to modify the strategic plan or strategic goals to make them compatible with the solutions. This kind of approach is consistent with what John Bryson called backward mapping. Backward mapping is essentially starting from an initiative to solve a problem (being proposed by professionals at or near the front-line of service delivery) and mapping back to strategies and the policies, and then making adjustments in them.

WHOLE SYSTEMS DEVELOPMENT

The increasing realization that good strategic decisions are based on as much consensus as possible has led some public service organizations to experiment with whole system events or large-scale strategic planning events to make a direct bid for a consensus. Such events can involve members of the public, representatives of partner organizations, as well as professionals and front-line staff. Mulgan (2007: Ev13) has made a specific statement in support of involving front-line staff, '. . . in all strategy work I would certainly encourage the close involvement of front-line staff, the people who have to live with it . . .'. A strong plea for involving a wide range of people was made by Sir Michael Bichard (2007: Ev17), who told a Parliamentary Select Committee:

> . . . strategic thinking happens when you involve a wide range of people with different experiences and approaches, because every strategic issue is a function of connectivity and it should not be a black art and it should not be done behind closed doors and public servants should be accountable.

Whole systems development events are interesting large-scale interactions of key stakeholder groups, in this case aimed at agreeing a strategic plan for a public services organization. They can be carried out with 200 or 300 people. The key stakeholders, taking the example of a local authority, can include elected politicians, managers, professionals, front-line staff, representatives of organizations with overlapping mandates and members of the public. The event might last one or more days. It could begin with the presentation of a draft strategic plan, including strategic vision and strategic goals. The various stakeholders, internal and external, could then be asked to react or respond to what they have heard. In turn, the top leaders of the organization are asked to respond to the views and judgements of professionals, front-line staff, those who use the services covered by the strategic plan, etc. The response of the leaders should take the form of proposals to revise the strategic vision and plan in order to take account of the stakeholders' contributions. In this way whole systems development planning enables service users to be involved at a very early stage, and actually involved in the development of strategic visions and plans. If the users are involved before strategic vision and plans are fixed, and when ideas are still very fluid, it may be hoped that their voice would influence in a significant way the development of the strategic vision and plans. Ideally, whole systems development events might be used to create strategic plans which are genuinely customer centric.

Whereas the programme planning model should ensure that strategic planning takes a consumer perspective, since it is focused on resolving the problems identified by service users, the whole system development event endeavours to modify the strategic visions and plans produced by leaders of the government organization by ensuring that stakeholders have their voices heard and the leaders respond to what they hear. Although it is very obvious if the strategic leaders in a whole systems development event are trying to avoid responding to uncomfortable feedback by stakeholders, the fact is that the leaders start the conversational process by outlining a leadership vision and plan. In this sense, these two techniques are quite different. On the face of it, it would seem that the programme planning model could support bottom-up innovation, whereas whole system development events could be seen as a more top-down approach, although it must be stressed that whole systems development processes do encourage the top strategic leaders to learn from those in front-line service delivery and from the public who use the services.

CASE STUDY

South Australia

The state of South Australia produced a strategic plan in 2004 called 'Creating Opportunity'. This plan had a number of sections to it: first, it set out objectives; second, it set out the current situation ('Where are we now'); third, it set out the targets the state wanted to achieve; fourth, it set out performance indicators; fifth, it set out priority actions; and, lastly, it set out who was responsible for the priority actions. So, the strategic plan provided not only a statement of strategic objectives, actions and performance requirements, but also information important for the management of the implementation of the action.

The plan had six objectives and 79 targets. Its objectives were:

1 growing prosperity
2 improving well-being
3 attaining stability
4 fostering creativity
5 building communities
6 expanding opportunity.

These sound like desired outcomes rather than outputs.

Questions for discussion

1 Was anything important missing from the list of contents?
2 What do you think of the six objectives – do you think these were suitable for a state government in Australia?

FROM STRATEGIC PLANNING TO STRATEGIC MANAGEMENT

During the 1970s, books on private sector management began to use the term 'strategic management' in preference to 'strategic planning'. This was done by some writers to underline the need in the 1970s to pay attention to the management of implementation of strategy, as well as the goal setting and analysis used to select strategic action. The reason for this increased attention to implementation might be attributed to at least two separate concerns. First, the business environment of the 1970s was much more volatile than that which had existed in the 1950s and 1960s, which were generally years of growth. Simple extrapolations of trends in the 1970s were less useful than they had been for planning purposes, and strategic leaders had to cope with more unpredictable circumstances and discontinuities. Logically, this implied that implementation needed more attention as adjustments were needed during the implementation phase and as lessons were learnt during implementation. Second, some of the early writers on strategic planning had also begun to realize that they had underestimated the degree to which implementation was also affected by resistance to change. It might even be said by some that strategic implementation was the most important stage of the process. One way of summing this up is to say that strategic implementation processes needed to be taken seriously and that, therefore, strategic management was strategic planning processes plus strategic implementation processes.

In fact, many of those who talk about strategic planning in the public services context are also concerned about effective implementation, and may simply be choosing to use a more widely used and familiar term – they are probably not using the term 'strategic planning' to suggest that implementation is unimportant.

SUMMARY

In this chapter we have looked at the existence of different types of strategic planning. We noted the existence of a type concerned with performance and results, and a type that seemed to be more tailored to the public sector and which was suited to strategic change and innovation. In relation to the latter type of strategic planning, we briefly examined the concept of public value that was actually anchored within Moore's discussion of the strategic triangle with its three elements to be aligned through strategic planning.

We looked at the benefits of strategic planning and management in the public services, which include helping managers to set direction and milestones, to make budget decisions and to improve the delivery of high-quality public services.

The chapter briefly reviewed methods of achieving responsiveness to service users through strategic planning. There is more than one way of including them in strategic plan development in the public services. We first explored lessons from the private sector and its approach to understanding customer needs. The use of the word 'customer' in the public services is sometimes controversial. Of course, this word can even be confusing when describing those who consume public services, but it has been justified at times by the need to underline the point that public services should serve the public. Within the discussion of responsiveness, we emphasized the importance of careful study of the needs of the public, and the use of what is called customer segmentation, and on the back of this how to review services and beneficiaries using a 'customer service matrix'. We also considered expeditionary marketing, the programme planning model and the whole systems development approach. The latter two were briefly described, and compared with each other in terms of their approximation to bottom-up and top-down processes.

The chapter was concluded by drawing attention to the distinction between strategic management and strategic planning. In brief, it was argued that strategic management is concerned with the development of strategic plans (strategic planning) and their successful implementation.

Work-based assignment: evaluation of public value

The work-based assignments in this book are for civil servants and other public services staff who have management experience.

This assignment is a qualitative study of the public value created by a public services organization you work for or you know well. It has three stages. First, investigate the needs, desires and aspirations of the service users who currently use the service or services. Second, assess the 'functionality' of the service or services – what needs, desires or aspirations does it actually meet currently? Third, compare the findings of the first two stages and comment on the public value being produced by the public services organization.

Work-based assignment: evaluation of the current strategy of a public services organization

Investigate and write up the following aspects of the public service organization you work for or you know well:

■　The strategic goals of the organization and the social needs addressed
■　The external support enjoyed by the organization
■　The structure, culture and capabilities of the organization
■　The strategic plan.

Assess the effectiveness of the strategic plan in aligning the goals, external support and capacities of the organization. Identify, if you can, any reasons for deficiencies in the alignments of these three aspects – is a reason, for example, a poorly designed strategic plan or a poorly implemented strategic plan?

DISCUSSION QUESTIONS

1　Do public services require their own version of strategic planning? What should be different or special about strategic planning and management in the public services?
2　Is the concept of 'public value' useful, and how does it help in thinking about or doing strategic planning?

 206

3   Is the evidence in favour of using strategic planning and management in the public services compelling? Please justify your opinion.
4   Is the public sufficiently involved with the process of strategic planning in public services? Are there viable methods for involving the public in strategic planning and could they be 'rolled out' generally?
5   Do we need to make a distinction between strategic planning and strategic management in the public services? If yes, what is the difference?

FURTHER READING

Ferlie E. and Ongaro, E. (2015) *Strategic Management in Public Services Organizations: Concepts, Schools and Contemporary Issues.* Abingdon: Routledge.

This book might provide useful background understanding to some of the material covered in this chapter. It focuses on different schools of thought about strategic management. It also contains a significant argument about the importance of context and suggests how successful strategic management can be transferred from one context to another.

REFERENCE LIST

Berry, F. S. and Wechsler, B. (1995) State agencies' experience with strategic planning: findings from a national survey. *Public Administration Review*, 55: 159–68.

Bichard, M. (2007) 'Oral evidence', in House of Commons Public Administration Select Committee, *Governing the Future, Second Report of Session 2006–07*, Volume II, HC123-II. London: The Stationery Office Limited.

Bryson, J. M. (2004) *Strategic Planning for Public and Nonprofit Organizations: A Guide to Strengthening and Sustaining Organizational Achievement.* 3rd edition. San Francisco, CA: Jossey-Bass.

Collier, N., Fishwick, F. and Johnson, G. (2001) 'The processes of strategy development in the public sector', in G. Johnson and K. Scholes (eds) *Exploring Public Sector Strategy.* Harlow: Pearson Education.

Eadie, D. C. (1983) Putting a powerful tool to practical use: the application of strategic planning in the public sector. *Public Administration Review*, 43: 447–52.

Flynn, N. and Talbot, C. (1996) Strategy and strategists in UK local government. *Journal of Management Development*, 15: 24–37.

Frost-Kumpf, L., Wechsler, B., Ishiyama, H. J. and Backoff, R. W. (1993) 'Strategic action and transformational change: the Ohio Department of Mental Health', in B. Bozeman (ed.) *Public Management*. San Francisco, CA: Jossey-Bass.

Gordon, G. (2005) From vision to implementation: the changing state of strategic planning. *Public Management*, 87(8): 26–8.

Heymann, P. B. (1987) *The Politics of Public Management.* London: Yale University Press.

Joyce, P. (2000) *Strategy in the Public Sector: A Guide to Effective Change Management.* Chichester: Wiley.

Miles, R. E. and Snow, C. C. (1978) *Organizational Strategy, Structure, and Process.* London: McGraw-Hill.

Moore, M. (1995) *Creating Public Value: Strategic Management in Government.* London: Harvard University Press.

Mulgan, G. (2007) 'Oral evidence', in House of Commons Public Administration Select Committee, *Governing the Future, Second Report of Session 2006–07*, Volume II, HC123-II. London: The Stationery Office Limited.

Osborne, D. and Gaebler, T. (1992) *Reinventing Government: How the Entrepreneurial Spirit is Transforming the Public Sector.* Reading, MA: Addison-Wesley.

Poister, T. H. and Streib, G. D. (2005) Elements of strategic planning and management in municipal government: status after two decades. *Public Administration Review*, 65(1): 45–56.

Sorkin, D. L., Ferris, N. B. and Hudak, J. (1985) *Strategies for Cities and Counties, A Strategic Planning Guide.* Washington, DC: Public Technology.

Thurley, K. and Wirdenius, H. (1989) *Towards European Management.* Pitman Publishing, London.

Toft, G. S. (2000) 'Synoptic (One Best Way) approaches of strategic management', in J. Rabin, G. J. Miller and W. B. Hildreth (eds) *Handbook of Strategic Management.* 2nd edition. New York: Marcel Dekker.

US General Accounting Office (1996) *Executive Guide: Effectively Implementing the Government Performance and Results Act*, GAO/GGD-96-118, Washington, DC.

Chapter 9

Implementation

LEARNING OBJECTIVES

■ To seek a better understanding of how to make strategic implementation successful

■ To examine the planning of strategic implementation

INTRODUCTION

Nowadays, a frequently made assertion is that implementation of strategy is harder than strategy formulation. This assertion was supported by evidence from a survey of 11 national libraries, including those in Australia, Britain, Canada, France, Germany, Ireland, New Zealand, Malaysia, the Netherlands, Singapore and the United States (Chalmers 1997). The most serious implementation problems appeared to be setting budget priorities in line with strategic priorities, and making changes in the competencies of staff and managers if required for the implementation of a strategy. Two critical sets of resources (financial and human) were not easily aligned with strategy. Summing up the significance of the survey, the analytical aspects of strategy are easier than strategic implementation.

Implementing strategy is not only hard to do, it is often unsatisfactory as well. A 2007 review of civil service capability in the UK made the following generalization (Capability Reviews Team 2007: 44): 'The reviews found excellent practice in setting direction and in developing outcome-focused strategy, but poorer performance on translating this consistently into delivery'.

At the present time, there are civil servants and public services managers in a number of countries who are struggling with implementation of strategy. They may have a sophisticated or a rudimentary knowledge of how strategic planning is supposed to work on paper, but they know successful implementation is not easily achieved. They wonder what they need to do to make strategic implementation work in their own organization with its specific history, culture, habits, pressures and problems. So, to some degree, they are struggling with not only understanding the theory of strategic planning but, probably more importantly, they want to understand how they can deliver it in practice.

In private sector oriented management books the concern with implementation emerged in the 1970s, when the name 'strategic management' started to displace the earlier name of 'strategic planning'. Until then, books on corporate strategy focused on formulating strategies and gave little attention to the learning that could occur during implementation or the need to address conflicting interests and resistance to new strategies. It was later in the 1980s and 1990s that there was more appreciation of the importance of the work of turning strategic plans into concrete action. One response to this might be to call for the management of implementation, beginning with the planning in detail of the strategic actions, responsibilities for action, budgets and the timing of actions. It could also require supporting the implementation of strategic action with communication by leaders, training, targets and rewards. For example, Hussey (1999) gave the following advice for managing strategic implementation:

1 Provide a vision statement of what the business will be like after change.
2 Involve others to get commitment to the changes; do this by holding meetings to explain the vision and plan the detail of the change.
3 Give support through training and coaching.
4 Plan and manage the actions needed to implement the strategy and align budgets and measure progress.
5 Monitor and control and set up special systems to do this.
6 Recognize those who make implementation successful by rewarding and thanking them.

Stonich (1982), basing an approach on consultancy experience, highlighted culture, organizational structure, management processes and human resources as key areas for the implementation of strategy (see Figure 9.1).

CULTURE

Culture is a much used word by leaders in public services. There is some research on it in the public services. Pettigrew, Ferlie and McKee (1992) identified organizational culture as one of the factors as they attempted to characterize receptive contexts. They did not think cultural change was easy to bring about, and they seemed to think that some organizational cultures enabled change, and some were an impediment to change.

Usually, organizational culture is equated to beliefs, expectations, values and norms. In former times there were public services leaders who were keen on employee programmes to inculcate new values and thus change the culture of the organization. Some saw the culture as the essence of the emotional life of an organization. If cultures develop over periods of time they can be seen as learnt from past experience, from both successes and failures. Culture can also be seen

210

Figure 9.1 *Implementation factors*

as a factor in the capacity of a public service organization, sitting alongside capabilities, helping to shape what people in the organization are willing or unwilling to do on the basis of their taken-for-granted assumptions and values (Heymann 1987).

Conversations and meetings may provide strategic leaders with the data they use to typify their organization's culture. It may be that often mentioned incidents from several years ago, or often repeated phrases that crop up over and over again in conversation, provide insights to the strategic leader on the nature of this culture. For example, the organization's top management may have taken a major decision five years ago with an impact on those who work in the organization, and people may often refer to this incident to explain or analyse everything that is happening now. The actions of top management may have been evaluated positively or negatively, but the incident is thought to say something important about the nature of the organization and how it can be expected to act. Front-line service managers may constantly, for example, use the word 'protective' to describe their responsibilities in relation to the staff; the word is repeated so often that it is clear that this is regarded as a norm for how front-line managers should behave.

What attitude could a leader have towards organizational culture during strategic implementation? Logically, the leader can ignore it and hope that it changes appropriately as a result of changes occurring because of strategic actions. If this approach is taken and the culture is a very strong impediment, a strategic leader may even feel during implementation that the culture is splintering the strategy. A second attitude is for the leader to make adjustments to the strategy to fit it to the existing culture, and, therefore, strategy is accommodating the culture. Third, the leader can try to change the culture using a range of

211

methods including, for example, human resources (HR) systems for recruiting new individuals who have the desired values and beliefs, and using reward systems to alter what is perceived as valuable.

ORGANIZATIONAL DIMENSION

Bryson (2004: 270) defined strategic management systems as 'ongoing organizational mechanisms or arrangements for strategically managing the implementation of agreed-upon strategies, assessing the performance of those strategies, and formulating new or revised strategies'. He provided a sketch of six different types of strategic management systems including ones we might say were appropriate for partnership situations and for use with market mechanisms; these were:

1 Integrated units of management
2 Strategic issues management
3 Contract
4 Collaboration
5 Portfolio management
6 Goal or benchmark.

The first of these systems seeks to integrate strategies at different levels and across functions. Bryson gave the following overview of the second system (Bryson 2004: 277):

> In this [strategic issues management] system, strategic guidance is issued at the top, and units further down are asked to identify issues they think are strategic. Leaders and managers at the top then select the issues they wish to have addressed, perhaps reframing the issues before passing them on to units or task forces. Task forces then present strategic alternatives to leaders and managers, who select which ones to pursue. Strategies are then implemented in the next phase. Each issue is managed separately, although it is important to make sure choices in one issue do not cause trouble in other issue areas.

The contract system is where one organization contracts other organizations to provide public services. Bryson suggests that both those commissioning and those providing public services use strategic plans. To Bryson's remarks on this type of system might be added the speculation that the concerns of the commissioning organizations' and providers' strategic plans are likely to be very different. For example, the commissioning organizations are likely to require strategic plans that maximize political support, and the provider organizations are likely to require strategic plans that focus on competitive advantage issues.

This contract system is also featured in Osborne and Gaebler's 1992 book, *Reinventing Government*. In it, they suggested the need to split steering (in effect, strategic planning) from rowing (service delivery), and to split regulation from enforcement. This split of steering and rowing was supposed to enable a more holistic approach to be developed, and to enable the introduction of competition in the provision of public services. Essentially, they were arguing for more multi-organizational systems and a move away from hierarchical linkages to the use of other coordination mechanisms, including commissioning and contracting to deliver services. This movement from organization based on hierarchy, perhaps, is partially conveyed in words such as 'steering' (rather than top-down command and control forms of directing) and 'governance' (rather than government).

Bryson's fourth type of system, the collaboration approach, may be partially underpinned by contracts, but in this case the emphasis is not on competitive contracting and may involve no organization being 'fully in charge'.

The portfolio management system is where, for example, the organization treats its activities or units as independent and makes corporate judgements about them individually on the basis of their attractiveness and importance (e.g. market share).

The final system is termed a goal or benchmark model. Bryson sees this as a system in which there is only loose integration between a set of organizations. He thinks that this system is suited to shared power environments and that it is used in most community strategic plans. It does offer some integration of participating organizations (Bryson 2004: 281):

> It is designed to gain reasonable agreement on overarching goals or indicators (benchmarks) toward which relatively independent groups, units, or organizations might then direct their energies. The consensual agreement on goals and indicators can function somewhat like the corporate control exercised in integrated models, although it is of course weaker.

Obviously, strategic implementation would be managed in very different ways for each of these six systems.

MANAGEMENT AND MANAGEMENT SYSTEMS

The PA Consulting Group highlighted management systems in its evaluation study of the Strategic Management Initiative launched by the Irish government in 1994. PA Consulting Group identified three management systems: human resources management (HRM), financial management and information systems (IS) management. The report stressed the importance of improving all these three areas: 'These three components are critical enablers of change ...' (PA Consulting Group 2002: 5). The study found that the management systems had not been fully developed by the time of the evaluation. Taking the case of HRM first, some weaknesses in the system included failure to tackle under-performance and lack of ability to recognize and reward good performance. In the case of financial management systems, one problem was the meagre financial commentary in Statements of Strategy. In the case of the IS manage-ment system, the report quotes the views of some of the managers in the Irish civil service that 'the part IT has to play in effecting change within SMI/DBG [i.e. two government reform programmes] is not fully appreciated at top management level' (*ibid.*: 77). Although not stated explicitly in the report, all of these management systems can be important for the implementation of strategy and for public services reform.

Recognition of the importance of management systems can be seen in the approach taken by the United States government when introducing strategic planning into federal government on a systematic basis. In this case it was quite clear that the intention was to forge a strong bond between strategic planning and performance measurement and management. In the case of France, in recent years, the drive in the public services in central government has been to link performance measurement and budgeting on the basis of a focus on mission. The same trend towards linking and integrating management systems is to be found in local government in the United States. Gordon (2005), drawing on much practical experience from American local government, stressed the trend to integrate strategic plans with budgetary and performance measurement sys-tems. Whereas, in the early 1990s, managers in local government in the United States were just beginning to use the concept of strategic planning in their services, a decade later, he reports 'local governments are becoming keenly aware that the vision and strategies of the strategic plan must be incorporated into budget preparation, review and approval' (Gordon 2005: 27).

Gordon illustrates this with the example of Worcester city government (Massachusetts).

> Simultaneous to the strategic planning initiative, a performance-based budgeting system was established internally for Worcester city government that identified service delivery inputs, outputs and departmental outcomes. These were linked to departmental performance, budget priorities and financial allocations. The system identified costs, benefits, efficiencies and constraints of municipal dollars and services. Goals, objectives and strategies of Strategic Plan 2000 were all tied to performance budgeting so that citizen priorities would be addressed when municipal departments established the annual agendas.
>
> (Gordon 2005: 27)

It is possible that some management systems are important in part because they ensure 'buy in' from managers in an organization, and their 'buy in' is important if implementation is going to be pursued with any vigour. For example, one way to get the managers motivated to implement strategic plans is to use the performance management system to integrate the individual objectives of managers and the strategic goals of the organization. This integration means at least two things: first, setting individual objectives for managers based on the strategic plan and, second, basing annual evaluations of the performance of managers on the contribution they make to accomplish the strategic goals. There is evidence from a major study of strategic planning in US local government that suggests that these two things help to improve the impact of strategic plans (Poister and Streib 2005).

Strategic leaders must also take care how they integrate budgetary processes with strategic planning. Integration may be achieved by timing the budget decisions to follow shortly in time after strategic decisions in the strategic planning process. But then strategic leaders need to communicate the strategic decisions effectively to managers so that the tight time linkage of strategic and budget decisions is reinforced by budget decisions being better understood, and thus, hopefully, the budgets are well managed. If managers do not understand, or are unaware of, the strategic decisions, then there will be problems in how budget decisions are implemented. If there is no tight linkage between strategic and budget decisions, the evidence from a study by Goodwin and Kloot (1996) of six Australian and New Zealand local authorities suggests this may be a result of the organization having traditional incremental decision making with budget decisions shaping the strategy (see Research Box 9.1).

RESEARCH BOX 9.1   STRATEGIC PLANNING AND BUDGETING PROCESSES

Goodwin and Kloot (1996) carried out interviews in three New Zealand local authorities and three Australian local authorities to investigate the relationships between strategic communication, budgetary response attitude and budgetary role ambiguity. They defined these concepts as follows:

- Strategic communication – this was communication of decisions made within the strategic process to managers
- Budgetary response attitude – this attitude could be one of support, withheld support or sabotage of the budget
- Budgetary role ambiguity – this was not having the information needed to carry out the budgetary role.

In the Australian cases, strategic planning and budgetary processes were only loosely linked, with a time gap, and often with no link at all reported. In the three New Zealand cases, they found that there was a tight link between strategic planning and the budgetary process. They reported that the strategic plan was first revised, followed closely by changes to the budget.

Their analysis of the data for New Zealand cases (tight linkages between strategic and budgetary processes) indicated that strategic communication was positively associated with budgetary response attitude. This could mean that managers were more supportive of the budget when they had received more communication on the decisions made within the strategic process. Furthermore, this positive relationship appeared to exist because communications on strategic decisions reduced the ambiguity or uncertainty of the managers in how they should understand and manage budget decisions.

Their analysis of the Australian cases (loose linkages between strategic and budgetary processes) also found that strategic communication and supportive budgetary response attitudes were positively associated, but in these cases it did not occur because of a reduction in budgetary role ambiguity.

What sense can be made of this? Goodwin and Kloot (1996: 202) draw attention to the nature of the budgetary process in the Australian cases, suggesting that incremental budgeting explained the results observed, and pointing out that budgeting decisions were informing or shaping strategy:

> For the Australian setting, however, while the processes were not found to be as tightly linked as those in the New Zealand bodies, in each case the planning was incremental and budgeting led the development of strategy. So long as no information was received that suggested a change in strategic direction was needed, budgeting allocations were seemingly predictable.

To sum up, strategic communications to managers with budgetary management responsibilities seems like a good idea, and seems to foster positive attitudes on their part to the budget decisions. In the case of local authorities that have tight linkages between strategy and budget processes, and in which the strategy shapes the budget, the strategic communication reduces uncertainty and ambiguity in the minds of the managers about how they should manage their budgets, thereby creating positive attitudes towards the budget.

There is evidence from Poister and Streib's (2005) study that the budgeting process, performance measurement and performance management were important influences on the impact of strategic planning. Conversely, their study implied that strategic plans have less impact if they are not integrated with budgetary decisions and performance measurement. This idea can be seen as implicit in Vinzant and Vinzant's (1996) model of four levels of strategic management capacity (see Figure 9.2).

In the Poister and Streib survey of US cities (2005: 49) only a third had got to level three as shown by having a budget tied to strategic priorities, and only a fifth had reached level four as indicated by using performance measures to track results against strategic goals and objectives.

216

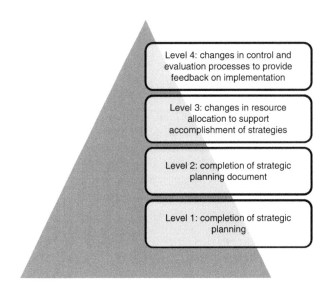

Figure 9.2 *Vinzant and Vinzant (1996) – levels of strategic management capacity*

There is also an issue about which of the systems (strategic planning, budgeting, and performance measurement and management) should take precedence over the others. So, even if the three are integrated, which system is determining or steering what is done? Ideally, strategic planning, with its concern for foresight and for being clear about the benefits (outcomes) to be delivered to the public service users and others, together with its concern for basing planning of action on a robust strategic analysis of the situation, should be steering both the performance management system and the budget allocation system. Looking at some experiences of public services strategic planning, it is possible to imagine that strategic planning is being used to supplement old fashioned incremental budgeting or even new style performance budgeting. This is the case where central government departments and public service organizations are, first and foremost, given performance targets and budget allocations and told to deliver those performance targets with the budget allocated. With this as the central top-down pressure on departments and organizations, it leaves public services leaders, at best, trying to get extra 'leverage' in their efforts by drawing on strategic planning ideas and techniques. Even in this scenario, it may still be the case that strategic planning processes and techniques can make an important contribution to reform and improvement of the public services. But there is a question to be answered about whether this use of strategic planning can achieve as much as would be achieved by an implementation system in which strategic planning was steering the performance management and the budgeting process. In the case of the UK between 1998 and 2010, for example, were performance targets driving central government departments, executive agencies and local government, or were strategic plans addressing cross-cutting issues and delivering outcomes that mattered?

HRM

Strategic implementation requires that people in the organization have appropriate skills and the motivation to deliver the strategy. In larger organizations, these requirements may be addressed through formal recruitment and selection processes and through human resource development programmes. As a result of a new strategy, an organization may well prepare new job descriptions, and these would be used in recruitment and selection and for training and development purposes.

PROJECTS, PILOTS, LEARNING AND CONFLICT

In recent years project management became a more important tool as more managers in public services found themselves leading strategic changes. They turned to project management as a useful process for structuring the planning of implementation of strategic projects.

At face value, project management is a relatively simple process. It involves clarifying the project's goals, identifying the activities that make up the project and allocating responsibility for each activity to a manager; setting the start and finish dates of each activity; and assessing the activities in terms of their budgetary implications and, therefore, working out a project budget. It is quite possible that skills in executing project management have increased in recent years, especially in those public services organizations that have been at the forefront of modernization efforts.

Bryson (2004) provided a useful discussion about the use of different methods of strategic implementation in organizations with multiple sites. He drew attention to the fact that, in such organizations, it is possible to introduce strategic changes in one or more sites and then extend the implementation of the changes to the remaining sites later. As an example of this, when the US government passed legislation in 1993 requiring federal agencies to produce strategic and performance plans, the Act required that at least ten agencies or departments be pilots for the use of annual performance plans and programme performance reports. (Interestingly, there was no requirement for pilot projects for the strategic plans.) These pilots were to take place over the years 1994–6, prior to the requirement that all agencies submit strategic plans and annual performance plans in late 1997.

In essence, Bryson suggested designing the appropriate implementation process using one or more of the following: pilot projects, demonstration projects and direct implementation. The choice and design of approach is based upon an assessment of the technical and political difficulty of the change process.

218

In cases where the political difficulty of the change is relatively low, but there are significant technical difficulties, this could be a good situation for a pilot project. This allows changes to be tried out in one site, and then the experience of this first pilot project is studied and evaluated. Bryson (2004: 262) advised that 'in the early stages, when the practical nature of the changes still needs to be worked out, it is important to attract implementers with enough experience, skill and desire to make the changes work'. One way to attract implementers with the desire to make it work is to call for sites to volunteer as pilots. The lessons learnt from the pilot project may be incorporated in the proposed strategic change so that the technical difficulties are reduced when implementation is extended.

In cases where there is some modest or low level of technical difficulty but significant political difficulty (e.g. some groups have expressed some degree of opposition to the proposed strategic change), leaders can consider a trial of the change in one site. As already noted, Bryson suggests careful attention to site selection. A site might be selected because it seemed to be the most likely to be receptive to the strategic change, and because it has the experience and capability of making a success of implementation. So, the strategic change is implemented at a favourable site, and then the project is used to reduce the opposition of those who were wavering or uncertain, for example, about the feasibility or its consequences. In other words, a demonstration project is carried out not so much because the organization does not know enough about how to carry out a strategic change, but because leaders want to prove to others that the strategic change is feasible and can be beneficial. Such a demonstration project is aimed, therefore, at overcoming some of the resistance to the change that exists.

In situations where the technical and political difficulty of the change are both relatively low, then leaders should consider the use of direct implementation, which is where changes are implemented at all sites at the same time. If the amount of resistance to proposed changes is massive, leaders might still consider a direct implementation approach, the idea being that direct implementation right across the board, in all parts of the organization, means that the resistance or opposition cannot be concentrated on one site. So, the resistance has to be spread right across the board and may, therefore, be more easily overcome.

One final situation will be considered. This is where there is some political difficulty, but not a high level, and some technical difficulty as well. Leaders might consider starting with a pilot project, or a set of pilot projects, to learn the lessons necessary to reduce the technical difficulties involved. Then they could launch a demonstration project to show that it is possible to implement the change successfully. Finally, the change could be implemented in other sites.

Even where there is no formal piloting of strategic changes in order to learn lessons, there is an important argument that those responsible for strategy implementation should keep an open mind when monitoring the implementation process, and should be ready to learn as they implement.

Is there a willingness to learn, during the process of implementation, by listening to stakeholders and revising the strategy as appropriate? The process of strategy implementation provides an ideal opportunity for learning and revising the strategy if management listens to staff and other stakeholders. Failure to do so can result in lost opportunity and may even prove more costly for the organization in the long term.

(Tuohy 1996: 82)

FITTING IMPLEMENTATION TO LOCAL CIRCUMSTANCES

Both local government and nationally run services that are delivered at local level often find themselves responsible for implementing strategy that has been shaped or determined nationally. It is important in these circumstances that implementation decisions are used, in effect, to refine strategy to suit the local public. The process of implementation requires many decisions to be made because the concepts and ideas contained in national strategic thinking have to be interpreted and applied locally. This fact alone means that the people who lead the implementation process can have a big impact on how the strategy turns out when it is realized. The strategy in practice is, therefore, the result of the intended strategy and its transformation into action through implementation. Seen in this way, implementation is not a neutral process of installation, but an active process of realization.

Public services managers often recognize the importance of local factors. Many Chinese government managers, for example, are highly conscious of the differences between the populations of the city areas and the populations in rural areas, and of the differences between the needs of people in the west of China compared with the people living around, say, Shanghai where economic growth has been relatively much faster. In the UK there has been an issue of an urban–rural divide, with the public living in the rural areas having felt that their specific needs are neglected by governments they thought were more interested in the needs of people living in the big cities. And, again in the UK, even populations in urban areas vary a great deal in their character and needs – within London, for example, the needs of people living in the East End are very different from those of people living in Kensington and Chelsea in the heart of the city.

So, strategy needs to be implemented in a way that applies it differently in different localities.

TECHNIQUES FOR STRATEGIC LEADERS FOR USE IN RELATION TO IMPLEMENTATION

In this section of the chapter, three very basic techniques are introduced that may be used by leaders for planning implementation of strategic actions. These techniques are stakeholder analysis, resource analysis and risk management.

220

Stakeholder analysis

Stakeholder analysis is a very simple technique to outline. However that should not fool anyone into thinking that, because it is very simple, it does not have great value. It is hard to exaggerate the value of stakeholder analysis when planning the implementation of strategic action.

Stakeholder analysis can be carried out in many different ways, but when it is being used as part of the process of planning the implementation of strategic action, it needs to address some specific issues. First, what is the relevant set of stakeholders in the case of this proposed strategic action? The point is, of course, that the set of stakeholders will vary according to the strategic action being considered. Therefore, for every major strategic action planned, you probably need to carry out a separate stakeholder analysis. It should not be assumed that stakeholders will respond always in the same way to proposed strategic action irrespective of its content. So, it is obvious that we need to question how stakeholder groups will respond to the specific strategic action we are proposing to take. Will they like the proposed action and show support and commitment to it, or will they find the proposed strategic action undesirable from their point of view?

We can graph stakeholder positioning on a strategic action using two dimensions – attitude towards the proposed action in terms of whether they are likely to assist or block strategic action, and the power of the stakeholder group. In regard to the first dimension, we can use a scale of −10 to +10. If we rate a stakeholder group as −10, this would mean that it would be very unhappy about the proposed action, and +10 would signify that it would be very pleased with the proposed action. A score of zero would indicate that it is neither in favour nor against what is being proposed. In the case of the power of the stakeholder groups, we can use a very simple rating scale, say 1 to 10 points, where 1 means that the stakeholder group is very weak, and 10 that it is very powerful. We can then plot all the stakeholders on a graph showing both how they are likely to feel about the proposed action (from against to for) and how powerful they are in relation to the proposed strategic action (see Table 9.1).

Making judgements about whether a stakeholder group is weak or powerful might involve a wide range of considerations. One might be the control a group has over a key resource that is needed for the successful implementation of the action. For example, many strategic actions need the support of the stakeholders who control the financial resources. Financial resources are often critical for the successful implementation of major strategic action. In the public services, elected politicians may be very important for this reason since it is they who have the power to approve budgetary allocations. Another key group might be professional staff working for the organization that has some special kind of expertise. Michael Crozier discussed the presence of such groups in public sector bureaucracies, and the power they have in the organizational system, in his classic book, *The Bureaucratic Phenomenon* (1964). Modern public health services contain high numbers of knowledgeable professional employees, and it is fairly

221

Table 9.1 Stakeholder analysis

Stakeholder group	Attitude towards the proposed action (−10 to +10)	Power of the stakeholder group (1 to 10)
1		
2		
3		
4		
5		
6		
7		
8		

obvious that governments are aware of the power and influence of such groups as doctors in health services. Such professionals are powerful, as we have said, by virtue of their professional expertise and they may feel very strongly that they have to be convinced about the need for strategic action before they will cooperate. So, strategic leaders cannot take their support for granted. In most countries strategic leaders cannot order highly skilled professional employees simply to implement proposed action, and time will have to be spent persuading the professionals. This is one reason why strategic planning in public services can be a slow and energy consuming process. But if this time is not invested in convincing professionals, strategic action may become stalled.

Professionals may sometimes appear individualistic, but they can also form powerful occupational groups and be very well organized. They, therefore, can respond not only individually, but also sometimes en masse to strategic change. Their power can also be expressed through their ability to lobby elected politicians through their networks. Their overall ability to exercise power and influence partly derives from their special knowledge base, partly from their high degree of organization, and partly as a result of their ability to lobby and pressurize politicians.

There may also be stakeholder groups in the community. They may have important political power bases exercised through the electoral process. Politicians may be very aware of this and nervous about ignoring the wishes of powerful constituencies in the electorate. Some groups in the public are very well organized, and capable of attracting media attention and putting pressure on the politicians through lobbying. In some localities, for example, voluntary organizations for physically disabled people can be very vocal in community level politics.

We are barely touching on the range and variety of ways in which individuals and groups can be influential and powerful. However rough and ready are the judgements made about the power and likely reactions of stakeholder groups to proposed strategic action, they are important so that leaders can think about their likely position on a strategic change, and think through the sorts of stakeholder management actions that might be deployed (Nutt and Backoff 1992).

Let us take the case of a stakeholder group that is both likely to be in opposition to a proposed strategic action, and also to have a high level of power or influence. One approach to stakeholder management in this case is to try to negotiate with the stakeholder group to see how much of an adjustment in the proposed course of action, or in the distribution of the benefits from the course of action, is needed to bring an alteration to its likely reaction to the change. It should be stressed that stakeholder management could mean changing the planned strategic action. This may be needed to get a currently antagonistic group to become, if not supportive, at least less antagonistic.

Groups that are powerful or influential, and are likely to be supportive of the proposed course of action, could be valuable in the implementation process as advocates of the action. So the strategic leadership may concentrate on trying to get supportive groups to be active advocates. This might be possible by involving influential members or representatives of the stakeholder group in the planning of the implementation of the action. This should make them feel that they are part of the change process and willing to move behind efforts to implement it.

For stakeholder groups that are basically in favour of the proposed strategic actions, but that do not have a significant amount of power or influence, then perhaps stakeholder management is best kept low key and focused on keeping them informed. The idea in this case is to maintain their favourable attitude towards the proposed strategic action. If there is a stakeholder group that is hostile to the proposed strategic actions, but does not currently have much power, stakeholder management may be aimed at not pushing them into the camp of powerful antagonistic stakeholder groups.

So, we see that stakeholder analysis and management can be used within the process of strategic implementation and is about defining the stakeholders, evaluating who they are, considering how they are likely to react, what their degree of power or influence is and then, crucially, going on to plan specific implementation actions in relation to stakeholder groups. The aim is to maximize the chances of successful implementation. As we have seen, this could include a decision to negotiate with antagonistic groups, a decision to call on active support of the spokespeople and representatives of positive stakeholder groups who support the proposed actions, a decision to keep some groups informed and briefed, and actions designed to reduce the chances of oppositional groups forming a coalition against strategic action (see Table 9.2).

Resource analysis and plan

A second aspect of planning implementation is planning the acquisition or deployment of resources as part of the realization of strategic action. Although there may have been some prior evaluation of the resources needed to make strategic action feasible – at the stage of choosing strategic action – the issue of

Table 9.2 *Stakeholder assessment and possible tactics (based on Nutt and Backoff 1992)*

Importance of stakeholder	Likely response to strategy	
	Opposition	Support
Low	Problematic stakeholders (take precautions)	Low priority stakeholders (educate them)
High	Antagonistic stakeholders (negotiate change with them)	Advocates (think about co-opting them)

resources has to be confronted again when planning implementation. Arguably, when it comes to planning implementation, even more work is needed to review and audit resources than when strategic choices are being made.

Some fairly simple questions need to be answered in order to provide the basis of an effective resource plan. As usual, the questions may seem simple, but arrival at the right answers may sometimes be more difficult. First, what types of resources are needed to implement the strategic action? The answer can take the form of a list of the basic resources needed. Second, what quantity of each of the resources is needed? We may have financing on our list, but how much money will be needed? In each case, we need a description of the resource and a calculation of how much of the resource is needed. Third, how important is the resource? If the resource is critical, it means that we cannot implement the action unless this resource is obtained. In some cases, the resource will not be critical; it may be just desirable and not essential. In other words, it is sometimes a matter of a leader feeling that ideally a specific resource is needed but, if necessary, the action can still be implemented if the resource cannot be obtained. In some cases the matter may be more complex – some level of availability of the resource is essential, but above this level the resource is desirable. For example, some level of funding could be critical, but we might be planning to obtain a level of funding beyond this because there are some desirable investments in the strategic action. Fourth, how can we obtain (buy, redeploy, borrow, access) the resources we need for the strategic action? Sometimes the resources may be obtained by bidding for funding from the organization's strategic budgets; with this funding we may then buy the needed resources from their current owners. Sometimes it may be a matter of re-using resources, which may mean freeing them up from an existing use. Sometimes the resources already exist as spare resources due to underutilized capacity, underemployed people, etc. Sometimes organizations may look for partners and external support to supplement in-house resources.

What else is involved in obtaining resources for proposed strategic action? If we currently have the resource we need, but are using it in some other way, there will need to be some kind of judgement about the relative returns from its current deployment, and returns that we would get from redeployment.

224

If stakeholders of the proposed strategic action hold the resources, you may need to think through how to turn them into partners as opposed to just stakeholders. Partnerships provide the possibility of getting access to resources that you have no intention of owning or buying, but you wish to see mobilized in support of the desired action. Persuading other organizations to engage in partnership working so you can mobilize their resources may require discussions to show they share similar goals, and that it is feasible to create synergy by combining to deliver the strategic action. If you can persuade or negotiate with stakeholders to become partners, and this allows you to mobilize the resources they control, you may then weave together the use of resources from different organizations in successful joint action.

So, summing up, the resource plan for strategic implementation begins with listing each of the resources that will be required. The plan then details how the resources might be sourced or obtained through redeployment of existing internal resources, through reallocation of budget, by buying, or by working with partners to weave together their resources with yours because they share some overall goal.

The description just offered of resource analysis and planning probably makes it all sound too easy. There will be issues in trying to resource strategic action. How can we focus our attention on the most important resource issues in implementation? We could decide in relation to each resource, first, whether it is easily or not easily obtained and, second, whether it is desirable or critical in its importance (Nutt and Backoff 1992). Obviously planning needs to be thorough, and action most determined, in relation to those resources that are not easily obtained, and which are of critical importance to the successful realization of the strategic plan (see Figure 9.3).

Risk management

Risk analysis was discussed in an earlier chapter as part of a discussion about how to choose strategic action. The suggested technique for risk analysis could be

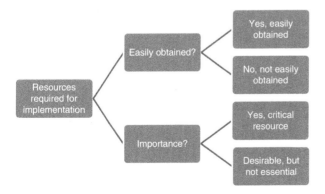

Figure 9.3 Assessing resource requirements

repeated as part of the implementation planning process to check that the strategic action had been sufficiently de-risked, and to check on the extent to which residual risk could be handled by means of contingency planning.

SUMMARY

As stated earlier in this chapter, implementation is not a neutral process of installation of strategy, but an active process of realization. In the end, the only strategic plan that matters is the one that is implemented, not the one that was intended. Interpreting the plan and making it concrete, inevitably, is more than simply imposing it as it is. Choices are always being made when making implementation decisions.

In looking at strategic implementation, this chapter looked at the familiar topics of culture, organization, management and management systems, and HRM. The discussion of the planning of implementation was explored in relation to projects and pilots, learning and conflict, and techniques for planning (stakeholder analysis, resource analysis and planning, and risk management).

Work-based assignment: planning implementation

The work-based assignments in this book are for civil servants and other public services staff who have management experience.

In this assignment you practice drawing up an action plan to implement strategic action in your own organization, or an organization you know very well. Select an idea for a strategic action. Draw up a plan using the following questions:

1 What is the name of the organizational unit or units involved?
2 To whom should reports of progress on implementation be made?
3 What is the overall strategy of which this specific action is a part?
4 What is the specific strategic action, its objectives, and the details of how it will be carried out?
5 What support or resources are needed?
6 Who is responsible for the strategic action and its component parts?
7 Who else needs to be involved?
8 When does strategic action need to be started and completed?
9 What is/are the performance indicator(s) you would recommend for monitoring purposes?
10 Do the data/management information systems currently exist to measure performance and identify performance gaps?

When you have completed the preparation of this plan, prepare some ideas for how it would be best presented to top management of your organization for approval.

DISCUSSION QUESTIONS

1 Why is strategic implementation so difficult?
2 What can be done to increase the chances of successful implementation?
3 Does a strategic leader make their most important contribution to successful implementation through planning implementation, or communicating the need for the change and the benefits that will result?
4 In addition to ideas presented in this chapter, what other things might a strategic leader do in order to manage stakeholders to make implementation a success?

FURTHER READING

Barber, M. (2015) *How to Run A Government: So that citizens benefit and taxpayers don't go crazy*. UK: Allen Lane. Chapter 2, 'Organization'.

Michael Barber was a top civil servant and Head of the UK Prime Minister's Delivery Unit between 2001 and 2005. He was responsible for making sure the government's strategic policies were implemented effectively. This model of a central unit concerned with making policy implementations more certain was much studied and sometimes copied by other governments. The chapter has some interesting figures on pages 35 and 36 concerning how to organize implementation within government. The book as a whole refers to experiences and experiments in different places, not just in the UK, including interesting case material on developments in public administration in the Punjab.

REFERENCE LIST

Bryson, J. (2004) *Strategic Planning for Public and Nonprofit Organizations: A Guide to Strengthening and Sustaining Organizational Achievement*. 3rd edition. San Francisco, CA: Jossey-Bass.

Capability Reviews Team (2007) *Capability Reviews Tranche 3: Findings and Common Themes. Civil Service – Strengths and Challenges*. London: Cabinet Office. Crown copyright. (Ref: 279915/0307/D2.4)

Chalmers, A. (1997) *Strategic Management in Eleven National Libraries: A Research Report*. Wellington: National Library of New Zealand.

Crozier, M. (1964) *The Bureaucratic Phenomenon*. Chicago, IL: The University of Chicago Press.

Goodwin, D. R. and Kloot, L. (1996) Strategic communication, budgetary role ambiguity, and budgetary response attitude in local government. *Financial Accountability and Management*, 12: 191–205.

Gordon, G. (2005) From vision to implementation: the changing state of strategic planning. *Public Management,* 87(8): 26–8.

Heymann, P. B. (1987) *The Politics of Public Management.* London: Yale University Press.

Hussey, D. (1999) *Strategy and Planning: A Manager's Guide.* Chichester: John Wiley and Sons.

Nutt, P. C. and Backoff, R. W. (1992) *Strategic Management of Public and Third Sector Organizations.* San Francisco, CA: Jossey-Bass.

Osborne, D. and Gaebler, T. (1992) *Reinventing Government: How the Entrepreneurial Spirit is Transforming the Public Sector.* Reading, MA: Addison-Wesley.

PA Consulting Group (2002) *Evaluation of the Progress of the Strategic Management Initiative/Delivering Better Government Modernisation Programme.* Dublin: PA Consulting Group.

Pettigrew, A., Ferlie, E. and McKee, L. (1992) *Shaping Strategic Change.* London: Sage.

Poister, T. H. and Streib, G. D. (2005) Elements of strategic planning and management in municipal government: status after two decades. *Public Administration Review,* 65(1): 45–56.

Stonich, P. J. (1982) *Implementing Strategy: Making Strategy Happen.* Cambridge, MA: Ballinger Publishing Company.

Tuohy, B. (1996) 'Strategic management choices and imperatives', in R. Boyle and T. McNamara (eds) *From Intent to Action: The Management of Strategic Issues in the Public Sector.* Dublin: Institute of Public Administration.

Vinzant, D. H. and Vinzant, J. (1996) Strategy and organizational capacity: finding a fit. *Public Productivity and Management Review,* 20(2): 139–57.

Chapter 10

Monitoring

LEARNING OBJECTIVES

- To investigate the monitoring of strategies
- To consider the trend towards outcome measures
- To look at various techniques relevant to monitoring including performance planning, scorecards and programme assessment

INTRODUCTION

The role of monitoring by government, or by a public sector organization, may seem completely obvious. The functions of monitoring have been to improve public governance and to serve the public better. There appears to be nothing objectionable in such functions. The public want their governments to keep their promises, get good value for taxpayers' money and run the public services professionally. How can governments tell if they are living up to these public expectations? How can governments tell if their top priorities for action are being successfully delivered? They need to obtain data on the performance of public services and measure the outcomes that are being achieved for the public. Performance data will need to be looked at on a regular basis so that the trends can be understood and gaps between intention and outcome can be identified. Then, of course, it will be important that this monitoring leads to action if the implementation is not succeeding as intended.

The introduction and application of performance monitoring in the public sector has many critics (and it sometimes feels like few supporters). Some critics complain that monitoring is top-down centralized government and centralized management. They appear to dislike it because it signifies top-down control. What is the alternative? One answer seems to be to dispense with monitoring and trust professionals in the public services to act responsibly by putting the interests of the public and their clients first. There are others who suggest performance monitoring is undermined by 'gaming', where people spend time trying to outwit the top-down control and defeat the purposes of the

229

monitoring processes. Data collection and reporting are falsified or distorted. Operating practices may even be adjusted to impact on the results being reported (i.e. effective service to the public is reduced to enhance apparent performance). Michael Barber, in his book *Instruction to Deliver* (2007), looks at these arguments against performance monitoring and suggests how those responsible for monitoring can respond to them.

In this chapter, we will be looking at different approaches to performance measurement and reporting. These can be politically owned, or owned by top civil servants or appointed public managers. We will be looking at the significance of different types of performance indicators and targets, especially output and outcome indicators and targets. This is followed by a consideration of performance plans and programme assessment tools. Finally we look at how issues of uncertainty and acceptability can be handled when setting performance targets.

THE EMERGING REALITY OF MONITORING

Strategic management and strategic capabilities have been spreading within government and the public sector, and so has performance management – in fact, performance management may have often preceded strategic planning. As a result, the issue is sometimes whether or not performance management is integrated into a strategic management system and supports strategic planning. It is highly desirable from the point of view of effective strategic planning that performance measurement, performance reporting and individual performance management are properly linked to strategic planning (Poister and Streib 2005).

For strategic leaders the matter may feel quite straightforward. If they have set clear strategic priorities, developed a vision statement based on these priorities and managed to articulate clear strategic goals, they are going to want to know on a fairly frequent basis if the organization is moving in the right direction. Is their public sector organization making the required rate of progress on the trajectory that was designed as part of the strategic planning? Without monitoring and reporting of progress, proper attention and persistence by strategic leaders and others to the task of delivering strategic change and reform seems unlikely to be sustained.

Some major developments in monitoring and evaluation have occurred in national social and economic planning systems in the last 10 or 15 years. Two prime examples are China and its five-year plans (changes taking place over the period 2003 to 2008) and Saudi Arabia with monitoring and evaluation being added to its five-year planning system to turn it into a strategic planning system at about the same time.

THE BASICS

In orthodox models of strategic planning, the monitoring of performance is a key part of a cycle of control. How does this cycle of control work? First, it assumes that the organization sets measurable strategic goals, linked to an organization's mission. These goals could be used as the basis for a gap analysis that feeds into the formulation of a strategic plan and its execution through budgetary and operational decisions. The analysis of current performance and past trends in performance would be needed to identify current or future performance gaps. So, in this way, performance assessment is an input to decisions on strategy and the strategic plan. The implementation of the strategic plan may then be followed up by measuring the impact of strategic decisions in terms of performance and by reporting findings up the management line. On the basis of this reporting, top managers could consider whether or not strategic goals or decisions about strategy and operational matters need revision. So performance measurement matters both at the beginning and the end of the cycle of strategic management. See Figure 10.1 for a simplified representation of the control cycle.

Monitoring can also be useful for learning. Politicians and other public service leaders may hope that the strategic plans are right, but they might realize that they need refining. The monitoring may help with the work of refining policies or strategic plans. We might call this type of learning making mid-course corrections as it is discovered how to adjust strategic plans to make them more effective.

Evaluation may get muddled up in our minds with monitoring, but the timing and purposes of evaluation of strategy and strategic management are different. Strategic leaders should be evaluating strategies and strategic plans after

Figure 10.1 Performance measures and control cycle

implementation in order to decide if they have been worthwhile (what was the value of this strategy?). They may also want to know if the strategic plan still has value, or whether the time has arrived to move on and develop new policies and strategic plans. Of course, evaluation can also feed into learning about policy and strategy.

Monitoring is not just an intellectual process. It needs to be organized and managed, and there need to be skills and capabilities in monitoring. From a strategic point of view, the monitoring needs to be focused on measuring results being achieved in priority areas of government. Monitoring can also help with the ongoing work of learning how to make refinements and adjustments to improve results.

We probably ought to distinguish the work of strategic monitoring of policies and strategic plans from the drive to improve performance through top-down performance management and performance budgeting. Strategic monitoring is concerned with checking on the implementation of new strategic policies and plans. This is quite different from standalone top-down performance management systems that are an intervention in their own right to 'sweat the assets'. It is probably safe to say that standalone top-down performance management rather than strategic monitoring has mainly caused the early growth of activity in collecting and reporting performance in the public sector.

While, as it has just been argued, performance measurement and management within government can be developed as interventions in their own right, if they do exist they can be taken over and used for monitoring strategic plans. In the United States, performance management was a part of strategic planning reforms in the early 1990s. Under these reforms the US federal agencies were, in fact, required to produce strategic plans and then, on the basis of them, to produce performance plans. The basic idea of performance management integrated with strategic planning is quite simple. Performance data is produced and reported to the appropriate committees and forums in a timely manner so that the effectiveness of strategic plans can be evaluated, implementation of strategic plans can be checked and poor performance can be challenged.

POLITICALLY OWNED PERFORMANCE MEASUREMENT

When there are targets and performance measurement and reporting, elected politicians can begin to hold civil service leaders of government departments and managerial leaders of public service organizations to account. Where politicians want an effective system of accountability for civil service leaders and public managers, the politicians may want to use their political manifestos and campaigning documents as the source of their priorities and performance indicators.

There are some obvious points that can be made about politically generated performance measures. First, when they are very specific and easily measurable, they carry a political risk. There could be a big improvement in government performance that just falls short of the promised achievement – this is potentially dangerous as political opponents can draw attention to the failure to achieve what was promised and portray the government as incompetent. It might seem much safer politically to make only vague promises.

Second, politicians are often accused of being short-term in their thinking because they are always worrying about how they are going to get re-elected, or are prone to getting distracted by crises and unexpected developments. It might be thought, therefore, that any politically led approach to performance measurement and reporting will be very short-term. In recent years, politicians appear to have become conscious of the dangers of short-term thinking. In the UK a new coalition government was elected in 2010, and their coalition agreement was very rapidly developed into structural reform plans that showed this longer time perspective. These structural reform plans were then made the basis of annual business plans by government departments. It was also true of earlier UK governments that there has been a desire to think long-term.

Third, just because performance measurement is based on the politicians' priorities, it does not mean that they are without interest to the public. It is possible for a politically led approach to performance measurement and reporting to be also a public-responsive approach. This requires that priorities are based on the top concerns of the public. In the UK, the government's emphasis on education and health as key areas for performance improvements matched the prominence of these two areas in public perceptions of key issues in the decade from 1997. Arguably, elected politicians could commission public opinion polling to track trends in public perceptions of national issues as a way of determining their strategic priorities and their selection of key performance indicators.

PERFORMANCE PLANS

Before we look at the long-running debate on whether you should monitor outputs or outcomes, let us first establish the idea of a performance plan that

Table 10.1 *Performance plan chart*

Strategic goal	Performance indicator	Annual performance target				
		Year 1	Year 2	Year 3	Year 4	Year 5

Table 10.2 *Targets in Government of South Australia Strategic Plan (SASP) 2011*

2011 Target	Measure	Data
1 Urban spaces: increase the use of public spaces by the community	The frequency in which people visit public spaces (2011 baseline)	SASP Household Survey
5 Multiculturalism: maintain the high rate of South Australians who believe cultural diversity is a positive influence in the community	Acceptance of cultural diversity as positive influence in the community (2008 baseline)	SASP Household Survey
7 Affordable housing: South Australia leads the nation over the period to 2020 in the proportion of homes sold or built that are affordable by low and moderate income families	Proportion of homes sold or built that are affordable by low and moderate income households (2010 baseline)	Council of Australian Governments Reform Council National Affordable Housing Agreement Performance Report (sourced from Australian Bureau of Statistics (ABS) Analysis of Survey of Income and Housing and Valuer-General sales data)
17 State-wide crime rates: reduce victim reported crime by 38% by 2014, maintaining or improving thereafter	Offences reported by victims, rate per 1,000 population (2002–3 baseline)	Office of Crime Statistics and Research
21 Greater safety at work: achieve a 40% reduction in injury by 2012 and further 50% reduction by 2022	Cumulative percentage reduction in income claim rate (2001–2 baseline)	WorkCover South Australia, SafeWork SA, Department of the Premier and Cabinet
35 Economic growth: exceed the national economic growth rate over the period to 2020	Growth in GSP/GDP from the baseline year (2002–3 baseline)	ABS Cat. No. 5220.0 – Australian National Accounts: State Accounts
75 Sustainable water use: South Australia's water resources are managed within sustainable limits by 2018	Water resource management areas in South Australia (2003 baseline)	Department for Water

provides a simple way of thinking about how to monitor the implementation of, say, a five-year strategic plan. Looking at examples of strategic plans in the public sector, it is evident that they are sometimes looking for changes over a five-year or, in some cases, longer period such as ten years. If the improvements in performance are to be monitored on an annual basis, the performance targets need to be set on an annual basis showing progress towards the achievement of the desired performance at the end of the planning period.

Table 10.1 is a performance plan chart; it shows how performance information for such a plan can be set out. For each strategic goal there may be one or more performance indicators, and for each performance indicator we can set targets on an annual basis.

The usual advice is to ensure performance targets are measurable and have timescales. An example of a set of performance targets is shown in Table 10.2. These are taken from South Australia's Strategic Plan for 2011, which was an update of a strategic plan first published in 2004 and updated in 2007 and 2011. The original strategic plan of 2004 had six objectives and 79 targets. For the 2011 strategic plan, the South Australian government carried out a community engagement exercise and tried to get the views of over 9,000 people. As a result of the process, issues around safety, affordable homes and water were identified. The government decided to keep most of its 2007 targets but to add some extra ones, resulting in 100 targets. The 2011 plan had three priorities: community, prosperity and environment. These were described as the 'organizing priorities' for the strategic plan.

It is obvious that the South Australia strategic plan tries to specify performance targets using numbers and also to set timescales.

One final point about performance plans – is it enough to monitor actual performance against planned performance on a year-by-year basis? There is a little evidence that it is important to track changes over time in actual performance and not just compare actual and planned performance (see Research Box 10.1).

RESEARCH BOX 10.1 PERFORMANCE MEASUREMENT IN US LOCAL GOVERNMENT

Poister and Streib's (2005) analysis of the experience of over 200 cities in the United States that had undertaken strategic planning efforts over the preceding five years found that only 60 per cent of them used performance measures to track the accomplishment of goals and objectives in the strategic plan. Slightly less than half reported performance measures related to the strategic plan to the city council on a regular basis. Only a third reported performance measures associated with the strategic plan to the public on a regular basis.

Many of the city councils that did use performance measures to track delivery of strategic goals and objectives also reported using performance data to monitor improvements over time. In fact, there was evidence to suggest that this particular practice was associated with the impact of strategic plans. They also found that making regular reports to the public on performance measures associated with the strategic plan was another practice linked to strategic plan impact.

So, a hypothesis might be proposed: it is not enough simply to compare planned performance with actual, it is better to track performance over time and appreciate the trends in performance. A second hypothesis might be: it is not enough to be accountable upwards to politicians; it is better to make yourself also accountable directly to the public for your performance.

INPUTS, OUTPUTS AND OUTCOMES

A key conceptual distinction in thinking about performance measurement in the public services is between outputs and outcomes. Ball (1994: 25), referring to New Zealand's public services reforms, said: 'We use these terms in a conventional fashion with outcomes being impacts on the community, such as a reduced level of crime, whereas outputs are services delivered by specific agencies, such as street patrolling, prosecutions and so on'.

The division of labour between politicians on one hand, and civil servants and public managers on the other, is often described as clear and reasonable. Politicians make policies, and civil servants and public managers deliver them. In practice, there are tensions between politicians and civil servants and public managers in terms of performance assessment, and these can emerge in the difference between outputs and outcomes. This has been noticed in the case of the New Zealand government. Some years ago, management reforms were made that were designed to ensure the accountability of the top civil servants for outputs. The chief executives of government departments (i.e. the top civil servants) were party to performance agreements that reflected the services their ministers wanted delivered. The performance agreements were linked to contracts that were concerned with the outputs of the departments. Ball (1994: 25) made the following comment about the New Zealand public service system:

While our system recognizes the critical nature of information relating outputs to outcomes in making policy decisions, there was a deliberate decision not to seek to use outcomes to define the accountability of chief executives and their departments. The reason for this is that the individual chief executive very rarely has sufficient control over outcomes to make accountability effective.

236

The distinction between outputs and outcomes, therefore, is partially important because of the accountability mechanisms and the incentives for senior civil servants and top managers in leadership positions in the civil service. The chief executives in New Zealand's public services clearly had an incentive to comply with their ministers. The ministers, as politicians, really wanted outcomes, but settled for outputs as the focus of accountability. The key point here is that politicians really wanted *outcomes* not *outputs*.

The importance of this point emerged a few years later when Schick (2001) wrote about the New Zealand government's introduction of strategic results areas (SRAs) and key results areas (KRAs). He suggested that they had only been partly successful in tackling weaknesses in directing budgetary allocations. He praised the New Zealand model for its focus on operational effectiveness but emphasized problems in respect of policy and strategy. It appears that there was a difference of perspective and interest between elected politicians and civil servants. Schick wrote (2001: 4):

> One way of making this point is that chief executives and ministers have different perspectives and interests. Although chief executives may be interested in outcomes and results, the system impels them to focus on outputs for which they are accountable; and although ministers have an interest in inputs and outputs, their political goals impel them to focus on outcomes and objectives.

These references to problems of accountability in the New Zealand case can be contrasted with the growing use of outcome performance measures in the federal agencies of the United States government. A decade after the Government Performance and Results Act (GPRA) of 1993, a report was produced by the US General Accounting Office (GAO) which looked, first, into the effects of the 1993 Act in terms of an increasing focus by government on results. Second, it looked into the challenges of performance measurement and the use of performance information. Third, it looked at how the US government could continue progress towards a more results-oriented government. The GAO report said the 1993 Act 'had established a solid foundation' in terms of achieving 'results-oriented performance planning, measurement, and reporting in the Federal government' (GAO 2004). It also found that strategic and performance plans were getting better, but there were areas that needed more work, such as the linking of results to the allocation of resources. There were also reported difficulties in setting outcome oriented goals, collecting useful data on results and linking performance measurement (at all levels from the institutional to the individual) to reward systems. Another issue was that the GAO believed there was an inadequate focus on crosscutting issues that were of concern to more than one federal agency. The Obama administration responded to various concerns about how GPRA was working in practice with the GPRA Modernization Act, which introduced federal priority goals, adjusted the planning cycle to the political process and made other changes to strengthen political oversight.

237

Table 10.3 *Outcome-based performance measures*

GAO surveys	1997	2000	2003
Percentage of federal managers having outcome-based performance measures	32%	44%	55%

The report summarized findings from surveys of federal managers for the years 1997, 2000 and 2003, showing that outcome-based performance measures were becoming more widespread in federal government. The evidence indicated that, whereas only a third of federal managers in 1997 had outcome performance measures, by 2003 just over half had outcome performance measures (see Table 10.3).

It is worth mentioning here that elected politicians may sometimes also want input performance measures to be featured in reporting systems. This may seem surprising given the evident point that outcomes have an obvious merit in being results that the public might experience and credit to the politicians as achievements. If patients have shorter waiting times for hospital operations, or school children achieve better exam results, the public can conclude that the politicians have made public services better. But input performance measures can also be highly important in political terms. A government may want to claim that it has made sure there are more doctors, teachers and police, which should reassure the public that core public services are not being starved of funding and have the capacity to deliver more public services.

PROGRAMME ASSESSMENT

Monitoring can also be carried out on the performance of government programmes that form parts of strategic plans. Programme assessment is not new and predates the era of strategic planning. In the 1970s, for example, programmes were assessed to see if they were achieving their objectives, and to understand the causes of success or failure of programmes (York 1982). The process could involve identifying the programme, formulating criteria (e.g. efficiency, effectiveness, impact, quality), deciding on a method, collecting data, analysing the data and then, finally, reporting.

In the United States in early 2002, the Office of Management and Budget (OMB) set up a task force to create a tool for assessing the performance of programmes – called the Program Assessment Rating Tool (PART). In the summer of 2002, OMB distributed the tool and instructions so that programmes carried out by federal agencies could be assessed by OMB. The assessments were made and sent to federal agencies, which were able to make written appeals to OMB in September of the same year. This process of programme assessment informed the President's budget for 2004, which was actually issued in February 2003. Subsequently, in 2004, an OMB official said that the performance information from PART had been useful for making budget decisions and had helped to identify opportunities to improve programmes.

The tool comprises a set of questions. Those used in the 2004 PART are reproduced in Table 10.4. The possible answers to questions in the first, second and third sections are: yes, no, or not applicable. The possible answers to section four are: yes, large extent, small extent, or no. (Specific questions according to the type of programme are ignored here.)

As can be seen by examining the contents of the PART, assessment is intended to be carried out in the context of the strategic plans for the federal agencies. This point was made, in effect, in guidance issued by the OMB. The OMB said that long-term performance measures and targets were the basis for assessing the results of programmes, and noted the strong focus on strategic planning in Section II of the tool. The linkage between strategic goals in the strategic plans of federal agencies and the outcome goals of programmes is conceived within the PART assessment as being a hierarchical one. Consequently, the strategic goals in the strategic plans should have been achieved if the programme outcome goals were achieved. More mundanely, this meant that federal agencies should have been using their strategic plan documents to complete Section II of the PART. OMB also indicated that changes in performance measures resulting from PART assessments should trigger consultation of stakeholders (OMB 2007: 8):

> Because of the importance of performance measures, OMB and agencies must agree on appropriate measures early to allow for review with relevant stakeholders if needed. If the agency intends to revise its strategic goals as the result of a PART assessment, the GPRA requires that relevant stakeholders be consulted during the strategic plan review.

In these ways, PART assessments were to have formal links to the strategic plans created under GPRA and, as the OMB suggested, it was possible that the PART assessments might lead to changes in strategic goals and stakeholder consultation. It was not clear from the examination of the PART, or the guidance issued by OMB, what long-term impact PART assessments might have on the nature of strategic planning by federal agencies, but because of the use of PART assessments for budgeting by the US government, it can be said that they potentially provided a way of connecting strategic planning to budgeting.

SCORECARDS

In some situations it may be civil services leaders or senior public managers who own performance measurement and reporting, and elected politicians who see these as mainly a managerial matter of little direct interest to them. In such cases, the balanced scorecard (which we looked at briefly in an earlier chapter) may appear to offer a useful approach that might be seen as very different from the

Table 10.4 *Programme Assessment Rating Tool*

Section	Questions	Answer		
		Yes	No	N/A
Section I: Program Purpose & Design	1. Is the program purpose clear? 2. Does the program address a specific interest, problem or need? 3. Is the program designed to have a significant impact in addressing the interest, problem or need? 4. Is the program designed to make a unique contribution in addressing the interest, problem or need (i.e., not needlessly redundant of any other federal, state, local or private efforts)? 5. Is the program optimally designed to address the interest, problem or need?			
Section II: Strategic Planning	1. Does the program have a limited number of specific, ambitious long-term performance goals that focus on outcomes and meaningfully reflect the purpose of the program? 2. Does the program have a limited number of annual performance goals that demonstrate progress towards achieving the long-term goals? 3. Do all partners (grantees, sub grantees, contractors, etc.) support program-planning efforts by committing to the annual and/or long-term goals of the program? 4. Does the program collaborate and coordinate effectively with related programs that share similar goals and objectives? 5. Are independent and quality evaluations of sufficient scope conducted on a regular basis or as needed to fill gaps in performance information to support program improvements and evaluate effectiveness? 6. Is the program budget aligned with the program goals in such a way that the impact of funding, policy, and legislative changes on performance is readily known? 7. Has the program taken meaningful steps to address its strategic planning deficiencies?			

Table 10.4. *(Continued)*

Section	Questions	Answer		
		Yes	No	N/A
Section III: Program Management	1. Does the agency regularly collect timely and credible performance information, including information from key program partners, and use it to manage the program and improve performance? 2. Are federal managers and program partners (grantees, sub grantees, contractors, etc.) held accountable for cost, schedule and performance results? 3. Are all funds (federal and partners') obligated in a timely manner and spent for the intended purpose? 4. Does the program have incentives and procedures (e.g., competitive sourcing/cost comparisons, IT improvements) to measure and achieve efficiencies and cost effectiveness in program execution? 5. Does the agency estimate the budget for the full annual costs of operating the program (including all administrative costs and allocated overhead) so that program performance changes are identified with changes in funding levels? 6. Does the program use strong financial management practices? 7. Has the program taken meaningful steps to address its management deficiencies?			

	Questions	Answer		
		Yes, large extent	Small extent	No
Section IV: Program Results	1. Has the program demonstrated adequate progress in achieving its long-term outcome goal(s)? 2. Does the program (including program partners) achieve its annual performance goals? 3. Does the program demonstrate improved efficiencies and cost effectiveness in achieving program goals each year?			

(Continued)

241

Table 10.4. *(Continued)*

Questions	Answer		
	Yes, large extent	Small extent	No
4. Does the performance of this program compare favourably to other programs with similar purpose and goals?			
5. Do independent and quality evaluations of this program indicate that the program is effective and achieving results?			

Note: 2004 PART (general questions only).

process of working from legal mandates to mission statements to performance indicators and targets. One argument for its use is that the balanced scorecard causes civil servants or public managers to consider a more diverse range of performance indicators, including indicators of relevance to service users, than they otherwise might. In other words, a balanced scorecard may encourage performance measurement to be less bureaucratic in nature and more 'customer-centric'.

So what is a balanced scorecard? It is a way of organizing performance data so that managers and staff at various organizational levels can monitor and discuss performance. The concept of a balanced scorecard is essentially very simple. It prompts organizations to formulate performance goals and measures using four perspectives. It has been considered for possible use in public services organizations for many years since its popularization in the early 1990s. For example, Boyle (no date: 8) suggested that it might be applied to the Irish civil service. In the case of the Irish civil service, as Boyle pointed out, the performance measurement system had to be linked to strategy since all government departments were working to a statement of strategy and mission, following the launch of the Strategic Management Initiative in 1994, and the passing of the Public Service Management Act of 1997:

> It is possible to see the ideas behind the balanced scorecard being adapted for use in the Irish civil service. Its focus on different stakeholders and their needs, on strategic management, and on presenting a balanced picture of key performance measures and indicators, is attractive for those concerned with performance measurement in the civil service.

The four perspectives of the balanced scorecard are the customer perspective, the financial perspective, the internal business perspective, and the innovation and learning perspective. Its value in any sector – public, private or voluntary – is that it encourages organizations to use a basket of goals and measures and not to rely simply on, say, a financial measure of performance.

We will briefly look at all four perspectives, taking note of possible examples and mentioning one or two considerations. First, there is the customer perspective, which has become more important in recent years. Boyle stresses the importance of the views of service users (i.e. the customer perspective). He says (no date: 9):

> Ultimately, most services are provided for the benefits of users, and their views on performance are important in determining how well or badly a service is provided. Defining users can be difficult at times in the civil service (Boyle 1996: 40), but a user perspective is important in judging performance.

This perspective might be reflected in a goal addressing the satisfaction of the public with the services they use, which may be assessed using surveys. Another option in measuring satisfaction levels is to monitor the number of complaints received from service users.

Second, there is the financial perspective, which might be reflected in a goal about containing spending within agreed limits or even making savings. Another financial goal may be earning revenue from user fees. It is worth considering how this goal may be seen as an aspect of modernization and reform. For example, public services have been exhorted to earn as well as spend (Osborne and Gaebler 1992). So, as well as receiving funding from government, organizations may set goals in terms of income from charging fees. Osborne and Gaebler (1992) directly challenge the traditional attitude of reliance on 'tax and spend' thinking.

> We can no longer afford this attitude, in an age of fierce resistance to taxes. This is not to say that most public services should be sold for profit – most shouldn't. But think of all the public services that benefit individuals: the golf courses, the tennis courts, the marinas. Typically, the taxpayers subsidize those services. Average working people subsidize the affluent to play golf and tennis or moor their boats. Why not turn such services into profit centres?
>
> (Osborne and Gaebler 1992: 199)

If such services are profitable, affluent service users can be charged so as to subsidize the public services that are necessary for the average citizen.

The internal business perspective is the third perspective. It relates to how well the organization is functioning. One goal in this area might be improved service quality, which might be measured in a benefits agency, for example, by how many correct benefits assessments are made.

Finally, the fourth perspective is an innovation and learning perspective, which is concerned with goals focused on improvements and developments. An organization might measure these in various ways, for example, the speed of process innovations (e.g. e-government) or spend on staff development.

Table 10.5 *Stakeholders and their interests*

Stakeholders	Service users, parliament, cabinet and government ministers	Resource controllers	Staff and management
Stakeholders' interests	Results	Financial management	Human resource management

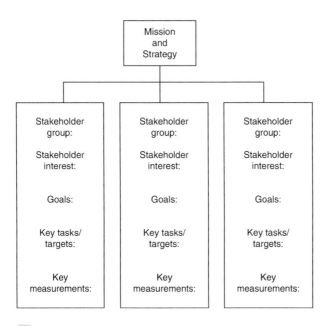

Figure 10.2 *Displaying performance measures*

Boyle suggested the use of what he called an integrated performance measurement framework focusing on three groups of stakeholders, rather than the four perspectives of the balanced scorecard. These are, first, service users and policy makers (the parliament, the cabinet and government ministers); second, resource controllers; and, third, staff and management. He claimed the first group is interested in results, the second is interested in financial management, and the third is interested in human resource management (see Table 10.5).

Whether a public service organization uses a version of the balanced scorecard or an adaptation of it (such as Boyle's), the performance measures need to be linked to the mission statement and strategy. Figure 10.2 shows a layout for displaying the linkages from mission and strategy through to performance measurement, which is more or less as suggested by Boyle (with some minor changes).

The display may be completed as follows:

1 The mission statement and strategy of an organization are written into the mission and strategy box at the top.
2 The key groups of stakeholders are identified and their interests clarified. These are summarized in the appropriate places in the performance measures boxes.
3 The goals rows in the performance measures boxes are completed by identifying what has to be accomplished if the mission and strategy are to be successful.
4 Key tasks/targets are time bound (have to be done by a specific date) and are 'operationalized' (i.e. more concrete) versions of the goals.
5 The key measurements are the actual performance indicators used.

The balanced scorecard cannot make up for poor quality financial and performance data and, even with good quality data, performance assessment still requires strategic leaders willing to devote time and effort to understanding the implications of the data and then willing to take tough decisions on the basis of it.

DEALING WITH FUTURE UNCERTAINTY

In order to complete a performance plan some judgement has to be made about the trajectory of performance improvement over, say, a five-year period. Because of uncertainty about the future, it is unlikely that it will be possible to predict the exact trajectory of performance improvement for each strategic goal, and the performance plan will have to be based on some guesswork.

Public managers sometimes find it difficult to think through guesses about the future annual performance targets in a performance plan. They sometimes just do not know how to start, especially if extrapolation from past trends is inappropriate or not possible. One way to get the thinking started is to ask public managers to choose one of three types of performance trajectory. Type one is that that there will be a steady increase in performance over the five years. Type two envisages that progress in improving performance will be initially rapid and then slow down. Type three is that performance will actually deteriorate as the organization changes over to a new process and employees and managers are trained in new methods, but then in the last part of the plan period progress is rapid. These three types of trajectory can be represented on a graph (see Figure 10.3). Such graphs – showing three trajectories – can be used in strategic planning workshops to facilitate discussions by management teams, and to prompt them to think about the actions needed to implement strategic measures.

- Which trajectory seems most likely to apply to a specific strategic measure?
- Why will performance improvement follow this trajectory?
- What implementation actions will be taken and when, to achieve this performance trajectory?

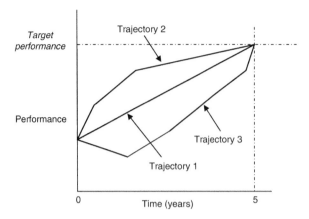

Figure 10.3 *Performance trajectory*

It is remarkable how this simple device can be used to prompt questions and cue thinking that enables management teams to confront the challenge of planning implementation. It is possible that public managers draw on tacit knowledge when they choose a trajectory and, having made the choice, they then surface their judgements about why the trajectory will be of that type.

ACCEPTABILITY

Performance targets in UK public services have been very controversial. One group that has often complained about targets are public services professionals. This can be illustrated by the response of the medical profession to the publication of performance information by the English NHS in the summer of 1999; this was published on the internet. The information had taken nearly two years to assemble and included data on mortality rates after surgery, detection and survival of cancer, teenage pregnancies and access to NHS dentistry. What was the response from the medical profession? One spokesman warned that it would put hospital consultants under pressure, and also raised a concern that doctors might refuse treatment because of the adverse effect on performance indicators of going ahead with treatment.

The justification for the exercise was that managers would use the statistics to improve health services and reveal variations in results. However, the English Health Secretary warned that this was the first time that information had been published in this form and so there would be some data quality issues. He also warned that the data required careful interpretation. He was quoted as saying (Revill 1999: 2):

> These indicators are not league tables – to use them that way would be misleading. There will often be very good reasons why one organisation appears to be performing differently from others.

While public service professionals in many sectors complained that performance measurement was creating wasteful bureaucracy and distorting behaviour, the counter arguments were that performance information was needed to improve the responsiveness of services to the public and should be used pragmatically to improve the public services even if some of the data was far from perfectly accurate.

It is not just professionals who are uncomfortable with the use of performance targets. Managers in public services have also often been uncomfortable either with the idea of performance targets, or with their use in practice. First, many managers dislike performance management systems – they are uncomfortable for the individual managers. This is because individual managers may be held to account for performance that is less than satisfactory. Second, there may be problems over the selection of performance targets. Managers may regard the performance targets they have been given responsibility for as crude and not suitable for judging the success of the services they manage. Third, the data collected against these performance indicators may be of poor quality. Fourth, the managers may not be provided with performance information they need on a timely or frequent basis.

But targets are useful (whether quantitative or qualitative) so government can decide if its actions have been successful. The real issue, therefore, should be how to set targets as effectively and sensibly as possible.

How can strategic leaders deal with the objections that may be put in the way of setting performance targets? First, what about the argument that performance targets were creating wasteful bureaucracy? While it is probably a good idea to be on guard against an excessive bureaucracy developing around performance targets, in the end governments need some priorities and performance targets to ensure the focus and persistence needed to achieve success.

Second, performance measurement is sometimes disliked because it distorts performance or has unintended effects. Barber (2007: 80–1) appeared not be impressed by these arguments on the basis of his experience of heading up the UK Prime Minister's Delivery Unit:

Here the debate is confused. If one purpose of a target is to enhance the priority of the focus area, it follows inescapably that some other areas will not be so prioritised and may suffer relatively ... Unintended consequences are another sort of risk. I found that whenever a new target or goal is set, those who defend the status quo instantly explain all the unintended consequences that will ensue. With the focus on literacy and numeracy, such people predicted that the science results would go down. (They didn't – they went up ...) When we focused on reducing street crime in 2002, senior police predicted that, as street crime fell, burglary and car crime would inevitably rise. (They didn't – they continued to fall ...) So in the Delivery Unit, our reaction to all these dire predictions was not to accept them at face value since they so often proved to be urban myths, but always to agree we would check. Then, if the fear proved unfounded, the urban myth would be exploded; and if it proved justified, a political choice could be made about whether it was a price worth paying.

CASE STUDY

Department of Agriculture and Rural Development (DARD) of Northern Ireland

This example is arguably a hybrid of a strategic plan undertaken voluntarily by managers as a way to improve their effectiveness and one that wraps around a performance budgeting framework. This is because, on one hand, the strategic plan contains vision, goals and actions, but on the other it has a set of targets and linked to them a budget allocation. This strategic plan is a five-year plan for the Department of Agriculture and Rural Development (DARD) of Northern Ireland, which covers the period 2006–11. The diagram at Figure 10.4 provides a summary of the strategic vision, aims and goals. The strategic vision offered a view of the aims of DARD whereas the aim statement seemed to be more of a statement of values (e.g. putting the customer first and valuing staff). Furthermore, while the strategic goals seem plausible in the light of the strategic vision, it is not clear that the strategic goals follow on from the aim. It may be that this diagram, which is based on an overview taken from the department's website, shows the process sequence rather than logical links.

For each of the strategic goals there was a set of strategic objectives and a set of key actions. For example,

Strategic goal: to improve performance in the market place
    Strategic objectives:

1   Farm-gate sales and ancillary land based industries to be competitive in a reformed market
2   A more competitive food processing industry
3   A more competitive fishing industry
4   A more competitive forestry industry.

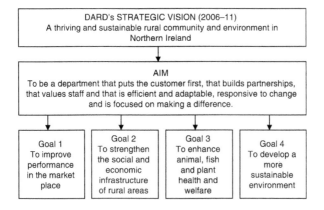

Figure 10.4 *Department of Agriculture and Rural Development (DARD) of Northern Ireland (2006–11)*

248

Key actions:

1 Deliver a targeted strategy for life-long learning
2 Deliver a targeted strategy for R&D and technology transfer
3 Implement the NI fit for Market food strategy
4 Deliver sectoral strategic plans and support in line with industry needs
5 Deliver the Single Farm Payment.

The department presented this five-year strategic plan as influencing its Public Service Agreements (PSA) (which was focused on performance targets and budget), an efficiency plan and the departmental reform plan, all of which were framed on an annual basis. The strategic plan also influenced the corporate scorecard which included the key performance targets of the department. The PSA also influenced the corporate scorecard. All this was then cascaded down the organization on an annual basis through the scorecard and business plan for groups and agencies, and then down to divisional branch level, and even down to individual personal performance agreements. So the intention was that, through this system, you could trace a formal link between the personal performance agreement with an individual all the way through to the department's overall five-year strategic plan (see Figure 10.5).

The published DARD strategic plan contained the PSA as an appendix. The PSA showed that the objectives were to promote sustainable development of the agri-food industry and the countryside and stimulate the economic and social revitalization of disadvantaged rural areas; reduce the risk to life and property from flooding; promote sustainable development of the sea fishing industry; and

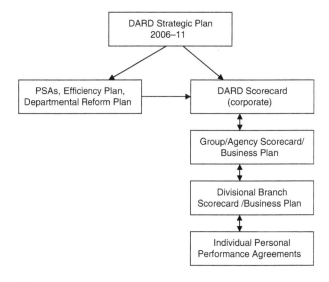

Figure 10.5 *Linkages*

maintain, protect and expand forests in a sustainable way. The PSA stated the current expenditure and investment levels in terms of millions of pounds for 2006/7 and for 2007/8. The PSA also attempted to indicate the planned outcome for citizens. In this case, it was stated that one result of the PSA was there would be a competitive agri-food industry and improved animal health. The PSA included a number of targets. One example was a target that was stated as: Create conditions for the agricultural industry to achieve a 10.5 per cent improvement in total factor productivity between calendar year 2001 and 2008. Another example of a target was: Create conditions to increase value added per full-time employee equivalent in the Northern Ireland Food and Drinks processing sector from £22,400 (1999/2001 average) to £33,100 by 2008.

It is possible that such a strategic plan was really based on the department's understanding of its mission (especially in terms of who were the intended beneficiaries and what the benefits should be), its strategic vision and its strategic situation. Alternatively, the strategic plan could have been merely a 'gloss' put on plans chiefly aimed at meeting performance targets set in the PSA, and thus important for securing budget allocations. In the former case, the PSA was absorbed into the work of a strategically led public service; in the latter case the PSA controlled the activity of the department and the strategic plan was in danger of being a waste of time or a paper exercise.

MINI CASE STUDY

The Delivery Unit (UK)

The Prime Minister's Delivery Unit, between 2001 and 2005, built up a powerful process of monitoring the performance of key departments against targets and ensuring an effective system of accountability to the Prime Minister. It also developed a system for fieldwork to identify specific initiatives to bring about performance improvements. Because of this, the UK government became more effective in managing performance in key strategic areas. The Prime Minister's Strategy Unit carried out a strategic audit in 2004 in which performance on the Prime Minister's priorities was reviewed. The results were very impressive (see Table 10.6).

SUMMARY

One choice for governments is whether to develop performance indicators and targets from political manifestos and surveys of public concerns, or whether to use a balanced scorecard approach. The balanced scorecard approach may be more suitable where there is little political leadership of strategic change and ministers have not developed the strategies or feel much sense of ownership of

Table 10.6 *Strategic audit of performance in 2004 (UK)*

Goal	Direction	Ahead of 1997?
Health:		
nurse numbers	positive	ahead
doctor numbers	positive	ahead
heart disease mortality	positive	ahead
cancer mortality	positive	ahead
waiting list	positive	ahead
waiting times	positive	ahead
accident and emergency	positive	ahead
primary care access	positive	ahead
Education:		
teacher numbers	positive	ahead
teacher recruitment	positive	ahead
11-year-olds' literacy	flat	ahead
11-year-olds' numeracy	flat	ahead
14-year-olds' English	positive	ahead
14-year-olds' maths	positive	ahead
five A–C GCSEs	positive	ahead
specialist schools	positive	ahead
truancy	flat	equal to
Home Office:		
police numbers	positive	ahead
overall crime	positive	ahead
burglary	positive	ahead
vehicle crime	positive	ahead
robbery	positive	worse
violent crime	positive	ahead
gun crime	negative	worse
antisocial behaviour	positive	worse
likelihood of being a victim	positive	ahead
asylum applications	positive	ahead
Transport:		
rail patronage	positive	ahead
rail punctuality	positive	worse

the strategies. In this case, the balanced scorecard is a useful framework for civil servants because it helps to broaden their work in monitoring and discussing performance. Critically, the balanced scorecard approach steers civil servants towards thinking about formulating performance goals and measures in ways that benefit users of public services. Boyle's (1996) view that a user perspective is important in judging performance may be noted here. But it is worth repeating that where there is strong and coherent political leadership, the performance measures may be more usefully – and more legitimately – directly drawn from manifestos and public opinion polling.

When developed as part of strategic planning reforms, monitoring through performance measurement and management can be used to empower civil servants within an accountability framework. This has important implications for the relationship between politicians and top civil servants, but these implications may also be influenced significantly by the decision to use output or outcome measures in setting performance goals for government departments and public services. In the past, there has been a view that it is technically difficult to focus on outcome measures and much easier to collect data and report on output measures. There is evidence showing that a government that persists in trying to base performance measurement on the basis of outcome measures can be successful in establishing their use.

We also looked briefly at the development in the US of the PART, which had taken federal agency strategic plans as the basis of programme outcome goals, and which enabled programme results to be assessed and taken into consideration when the budget-setting work was being done. It seems that the PART process could lead to changes in strategic goals, but it was not clear from the official guidance issued how else the nature of strategic planning might be affected by this development.

We looked at how performance plans may be drawn up on the basis of strategic goals, and we noted that public services managers are faced by problems of uncertainty when producing annual performance plans for, say, five years ahead. Finding ways to help managers to develop an understanding of the possible trajectories of annual performance targets that will lead to the accomplishment of strategic goals is important.

There are a number of technical and other issues in performance measurement and management. There are technical issues about the selection of performance indicators and problems of poor data availability and quality. The former problem will probably always be a source of argument, but data availability and quality can be significantly improved if there is the will to do so, as was shown by the UK experience when the Prime Minister's Delivery Unit was established in 2001 (Barber 2007).

In this chapter we have also briefly considered why performance measurement is resisted, and how those responsible for measuring and managing performance in government may respond to doubts and criticisms of performance targets. Behind the resistance may be issues that are not so much technical as ones of acceptability to those affected by performance measurement. They threaten individual professionals and managers and make them feel uncomfortable. Such systems not only make managers results more transparent, but can also expose them to criticism if the performance of the organization they are managing falls short of political or public expectations.

Work-based assignment: mission statements and performance measures

The work-based assignments in this book are for civil servants and other public services staff who have some management experience.

Reflect on your organization's mission statement. Can you identify three or four key performance indicators based on this mission statement that could be used to evaluate the strategic effectiveness of the organization?

If this assignment is reviewed in class, present your conclusions on a flip chart and discuss with others. Compare performance indicators in a plenary discussion and identify the best ones. Discuss the basis for selecting the best ones – that is, what criteria were used for selecting them?

Work-based assignment: balanced scorecard

Use the balanced scorecard to classify the performance indicators you developed in the previous assignment. Reflect on the results of this. Did you have a performance indicator for each of the four perspectives, or were there gaps in your coverage of the balanced scorecard?

DISCUSSION QUESTIONS

1 Which type of performance measures should public services use – output or outcome measures?
2 How helpful in exploring the idea of monitoring is the concept of the control cycle? Has it any disadvantages as a way of representing monitoring?
3 Should programme assessment be used to change strategic goals? How does programme assessment carried out by ministry of finance officials affect strategic management? Are the officials inevitably too focused on budget setting?
4 Is a scorecard approach the best approach to performance monitoring?
5 How do vested interests affect discussions of the value of performance targets?

FURTHER READING

Barber, M. (2007) *Instruction to Deliver*. London: Politico's.

> The ideas in this book are relatively simple but the book offers a very convincing case for performance monitoring and learning from it. It is especially interesting because it looks at all the issues from a practical perspective. It also has some very interesting ideas about coherence in the centre of government.

REFERENCE LIST

Ball, I. (1994) Reinventing government: lessons learned from the New Zealand Treasury. *The Government Accountants Journal*, Fall: 19–28.

Barber, M. (2007) *Instruction to Deliver*. London: Politico's.

Boyle, R. (no date) *Developing an Integrated Performance Measurement Framework for the Irish Civil Service*, Committee for Public Management Research, Research Paper 3. Dublin.

Boyle, R. (1996) *Measuring Civil Service Performance*. Dublin: Institute of Public Administration.

GAO [US General Accounting Office] (2004) *Results-Oriented Government: GPRA Has Established a Solid Foundation for Achieving Greater Results*, GAO-04-38, Washington, DC.

Government of South Australia (2011) *South Australia's Strategic Plan*. Adelaide: Government of South Australia. [Online]. Available from: http://saplan.org.au/media/BAhbBlsHOgZmSSIhMjAxMS8xMS8wNC8wMV8wMl8xNF8yMjNfZmlsZQY6BkVU/01_02_14_223_file [Accessed: 4 April 2016].

OMB [Office of Management and Budget] (2007) *Program Assessment Rating Tool Guidance No. 2007–02*.

Osborne, D. and Gaebler, T. (1992) *Reinventing Government: How the Entrepreneurial Spirit is Transforming the Public Sector*. Reading, MA: Addison-Wesley.

Poister, T. H. and Streib, G. D. (2005) Elements of strategic planning and management in municipal government: status after two decades. *Public Administration Review*, 65(1): 45–56.

Revill, J. (1999) Anger at new Dobson hospital `death scores', *Evening Standard*, Wednesday 16 June, pp. 1–2.

Schick, A. (2001) *Reflections on the New Zealand Model*. Lecture at the New Zealand Treasury.

York, R. O. (1982) *Human Service Planning: Concepts, Tools, and Methods*. Chapel Hill, NC: The University of North Carolina Press.

Chapter 11

Evaluating

LEARNING OBJECTIVES

■ To clarify the nature of the evaluation process
■ To look at approaches to evaluation
■ To look at an approach to evaluation based on Mintzberg's ideas of emergent strategy
■ To explore some evaluation tools

INTRODUCTION

Patricia Patrizi and Michael Patton introduce their edited book on evaluating strategy with an interesting anecdote about how they came to produce the book. In about 2008, chief executives of philanthropic foundations wanted evaluations of their organizations' overall strategy. Evaluation had in the past been focusing on projects, programmes, products, policies and personnel. Patrizi and Patton could find 'no evaluation literature that directly addressed evaluating strategy' (Patrizi and Patton 2010: 1).

On the other hand, they did find an emphasis on strategy everywhere (Patrizi and Patton 2010: 1):

> But once strategy had emerged as the focus, we noticed an emphasis on strategy wherever we looked, in government initiatives, not-for-profit conferences, international collaborations and, especially, private-sector leadership and management . . . Everywhere we looked, we saw a concern with being strategic: thinking strategically, acting strategically and being strategic, all of which led quite directly to evaluating strategically.

So, it looks like strategic leaders in the public sector who have been evaluating strategy and strategic plans in the last five to ten years must have been pioneering how to do it in practice without the help of a literature on evaluating strategy!

255

Both the planning process and the strategic plan can be evaluated. Evaluation can be undertaken at the end of implementation and obviously this suggests that it is not the same as monitoring (see Concept Box 11.1).

CONCEPT BOX 11.1   MONITORING AND EVALUATION DISTINGUISHED

Monitoring can be defined as an assessment process that helps to keep strategic leaders informed of what is happening and whether implementation of a strategic plan is on track, and it helps those managing implementation to make necessary adjustments in good time when implementation is not as successful as it should be.

Evaluation can be defined as a process of making judgements, usually at the end of implementation (although it might occur part way through), to judge the worth of the strategic planning effort.

Both monitoring and evaluation may involve learning lessons.

It is difficult to find much attention paid to the deliberate and organized evaluation of a strategic plan or the results of implementing a strategy in most public services organizations. This is despite the fact that the question to be answered is simple enough to state: was the cost and effort of designing and implementing a strategy worthwhile? As York (1982: 140) put it, 'evaluation is basically a judgement of worth or an appraisal of value'. This could be taken to mean that evaluators of a strategy need to identify all the costs and all the benefits of undertaking strategy formulation and implementation, and appraise them to calculate the net benefit.

But evaluators of a strategy will normally want to answer other questions as well. For example, if strategic goals had been set as part of the strategy process, were all of them achieved? If the strategic goals were achieved, what can be learnt about the causes of success? If some goals were not achieved, what can be learnt about the causes of failure? If answers can be found to these questions then evaluation is important for strategic leaders so they can learn how to be more successful in the future.

In this chapter we will be looking at what is evaluated, approaches to evaluation and some tools for carrying out evaluation.

WHAT IS EVALUATED?

Strategic leaders can ask the questions: was the effort to create and deliver the strategic plan worthwhile? How valuable was it? The strategic planning cycle can include setting priorities, formulating missions and goals, writing a strategic plan, implementing it and then producing outcomes. All of this can be covered in evaluation.

It is quite possible for political leaders to judge at the end of a planning period that results were not significant enough and that plans and action should have been bolder. They can do this even though a strategic plan was successfully implemented and measured outcomes were in line with expectations. The politicians may belatedly realize that although desired outcomes were completely achieved, they simply did not produce the degree of public satisfaction or appreciation that had been expected. The politician could say the outcomes were achieved, but so what?

Politicians may also judge that the outcomes delivered were much more modest than hoped for. The evaluation might then look for a mistaken strategy or poor execution of the strategy. Did we have the right strategy, but implementation was poor? Or was implementation done well, but the strategy was wrong? Politicians may decide the strategy needs changing even if the mission and strategic goals remain appropriate. We can illustrate this by a quote from a speech of David Cameron, the UK's Prime Minister, who, like the Blair Government (1997–2007), made public services reform and modernization a high priority. In early 2011, he said:

> So we are determined to modernise our public services and make them better for everyone … If we have learnt anything about public service reform in the past few decades, it's that simply setting standards and issuing diktats from Whitehall doesn't mean they actually happen. We do need structural changes – not just edicts about standards.
>
> (Cameron 2011)

APPROACHES AND BASIC POINTS

There are different approaches to strategy evaluation. One approach we might call a goals-based model; this is where the view is taken that strategic goals were clearly defined at the beginning and strategic options were evaluated before strategic choices were made, and so any strategic action that is successful must, by definition, have been worthwhile. In this model of evaluation the process is about checking that desired outcomes have materialized (see Concept Box 11.2). A stakeholder-based model may also assume that strategy formulation and implementation started with the definition of clear strategic goals, but assumes that the consequences of the process are not fully anticipated and that the valuing of the consequences can be appreciated from a variety of perspectives. There may have been important costs and benefits experienced by stakeholders that were not foreseen by the architects of the strategy. In a strategic planning process that tries to put the public first it may be useful to use a third approach, which we will call the satisfaction-audit model, and find out if citizens and service users actually were left feeling satisfied. A fourth evaluation model could be defined as assessing strategic processes from a normative point of view – was the strategic plan developed according to some rules or standards about how these things should be done? This is called here a normative model of evaluation.

CONCEPT BOX 11.2   GOALS-BASED EVALUATION

The simplest form of impact evaluation is what is sometimes called a 'goals-based evaluation' (Patton 2002), in which policy makers want to know whether a desired outcome, target or goal has been achieved. This is a fairly straightforward issue of defining a desired outcome at the outset of a policy initiative and checking at some agreed future time whether this outcome has or has not been achieved . . . One limitation of goals-based evaluations is that they may not also consider the unanticipated outcomes or consequences of a policy initiative and, consequently, may give a partial, if not biased, view of the policy's outcomes.

(Davies 2004: 3)

We can make some more points briefly about strategy evaluation. First, while the aims of monitoring and evaluation are different, superficially some of the activities to carry them out may seem similar.

Second, evaluation is unlikely to be a purely analytical process. For a start, leadership credibility might be at stake as a result of the evaluation – a strategy that is evaluated as a failure and as a costly mistake is unlikely to be welcomed by strategic leaders responsible for its design and implementation. Evaluation may result in the allocation of praise and blame, and this will matter to incumbent strategic leaders as well as their rivals. Then there is another political dimension, in terms of factions and cliques within an organization that may be arguing about the strategy to be evaluated with, for example, one management faction wishing to stick with the existing strategy (to whom it may seem highly important that the evaluation shows the strategy has been very successful and very worthwhile), and another management faction favouring a new strategy and wishing to see a strategy discredited. Obviously it is difficult to imagine a situation where there is no political rivalry, or even no open conflict at all, but some situations can be ones where the level of internal conflict and wrangling has become very dysfunctional and is preventing the existence of a cohesive and confident strategic leadership within the organization. When this is the case, the determination of who will carry out the evaluation, its terms of reference, the forum that will discuss and act on the evaluation, the public visibility of the evaluation process, etc., will become contested.

Third, it seems obvious that evaluation should piggyback on a performance measurement and performance management system as much as possible, but this will only be easily achieved if the strategic plan has been used to specify the performance data in the performance management system. In some cases it will not be possible because the strategy and the performance management system are disconnected. The evaluation process might need to involve interviews and other data collection methods with a range of stakeholders of the strategy – including elected politicians, managers, professionals and members of the public.

Fourth, an organization should be prepared to commit the necessary time and effort to collecting and analysing data for strategy evaluation, if it can only partially piggyback on existing performance management systems. The organization may also want relatively subjective data obtained through interviews and questionnaires. For example, evaluation data might be collected by carrying out an online survey of an organization's managers in which they are asked to rate the impact of the strategy on the services they manage and the satisfaction of the public that use the services.

Fifth, as well as making comparisons of goals and outcomes, organizations should consider using time trend analysis in which pre-strategy and post-strategy data is compared. The use of time trend analysis to carry out an evaluation is not without its complexities, but it is a very useful complement to evaluations that compare target results and actual outcomes. In Figure 11.1, the time trend analysis appears to show that a new strategy has been successful because the results do not follow the past trend in a straight line, but show a steeper upward movement in performance.

NORMATIVE EVALUATIONS OF STRATEGIC PLANNING PROCESSES

An interesting approach to evaluating planning processes was developed as part of the implementation of the United States Government Performance and Results Act of 1993 (GPRA) (see The Director of the Office of Management and Budget 1997 for a report to the President and Congress

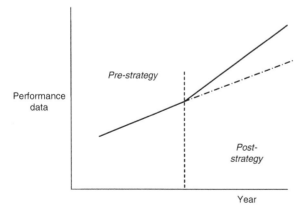

Figure 11.1 *Time trend analysis*

on this legislation). The act was aimed at improving the focus of federal activities and at better measurement of results. The key requirements were that federal agencies produced strategic plans and annual performance plans. The strategic plans enabled better focusing of activities by getting agencies to rethink and clarify their missions, and the annual performance plans were the basis of performance measurement that allowed progress to be evaluated and also provided important information for budgeting purposes. The performance plans were intended to deliver the strategic plans, which were required to cover five fiscal years in the future. The strategic plans and performance plans were to be submitted to the US Congress for the first time in late 1997.

In the summer of 1996, the Office of Management and Budget carried out a review of the strategic plans of federal agencies (including those that were under development). This produced four concerns (Koskinen 1997):

1　The annual performance goals were not adequately linked to the general goals in the strategic plans.
2　There was a lack of interagency coordination to ensure consistent goals.
3　Where the leadership of a federal agency was not involved in the preparation of the strategic plan, the plan was poorer.
4　There were few signs of extensive consultation with stakeholders in the preparation of strategic plans.

These concerns were clearly reflected in an evaluation worksheet which was developed for use by the US Congress to evaluate the strategic plans of federal agencies. The evaluation was concerned with compliance with the GPRA. In late 1997 this worksheet had ten evaluation factors:

1　mission statement
2　general (strategic) goals and objectives
3　strategies to achieve general goals and objectives
4　relationship between general goals and annual performance goals
5　external factors
6　programme evaluations
7　treatment/coordination of cross-cutting functions
8　data capacity
9　treatment of major management problems/high-risk areas
10　congressional and stakeholder consultations.

Each strategic plan was to be scored on all these factors, and a strategic plan could be awarded a total of 100 points (ten points for each factor). In fact, there were five bonus points given for the inclusion of realistic performance measures.

The scoring of each factor involved assessing a number of items and each of these had varying maximum scores. For example, the mission statement factor

260

had four items, two of which were worth a maximum of three points and two worth a maximum of two points. A mission statement that covered the federal agency's major functions and operations could score up to three points; if it reflected the agency's statutory authority it could score up to another three points; if it was results oriented it could get two more points; and if the mission statement made it clear why the agency existed and what it did, it could score another two points. Thus the maximum score of ten points could be achieved on this factor by scoring the maximum number of points on each of the four items.

The 20-item worksheet, at Table 11.1, to evaluate strategic planning aimed at performance improvement is inspired by the Congress worksheet. Some of the Congress items are paraphrased or combined together, but some new items have also been introduced (see United States General Accounting Office (1997).

This is what might be termed a 'normative' evaluation. A strategic plan that scores highly using the worksheet is demonstrating conformance to a set of ideas about what would be a good process for producing a strategic plan and is not being judged in terms of the consequences of the strategic plan. Since the 1993 legislation was using strategic planning as an essential framework for results-oriented government, the evaluation worksheet concentrated on the features of the strategic planning process crucial to that agenda. Obviously, if the law had been aiming at the development of federal agency strategic planning for different purposes, the construction of the evaluation worksheet would have been significantly different.

AN ACADEMIC FRAMEWORK FOR EVALUATING A STRATEGIC PLAN (HEYMANN 1987)

Heymann's (1987) model of strategy, in which the plan is used to align organizational capacity and external support with desirable strategic goals to meet social needs, offers another approach to assessing a strategic plan (see Figure 11.2).

Consider, for example, the following evaluation questions suggested by Heymann's framework:

1 Do the organization's strategic goals still correspond to current social needs, or have the goals lagged behind changes in social needs?
2 Did the strategic plan bring the following into a consistent alignment: desirable strategic goals linked to the political objectives of elected politicians and public and social needs; external support from politicians, the public and other external stakeholders; and organizational capacity?
3 Was the strategic plan developed through a process that created the support of partner organizations?

Table 11.1 *Evaluation worksheet – for strategic planning aimed at performance improvement*

Worksheet	Item	Score
Factor 1: mission statement	1 Does the mission statement make it clear who are the intended beneficiaries of the activities of the organization? 2 What benefits are intended as outcomes? 3 Does the mission statement identify the main activities of the organization? 4 Does the mission statement explain what the organization does and why in terms of its legal mandates?	Maximum 10
Factor 2: strategic goals	5 Are strategic goals logically related to the organization's mission? 6 Are strategic goals results-oriented and measurable?	Maximum 10
Factor 3: strategies	7 Do strategies logically realign or develop programmes and services to achieve the organization's strategic goals? 8 Do strategies logically realign or develop the capabilities of the organization to achieve the organization's strategic goals? 9 Do strategies logically realign or develop the alliances and cooperative activities of the organization (e.g. with other public service organizations)?	Maximum 10
Factor 4: relationship between strategic goals and annual performance goals	10 Are annual performance goals logically linked to strategic goals?	Maximum 10
Factor 5: situational analysis	11 Does the strategic plan identify and take external factors into account as threats and opportunities?	Maximum 10
Factor 6: performance and programme evaluation	12 Does the strategic plan explain what performance and programme evaluations were used?	Maximum10

Table 11.1. *(Continued)*

Worksheet	Item	Score
Factor 7: partnership working	13 Does the strategic plan provide evidence of discussion and planning with other public services organizations that have similar functions/programmes/ services?	Maximum 10
Factor 8: public consultation and involvement	14 Did the organization consult or survey the public as part of the strategic planning process? 15 Did it consult the public on the strategic plan in an open-minded, constructive and good faith manner? 16 Was the organization responsive to the views and suggestions of the public in finalizing the strategic plan?	Maximum 10
Factor 9: performance measurement and reporting systems	17 Does the strategic plan contain baseline data relating to all the strategic and annual performance goals? 18 Does the organization have the capacity to collect and report reasonably accurate data in relation to all the strategic and annual perform-ance goals?	Maximum 10
Factor 10: feasibility assessment and risk analysis	19 Were the strategies contained in the strategic plan subjected to rigorous assessments of feasibility before being approved or authorized? 20 Was a risk analysis of proposed courses of action (strategies) part of the strategic decision-making process?	Maximum 10

FRAMEWORK FOR EVALUATING EMERGENT STRATEGIES

Patton and Patrizi (2010) put forward an approach to evaluating strategy that is inspired and, almost entirely, influenced by their interpretation of the ideas of Henry Mintzberg. They were trying to find a basis for an approach to evaluating strategy (Patton and Patrizi 2010: 12): 'In looking at various frameworks that might inform evaluating strategy, we resonate to a behavioral approach in which strategy is evaluated by examining patterns of behavior – what the organization

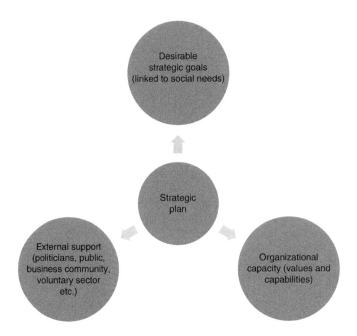

Figure 11.2 *Heymann's model – the strategic plan should align goals, support and capacity*

actually does – not just its rhetoric about strategy and strategic plans'. They found a starting point in Henry Mintzberg's view of strategy. They say (2010: 12–13):

Mintzberg's approach is to define strategy as systematic patterns of organizational behavior that determine overall direction, how the organization's work is carried out, and where it is carried out. He distinguishes "intended strategy" from "realized strategy". When examined, "realized strategy" (or what was actually done) reveals patterns of behavior and commitments, the ways that problems are framed, and how an organization relates to the external world. In combination, these patterns constitute strategy.

They also respond to Mintzberg's definitions of strategy as position and strategy as perspective. As a result of the first type of strategy (as position) they acknowledge the importance of looking at outcomes of the strategy. They say (2010: 15):

... strategy as position focuses attention on where an organization aims to have an effect and contribute to outcomes. ... In the worlds of government, philanthropic, and not-for-profit organizations, strategic position has to do with niche. Debates about strategic position in government focus on what the private sector can and should do, what the public sector can and should do, and what they should do together.

In this quote they suggest that strategic position 'has to do with niche' and then suggest debates in government focus on what the public sector can and should do, and so on. Their suggestion of the interpretation seems to be focused on the issues of commissioning, purchasing and partnership working in the context of public services being provided by organizations from all sectors of the economy (public, not-for-profit and private sectors). This seems an unduly narrow scope for the work of evaluating strategy in the public sector.

They also make the following observations on strategy as position (Patton and Patrizi 2010: 16):

> Strategy as position can productively test how an organization deals with its understanding of its own potential to be effective. Without position it is fairy difficult to even consider an outcomes framework, as position sets the terms of performance – where you will succeed, how much, and in what way. Commitment to a position makes success or failure more obvious than in its absence.

Their interpretation of Mintzberg's strategy as perspective seems to focus on how an organization *thinks* about itself (2010: 15):

> Evaluating strategy as perspective means examining how the organization thinks about itself, including the extent to which the organization's leadership, staff, and participants in the organization's programs articulate a consistent view of strategic perspective. Perspective is the core set of values and theories about how change comes about that shape what an organization is – reflecting its sense of how and where it can be effective. [. . .] We would posit that most organizations have perspectives – some weak or strong, but more often than not, largely undeclared and therefore unexamined and untested. Organizations with strong and clear perspective can use it to make decisions about where it can work most effectively and how. Clear perspective allows an organization to think about the staff it needs, communicate more effectively with its partners and stakeholders, identify where it can work effectively (or not), and deploy its resources accordingly.

This interpretation, stressing examining how the organization thinks about itself, may seem slightly surprising given Patton and Patrizi's earlier statement about resonating with a behavioural approach. It might also be regarded as strange that they propose to examine values and theories and think that a clear perspective allows the organization to think about various things, but they do not propose examining the strategic plan for evidence of how the organization thinks about itself, especially since the strategic plan might have the backing and support of a powerful group within the organization – i.e. the strategic leaders.

From this point they proceed to identify four groups of questions for evaluation (shown in Table 11.2).

Patton and Patrizi believed that basing evaluation on Mintzberg's framework for thinking about strategy (deliberate strategy, emergent strategy, unrealized strategy, realized strategy) offered an alternative approach to what they called the classic accountability-oriented approach of evaluation. By the latter they meant that evaluation looks at what was 'planned to do and achieve (intended outcomes)' (Patton and Patrizi 2010: 18).

Table 11.2 Patton and Patrizi's evaluation questions (2010)

Group 1: Strategic perspective	1 What is the organization's strategic perspective? 2 How aligned are understandings about the organization's strategic perspective across different stakeholder constituencies (leadership, staff, program participants, funders)?
Group 2: Strategic position	3 What is the organization's strategic position? 4 How aligned are understandings about the organization's strategic position across different stakeholder constituencies (leadership, staff, program participants, funders)?
Group 3: Interaction between strategic perspective and strategic position	5 What is the relationship between strategic perspective and strategic position? 6 How does the strategic perspective inform strategic position? To what extent and in what ways does a strategic position flow from perspective? 7 What tensions, if any, are manifest between perspective and position? How are these managed?
Group 4: Tracking strategy over a period of time	8 What was the intended (planned) strategy? 9 What aspects of the intended strategy were implemented as planned, becoming realized strategy? 10 What planned strategy elements were dropped? Why? 11 What unplanned and emergent strategies were implemented, becoming part of a realized strategy? Why? How? With what implications? 12 What has been learned (over some period of time) about the relationships among intended, implemented, dropped, emergent, and ultimately realized strategies?

For the public sector, however, there does need to be an accountability orientation somewhere within the evaluation of strategy. It is not clear to what extent Patton and Patrizi were suggesting that evaluation should be exclusively concerned with learning. They do suggest that Mintzberg was making a choice in favour of learning and adaptation and a choice to reject accountability (Patton and Patrizi 2010: 19):

> Mintzberg emphasizes that ongoing attention to the strategy should focus on learning and adaptation, not accountability (i.e., whether what was planned was actually implemented as planned with the planned results). In Mintzberg's model, strategy is an ongoing process of venturing and learning that supports how an organization creates strategy over time. "Doing" is the precursor to "learning," and learning is the precursor to developing a robust vision for the work to be done going forward.

They seem in this statement to be implying that learning is evaluation in the Mintzberg way of looking at things. In the public sector, because of the importance of good public governance, transparency and accountability to the citizens are increasingly asserted as critical in the public sector. But does there have to be a choice? Surely, good public governance would mean that strategic leaders would be designing and using evaluation for both learning/adaptation *and* accountability? It may take more will and expertise to make it both learning and accountability, but there seems to be no good reason to rule out either one as a goal of evaluation.

A FRAMEWORK FOR STRATEGIC LEADERS BASED ON INCLUSIVENESS

There is a risk that strategic leaders who are influenced by Mintzberg's ideas of informal learning will neglect the importance of evaluating formal strategic plans, both in terms of the process and the outcomes of formal strategic plans. If they are sympathetic to Mintzberg's position on strategic plans, there is a risk that their ongoing attention is given mostly to unintended patterns of consistency over time.

If, however, strategic leaders see strategic plans as vehicles for conscious and purposeful thinking and action, and if they also have responsibilities for leading in a way that supports public sector values of transparency and accountability to the public, an approach based on Mintzberg's view of strategy will be unsatisfactory. A framework for evaluating strategy, which takes account of the public governance agenda, needs to answer a relatively small number of overarching questions. The overall question to be answered might be: was it worth making the effort of creating and delivering the strategic plan? But in answering this question it is important to provide a comprehensive assessment of worth and also to evaluate on a normative basis the strategic planning process (from goal setting through to implementation, monitoring and evaluation). The overarching questions can be framed as shown in Table 11.3.

The first evaluation question can be seen as of direct and immediate importance in public governance systems where transparency is important and the public should be able to get (or be provided with) information on progress in delivering priority outcomes. Effective and honest reporting on strategic goals and results by government to the public can be seen as part of a democratic culture. As noted previously, many members of the public expect governments to keep their promises: politicians that make promises to the electorate at election time need to report back to the public on how successful they have been in delivering their promises. This is, in fact, putting the elected politicians on the line. Reporting back to the public is likely to make it more likely that the politicians are subject to public censure if they have failed to do what they promised to do. On the other hand, if the promises are kept then this is part of the way in which politicians can build their credibility in the eyes of the public. In fact, there is some evidence from research into strategic planning in local government that reporting on performance to the public is linked to strategic plans being more effective (Poister and Streib 2005). (Of course, there may be an issue about direction of causality there!)

The second evaluation question is prompted by the need for evaluation to include both types of consequences – intended and unintended. It is possible that there might be unintended benefits from the implementation of a government strategic plan. It is essential that evaluation includes people, groups and organizations outside of the public sector. It is what a public sector organization or government should do. The third question reinforces the importance of modern public governance producing and delivering government strategies that are responsive to citizens. The fourth question should generate evidence that could be useful in improving the future effectiveness of strategy and the strategic planning process.

To sum up, accountability does matter, including accountability to the public. Formal strategic planning needs to benefit from strategic learning *and* be

---

Table 11.3 *Evaluation for conscious and purposeful strategic leaders*

Framework for evaluation for use by strategic leaders

1 Were strategic goals (outcomes) achieved?
2 What were the costs and benefits (intended and unintended) for various stakeholders?
3 Were citizens and service users (if applicable) left feeling satisfied as a result of the strategic changes delivered?
4 Was the strategic planning process done well? Was strategy refined (or changed) along the way? Why? Did refinements (or changes) in strategy incorporate lessons from strategic learning?

accountable and responsive to citizens. It is worth noting again the observation of Norwegian researcher, Aage Johnsen (2014), who suggested that there was an alignment of the strategic planning approach in Norway's public sector with important expectations about transparency and accountability.

THEORY INTO PRACTICE

Concept Box 11.3 examines a practitioner's views on evaluation.

CONCEPT BOX 11.3   A PRACTITIONER'S VIEWS ON EVALUATION

By Adrienne Roberts, who has held senior positions in local and central government and now works independently in the public sector as an adviser and interim executive from her company Guy Harlings Consultancy.

On the face of it, the answer is simple. Against the objectives, assess the delivery and put either a tick or a cross in the box. There are occasions when this is what happens, but there are lots of considerations and challenges that can get in the way.

What is the big picture for your strategy? How clear are you about the overall landscape in which your strategy is intended to be implemented? Are all the levers and connectivities mapped and understood? Do we see which are the short cycle processes and systems, and which are the long-term intergenerational cycles?

A whole systems approach gives us a mechanism for assessing these questions, but it is rare, in my experience, that much effort is put into that meta level strategic appraisal. There is a job to be done and we want to get on with it! The challenge, however, is there may well be unintended and long-term consequences of the strategy that never get evaluated.

In the 1980s, local government was under severe pressure to reduce cost, reduce size, and reduce overheads. The strategy was to open services up to the market, and the theory was that market forces would create an equilibrium that would give value and more efficient service. Schools sold their playing fields, the meals they produced for our children were done at the lowest possible cost, public transport was deregulated, and our parks and open spaces were contracted out. How was that strategy evaluated? Costs were reduced and new markets were developed, but what of the total impact on our public realm, on children and young people – their ability to exercise and eat well? Those long-term effects are possibly only now coming to the fore and causing great concern.

Who is doing the evaluating? Best practice would say that independent evaluation is best. It brings a degree of rigour and objectivity that those who were involved from the start would be hard put to achieve. For statistical, demographic, and scientific evaluations that is probably right – but what about the passion, the experience, the relationships, and the arrangements that went with the delivery and the achievements or failures? There is often real learning and culture change that comes about through new ways of working and problem solving that is felt and understood most strongly by those who were involved. This 'naturalistic' approach is, of course, potentially dangerous for the objectivity of the evaluation, but it might make one think that in setting any strategy the 'how' as well as the 'what' are worth evaluating for benefits and learning. Relationships can be tested and strengthened, new means of communicating and sharing information evolve, an appreciation of differing perspectives and histories can grow, all of which have a qualitative impact on delivery, but may not necessarily get evaluated.

There are other pros and cons to the issue of who does the evaluation around the ability of the strategy sponsors to hear and see the messages coming from the evaluation. This stems not so much from the rigour of the exercise, but the positioning and communicating of the evaluation.

Internal evaluation feels different to recipients. It is 'evaluation of us' not 'evaluation for us' and it can feel part of an ongoing narrative rather than a real opportunity to stand back and reflect. The organization just gobbles it up, digests it, and moves on; and the formalities or starkness of an external evaluation are not there to create any uncomfortable feelings in the stomach! So there is a real chance that the lessons are not heard or learnt. It is possible that the regime is such that the evaluation produced provides only acceptable messages and some of the trickier issues go unremarked.

On the other hand, external evaluation is sometimes hard to place, especially when it has had a long-term perspective, reviewing activity and outcomes over a long period. Life has moved on, the original protagonists are long gone, who is there to hear the message? Equally, in a society where today's news is everything, the short-term drives our decision making. What processes do we have at our disposal to look back over a generation and project forward over a generation to plan what next?

Really hearing the conclusions of an external evaluation of a long-term strategy takes some doing. Making decisions on a new strategy as a consequence takes even more effort because it is like turning an oil tanker.

A strategy may have been in place for some time, possibly years. It is now part of the infrastructure and fabric of partnerships, job design, and resource allocation. In other words it has become a way of life and the evaluation may mean a fundamental redesign. How often do we properly plan for this stage that may not fit neatly with our strategic planning processes and will require a programme of work in its own right in order to reconfigure or refocus the strategy and subsequent implementation?

How specific is the implementation? How real is it to attribute outcomes to the actions taken? Sometimes good things happen; sometimes bad things happen. It is not uncommon for things to be attributed to the plan when, in fact, it is sheer accident or serendipity. There are occasions when the public commitment to a strategy, and the sheer force of energy behind it, make it too sensitive or embarrassing to be able to make rational assessments of practical consequences. The force of an individual's experience, in any event, outweighs their willingness to be swayed by a subsequent dispassionate analysis of outcomes. The chain of events that may be triggered can, in real life, lead in all sorts of interesting directions, and create tensions and dynamics that were not planned or required by the strategy. Programme management is a good tool and, used well, helps keep a project on track, but real people, their energies, and conversations and actions exist outside the standard proforma given to them to return to the project manager!

Who is listening? Solutions are what we want. We can see the problems and often leaders may feel they just know the solution and that is the right thing to do. Evaluation and reflection is not on their radar and, anyway, the type of work envisaged in the solution sits comfortably with their view of life. This is a linked point to the issue of 'how big the picture is', but it can also be an emotional tussle. Sometimes, we just do not want to give up our pet theories. We are emotionally, if not intellectually, wedded to them and believe that if we just work hard enough, put in enough resource, go that extra mile, it is bound to work!

Who needs evaluation? There is a darker aspect to this problem. Evaluating a strategy in the environment I have described can be quite dangerous to the evaluator, particularly if it is an internal person. Objective assessment of the benefits and disadvantages may be heard as disloyalty and lack of commitment to the programme. In that case, it is worth planning the manner in which the evaluation is fed back, and playing a longer game. There may be some credible stakeholders who can play a role and are less likely to be seen as partisan. Creating a context and environment where the messages are being fed in gradually can be a more productive way of getting the key players to listen. Evidence, facts and figures, and national and international trends, may assist in putting the evaluation on a non-emotional footing and provide an opportunity to be open and honest in the challenges. But beware! In the public sector whether in executive or non-executive roles, passion and emotion lie not far below the surface in us all. Sometimes none of us are listening – we just want it to work.

SUMMARY

In this chapter we noted the possibility of different approaches to strategy evaluation, which is concerned with judging strategy processes and whether a strategy has been worthwhile or not. We distinguished evaluation from monitoring activity, which is used during implementation and for the realization and maintenance of the strategy.

We presented four models to indicate some of the choices strategic leaders have in designing practical evaluations.

- Goals-based model: evaluation is about checking that desired outcomes have materialized
- Stakeholder-based model: evaluation is based on appreciating that the valuing of the consequences can be from a variety of perspectives

■ Satisfaction-audit model: evaluation researches the satisfaction of citizens and service users
■ Normative model: evaluation checks the process to see if the strategic plan was developed according to some rules or standards about how these things should be done.

This chapter included a brief note on the use of trend data for evaluation rather than just data comparing intended and actual outcomes.

Two different evaluation tools were presented. One was based on Mintzberg's framework for understanding strategy. The second was a very simple tool consisting of four overarching questions that were justified as being relevant to strategic leadership that was purposeful and conscious and relevant to modern ideas and values of public governance.

The chapter was concluded with a contribution of a practitioner who drew attention to the meaning and impact of evaluation for managers and professionals. She provided an alternative perspective on evaluation – quite different from cool and analytical guidance on how to do evaluation as if it is just a matter of data, evidence and analysis. She also stressed that it is not easy for those who have a stake in a strategy evaluation to really hear the conclusions of an evaluation.

Work-based assignment: evaluating your own organization's strategic plan

The work-based assignments in this book are for civil servants and other public services staff who have management experience.

Does your own public service organization have a strategic plan produced in the last five years? If it does, review the evaluation worksheet with 10 factors and 20 items presented in this chapter (which was based on the draft of a US Congress evaluation tool). Prepare your own version of this evaluation worksheet, changing any items you think need to be changed, and work out a detailed scoring system (so that the maximum score on each item is clarified). Then use it to evaluate the strategic planning effort in your own public services organization. You may need to collect information and study strategic documents to carry out this evaluation. Based on your evaluation, identify any shortfalls in the way the strategic planning process was carried out in your own organization.

DISCUSSION QUESTIONS

1 Is there really a difference between monitoring and evaluation as suggested at the outset of this chapter? Would it be better to combine monitoring and evaluation as a single activity? What are the advantages, if any, of keeping monitoring and evaluation as separate activities?

2   Is there a best model for evaluating strategy?
3   Do elected politicians learn lessons from studying the previous government's mistakes? What factors make it difficult for a new government to learn from what the previous government did?
4   Who should do evaluations of strategy? Should organizations pay outsiders to come in and do evaluations?
5   Is it dangerous for your career to be an internal evaluator of an existing strategy? Why?

FURTHER READING

Patton, M. Q. and Patrizi, P. A. (2010). 'Strategy as the focus for evaluation', in P. A. Patrizi and M. Q. Patton (eds), *Evaluating strategy: new directions for evaluation*, 128: 5–28.

This provides an approach to evaluating strategy based on Henry Mintzberg's ideas of emergent and deliberate strategies. Although Patton and Patrizi's ideas on evaluating strategy have been briefly outlined in the chapter, this is also worth reading because it champions the approach they set and provides more explanation and justification for it.

REFERENCE LIST

Cameron, D. (2011) *Prime Minister's Speech on Modern Public Service*. [Online]. Available from: www.gov.uk/government/speeches/prime-ministers-speech-on-modern-public-service [Accessed: 14 May 2016].

Davies, P. (2004) *Policy Evaluation in the United Kingdom*, [UK Cabinet Office] Paper presented at the KDI International Policy Evaluation Forum, Seoul, Korea, 19–21 May 2004.

The Director of the Office of Management and Budget (1997) *The Government Performance and Results Act. Report to the President and Congress*. [Online]. Available from: http://govinfo.library.unt.edu/npr/library/news/gprarpt.html [Accessed: 4 April 2016].

Heymann, P. B. (1987) *The Politics of Public Management*. London: Yale University Press.

Johnsen, A. (2014) 'Strategic management schools of thought and practices in the public sector in Norway', in P. Joyce and A. Drumaux (eds) *Strategic Management in Public Organizations: European Practices and Perspectives*. New York & London: Routledge. pp. 34–40.

Koskinen, J. A. (1997) Statement of John A. Koskinen, Deputy Director for Management and Budget, before the Subcommittee on Government Management, Information, and Technology of the House Committee on Government Reform and Oversight, 105th Cong. (June 3, 1997).

Patrizi, P. A. and Patton, M. Q. (2010) 'Editors' Notes', in P. A. Patrizi and M. Q. Patton (eds), *Evaluating Strategy: New Directions for Evaluation*, 128: 1–4.

Patton, M. Q. (2002) *Qualitative Research and Evaluation Methods*. 3rd edition. Thousand Oaks, CA: Sage.

Patton, M. Q. and Patrizi, P. A. (2010) 'Strategy as the focus for evaluation', in P. A. Patrizi and M. Q. Patton (eds), *Evaluating strategy: new directions for evaluation*, 128: 5–28.

Poister, T. H. and Streib, G. D. (2005) Elements of strategic planning and management in municipal government: status after two decades. *Public Administration Review*, 65(1): 45–56.

United States General Accounting Office (1997) *Agencies' Strategic Plans Under GPRA: Key Questions to Facilitate Congressional Review*. GAO/GGD – 10.1.16. Washington: United States General Accounting Office.

York, R. O. (1982) *Human Service Planning: Concepts, Tools, and Methods*. Chapel Hill, NC: The University of North Carolina Press.

Part 3

Leading and the new public governance

INTRODUCTION

In this last part of the book a particular public sector reform movement is examined, one that is modernizing the institutional characteristics of public governance, and one that seems to be underway in many different countries. It is a reform movement in which public sector leaders have been assumed to have a major part to play. It is a reform movement that looks likely to reset the situation, relationships and challenges of public sector leaders.

We can describe this movement as one in which public governance is being modernized by reinventing it around strategic management. To accomplish this reinvention the state has to be equipped with a strategic dimension, has to develop new 'strategic-state' capabilities and has to be invested with a new set of relationships. Every part of the public governance system is being reconfigured to enable the state to become more effective, to be more engaged with stakeholders in society, and to develop closer and less paternalistic, or authoritarian, relationships with citizens. There is no doubting that some governments are keen to see this new public governance create more responsiveness to the public with citizens more consulted, more empowered, and feeling more ownership of long-term national development visions and government strategies.

For some politicians good governance is a set of huge and hegemonic ideas that will transform society, and in a sense the antithesis of the 1980s' idea of a neoliberal state, as in the following 2015 statement made by the Government of India (2016):

> Governance, across the public and private domains, is the concern of society as a whole. Everyone has a stake in ensuring good governance and effective delivery of services. Creating Jan Chetna, therefore, becomes crucial for people's initiative. In the past, governance may have been rather narrowly construed as public governance. In today's changed dynamics – with 'public' services often being delivered by 'private' entities, and the greater scope for 'participative citizenry', governance encompasses and involves everyone.

Arguably, the issue for many countries was not only that governance was narrowly construed but rather that public governance was narrowly construed and there was much less ambition for government–society relationships and for mobilizing both private and public action in line with society's aspirations.

In Chapter 12 the new public governance is introduced and examined. This is followed, in Chapter 13, by a consideration of the new terrain for public sector leadership in relation to economic growth and in relation to two spheres of public governance – regulation and service delivery. For example, this last chapter will look at how the drive for coherence and integration challenges the leaders of regulatory bodies pursuing better regulation and how the search for vertical accountability and horizontal cooperation challenges the leaders of public service systems.

REFERENCE LIST

Government of India (2016) *Government Constitutes National Institution for Transforming India (NITI) Aayog.* [Online]. Available from: http://pmindia.gov.in/en/news_updates/government-constitutes-national-institution-for-transforming-india-niti-aayog/?tag_term=niti-aayog&comment=disable [Accessed: 31 January 2016].

Chapter 12

The strategic state

INTRODUCTION

In 1999, an OECD symposium, looking at the future shape of government reform, made the following suggestion about the significance of reforms taking place in many countries (OECD 2000: 11):

> The purpose of reform is to make government more responsive to society's needs. People want government that does more and costs less. Much of current public reform is an effort to meet society's needs by providing better, faster and more services from government.

The OECD symposium not only framed much of the analysis and conclusions in terms of being strategic, it also endorsed the role of leadership in reform. Leaders, the symposium report said, were important for the reform process: 'Leaders within government are key to bridging the gap between the development and the implementation of reform. OECD countries have used leaders at many different levels of government as drivers of reform' (OECD 2000: 15).

Governments involved in reform and modernization were recommended to make use of leaders acting as change agents 'to help their colleagues understand the strategy and values underlying reform efforts' (OECD 2000: 76). In effect, the OECD report's ideas were built around seeing relationships between reform, strategy and leadership, and this entailed leaders changing the institutions of public governance to enable government to be more strategic. In turn, the change in public governance institutions might affect the potential for strategic leadership (by politicians and appointed administrators) in the public sector. See Figure 12.1.

It may be useful here to emphasize three key points about the strategic state. First, the strategic state probably requires capability to be developed in both strategic thinking and performance management at the centre of government, and also in individual government departments. Second, the effectiveness of political and civil service leadership through the development of a strategic state will depend on the coherence and integration that can be achieved. Third, strategic planning will be an important public management tool used in the strategic state for service innovation and transformation.

The UK government elected in 1997 experimented with a lot of the component ideas that were to coalesce into the idea of the strategic state. Ideas such as the importance of the centre of government being selective (focused) and setting priority areas for reform, the importance of long-term thinking, the use of long-term plans (e.g. for health and transport), the promotion of joined-up government and partnership working, and much more. This government also took various initiatives to build strategic capabilities; for example it created specialist central units (e.g. Prime Minister's Strategy Unit, which was also required to build strategic capability in government departments) and it launched the Departmental Capability Reviews that were, in part, designed to assess the ability of government departments to deliver the strategies of ministers. The National School of Government delivered training to civil servants on strategic thinking. In 2004 all of the government departments in Whitehall produced a five-year strategic plan containing the department's vision, its priorities and actions.

There was also considerable work done in the Civil Service to create more of a culture of looking ahead. After a review in 2000, the government's Foresight Programme worked on a number of specific projects. Its work included horizon scanning, trend analysis, modelling, scenarios, visioning and more.

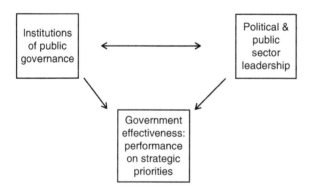

Figure 12.1 Leadership and public governance

In 2007 the Prime Minister's Strategy Unit produced a report on the 'strategic and enabling state'. This report suggested (Prime Minister's Strategy Unit 2007: 4):

The modern state needs to work in a new way – less about command and control and more about collaboration and partnership. This reflects the kind of citizen we have today: inquiring, less deferential, demanding, informed.

[. . .]The core idea of the strategic and enabling state is that power is placed in the hands of the people. It is a vision of the state in which we increase the range of opportunities for engagement; we empower citizens to hold public institutions to account; and we ensure that citizens take joint responsibility with the state for their own well-being.

In the same year as the Prime Minister's Strategy Unit produced its report on the strategic and enabling state, Michael Barber, previously head of the Prime Minister's Delivery Unit, developed ideas for the UK's 'centre of government' to address his concerns about its coherence and integration, and also provided a schematic model of a strategic state (see Figure 12.2).

AN EMERGING ANALYTICAL FRAMEWORK FOR THE STRATEGIC STATE

Attention to the idea of the strategic state and interest in reforming public governance were both very evident in the ten years and more leading up to the 2007–9 banking and finance crisis. In the aftermath of the crisis there seemed to be no loss of interest in the concept of the strategic state or in public governance reform. The OECD carried out many public governance reviews at the request of governments from 2007 onwards. As a result, by the years 2013 and 2014, the OECD was beginning to be very clear about the features of a type of modern public governance suitable for a strategic state.

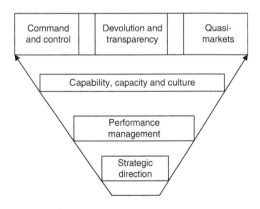

Figure 12.2 Barber's concept of the modern state (2007)

In 2013 the work of the OECD had led them to the following definition of the strategic state (OECD 2013: 7):

> The Strategic State framework emphasises leadership and stewardship from the centre, integrity and transparency, the importance of networks and institutions (both inside and outside government), the need to draw inspiration from sub national initiatives and citizens and crucially, the importance of effective implementation of strategies and policies in support of positive outcomes and impacts for a country's economy and society.

There are a lot of points being made in a concise way in this definition. It might help with understanding the concept to know that the OECD did not think that the strategic state was in any way connected to, or part of, what people had been referring to for some years as the New Public Management (NPM). The strategic state concept should not be seen as a type of management innovation or just about management or just about making the management hierarchy stronger and so on. It is about governance being strategic. To understand the concept of the strategic state, we will clarify and elaborate some of its features; in part this draws on the OECD experience.

Long-term priorities and visions

In the case of a strategic state, public governance was required to create and deliver a vision of the future and a strategy that would bring about national development and improved social and economic outcomes for a country.

Central steering and coordination

The OECD has championed a 'whole of government' approach. So, for example, inter-ministry cooperation is very important. The OECD has developed its ideas of a centre of government and the special responsibility that the centre has for ensuring the coordination, integration and coherence that enables the work of different parts of government to contribute in a joined-up way to delivering the long-term vision and strategy of the government.

Integrated systems in government (performance monitoring, budgeting, ICT, HRM etc.)

Increased levels of coordination and alignment and effective implementation in a strategic state are secured by integrating key systems and processes, such as monitoring and evaluation, budgeting, auditing, human resources management (HRM) and ICT, into the strategic agenda of government. For example, monitoring and evaluation and budgeting should reinforce the strength of the whole of government strategies and help to deliver the long-term strategic priorities.

Multi-level governance

The need to draw inspiration from subnational initiatives might include national level governments listening to the views of subnational governments, to their issues, problems and preferences, rather than national government seeing the subnational governments as merely delivery partners for centrally decided strategies and policies. All in all, multi-level governance shifts towards more cooperation up and down the levels of governance.

Partnerships and stakeholders

The government needs the support and cooperation of bodies and interest groups beyond the state (government). These are sometimes referred to as civil society. The relationships with stakeholders in civil society are not ones in which the state can be autocratic. For, 'the central State cannot directly implement most or even any policies alone' (OECD 2013: 8). If the state cannot simply tell everybody what to do, then it must be willing and able to cooperate. This may mean partnerships. It may mean being part of networks of organizations, including organizations outside the state. To deliver on vision and strategy the state has to work with partners, to work in networks.

Engaging citizens: consultation and participation

The views and opinions of citizens matter to government. Citizens should be invited to help shape and update strategies. Government has to give attention to citizen engagement, access to information and open government. This is not only appropriate in democratic culture, it is also useful pragmatically since it can help to make government strategies and policies more informed. The last word on the strategic state is that in a strategic state the processes of public governance should be designed to serve citizens.

The OECD thinking on strategic states over the years 2007–15 has been a work in progress. As more work has been done, more issues have emerged. For example, the working of a strategic state can be severely hampered if key relationships are not working properly, such as the relationship between political leaders and civil servants, and the relationship between government executives and parliamentary bodies. It is also clear that strategic states need not only to have strategic capabilities that allow them to focus and persist at delivering long-term national development priorities and visions, they also need to be able to deal strategically with periods of major crisis or the sudden onset of a 'wicked problem'. So, it is important we do not restrict our concept of the strategic state to a situation in which the experiences and challenges are mainly ones of steady strategic performance management. Ideally, we would also be clear about strategic crisis management capabilities and problem-solving capabilities.

THE IMPLICATIONS OF THE STRATEGIC STATE FOR PUBLIC ADMINSTRATION REFORMS

The idea of the strategic state is also clearly embedded in some recent thinking about the quality of public administration that should be expected of countries applying to join the European Union. The result of this thinking appears in a report on principles of public administration published by OECD/SIGMA (2014). The same report advocates reform of public administration based on a whole of government approach (OECD/SIGMA 2014: 9):

> Achieving the necessary standard of public administration requires reforms in many areas of policy and administration. [. . .] Achieving results requires the Government to steer and co-ordinate the implementation of an overall reform vision and prioritised objectives. It is therefore important to approach public administration reforms sequentially and in a coherently planned way and to compile a reform agenda from a whole-of-government perspective.

Reform should also be politically and administratively led and make use of strategic planning documents (OECD/SIGMA 2014: 10):

> In addition to top-level ministerial and official leadership, PAR [public administration reform] also requires strategic and business planning documents that provide a clear roadmap for implementing individual policies. These planning documents should translate political-level priority statements into clear objectives, establish performance indicators to measure their level of achievement, designate actions and institutions responsible for realising them, allocate the necessary resources and provide other information for implementing the reform agenda.

MINI CASE STUDY

Developments in India

The Government of India, in 1944, created a Department of Planning and Development. Five years later there was a recommendation that there should be a Planning Commission to provide continuous attention to development from a central government perspective. In 1950 the Indian government, by means of a cabinet resolution, set up a Planning Commission and a system of national development planning was started which was to see the introduction of 12 successive Five-Year Plans. The cabinet resolution of 1950 stated (Government of India 2016):

> The need for comprehensive planning based on a careful appraisal of resources and on an objective analysis of all the relevant economic factors has become imperative. These purposes can best be achieved through an organization free

from the burden of the day-to-day administration, but in constant touch with the Government at the highest policy level. Accordingly, as announced by the Honourable Finance Minister in his Budget speech on the 28th February, 1950, the Government of India have decided to set up a Planning Commission.

The Planning Commission was tasked with assessing the country's resources and formulating a plan to make effective and balanced use of them. It was also to make a determination of priorities, and identify a series of stages in the plan, and then plan the resources needed for each stage.

Since we are concerned with public governance in this chapter, it is interesting to appreciate the Indian government's thinking about how this new Planning Commission based in Delhi would function in terms of its key relationships. The Commission's key relationships were expected to be with the ministries of the central government, the governments of the states, and two major interest groups, which were named as industry and labour. The Planning Commission was not given the power to make and implement decisions; this was the responsibility of the central government and the state governments. Therefore, the cabinet resolution talked about the Planning Commission acting in close consultation with the ministries and the state governments. The government hoped 'that in carrying out its task the Commission will receive the maximum support and goodwill from all interests and in particular, from industry and labour'.

Figure 12.3 shows the Planning Commission at the heart of things but actually just on the outside of central government and the state governments of India – close to government but not part of the governance system itself. Sixty-five years later the Government of India launched a new idea for governance, not just of the public sector, but of the whole of society, and with a proposal to put a strategic input into the governance process. Planning would no longer be on the outside.

The Government of India abolished the Planning Commission part way through the 12th Five-Year Plan (2012–17). The plan was still to be completed but it was envisaged that this would be the last of the Five-Year Plans. At the same time the Government of India launched a new body, to be chaired by the Indian Prime Minister. In fact, the government was replacing the Planning Commission with this new body, which was called NITI Aayog (National Institution for Transform-ing India). The Government of India formulated a whole new system of governance, which it said was not just public governance, because it was to be a new all-inclusive process of governance involving everybody. There were some very big ideas and ambitions surrounding this institutional change, as can be appreciated in the description below, which is based on a government statement published in 2015 (Government of India 2016).

The new concept of governance as articulated by the Government of India is summarized under eight sub-headings.

Long-term key priorities
India was to develop its own strategy for economic growth. The social priorities were to eliminate poverty and to create the opportunity for every Indian to live a life

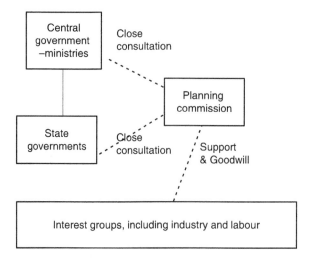

Figure 12.3 *The Government of India's ideas for the relationships of the Planning Commission (1950)*

of dignity and self-respect. India was to be a society of equal opportunity and inclusiveness. India was to achieve environmentally sound development so that the quality of life of existing and future generations was safeguarded.

Institutional character of development work
India was to shift away from central to strategic planning. (This was confirmed a month after the cabinet resolution establishing NITI Aayog. The new Vice-Chairman of NITI Aayog, Arvind Panagariya, is reported to have said that India was likely to switch over to strategic planning and away from the traditional five-year planning system.) The government's logic for the shift from central planning was that many changes were now the result of market forces and global developments and that Indian institutions and its polity had in any case evolved and matured.

So, with the passing of central planning, the new system would involve NITI Aayog developing a 'shared vision of national development priorities with the active involvement of States in the light of national objectives'.

Provision of strategic input into the governance process
The brief given to NITI Aayog by the Indian government was to 'provide the strategic policy vision for the government' and to 'provide a critical directional and strategic input into the governance process' (Government of India 2016). The government perceived a need to use the 'strategy' of governance to energize the 'process' of governance. (It is not exactly clear what this means: we might speculate that it means that strategic thinking and strategic capabilities will energize the process of governance. A good strategy, pursued with will and persistence, might then be seen as the content of governance.)

It is important to be clear that NITI Aayog is not a relatively unimportant group of technical experts giving advice to the Indian government. The NITI Aayog has as its chairperson the Prime Minister of India. Its Governing Council comprises the Chief Ministers of all the States in India and the Lieutenant Governors of Union Territories. The chief executive officer is appointed by the Prime Minister at a rank of Secretary to the Government of India. The Prime Minister will also nominate four members of the Union Council of Ministers.

Integration of ministries/whole of government approach
NITI Aayog will be trying to make the implementation of the national development agenda fast. In order to do this the government brief says they are to 'offer a platform for resolution of inter-sectoral and inter-departmental issues' (Government of India 2016). So, it will be helping to transform India through overcoming the obstacles created by silo working.

Integration of management systems (strategy and monitoring)
The Government of India wants NITI Aayog to carry out monitoring to check on the delivery of strategic and long-term policy and programme frameworks and initiatives. This monitoring will check not only on progress but also on the efficacy of them. This is not just about checking up and accountability – the government also wants learning to result. 'The lessons learnt through monitoring and feedback will be used for making innovative improvements, including necessary mid-course corrections' (Government of India 2016).

Multi-level governance
A highly significant feature of these proposals concerns the intended transformation of the multi-level governance arrangements. It is worth quoting the government statement at length – there is no doubt about the direction of travel in terms of multi-level governance – it is towards partnership (Government of India 2016):

> An important evolutionary change from the past will be replacing a centre-to-state one-way flow of policy by a genuine and continuing partnership with the states. The States of the Union do not want to be mere appendages of the Centre. They seek a decisive say in determining the architecture of economic growth and development. The one-size-fits-all approach, often inherent in central planning, has the potential of creating needless tensions and undermining the harmony needed for national effort. Our development model has to become more consensual and co-operative. It must embrace the specific demands of states, regions and localities. A shared vision of national development has to be worked out based on human dignity, national self-respect and an inclusive and sustainable development path.

Working with partners/stakeholders/civil society
The government intentions here are examples of pure 'reinventing government' thinking (Osborne and Gaebler 1992). The government is to do less producing and

delivery (in the industrial and service sectors) and is to become an 'enabler' rather than a provider of first and last resort.

Active participation of the public
The government took the view that the people of India wanted improvements in governance; they wanted institutional reforms in governance and large-scale change. The intention was to be inclusive in setting the national agenda – everyone was to be given the ability to have their say in setting the agenda. The government plainly declared that the new governance would be based on anticipating and responding to the needs of the people, participation (involvement of citizens), inclusion of all groups and transparency to make the government visible and responsive.

Reflecting on the statements of the Indian government, it appears consistent in all respects with the analytical framework of the strategic state developed by OECD. More than that, it also seems to be consistent with the idea of strategic planning by government being different from central planning because it is selective and interactive (Budd 1978).

INTERNATIONAL COMPARISONS

Public governance is now widely perceived to be important. Dr Rolf Alter, Director for Public Governance and Territorial Development at the OECD, wrote in 2013 (Alter 2014):

Public Governance has moved up in the awareness of the public policy community for quite some time now ... In development economics, institutional weaknesses and lack of good governance are equally identified as the critical bottlenecks for sustainable growth.

In fact, one can get the impression that good public governance is elevated to the all around response, from improving policy performance, achieving better outcomes of development, to more effective sector policies and rebuilding or maintaining trust in government. And its capacities to deliver are expected at all levels of government, including the supra or international level ...

So, there are high expectations that various benefits will flow from improving public governance. It is possible that some of the expectations will prove too high. But what is the evidence that modernizing public governance by infusing it with a strategic dimension improves government effectiveness and then leads to better results in terms of important policies, such as economic growth and environmental performance?

We do not have direct evidence on this, but looking at the data in Table 12.1 suggests some possible conclusions. First, we have a group of countries

Table 12.1 Fifteen countries

Country	Government effectiveness (percentile rank) (high scores are good)		GDP per capita (constant 2005 US$)		Environmental Performance Index (EPI)	
No Name	2000	2014	2000	2014	EPI score published in 2016 (high scores are good)	10-year % change (2016 EPI Report)
1 China	54	66	1,128	3,866	65	13
2 Russian Federation	23	51	3,870	6,844	84	24
3 Saudi Arabia	46	62	12,089	16,944	69	25
4 Turkey	57	67	6,113	8,861	68	7
5 Argentina	59	46	5,450	7,738	80	5
6 Brazil	58	47	4,407	5,853	79	17
7 Ghana	58	44	446	766	59	23
8 South Africa	76	65	4,854	6,087	71	15
9 India	51	57	572	1,236	54	21
10 Singapore	100	100	24,921	38,088	87	0
11 Sweden	97	96	38,516	46,061	90	6
12 UK	94	93	35,445	40,968	87	7
13 Australia	92	92	30,854	37,835	87	22
14 Canada	96	95	33,372	38,259	85	5
15 United States	93	90	40,946	46,405	85	11

Definitions and sources of data:

■ Government effectiveness: data consists of percentile ranks. Based on perceptions of the quality of public services, the quality of the civil service and the degree of its independence from political pressures, the quality of policy formulation and implementation, and the credibility of the government's commitment to such policies. Detailed documentation is available at www.govindicators.org

■ GDP per capita (constant 2005 US$) source: World Bank national accounts data and OECD National Accounts data files. Last updated: 10/14/2015.

■ EPI source: Hsu, A. *et al.* (2016) *2016.*

(Argentina, Brazil, Ghana and South Africa) where government effectiveness dropped over a period of time while economic growth was respectable. This is the opposite of what might be expected. On the other hand, we have a number of countries where government effectiveness increased markedly over the period and so did economic performance (as measured by GDP per capita). In fact, all but one of these countries (China, India, Russian Federation, Saudi Arabia and Turkey) had quite an interesting story to tell in relation to governance and strategic capabilities. Between 2003 and 2008 China added a system of monitoring and evaluation to its five-year planning system, and this was seen as meaning that the planning was becoming a strategic planning system. The Russian Federation went through a period in the 1990s when there was little long-term orientation in the national government, but around the turn of the century there was a distinct move towards a strategic approach; the more strategic approach was applied to the planning of investment by the government. The Russian Federation's seriousness about strategic planning can be inferred from the fact that a new law on strategic planning was signed by the President in 2014, and that made it compulsory in the government system. Saudi Arabia, beginning in 2003, shifted towards a more strategic approach to national development planning, consciously developing monitoring and evaluation for its five-year plans, but also developing a long-term strategic vision. Turkey, also in 2003, began to introduce strategic plans for central government ministries and other public sector organizations (e.g. universities, municipal government), partly linked to a much stronger public financial management framework, and partly to support the national development planning system facilitated by the government's State Planning Organization. So, for all these countries, the planning was becoming more strategic and serious, in one sense or another, at the same time that perceptions of government effectiveness increased. It cannot be assumed, however, that the changes in government effectiveness were necessarily linked to the impressive trends in economic growth.

CASE STUDY

Strategic Leadership in the Public Services of Turkey

By Nahit Bingöl, Director General, Regional Development and Structural Adjustment, Turkish Government, Turkey.

Gaining momentum after the middle of the last decade, Turkey has embarked upon a comprehensive and ambitious set of public sector reforms. Several domestic and external dynamics led to change efforts. Among them were the substantial change in the political establishment due in part to the severe financial crisis in 2001 and the aftermath, the EU Accession process and the tacit societal demand that is manifest especially in urbanization. Major reform processes addressed, among others, Public Management, Public Financial Management, Personnel Regime, Social Security and Health. The proliferation of these initiatives called for effective leadership on all fronts, and provided a fertile ground for those who have the ability to take responsibility.

Change in the public sector and any strategic ingredient of it have operated at two levels in Turkey. Design and management of public sector reforms make up the macro level, whereas those at a given public organization correspond to the micro level, the critical factor being the interplay between them. Experience in Turkey confirms that strategic leadership is a concomitant prerequisite. Strategic management, for instance, could apply to both levels; one may talk about strategic management in reform in the public sector at large, while it may be possible to refer to strategic management as reform for a particular agency. Change efforts required effective leaders both in the management of reforms and in individual organizations to realize them as intended.

Political leadership is the foremost prerequisite as rubber-stamped initiatives have not got rooted. As political and administrative realms operate on different rationalities, striking an effective balance between them is a preferred state. Bureaucratically led reform proposals have not worked unless political buy-in takes place, though political ambitions have also encountered resistance unless bureaucratic consultation is carried out.

Studies and practice concur that the attributes of strategic leadership in the public sector could be summed up in three characteristics: a visionary attitude, an ability to create and sustain motivation for self and others, and a demonstrated belief and practice in collectivism. Design and management of reforms in Turkey have required, in addition to these qualifications, the ability to adapt universal experience to domestic structures. Leadership is instrumental in creatively blending universally accepted merits with those of the domestic requirements to be able to convince and steer the change resistant milieu. Context-blind adoption of change tools have always been faced with ineffective implementation of change initiatives. Many pragmatic adjustments are needed for a meticulously crafted change and risk management plan. People have expected quick results, yet the results required time. It has, therefore, proved critical to manage the trade-off. Ultimately, if leaders of change are successful in creating a critical mass of people and discourse that will, in turn, create its own momentum for sustained change, change takes place.

Experience in Turkey has vindicated the validity of universal principles of change, yet it also confirmed that cultural background and conditions matter equally. Visioning and passion, having in-depth knowledge of legislation and public organizations, and creating a team of good calibre have been essential components and qualifications. The first is critical because, in the absence of it, the change movement becomes erratic. The second proves that, without this knowledge, the movement will not be authoritative enough to overcome resistance. Without the third the movement will not be put into action effectively.

It might be relevant to frame the lessons learnt in the Turkish experience by way of questions that follow:

What is the orientation of strategic leaders to change? In Turkey it was a wholehearted answer to the needs of a vibrant society that has been going through modernization and urbanization.

What strategic management tools, if any, should they use? Political and public sector leaders should definitely make use of change management knowledge and practice, and be competent in risk management as many unprecedented details hinder implementation along the way.

What strategic leverage points can leaders use for bringing about modernization and innovation? Design and management of reforms cascade from political leaders through front line employees. Establishing a network of change champions at all levels, and being able to create a network among them, would certainly be useful in building channels to facilitate the flow of passion. Professional consultation services in public relations and communication is *sine qua non* as public officials may not be versatile enough to administer this very critical aspect of reform management. However, any abilities that the digital world offers should be accepted.

What are the costs and benefits of being a strategic leader in today's public services in Turkey? Change is a challenge to power and interest groups. It poses political and personal risks of rapid elimination. If not carefully administered and effectively communicated, it may backfire. It is a real test of stress and passion. The most rewarding benefit is self-discovery.

MINI CASE STUDY

Reform and the Governance of Scotland (2007–11)

Scotland, between 2007 and 2011, appears to have engaged in a whole of government reform of its public governance that was, in effect, creating what we have been calling a strategic state. It was a step-change in how Scotland was governed. Importantly, this case appears to suggest that the ideas for the change came partly from political leaders and partly from civil service leaders. Furthermore, the changes made created a new institutional framework in which political and civil service leaders could operate in a more integrated way in pursuit of national outcomes.

What happened? The Scottish Nationalist Party (SNP) formed a minority government in 2007 (with only 36 per cent of the seats in the Scottish Parliament). It began its period in office with a commitment to an outcome-based approach to government and the idea of a slimmed down cabinet. During 2007 the Scottish Government set five outcome-based strategic objectives – the country was to become wealthier and fairer, safer and stronger, smarter, greener and healthier.

Many changes were made to enable effective delivery of these five objectives. In line with SNP thinking, a smaller cabinet was established. A new 'Strategic Board' was created at the top administrative level. The Board had the function of supporting the Cabinet. Its members included the Permanent Secretary to the Scottish Government, five directors general and others. The number of directors general was significant. Each of them was responsible for one of the five top-priority strategic objectives.

Changes were made to the structure of the Scottish Civil Service. In place of the old departmental structure there was an attempt 'to create a stronger sense of a single coherent organization' (Elvidge 2011: 33). The Permanent Secretary saw this as an attempt to overcome organizational silos that are a problem in many civil service structures.

Management systems were also redesigned. As a result of the Scottish Budget Spending Review of 2007, a National Performance Framework was introduced that was intended to enable the performance of the Scottish Government to be tracked against its strategic objectives.

An attempt was made to integrate local government and other public sector bodies into the delivery of the overall strategic objectives. Elvidge (2011: 35) described this as an attempt to 'link the new concept of a single framework of national purpose, the Purpose and National Outcomes, to the established arrangements for providing varying degrees of Ministerial direction to the many organisations which comprise the totality of Scotland's public sector'.

The government's desire to reconstruct its relationship with stakeholders and citizens was also evident in two initiatives. First, the government set up a Council of Economic Advisers and a National Economic Forum, signalling not only its intention to consult beyond government but also the importance it placed on economic strategy. Second, in June 2008, the Scotland Performs website was launched, which was the basis of a reporting system to the public on progress in delivering the strategic objectives.

Using the Scottish Government's own reports on its performance, and taking into account a wide selection of indicators, it appeared by 2012 that government performance had been relatively good and many of the performance trends were positive, including those for GDP growth and economic productivity. Judged in this way, the Scottish Government performed well over the period from 2007 to 2011. At least one external report suggested that the government had governed in a very strategic way: 'Scotland was the only jurisdiction where we were able to clearly observe a strategic approach and trace it to a series of cross-cutting policies' (Wallace, Mathias and Brotchie, 2013: 9).

One of the most interesting insights into this Scottish experience of modernizing public governance came from one of the leaders at the heart of the developments, Sir John Elvidge, who was Permanent Secretary to the Scottish Government from 2003 until 2010, when he retired. According to him, the ideas behind the redesign of public governance came from both the political leadership and the civil service leadership (Elvidge 2011: 34):

> So, in May 2007, two separate analyses of ways to define and pursue the objectives of government more effectively by changing the organisation and functioning of government – that developed by the SNP outside government and that developed by me, with my senior colleagues, within government – came into conjunction.

The model, according to Elvidge, had strategic leadership and cooperation as essential ingredients (2011: 4):

> In partnership between Civil Service and political leadership, a radical Scottish model of government has developed since 2007, building on the learning from the earlier period of devolution. [...] It places strategic leadership and the facilitation of cooperation between organisations and

sections of society at the heart of the role of central government, rather than a managerialist view of the relationship of central government to others.

Elvidge (2011: 25) highlighted the issue of leadership styles as an influence on the success of the model, which he discussed in relation to the move to a small cabinet.

SUMMARY

The last 20 years have been rather surprising, really. People have rediscovered the idea that the state is important and that it needs reforming to be more effective. Perhaps more surprising still is that the core idea for creating more effective government is to redesign governance (and to reenergize it) around strategic management and by making use of ideas of vision and strategy in the governance process. This view of the way to reform public governance was shown very clearly by the decision of the Government of India in 2015 to change away from central planning and to switch to strategic planning.

Public governance reforms are occurring in a wide range of countries. It is quite likely that it will prove to be of the utmost importance to public sector leaders. Being a public sector leader in a country at the pre-reform stage of public governance and being a public sector leader in a country where the reform of public governance was complete would be very different. The challenges facing the leader would be completely different. For example, to be a public sector leader where there is a whole of government approach will be quite different from being a leader where silo working continues. Being a public sector leader in which transparency and accountability to the public are high on the agenda and where there is a genuine level of public engagement is presumably very different from a public governance situation in which paternalism and bureaucratic secrecy still prevails. Will we need new theories of public sector leadership for post-reform situations – theories for example that reflect much greater levels of partnership working across organizations in a public service system? They may already be arriving, as shown by the recent interest in systems leadership theory.

Technique-based assignment

Scenario planning can be used to explore a range of different possible futures. It is in principle quite simple to do (see Chapter 6), although it can take a long time when it is carried out in a participative way.

You begin by identifying a small number of drivers for change (e.g. climate change, global economic developments); six to eight is sufficient. You then rank them in terms of uncertainty. Then they are analysed to work out what issues they create for a specific public sector organization or a specific government.

The next step is to group the drivers into themes (so there is, say, only four themes). Then select two of them and imagine how they might turn out. The example below (Figure 12.4) was produced at the instigation of Lord Treasman, a new minister in the UK Department for Innovation, Universities and Skills. He wanted both new ideas and to test legacy policies. Evidence collection and scenario preparation took place in late 2007 and early 2008. Two 'axes of uncertainty' were used: social values (individualistic-collective) and globalization (open-closed). In the example you will see this meant that there were four possible scenarios and each was given a name. The scenarios were elaborated by incorporating other things in to each of them – both forces and issues – to create richer narratives.

The 'perpetual motion' scenario can be summarized as follows. There were global free markets; there were open markets in resources; market supply of resources was not always secure; people were quite self-reliant; and there was a lot of poverty.

Such scenarios can be used to evaluate an existing strategy. Would a proposed strategy work in all four scenarios? Would it be very risky in one or more scenarios? Would it be a disaster in any of the scenarios? And so on.

Sometimes people prepare such scenarios and use them to generate ideas for strategies by trying to imagine what strategy might be needed in such a scenario. They can also be used to think about the impact of future changes on various stakeholders.

Select a specific country and prepare your own set of scenarios. Now consider how well a strategic state would do in each of them.

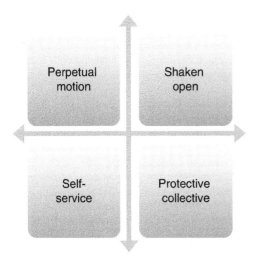

Figure 12.4 *Four scenarios*

DISCUSSION QUESTIONS

1 Is the development of a strategic state a good thing? For whom?
2 Are there any elements of the strategic state framework you think will be unlikely to work very well?
3 Do we need to think about public sector leaders differently from private sector leaders because of the public governance context of public sector leaders?
4 If the strategic state idea becomes a living reality, how will it transform the role of public sector leaders compared to the past?

FURTHER READING

Bezes, P. (2007) The "steering state" model: The emergence of a new organizational form in the French Public Administration! *Sociologie du travail*, 49S: e67–89.

There are a few academic articles and book chapters on the strategic state or the steering state – this is one of them. It contains an empirical analysis of how new organizational principles were imported, reworked, negotiated and slowly implemented throughout the 1990s.

REFERENCE LIST

Alter, R. (2014) *Public Governance: All About Solving Public Problems or Something More?* [Online]. Available from: www.globalpolicyjournal.com/blog/19/04/2013/public-governance-all-about-solving-public-problems-or-something-more [Accessed: 7 January 2014].
Barber, M. (2007) *Instruction to Deliver*. London: Politico's.
Budd, A. (1978) *The Politics of Economic Planning*. London: Fontana.
Elvidge, J. (2011) *Northern Exposure: Lessons from the First Twelve Years of Devolved Government in Scotland*. London: Institute for Government.
Government of India (2016) *Resolution (Planning) – New Delhi, the 15th March*, 1950. [Online]. Available from: http://planningcommission.gov.in/aboutus/history/PCreso-lution1950.pdf [Accessed: 1 April 2016].
Hsu, A. *et al.* (2016) *2016 Environmental Performance Index*. New Haven, CT: Yale University. [Online]. Available from: http://epi.yale.edu/sites/default/files/EPI2016_FINAL%20REPORT.pdf [Accessed: 1 April 2016].
OECD (2000) *Government of the Future*. Paris: OECD.
OECD (2013) *Strategic Insights from the Public Governance Reviews: Update. GOV/PGC(2013)4*, Public Governance and Territorial Development Directorate. Public Governance Committee. Paris: OECD.

OECD/SIGMA (2014) *The Principles of Public Administration*. Paris: OECD.
Osborne, D. and Gaebler, T. (1992) *Reinventing Government: How the Entrepreneurial Spirit is Transforming the Public Sector*. Reading, MA: Addison-Wesley.
Prime Minister's Strategy Unit. (2007) *Building on Progress: The Role of the State*. London: Prime Minister's Strategy Unit.
Wallace, J., Mathias, M. and Brotchie, J. (2013) *Weathering the Storm? A Look at Small Countries' Public Services in Times of Austerity*. Dunfermline: Carnegie UK Trust.

Chapter 13

Economic growth, better regulation and services

LEARNING OBJECTIVES

■ To consider the nature of national economic strategy and how it should be led
■ To look at the distinctive challenges of strategic leadership in a regulatory body
■ To consider the principles and meaning of systems leadership in a public services context

INTRODUCTION

At least three new challenging locations for public sector leaders come to mind when thinking about the leadership in a public sector characterized by new forms of public governance. First, with the shift of government's focus from service delivery to an enabling role, government leaders have to become strategists who can work on important long-term goals that will depend for their success on the actions of citizens, partners and stakeholders in civil society. One of the most important challenges today concerns the creation of sustainable economic growth, which government will often try to do by supporting businesses and creating a business-friendly environment for the private sector.

Second, with the rise of the strategic state there has been much rethinking – especially during the period from 1997 to 2010 – of the aims and methods of government regulation. What has emerged is a concern for 'better regulation' and regulatory impact assessments. But we still live in a world where people and organizations do not really like being regulated. The leaders who lead regulatory bodies have to use their organization's room for manoeuvre and capabilities to find a middle way between regulation being too lenient and too tough. The leaders may give their attention to building organizational reputations that mean they are respected for their expertise, and for being fair, independent and objective.

Third, however much governments have aspired to reinvent themselves and become enablers, they are still directly involved in some public service delivery.

In some countries, austerity pressures mean that leaders of public services organizations may face constant pressures to ensure that the services of their organization are designed and delivered efficiently. There may even be an expectation that leaders will drive productivity gains and find ways of 'doing more with less'. Leaders of these public services are now very frequently faced by requirements to work in partnerships while delivering an efficiency conscious and responsive service.

In this chapter we look at each of these three leadership locations in turn.

NATIONAL STRATEGY FOR SUSTAINABLE ECONOMIC GROWTH

What might a strategic leader with a newly acquired responsibility for a national economic growth strategy think about at the outset?

1 How do I find the right strategy or create the right strategy?
2 How do I get the necessary funding and other resources for the strategy?
3 Where do I get the necessary allies and support for the strategy?
4 What are the barriers to the strategy working successfully?
5 How should I personally lead the development and delivery of this strategy?

The answers they might grope towards could depend on whether they are a politician or a civil servant. There are occasions when the minister, working with cabinet colleagues, is actually the architect of strategies. There are occasions when ministers and civil servants are working 'in tandem' (Limbach-Pirn 2014) and in some of these occasions the civil servants may play a critical role in driving the momentum of strategic policy change. (See the mini case study, T. K. Whitaker in the Irish civil service.)

MINI CASE STUDY

T. K. Whitaker in the Irish Civil Service

Ken Whitaker might be introduced as the strategic leader who transformed the Irish economy, bringing about a shift in 1958 from the economic protectionist policies to free trade policies. Born in 1916, he became a civil servant in 1934, enjoyed fast promotion in the 1950s, and became, at a comparatively young age, the secretary of the Department of Finance in 1956. His biographer described the significance of this promotion as follows (Chambers 2014: 119):

> For the country at large, however, the appointment of Ken Whitaker as Ireland's premier public servant was of huge significance. It changed the direction of economic policy, spearheaded the move from protectionism to

free trade, and guided the country on its momentous journey towards European integration.

In 1957 Eamon de Valera, now 75-years-old, was re-elected as Taoiseach (i.e. prime minister) at the head of a Fianna Fáil government. This did not seem to augur well for new thinking on economic policy. The Irish economy had been falling behind the rest of Europe: Irish GNP had increased by about 10 per cent between 1949 and 1955 compared to more than three times that much in the rest of Europe. It appears that de Valera was indifferent to the economic realities of the situation and their social consequences for the people of Ireland: high unemployment and mass emigration. However, Sean Lemass, a close political ally of de Valera, persuaded him that there needed to be a change of economic policy, and James Ryan, also a close ally of Lemass, became the minister for finance. On their first meeting, Ryan apparently told Whitaker that he would look after the politics and Whitaker should look after the administration.

Lemass, as minister for industry and commerce, came up with a new and ambitious vision for the economy, including a state financed capital programme, abolition of import tariffs, amendments to the Control of Manufactures Act, provision of capital investment and modernization of agriculture.

Whitaker had begun working on a study of national economic development from early 1957. Jack Ryan, Whitaker's new minister, was presented on 21 March 1957, his first day as minister, with a document written by Whitaker on the Irish economy. In it Whitaker advised that the current economic policies had not produced a viable economy and he advised a turn away from protectionism to free trade.

Whitaker took the view that 'planning' the national economy was the way forward; to him planning represented reason and order. He was convinced that there was a need for national targets, although the targets should be reasonable and consistent. By early December 1957, Whitaker and his civil service colleagues had virtually completed a study titled *Economic Development*. His minister agreed to present Whitaker's idea for an integrated programme of national development to the cabinet. In December the cabinet considered Whitaker's request to continue the study of economic development through to completion. An interesting glimpse of the internal politics of the civil service can be found in the following description of the role Whitaker wanted in the process of completing the study (Chambers 2014: 135–6):

> Anxious, too, that the other public service departments would not feel left out in the cold, to complete the project he proposed that his team should have free access to the advice and assistance of other departments and semi-state organizations. Knowing from experience that old habits and territorial jealousies were entrenched in some departmental thinking, he was insistent that the study should continue under his direction and under the auspices of the Department of Finance, whose 'central position ... gives us a special responsibility for studying how economic progress can be promoted ... '.

It appears that, even so, there was some opposition from the secretary of the Department of Industry and Commerce who may have felt threatened by the study and may have wanted to defend the policy of economic protectionism that had been supported by his department.

The study was completed and in July 1957 Whitaker's programme for economic development became government policy. Sean Lemass, the government minister who had persuaded the Taoiseach that a new direction was needed, chaired the committee that turned Whitaker's study into a White Paper.

As a final thought on this case, it is interesting to understand how Whitaker saw the working relationship between ministers and civil servants in Ireland (Chambers 2014: 35–6):

> ...there was no question, in Ken's mind, of government ministers being coerced or cajoled into policy decisions by their senior advisers. The civil service was, as he saw it, 'an integral part of a democratic constitutional system of Government ... but [one] which has no policy commitments of its own', accordingly, its promotion of national development 'must always be a subordinate one – the responsibility for economic policy rests with the Government ... but the Government rightly expects a significant contribution from the public service, if only because of its special qualifications, experience and access to information'.

A new strategic leader on an economic growth strategy would need to check if there was an existing strategy and how well it was working. If there is an existing strategy for growth the leader might need to check whether people know about it – especially people in the business community. If there is an existing strategy, the leader would probably need to find out if it had produced any consequences. If a new strategy were to be developed, they would need to decide on a time frame for the strategy and what strategic issues might have to be factored into the strategy. They would need to decide if the strategy would be taken to parliament and how elected politicians would decide the priorities.

In a strategic state, a strategic leader in central government would need to engage with the business community and consult them on the future strategy for growth. Would the business world welcome a government strategy setting out a vision for sustainable economic growth and the government's plan to ensure it was successfully delivered on a whole of government basis? Probably, if they thought the government could create a good infrastructure for business.

A second key consultation requirement in the early stages of strategy for-mulation would be to interact with subnational levels of government. This would have several functions. The first, and most important, would be to establish a cooperative relationship between national and subnational govern-ment in relation to sustainable growth. How the lower levels of the governance system might see this will probably depend on the history of multi-level governance and the constitutional position. A second function of interaction would be to develop sensitivity to local variations in the issues and causes of economic growth. A third function would be to elicit ideas and proposals from lower levels of governance about what they would like to see in the national growth strategy.

The leader would also need to consider how the main opposition parties in parliament would be able to contribute their ideas to the strategy.

A national growth strategy would probably identify growth priorities. It would probably seek to take a whole of government approach to economic growth and therefore require the involvement of a number of government departments. It would contain commitments and there would be a need to decide how to communicate the strategy and the commitments to the business community, the public and other stakeholders.

One of the issues a strategic leader may need to think about is the response of central government departments (ministers and civil servants) to a new strategy. Some ministers and departments might resist changes required by the new strategy. Or they might see a growth strategy as of little concern to their department, assuming it is of interest only to the business department and the ministry of finance. The strategic leader might, therefore, have to think about how they are going to get ministers and civil servants to support the strategy and work together in a joined-up way, and how decisions taken by different government departments can be coordinated to support the national growth strategy.

A strategic leader in central government leading on the national growth strategy is quite likely to assume that there would need to be a plan focused on a vision for economic growth and on the national growth strategy. They are also quite likely to be concerned to be clear on the scale and sources of funds available for the plan. It may be useful to think of the plan also as an investment plan.

They will, in due course, prepare proposals for the governance of the strategy, meaning how it will be led and by whom, and how it will be monitored and evaluated. The proposals could have a number of elements to them, which will be designed to achieve integration and coherence that is the hallmark of the new public governance. For example:

■ A forum to ensure cross-departmental cooperation to properly support the sustainable growth strategy might need to be set up. This forum would have senior people from relevant government departments and would need to be chaired by a person with a level of authority that meant the ministers of government departments would take seriously decisions made by the forum. The forum might be tasked with intervening to get departmental decisions made that have taken too long and with resolving inter-departmental disputes on aspects of the strategy. The forum would probably require dedicated administrative support since the economic growth strategy is bound to be a very high priority for a government.

■ Government departments might be encouraged or required to indicate in their own business plans or strategic plans the actual actions that will be taken as part of the national sustainable growth strategy.

■ A visible system of annual monitoring of the delivery of the sustainable growth strategy. One model for this might be the European Semester used by the European Union to track progress on the Europe 2020 strategy, which is a sustainable growth strategy that was approved in 2010 and is due to be completed in 2020. This monitoring system not only assesses progress but also makes recommendations for changes in the actions and policies of the governments that form the European Union (European Commission 2015). If this model was applied it could involve the various government departments submitting an annual report on the actions they are taking as part of delivery of the sustainable growth strategy and with data showing exactly what has been achieved and how much more is to be done. This monitoring process could also involve recommendations being made to departments as a part of this annual process. These recommendations might include suggestions for corrections or enhancements of departmental action.

■ A business advisory council might be formed to provide advice as needed during the development and implementation of the strategy.

THE ANALYTICAL SIDE OF DEVELOPING AN ECONOMIC GROWTH STRATEGY

Richard D'Aveni (2012) took ideas from private sector strategic management tools and used them to develop a way of thinking about economic strategy for government. He included ideas of generic strategies and business models. He also made use of the idea of disruptive technologies that impact on incumbent industry leaders. He applied this idea to suggest that government has to plan an offensive strategy to disrupt the progress of major rival countries. His overall approach to analysis has some face validity as a way of formulating a national growth strategy. The 'sustainable' aspect would need to be added in to the analytical processes he suggests.

His analytical approach involved (among other things):

1 Setting long-term economic goals
2 Choosing performance indicators
3 Benchmarking
4 Long-term plans
5 Designing an economic model for the country's strategy
6 Monitoring
7 Graphing industry profitability and industry growth
8 A matrix for planning geo-economic strategic moves.

Long-term economic goals

He suggested that only by making tough choices about priorities could proper long-term economic goals be set. He argued to set them so that free resources will be created or increased in the future.

By way of illustration, the sort of things he had in mind as long-term economic goals were:

1 To ensure the availability of resources from the economy
2 To conserve resources by ensuring efficient government
3 Not squeezing selected taxpayers too much
4 To create new resources – competitive advantages – for the country
5 To shift the economy from spending money to investing in the future.

D'Aveni considered that politicians should be held accountable for delivering results. He argued that politicians and civil servants should have financial incentives to achieve the stated goals in the future.

Performance indicators

Some of the indicators he suggested were as follows:

1 A healthy GDP growth rate; a modest unemployment rate
2 Efficient operation of government's social programmes; efficiency in public service
3 Taxes spread across all citizens
4 Investment in research and development; investment in infrastructure; strong manufacturing base
5 A national savings rate that is high enough; optimal level of personal consumption.

With respect to efficiency in public services, D'Aveni proposed that the government services should consume no more than 25 per cent of GDP.

Benchmarking

He advocated using benchmarking of economic performance against other countries to improve the competitiveness of the system.

Long-term plans

He specified the need for long-term plans to deliver long-term goals.

Designing an economic model for the country's strategy

D'Aveni argued that countries could plan by design an economic model for a strategy based on a combination of four generic types of capitalism (Figure 13.1).

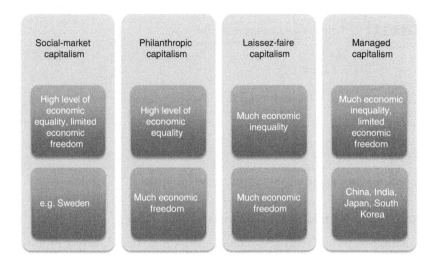

Figure 13.1 D'Aveni – four generic types of capitalism (2012)

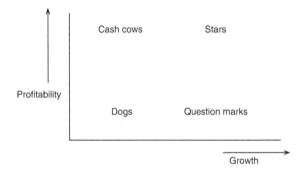

Figure 13.2 D'Aveni – graphing profitability and growth of industries (2012)

Monitoring

He argued for monitoring the implementation of plans and goals.

Graphing industry profitability and industry growth

A country's industry portfolio can be graphed in order to show industry profitability and industry growth (Figure 13.2). And just like the Boston Consulting Group Matrix used by large complex companies, the industries of a country can be named 'stars', 'question marks', 'dogs' and 'cash cows'. Obviously, a government might use this when allocating investment funds for research and development into priority growth areas.

Table 13.1 D'Aveni – a grid for geo-economic moves

	Region 1 (e.g. Europe)	Region 2	Region 3	Region 4	Region 5
Industry 1					
Industry 2					
Industry 3					
Industry 4					
Industry 5					

Note: adapted from Figure 8.1 in D'Aveni (2012), page 224.

A matrix for planning geo-economic strategic moves

D'Aveni explained the idea of geo-economic strategy as concerned with regions and industries (Table 13.1). A government may think about which combinations of industry and region it wants its businesses to be paying attention to. They may be selected for reasons of their attractiveness or reasons of disrupting businesses of rival economies. He also suggested that this tool can be used to plan the evaluation of the costs and benefits of trying to control fast-growing or the most profitable geo-economic categories, or of trying to weaken the economic power of rivals.

THE TOP SECTORS APPROACH: A DUTCH EXAMPLE (2011)

Selectivity (focus) and partnership were the key features of the new industrial policy introduced by the Netherlands in 2011, which are obviously features in keeping with a strategic state approach to industrial strategy. The essence of this policy was summed up as follows (OECD 2014: 388): 'The top sectors approach, a new form of industrial policy announced in 2011, focuses public resources on specific sectors and fosters co-ordination of activities in these areas by businesses, knowledge institutions and government'.

The Dutch government chose nine industrial sectors in which their country had a strong competitive position. These sectors were agri-food, horticulture and propagating stock, high-tech materials and systems, energy, logistics, creative industry, life sciences, chemicals and water. The government strategy was to provide support to these nine sectors in terms of investment and R&D tax reductions. This government policy also involved enhanced exchange between business, knowledge institutes and government. Each sector has a place where businesses and research organizations can work together (innovation hotspot). In addition there have been joint action plans for each sector (opportunities and problems) and innovation contracts covering the financial arrangements between businesses, scientists and governments.

BETTER REGULATION

Regulators may be found in different types of public sector organization. They may be found working within multi-function government organizations or in standalone regulatory bodies. In the UK, for example, local government has provided public protection services in relation to health and environment issues whereas health and safety at work and health and adult social care services have both been covered by standalone regulatory bodies (Local Government Association 2015).

In the 1980s there was often a policy of rolling back government regulation of business. Then, in the mid to late 1990s, new national regulation policies began to emerge. The aim of the new policies was better regulation and not simply deregulation. For example, in the UK a better regulation unit was established within the Cabinet Office (see mini case study).

MINI CASE STUDY

National regulatory policies in the UK
The focus of national policy on deregulation, which had been established in the 1980s, was ended in 1997 when a newly elected government brought in the concept of 'better regulation'. In essence, the argument went from saying that all regulations were bad to saying that it was bad regulation that was the problem. A better regulation task force and a better regulation unit were set up during 1997, based in the Cabinet Office in London. Regulatory impact assessments were introduced in 1998. The better regulation unit became the regulatory impact unit in 1999.

As can be seen from Table 13.2, developments in terms of regulatory oversight bodies were concentrated between the years of 1998 and 2008. It is also evident that oversight units were often set up so that they reported to the centre of government. This relationship to the centre of government can be expected to have helped these new units in terms of their power and credibility (Cordova-Novion and Jacobzone 2011).

Changes in national policies on government regulation coincided with other reforms that were helping to create governments with strategic-state capabilities. It is interesting, therefore, that Cordova-Novion and Jacobzone (2011: 57) conclude:

Regulatory oversight bodies are as strong as the political leadership behind them. The success of these institutions is dependent on underlying political forces and external drivers of the policy. In addition to the obvious "political will" required, some oversight bodies have performed better thanks to their efforts to coordinate and ensure coherence with other policies and reform institutions.

Table 13.2 *Regulatory oversight bodies in government*

Country	Name of regulatory oversight body	Nature of body	Reports to	Year created
Australia	Deregulation Group in the Department of Finance and Deregulation	Unit	Finance	2006
Canada	Regulatory Affairs Sector in Treasury Board	Unit	Centre of government	2006
Germany	Better Regulation Unit	Unit	Parliament and centre of government	2006
Italy	Unit for Simplification and Better Regulation	Unit	Centre of government	2008
Japan	Subcommittee for Regulation and System Reform	Council	Centre of government	2010
Korea	Regulatory Reform Bureau & Regulatory Reform Committee	Unit & Council	Centre of government	1998
Netherlands	Regulatory Reform Group	Unit	Finance and economy	2007
UK	Regulatory Impact Unit in the Cabinet Office (further developments occurred in 1999 and later)	Unit	Centre of government	1997
USA	Office of Information and Regulatory Affairs	Unit	Centre of government	1980

Source: Mostly adapted from Cordova-Novion and Jacobzone (2011).

LEADERSHIP ISSUES FOR REGULATORS

Do leaders in government regulators have just the same issues as other leaders in the public sector or are there issues that are distinctive to them? Mostly leaders working in regulator organizations are probably doing more or less the same as their counterparts in other public sector organizations.

They probably now spend significant amounts of time interacting with partners and other stakeholders. They may spend time explaining to partners their new strategic ideas and getting their responses. They probably spend some time attending partnership forums, and they probably publicize their organization externally, promoting a positive reputation.

They discuss future directions with their own staff. They try to keep staff morale up when people feel that they have been through more than enough organizational change. They can probably be found greeting new members of staff on induction programmes.

They are also inevitably going to be involved in sorting out new processes and systems, planning budgets, ensuring that the budget decisions support the strategic plan and trying to assess the way the funding environment is changing.

All this, and probably much more that has not been mentioned, may fill much of their working time. It is probably not fundamentally different in nature from what fills the time of other leaders in the public sector. But leaders of regulatory organizations face at least two issues that are fairly unique and are a result of the function their organizations carry out. First, they need to create and sustain a culture of expertise, independence and objectivity in their operational judgements (i.e. when they are regulating). Second, they have a special proneness to being attacked because they have made decisions as regulators that people do not like. The reaction of people when a regulator's decision goes against them, or when a regulator tells a provider that their services are not meeting required standards, is on occasion going to be one of attacking the regulators. Regulators need to keep their organizational composure in the face of attacks on the quality of their regulatory decision making – they need to do this to sustain their credibility for independent and objective judgements. They need to be clear that people who do not like a decision often attack the organization that made the decision.

WHAT IS SYSTEMS LEADERSHIP AND WHY IS IT NEEDED?

Systems leadership is a comparatively new perspective on public sector leadership, one that has been attracting increasing attention. Rutter (2015) introduces it as follows: 'A new model of leadership that has collaboration and citizens' needs at its core is starting to take hold across public services'.

Ghate, Lewis and Wellbourn (2013: 6) argue: ' . . . systems leadership by definition is the concerted effort of many people working together at different places in the system and at different levels, rather than of single leaders acting unilaterally'. One implication of this particular variant of systems leadership was that leaders might be seen as working across boundaries and 'well beyond the usual limits of their formal responsibilities and authority' (Ghate *et al.* 2013: 6).

Ghate *et al.* (2013: 7), who carried out interviews with public services leaders in England, noted that, 'systems leadership was described as a mindset, or a way of thinking about and approaching the leadership role, rather than a set of technical skills or competencies'.

So, systems leaders believe in cooperation and partnership and they are good at putting the collective interests above the interests of their own organization. The systems leaders are also said to be good at coping with the uncertainties that are a feature of situations in which there are complex systems, wicked issues and paradoxes. They are also good at the relationships involved in systems leadership, having empathy, listening, being honest and authentic, and having humility and magnanimity. According to Ghate and colleagues (2013), systems leadership involves more than effective alignment or coordination of individual contributions (by partner organizations). It involves trying to achieve things through the relationships between partners. See Figure 13.3.

Systems Leadership may be seen as vital for the functioning of public services. Rutter quotes a director of organizational development at Public Health

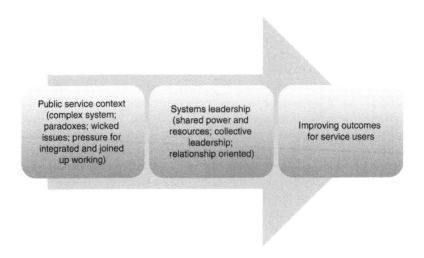

Figure 13.3 *Shared power systems leadership (Ghate et al. 2013)*

England as saying, 'Most major incidents where we see care breaking down in any part of the public sector are about a failure to work together effectively. The impact varies from delivering poor services to the most heartrending outcomes imaginable'.

Care services are often not good enough or not right (Department of Health 2012: 5):

> Children, young people and adults with learning disabilities or autism and who have mental health conditions or behaviour that challenges have for too long and in too many cases received poor quality and inappropriate care. [. . .] All parts of the system – commissioners, providers, the workforce, regulators and government – and all agencies – councils, providers, the NHS and police – have a role to play in driving up standards for this group of people. There should be zero tolerance of abuse or neglect.

HOW DOES SYSTEMS LEADERSHIP WORK?

Arguably, at the present time, the concept of systems leadership is more of a response to a need for more integration and coherence than a well-defined and empirically verified type of leadership. The presentation of its key features seems at times to assume precisely what needs explaining. It may be argued that this spirit of cooperation has to be based on values. Ghate *et al.* (2013: 9) put it like this:

> Systems leadership was described as being as frequently about 'willingness to give things away' as it was concerned with achievement of one's own

goals or promoting of one's own agency agenda . . . Some participants [in the research study] talked of this requiring the nurturing of a stronger spirit of public service that emphasises wider public service goals over the goals of or working practices of the specific existing professions or agencies.

But even if they have public service values, how do systems leaders cope with the conflict between the collective interest and the interest of their own organization? How do they make decisions if the systems are very complex and the issues are very wicked? How do public services leaders manage issues of accountability and democracy while at the same time taking care to protect and nurture the relationships of collective leadership? Is it as simple as them just having the right mind-set and attitudes?

SYSTEMS LEADERSHIP AND THE LONG-TERM

An interesting point has been made about the time frames used by systems leaders. It seems that systems leadership is concerned with the longer term (Ghate *et al.* 2013: 10):

> . . . what they described in systems leadership is a 'long game' . . . where patience and confidence and a degree of resilience were needed to accommodate the sometimes lengthy and/or unpredictable time lines over which systems change occurs, and rewards and payoffs are realised. Many people will be working towards the ultimate goal but, 'you have to recognise it may not be in your own lifetime.'

The director of organizational development at Public Health England made a similar point. She argued that systems leaders might need government to work to longer time frames (Rutter 2015): 'Part of our challenge is our budget cycles are annual so we often think and act in 12-month cycles – rather than over three to five years. Perhaps we should lobby for longer policy time frames'.

SYSTEMS THINKING

The use of the word 'system' may also evoke the idea of 'systems thinking'. Attwood, Pedler, Pritchard and Wilkinson (2003: 22) explain systems thinking as follows:

> It is a discipline or methodology for recognizing the interrelatedness of parts in wholes and for working with these. The importance of this perspective is underlined by Senge's dramatic 'We are literally killing ourselves through being unable to think in wholes' (1990) . . .

Using a system perspective can expose the lack of joined-up thinking. This is illustrated in the following commentary on the US federal government (Osborne and Gaebler 1992: 37):

> In 1986, a White House report . . . concluded:
>
> 'Each program began with its own rationale, representing the intent of public officials to address a perceived need. But when the programs are considered as a system they amount to a tangle of purposes, rules, agencies and effects.'
>
> . . . The only realistic way to develop such holistic strategies is to separate steering from rowing, so the policy managers can define a comprehensive strategy and use many different oarsmen (oarspeople?) to implement it.

If public service systems are to change, how is this to be done? Attwood *et al.* (2003) state: 'Effective leadership is vital to the achievement of systemic change'. Which brings us back to the need to better understand systems leadership

SUMMARY

This chapter has covered a lot of ground, some of it very briefly. In the new public governance the strategic leaders might be politicians and they might be civil servants and managers. The politicians and the civil servants may work together, in tandem, to develop new economic strategies. We have looked at some of the practical questions that a strategic leader might need to consider when working on a new strategy. We have noted the governance arrangements that might be needed, especially to deal with issues of inter-ministerial and inter-departmental cooperation.

We outlined the concepts and tools that might be used to construct a national economic strategy, tools that had been largely borrowed from the private sector strategic analysis toolbox. We turned to Dutch experience to find a recent example of a national policy on economic growth in which there were priority sectors receiving government support.

The discussion of regulation noted the policy turn to 'better regulation' in the period from 1997 to 2010 and some special challenges for strategic leaders of regulators were identified.

Finally, we set out some basic ideas about the nature of systems leadership, which may be rooted in identification with public service values. It was noted that systems leadership is a comparatively new perspective on public sector leadership, one that has been attracting increasing attention.

Work-based assignment: regulatory impact assessment

Write a brief about changed or new government regulations in a country or subnational territory of your choosing. Collect as much information as you can on the changed/new regulations. Use the data collected to complete a simple regulatory impact assessment (see the Worksheet below) and then review it and come to a conclusion about whether the changed/new regulations are an example of 'better regulation'.

Notes on regulatory impact assessment:

1 Regulatory impact assessment is a technique used by governments in many different countries. It is a systematic and disciplined investigation of the consequences of proposals to introduce or change government regulations.

2 The results of a regulatory impact assessment can be used to inform strategic leaders' judgements of the likely acceptability of proposals for new or changed regulations that are seen as necessary to deliver a government strategy. The results can also be input into cost-benefit analysis and used to decide if it is worthwhile to proceed with proposed government strategies.

3 The assessment may investigate impacts on businesses and other stakeholders. Governments have used various methods of data collection for regulatory impact assessment, including surveys, advisory bodies, consultations of affected parties, business test panels, talking to other governments, literature reviews, etc.

Worksheet: regulatory impact assessment

Relevant stakeholders (individuals, communities, organizations, etc. impacted by new or changed regulations)	Description of impact on stakeholder	Assessment of impacts		
		Size of impacts (measurements of consequences)	Numbers of people impacted	Duration of impacts (how long will consequences persist?)
1				
2				
3				
4				
5				
6				

FURTHER READING

Crosby, B. C. and Bryson, J. M. (2005) *Leadership for the Common Good: Tackling Problems in a Shared-Power World.* 2nd edition. San Francisco: Jossey-Bass.

This reading offers a practical perspective on leading in a 'shared-power' world. It is concerned with action to address important public problems. Many situations faced by public sector leaders are challenging in terms of reconciling their accountability in the public governance system and cooperation with partners who may be representing other public sector organizations but might be in the voluntary or private sector. Among other things this book suggests the leadership capabilities suitable for situations when nobody is in charge.

REFERENCE LIST

Attwood, M., Pedler, M., Pritchard, S. and Wilkinson, D. (2003) *Leading Change: A Guide to Whole Systems Thinking.* Bristol: The Policy Press.

Chambers, A. (2014) *T. K. Whitaker: Portrait of a Patriot.* Dublin: Doubleday Ireland.

Cordova-Novion, C. and Jacobzone, S. (2011) Strengthening the Institutional Setting for Regulatory Reform: The Experience from OECD Countries. *OECD Working Papers on Public Governance*, 19. OECD Publishing. [Online]. Available from www.oecd-ilibrary.org/governance/strengthening-the-institutional-setting-for-regulatory-reform_5kgglrpvcpth-en [Accessed: 1 April 2016].

D'Aveni, R. (2012) *Strategic Capitalism: The New Economic Strategy for Winning the Capitalist Cold War.* New York: McGraw-Hill.

Department of Health (2012) *Winterbourne View Review: Concordat: A Programme of action.* London: Department of Health.

European Commission (2015) *2015 European Semester: Country-specific recommendations.* COM(2015) 250 final, Brussels, 13 May 2015. [Online]. Available from: http://ec.europa.eu/europe2020/pdf/csr2014/eccom2014_en.pdf [Accessed: 1 April 2015].

Ghate, D., Lewis, J. and Wellbourn, D. (2013) *Systems Leadership: Exceptional leadership for exceptional times.* Nottingham: Virtual Staff College.

Limbach-Pirn, E. (2014) 'What are the competencies for effective strategic leadership in Estonia?', in P. Joyce and A. Drumaux (eds) *Strategic Management in Public Organizations: European Practices and Perspectives.* London: Routledge. pp. 115–32.

Local Government Association (2015) *Remodelling Public Protection: The Future of Council's Regulatory Services.* London: Local Government Association.

OECD (2014) *OECD Science, Technology and Industry Outlook 2014.* OECD Publishing. [Online]. Available from: http://dx.doi.org/10.1787/sti_outlook-2014-en [Accessed: 1 April 2016].

Osborne, D. and Gaebler, T. (1992) *Reinventing Government: How the Entrepreneurial Spirit is Transforming the Public Sector.* Reading, MA: Addison-Wesley.

Rutter, T. (2015) *How Leaders From Across Public Services Can Work Together Better.* [Online]. Available from: www.theguardian.com/public-leaders-network/2014/may/13/leaders-public-services-work-together-better [Accessed 28 December 2015].

Senge, P. (1990) *The Fifth Discipline.* London: Century Press.

Appendix 1

Strategy workbook

This workbook is designed for use in the public sector to help strategic leaders to capture their strategic thinking and planning for a strategic plan to deliver the outcomes sought by elected politicians.

The workbook consists of a number of worksheets that support a process with seven main steps:

1   Identification of strategic goals from top policy outcomes and formation of strategic management groups
2   Stakeholder analysis
3   Situational analysis
4   Mapping context of strategic priorities, envisioning strategic success and generating ideas for strategic action
5   Idea appraisal
6   Planning delivery of the strategic plan, information requirements and reporting systems
7   Integrating strategic planning processes with other management systems.

This process should deliver all the basic elements of a strategic planning process that incorporates a concern for issue management as well as performance management (see Figure A.1).

CONTENTS: PROCESS STEPS AND WORKSHEETS

Identification of strategic goals from top policy outcomes and formation of strategic management groups:
Worksheet 1 – Listing of strategic goals
Worksheet 2 – Forming strategic management groups (SMGs)

Stakeholder analysis:
Worksheet 3 – Stakeholder analysis

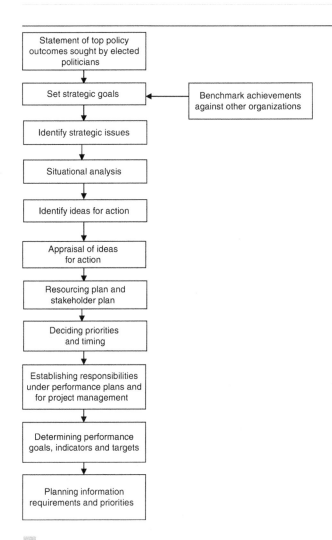

Figure A.1 *Strategic performance management with an issue management element*

Situational analysis:
Worksheet 4 – Exploration of public/community problems
Worksheet 5 – Opportunities and constraints

Mapping context of strategic priorities, envisioning strategic success and generating ideas for strategic action:
Worksheet 6 – Trend analysis
Worksheet 7 – Interpretive structural modelling (strategic goals)
Worksheet 8 – Vision of success statement
Worksheet 9 – Forming strategic issue agendas
Worksheet 10 – Generating ideas for strategic action

Idea appraisal:
Worksheet 11 – Evaluating ideas for strategic action

Planning delivery of the strategic plan, information requirements and reporting systems:
Worksheet 12 – Stakeholder plan
Worksheet 13 – Resources analysis
Worksheet 14 – Defining strategic performance goals, indicators and targets
Worksheet 15 – Identifying information requirements for reporting systems
Worksheet 16 – Allocating management responsibility

Integrating strategic planning processes with other management systems:
Worksheet 17 – Developing a calendar for integration of strategic plan processes with budgetary and other processes

WORKSHEET 1: LISTING OF STRATEGIC GOALS

This worksheet is the foundation for the success of the whole process. The top priority policy outcomes sought by elected politicians are written into the left hand column. Now formulate up to three strategic goals per policy outcome. For each strategic goal suggest how achievement of the goal can be measured – using what performance indicator?

Top priority policy outcomes sought by elected politicians	Description of high level strategic goals	Performance indicator
	1	
	2	
	3	
	1	
	2	
	3	
	1	
	2	
	3	
	1	
	2	
	3	

WORKSHEET 2: FORMING STRATEGIC MANAGEMENT GROUPS (SMGS)

The initial assumption is that there should be a SMG for delivery of all the strategic goals, and who needs to be involved can be decided by looking at the top strategic goals and answering the three questions:

Top strategic goals	What expertise or experience would be useful in respect of this strategic goal?	Who is best equipped to lead on this strategic goal?	Who needs to be involved in addressing this strategic goal? Suggest some possible names

WORKSHEET 3: STAKEHOLDER ANALYSIS

Stakeholders are anybody who is likely to be affected by, or who can affect, the strategic plan. Obvious stakeholders include the public, service users, employees, suppliers, other public services, businesses, the voluntary sector, etc.

To complete this worksheet, first, name all the key stakeholders of the organization.

Next, suggest the top two or three criteria used by each stakeholder to assess the effectiveness of the organization. For example, do service users care most about the level of customer care or quality or are they only interested in the reliability of a service? Is the tax they pay for public services in their top criteria?

The list of stakeholders may need to be reconsidered as you complete the worksheet. For example, it may be necessary to distinguish different groupings among service users or employees if they vary in the criteria they use to judge the organization or if they vary in their relative importance. For example, do people living on pensions have different criteria from other users of services?

Finally, assess the relative importance of each stakeholder. You could use a simple scoring system to rate importance:

1 = not important; 2 = slightly important; 3= very important; 4 = most important.

317

Please note that you may need to define what you mean by 'important'. For example, does important mean powerful or does it mean a stakeholder whose needs or wants the organization intends to make a high priority?

Summarize the results of your analysis in the worksheet – include only the eight most important stakeholders.

Stakeholder	What criteria do stakeholders use to judge effectiveness of the organization?	Relative importance of each stakeholder
1	1	
	2	
	3	
2	1	
	2	
	3	
3	1	
	2	
	3	
4	1	
	2	
	3	
5	1	
	2	
	3	
6	1	
	2	
	3	
7	1	
	2	
	3	
8	1	
	2	
	3	

WORKSHEET 4: EXPLORATION OF PUBLIC/COMMUNITY PROBLEMS

This worksheet is designed to produce a 'problem brief'. This may be based on interviews with key people and key stakeholder groups as well as discussions in workshops. The brief provides a concise summary of the main public or community problems that the organization wants to solve (e.g. teenage pregnancies, community safety issues, anti-social behaviour). This is informed, where possible, by empirical data on the problems. The data may provide a baseline against which improvements can be measured. It may describe in some way the nature of the problem and show its trend over the last five years. The worksheet may be copied and used for further problem briefs.

Public/Community problem brief 1   Date prepared: ....

1   Name of public/community problem:

2   Indicators of development of the problem (empirical data) and evaluation of future trend if no new action is instigated:

3   Impact of problem on public/community (empirical data):

4   Analysis (why is this problem difficult to solve?):

5   Current measures being taken by organization:

WORKSHEET 5: OPPORTUNITIES AND CONSTRAINTS

The data for this worksheet can be pooled from interview data and discussion groups in strategic workshops. If the data is being generated in a workshop, individuals should be asked, first, to silently brainstorm their perceptions of the opportunities and constraints for the strategic plan. This ensures that a wider range of opinions surfaces.

Definitions

An **opportunity** might be some external event or development that could be exploited to make the strategic plan more successful. For the purposes of this worksheet, an opportunity might also be some strength or resource that the organization could use to achieve more success through the strategic plan.

A **constraint** could be a weakness or a deficiency that might prevent or impede success in relation to the strategic plan. But it could also be something external – some event or a trend – that will make achieving a successful strategic plan more challenging.

Both the opportunities and constraints should be ranked in order of importance and this ranking discussed with elected politicians and senior managers. Importance may need to be defined. For example, a specific opportunity or constraint might be rated as more important if there is a widespread consensus that it could impact in a big way on the hopes for a successful strategic plan.

The 8 top opportunities (ranked)	The 8 top constraints (ranked)
1	1
2	2
3	3
4	4
5	5
6	6
7	7
8	8

WORKSHEET 6: TREND ANALYSIS

This worksheet summarizes the trends affecting the whole of the organization over the last four to five years. Will these same trends continue impacting over the next four to five years? Checklist: How is the public changing? How are lifestyles in the county/locality changing? Is the organization meeting different public needs now compared to five years ago? If it is meeting different needs, are there any trends evident in this? Have there been any trends in the changes of who the users of services are? Are the services or service delivery processes the same now as five years ago? Are the key partners the same as five years ago? Have the organization's suppliers changed – if so, is there any trend in this? Have the organization's capabilities changed in any way over the last five years? Have management capabilities changed? Have IT capabilities changed? Are there any changes/trends in the organizational structure? Have there been any important trends in the availability of financial and other resources? Have the main types of interface with the public changed – is there any trend towards different patterns in how the public access services? Have there been any trends in changes in the workforce? And so on.

Trend no.	Description of trend over last 4–5 years and empirical evidence on the trend	Impact of trend on organization	Expectation of direction of trend over next five years
		Low/Medium/High	Continue/Reverse/Other
1			
2			
3			
4			
5			
6			
7			
8			

WORKSHEET 7: INTERPRETIVE STRUCTURAL MODELLING (STRATEGIC GOALS)

Interpretive structural modelling can be used in a variety of ways in a strategic planning process. It can be used to capture judgement about cause and effect relationships between strategic goals and/or strategic issues, which can be useful in deciding on the best points of leverage in bringing about change. It can be applied to explore causal linkages between multiple strategic actions, which can be useful when planning the implementation of a strategic plan. In this case, the intention is to use it to think about cause and effect relationships between strategic goals (see Worksheet 1).

The interpretive structural model in this worksheet depicts the cause and effects linkages between the main strategic goals. This model could be presented in a narrative form, but there are important advantages in presenting it as a diagram – as shown in the box below.

*Note: A diagram of a **model** consists of arrows and boxes. Each of the top strategic goals is represented as a box. Each arrow is taken to mean that obtaining results with one goal will also produce results in terms of another. So, if it is thought that making progress with one strategic goal will have positive consequences for another, then this is shown as an arrow between them (see Figure A.2).*

This worksheet is probably best based on discussions by the SMG (see Worksheet 2). The SMG should discuss possible 'patterns' of cause and effect between the strategic goals. This discussion may draw on evidence regarding cause and effect linkages, but it is to be expected that the SMG will have to use their experience and judgement and this will inevitably contain some subjectivity. This subjectivity is not a problem and is unavoidable. The SMG should diagram their model.

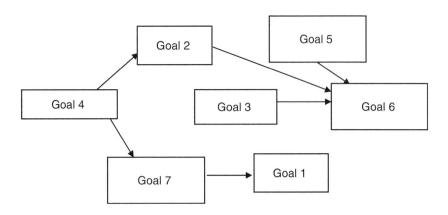

Figure A.2 *Abstract version of an interpretive structural model*

Model for set of strategic goals

Please draw your interpretive structural model in this box

WORKSHEET 8: VISION OF SUCCESS STATEMENT

This worksheet could be done by the SMG. Note: The vision of success statement is NOT a strategic vision statement in the usual sense. The usual vision statement acts as a challenge or target for strategic change. In this strategic planning process the strategic challenges have been set by the elected politicians as policy outcomes. Thus the vision of success statement provides managers with a narrative about what things will look like when the challenges have been met. The vision of success statement helps to imagine and create ideas for management action in order that the policy outcomes of politicians are realized.

The SMG should write this statement as an optimistic scenario of the future based on **'reasonable hope'**. *It is important that the SMG make explicit in the statement the chief benefits that the public or service users will enjoy (as a result of strategic action) in five years' time. Also the statement might contain references to new activities and 'interfaces' between the organization and the public/service users. Mention might also be made of any critical new capabilities the organization will have developed to deliver the benefits and any new partnership working that will be established. The SMG should write this positive scenario as a very short paragraph of 5–15 lines only.*

The SMG should also prepare a pessimistic scenario for five years' time. This would spell out gaps or shortfalls in the chief benefits for the public and/or service users of the organization's activities, dysfunctions in the organization's main activities, and problems with the main interfaces between the organization and the public/service users. The SMG prepare this by making negative assumptions about what is achieved over the next five years. This should influence the SMG's planning in the sense that the SMG will be clearer about the kinds of developments the organization needs to avoid.

WORKSHEET 9: FORMING STRATEGIC ISSUE AGENDAS

This worksheet should be a summary of work done by the SMG.
The SMG is asked to look at its strategic goals and its associated performance indicators. For each strategic goal, the SMG asks: Why do we think it might be difficult to succeed with this specific goal? What might make achieving success with this goal difficult? In other words, what are the top strategic issues for this strategic plan? What evidence have we got, or could we get, to substantiate the existence of each issue? After checking on the evidence about the existence of the issues, the SMG should rank in order of importance the issues for each goal.
It would be good to have at least one top strategic issue identified for each strategic goal.

Policy outcome	Strategic goal	Issues: why is it difficult to achieve success on this goal?	Evidence that difficulties (issues) really exist?
	1		
	2		
	3		
	1		
	2		
	3		
	1		
	2		
	3		
	1		
	2		
	3		
	1		
	2		
	3		
	1		
	2		
	3		

WORKSHEET 10: GENERATING IDEAS FOR STRATEGIC ACTION

Brainstorming ideas

Very often managers are asked to simply brainstorm ideas for actions to achieve strategic goals. Sometimes they are asked to do this brainstorming on the basis of a SWOT (strengths, weaknesses, opportunities and threats) analysis. In this strategic planning process we want to 'cue' the creativity of the SMG by asking them to construct 'narratives' (Figure A.3) based on three contributory sources of ideas already generated by them (Nutt and Backoff 1992):

1   *Vision of success statement*
2   *Ideas about opportunities and constraints*
3   *Ideas about the top strategic issues.*

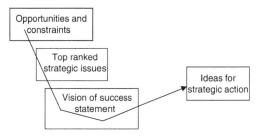

Figure A.3 *Three contributory sources of ideas*

A question to cue the brainstorming of ideas might be framed as follows:

How can the organization act to use an opportunity so that it will reduce or solve a strategic issue in such a way as to take us towards the vision of success statement?

Another question to cue the brainstorming could be:

How can the organization act to deal with a constraint so that it will reduce or solve a strategic issue in such a way as to take us towards the vision of success statement?

Ideas that are formed in such a way should be especially powerful – they should be strategic, not only in the sense of bringing into being the future desired by the elected politicians, but also in the sense of 'lever' more change than other alternative actions would.

Note: Brainstorming should be imaginative and creative and will therefore produce many poor ideas that need to be weeded out at a later stage through careful evaluation of the ideas. The SMG should be warned not to be discouraged by this. The SMG should be assured that if there is one really good idea in 20 poor ideas that this will be enough to make the difference.

Strategic goal	Description of idea for strategic action under the strategic plan	Short name for idea	Check: how much impact on the strategic goal will this action have?
	1		
	2		
	3		
	4		
	5		
	6		
	7		
	8		
	9		
	10		
	1		
	2		
	3		
	4		
	5		
	6		
	7		
	8		
	9		
	10		
	1		
	2		
	3		
	4		
	5		
	6		
	7		
	8		
	9		
	10		

1

2

3

4

5

6

7

8

9

10

1

2

3

4

5

6

7

8

9

10

WORKSHEET 11: EVALUATING IDEAS FOR STRATEGIC ACTION

Each proposal – idea for strategic action – needs to be evaluated. (If the list of ideas for each strategic goal is too long, some screening criteria may be needed to bring the list down to a manageable length of, say, 10 to 12.) Suggestion: group together into programmes of action those ideas which seem to be related ideas for action.

The first step is to decide the criteria to be used in appraising each idea. The selection of criteria may be influenced by the need to devise a strategy to suit the specific situation, but commonly used criteria are:

■   *Feasibility: Can the strategic action be delivered? Can it be made to happen?*
■   *Suitability: Will the strategic action lead to the right results in terms of a strategic goal?*

- *Acceptability: Will the strategic action produce results that will be perceived as satisfactory by important stakeholders?*
- *Timeliness: Will the strategic action have its beneficial impact in the required timescale?*

Each idea for strategic action is appraised using selected criteria. This can be done using a table – see the example below. The selected criteria are entered in the left hand column. A weighting is decided for each criterion: a weighting of 1–4 is used, with 4 being the highest to indicate that the criterion is very important. Each proposal is scored on a scale of 1–10 for how well it meets each criterion. The scale is defined as follows: 1 = totally fails criterion; 4 = just meets criterion; 6 = meets it comfortably and 10 = ideal. This is then multiplied by the weighting to give the weighted score on this criterion. In order to make comparisons, the same criteria, weightings and scales need to be retained for each evaluation.

A made up example of a possible set of criteria and scores for a fictitious proposal for strategic action is shown below. In this example there are eight criteria and the maximum total score is 50. However, the number of criteria can be varied and the maximum score will vary depending on weightings used.

The total scores are meant to aid discussions by the SMG about the relative merits of different courses of action. The total score should be taken into account, but not seen as decisive in the discussion of the courses of action.

Proposal: 'example'

Criteria		Weighting (1–4)	Raw score (1–10)	Weighted score
1	Acceptability to the general public	2	4	8
2	Acceptability to other key stakeholders	1	7	7
3	Benefits to service users	2	6	12
4	Consistency with mission	1	6	6
5	Technical feasibility	1	5	5
6	Cost and financing	1	2	2
7	Cost effectiveness	1	8	8
8	Timeliness	1	2	2
			Total score = 50	

Proposal 1: (name)

Criteria	Weighting	Raw score	Weighted score
1			
2			
3			
4			
5			
6			
7			
8			
			Total score =

Proposal 2: (name)

Criteria	Weighting	Raw score	Weighted score
1			
2			
3			
4			
5			
6			
7			
8			
			Total score =

Proposal 3: (name)

Criteria	Weighting	Raw score	Weighted score
1			
2			
3			
4			
5			
6			
7			
8			
			Total score =

Proposal 4: (name)

Criteria	Weighting	Raw score	Weighted score
1			
2			
3			
4			
5			
6			
7			
8			
			Total score =

Proposal 5: (name)

Criteria	Weighting	Raw score	Weighted score
1			
2			
3			
4			
5			
6			
7			
8			
			Total score =

Proposal 6: (name)

Criteria	Weighting	Raw score	Weighted score
1			
2			
3			
4			
5			
6			
7			
8			
			Total score =

WORKSHEET 12: STAKEHOLDER PLAN

When an organization has decided on a strategic action, it needs to decide how it will implement it. This should be informed by an analysis of the likely reactions of stakeholders to the implementation of the strategic action. This analysis involves identifying stakeholder groups in terms of their likely attitude to the chosen strategic action and in terms of their power. Based on this analysis managers need to think about how they will communicate and promote the plans to carry out strategic actions. Managers may need to think about the timing of such actions and even think about revising the action itself to make it more acceptable to groups currently likely to be opposed to it.

Definition

Stakeholders: individuals, groups or organizations who are likely to affect or be affected by the strategic plan and its associated strategic action.

The analysis:

1 *Stakeholders are listed for the strategic action (note that the list may change for different strategic actions).*
2 *Then, <u>for the specific strategic action</u>, the stakeholders' likely reactions are rated on a scale of −5 to +5. Those who are likely to welcome or support the strategy are rated as +5, and those who are most likely to be strongly opposed are rated −5. When stakeholders are unlikely to react either positively or negatively, they are rated as 0.*
3 *Finally, rate the power of stakeholders. Using a scale of 1−10, rate them as 10 if they are extremely powerful; if they have little power rate them as 1 or thereabouts.*

Stakeholder	Attitude to proposed action (rated on scale −5 to +5)	Power (rated on scale 1 to 10)

The stakeholders can be mapped using these scores; this seems to help in various ways when thinking about a stakeholder plan for implementation (see Figure A.4).

The stakeholder plan may entail negotiations with stakeholders who are likely to oppose proposed strategic action. Supporters may be asked to help sell the idea to others who are less sure about the desirability of the action. Demonstration projects may be used to win over those who are important but are not yet convinced that the idea for a strategic action is a good one. And so on.

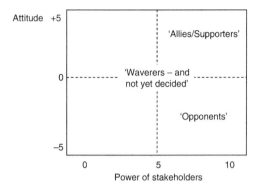

Figure A.4 *Stakeholder attitude and power relationships*

WORKSHEET 13: RESOURCES ANALYSIS

A resources analysis is useful in planning the implementation of action. A careful assessment needs to be made of the resources required for each strategic action and how they can be mobilized. The basic approach is to identify the required resources, who controls or owns them, their availability and their criticality to the implementation of change.

The most obvious resources needed to implement strategic changes include money, skills, legitimacy, power, time, commitment, etc.

In the table below rate availability of each resource on a scale of 1–10. Resources with uncertain availability are rated as 10. Resources that are definitely available are rated as 1. Rate the criticality of resources from 1–10 with 1 representing resources which are not important and 10 representing essential resources.

This table helps you to identify systematically which resources need most attention (i.e. those which are not available but are highly critical) and draws attention to where those resources are currently located. This is important information for planning strategy implementation.

Required resource	Owner, supplier or controller of resource	Availability of resource (scale 1–10)	Criticality of resource (scale 1–10)

WORKSHEET 14: DEFINING STRATEGIC PERFORMANCE GOALS, INDICATORS AND TARGETS

This worksheet needs to be completed for each strategic goal. You need to think about performance indicators and for each strategic goal you need a series of annual performance targets set for years 1–5. Target performances should be feasible but challenging.

To begin completing this worksheet, first identify the strategic goals which may be used to draw up a list of the performance goals. Then identify a performance indicator and a target performance (for year 1) for each of them. For example, a public services organization might have a performance goal to 'improve the way we deal with the public'; the performance indicator could be 'speed of answering the phone', and the target performance could be 'answering within six rings'.

To finish the process you need to set annual performance targets for the period of the strategic plan. The worksheet asks you to identify target performances for years 2, 3, 4 and 5. As before, try to set targets which are feasible but challenging.

Strategic performance goals and performance indicators	Annual performance targets (year)				
	Year 1	Year 2	Year 3	Year 4	Year 5
1					
2					
3					
4					
5					
6					
7					
8					
9					
10					
11					
12					
13					
14					
15					
16					
17					
18					

WORKSHEET 15: IDENTIFYING INFORMATION REQUIREMENTS FOR REPORTING SYSTEMS

This worksheet also needs completing for each strategic goal. There has been considerable criticism that managers fail to monitor and evaluate the results of their organizations. One important barrier to monitoring and evaluation is the lack of information. This worksheet helps you to plan how to meet your information requirements.

The organization needs to set up reporting systems and organize at least an annual meeting to review actual performance against target performance. Ideally the reviews of performance should also look at performance trends over several years and there should be annual reports of strategic performance results to the public and employees. Academic research (Poister and Streib 2005) shows these two ideals are associated with better performance by local authorities.

Setting up reporting systems involves ensuring the supply of required information to scheduled meetings of management groups on a regular basis, to study reports and decide on corrective action, and report back to more senior management.

In terms of planning information requirements, the main thing here is to think through systematically what information you require in relation to each of the strategic goals you have established. The worksheet invites you to assess the availability of information required for evaluating achievement of the target performance, and rank the strategic goals in order of priority. After carrying out this assessment you should be clearer about what actions are needed to set up information systems and their relative importance based on the importance of the strategic goals.

Strategic goal	Availability of information required to evaluate achievement (circle answer which applies)	Priority of strategic goal (show rank order of importance)
1	Available/need to collect information	
2	Available/need to collect information	
3	Available/need to collect information	
4	Available/need to collect information	
5	Available/need to collect information	
6	Available/need to collect information	
7	Available/need to collect information	
8	Available/need to collect information	

WORKSHEET 16: ALLOCATING MANAGEMENT RESPONSIBILITY

Having decided on one or more strategic actions, the organization needs to assign responsibility for successful implementation of the action. The managers may be in an operational role and the action may be implemented through operational planning. Alternatively the implementation of strategic actions may be organized through project management and then a project manager may be given responsibility for their delivery. It is also possible to identify to whom progress is to be reported and by when.

Strategic action or pro-gramme (brief title)	Manager responsible for implementation	Progress reporting	
		(a) To whom	(b) How often
1 _____	_____	_____	_____
2 _____	_____	_____	_____
3 _____	_____	_____	_____
4 _____	_____	_____	_____
5 _____	_____	_____	_____
6 _____	_____	_____	_____
7 _____	_____	_____	_____
8 _____	_____	_____	_____

WORKSHEET 17: DEVELOPING A CALENDAR FOR INTEGRATION OF STRATEGIC PLAN PROCESSES WITH BUDGETARY AND OTHER PROCESSES

There is evidence that strategic plans need to be integrated with other management systems to ensure their effectiveness. Most critical among these other management systems are budget processes and performance measurement and management systems.

One measure for improving integration (tight linkages) is to produce a calendar showing the linkages between the strategic planning and other processes.

This worksheet is therefore a matrix that can be used to produce the first draft of a calendar to suit the specific needs of your organization.

Processes	Month											
	Jan	Feb	Mar	Apr	May	Jun	Jul	Aug	Sep	Oct	Nov	Dec
Political processes												
Strategic planning processes												
Budgetary processes												
Performance management processes												
HR processes												

REFERENCE LIST

Nutt, P. C. and Backoff, R. W. (1992) *Strategic Management of Public and Third Sector Organizations*. San Francisco, CA: Jossey-Bass.

Poister, T. H. and Streib, G. D. (2005) Elements of Strategic Planning and Management in Municipal Government: Status after Two Decades. *Public Administration Review*, 65(1): 45–56.

'Silent planning' exercise for SMG: generating ideas for action

This exercise exploits the use of nominal group technique to make planning a very inclusive process. There is also a very interactive element; it needs to be facilitated.

The process is as follows:

Each member of the SMG is asked to review Worksheets 5, 8 and 9 and note the top opportunities, the top constraints, the benefits for the public/service users and the top strategic issues. Each member of the SMG is given a pad of sticky notes and told that they should write only a single idea on each sticky note and that the idea should be expressed as concisely as possible – preferably in one or two words. They should also be warned that their sticky notes will be read by others so they should write their ideas clearly in capital letters.

The next steps are conducted in complete silence.

First, they are given four questions and asked to brainstorm as many answers as possible to each of them and to write these on their sticky notes until they can think of no more ideas. It would be good if each person comes up with at least eight ideas per question. The four questions are:

- What are the key opportunities for achieving the strategic goals on which we are working?
- What are the key constraints for achieving the strategic goals on which we are working?
- What new or better benefits should we be offering the public/service users in five years' time?
- What key strategic issues do we need to solve?

Four charts are placed on a wall close to where the SMG is working. Each is headed by one of the four questions. Sticky notes are placed on the wall to the left of the relevant chart.

The SMG members queue up and visit each chart in turn; they take a sticky note blindly (without looking to see which of the sticky notes they have picked up). They place them on the flip chart. This involves them comparing the idea on the sticky notes with those already put on the chart. If a sticky note with a similar idea is already *on the chart they place the new one to its immediate right. If there are no similar ones up already, they start a new line. They place only one sticky note on a chart before moving on to the next chart and repeating the process. The members of the SMG continue to do this until all the sticky notes are on the four flip charts. No one is allowed to move any sticky note already placed on a chart. Nor is anyone allowed to speak during all this.*

The remainder of this exercise is carried out as a group discussion. First the SMG looks at each line of sticky notes and labels it with a short name. Then the SMG comments on the relative lengths of each line of sticky notes. The most interesting ones are possibly the longest lines. Then the SMG notes the longest lines on each of the four charts and begins to discuss how they might be woven together into a narrative about possible courses of action. The discussion should also identify which strategic goals are likely to be impacted and which goals have still not been addressed.

This may sound complicated but people usually get the hang of it pretty quickly. During the last stage you need people to be imaginative and open minded about the possibility of weaving together a story about courses of action. Groups can become quite engrossed in this exercise and find it very enjoyable. Sometimes there are individuals who feel it is childish. This can sometimes depend on the professional background of the individual.

INDEX